Implementing Microsoft Dynamics 365 Business Central On-Premise
Fourth Edition

Explore the capabilities of Dynamics NAV 2018 and Dynamics 365 Business Central and implement them efficiently

Roberto Stefanetti
Alex Chow

BIRMINGHAM - MUMBAI

Implementing Microsoft Dynamics 365 Business Central On-Premise
Fourth Edition

Commissioning Editor: Richa Tripathi
Acquisition Editor: Chaitanya Nair
Content Development Editor: Rohit Singh
Technical Editor: Romy Dias
Copy Editor: Safis Editing
Project Coordinator: Vaidehi Sawant
Proofreader: Safis Editing
Indexer: Pratik Shirodkar
Graphics: Alishon Mendonsa
Production Coordinator: Priyanka Dhadke

First published: January 2009
Second edition: February 2013
Third edition: April 2016
Fourth edition: December 2018

Production reference: 1171218

Published by Packt Publishing Ltd.
Livery Place
35 Livery Street
Birmingham
B3 2PB, UK.

ISBN 978-1-78913-393-6

www.packtpub.com

To my mother, who unfortunately left us far too soon. We always think of you, every day. From heaven, you always protect us.

To my son, Luca; my wife, Monica; and their patience.

– Roberto Stefanetti

`mapt.io`

Mapt is an online digital library that gives you full access to over 5,000 books and videos, as well as industry leading tools to help you plan your personal development and advance your career. For more information, please visit our website.

Why subscribe?

- Spend less time learning and more time coding with practical eBooks and Videos from over 4,000 industry professionals

- Improve your learning with Skill Plans built especially for you

- Get a free eBook or video every month

- Mapt is fully searchable

- Copy and paste, print, and bookmark content

Packt.com

Did you know that Packt offers eBook versions of every book published, with PDF and ePub files available? You can upgrade to the eBook version at `www.packt.com` and as a print book customer, you are entitled to a discount on the eBook copy. Get in touch with us at `customercare@packtpub.com` for more details.

At `www.packt.com`, you can also read a collection of free technical articles, sign up for a range of free newsletters, and receive exclusive discounts and offers on Packt books and eBooks.

Contributors

About the authors

Roberto Stefanetti is a functional and technical consultant, who has worked on education and training for companies, partners, and clients. He currently works on Microsoft systems, especially ERP and related environments.

He started working on Navision in 2004, both as a developer and as a functional consultant, and he is now more involved in consulting and managing projects than in development. He has been an MVP in business application since 2016 and a Microsoft Education Influencer since 2017.

Roberto's blog is one of the most widely read in the world (with more than 1 million page visits). He has also published articles on many digital publications (such as MSDynamicsWorld, NAVUG Magazine, and others) and reviewed a number of books.

> *Special thanks to the reviewers for reviewing this book, and thank you to my company for giving me the "free time" to complete it. Many thanks also to my wife and my son for their patience; even if it is only a re-edition of the book, writing it takes time. And finally, thanks to everyone who bought this book and who will have the patience to read it.*

Alex Chow has been working with Microsoft Dynamics NAV, formerly Navision, since 1999. His customers range from $2 million a year small enterprises to $500 million a year multinational corporations. With a background in implementing all functions and modules inside and outside of Microsoft Dynamics NAV, Alex has encountered and resolved the most practical through to the most complex requirements and business rules. He founded AP Commerce, Inc. in 2005, a full-service Dynamics NAV service center. Alex has also written the books *Getting Started with Dynamics NAV 2013 Application Development* and *Implementing Dynamics NAV, Third Edition*, both by Packt. He lives in southern California with his wife and two lovely daughters.

About the reviewers

Stefano Demiliani is a Microsoft MVP on Business Application, a Microsoft Certified Solutions Developer, and a long-time expert on different Microsoft technologies. He has a master's degree in computer engineering from Politecnico of Turin, and works as a CTO for EID/NAV-lab (one of Microsoft's principal partners in Italy). His core responsibilities include architecting and developing solutions with Microsoft Dynamics ERPs and the Microsoft technology stacks (such as .NET and Azure solutions).

He has worked with Packt on many IT books, having recently authored *Dynamics 365 Business Central Development Quick Start Guide*, the first development guide for Dynamics 365 Business Central. You can reach him on Twitter (@demiliani) or on LinkedIn.

Duilio Tacconi is a Microsoft Dynamics 365 Business Central Escalation Engineer at Microsoft EMEA Customer Support and Services. He joined Microsoft in 2008, after working for end customers with a primary focus on the technical side of Microsoft Dynamics NAV. Despite being graduated with highest vote in agricultural science, he has worked on the ERP circuit since 1998 as a developer for several companies, with Microsoft and non-Microsoft technologies. Currently, he is a subject matter expert in the EMEA region for RDLC reports, Microsoft EMEA CSS senior reference for Managed Service for Partners, and an EMEA CSS reference for modern development with Dynamics 365 Business Central.

Three times Ironman competition finisher, Duilio lives in Cernusco sul Naviglio, Italy, with his beloved wife, Laura, and their son, Leonardo.

Packt is searching for authors like you

If you're interested in becoming an author for Packt, please visit `authors.packtpub.com` and apply today. We have worked with thousands of developers and tech professionals, just like you, to help them share their insight with the global tech community. You can make a general application, apply for a specific hot topic that we are recruiting an author for, or submit your own idea.

Table of Contents

Preface

Let me start out by saying congratulations on your decision to work with **Microsoft Dynamics NAV** and **Microsoft Dynamics 365 Business Central.** Microsoft Dynamics NAV is a wonderful historical product, and Microsoft Dynamics 365 Business Central is the new release of Microsoft Dynamics NAV, available in cloud (**Software as a Service—SaaS**) and on-premise releases.

In this book, we will talk about both Microsoft Dynamics NAV and Microsoft Dynamics 365 Business Central because we cannot forget the past when talking about the future Microsoft Dynamics 365 Business Central is the new release of Microsoft Dynamics NAV and is based on NAV (which reports all the features).

When it was created, Microsoft Dynamics NAV (formerly known as Navision) was nothing more than an accounting system from Denmark. Following a couple of releases, its acquisition by Microsoft, and a couple of further releases, Microsoft Dynamics NAV has become a full Enterprise Resource Planning (ERP) software with rich functionalities. With every release, we are seeing improvements in both the technical and functionality aspects. And they're not done yet. Microsoft Dynamics 365 Business Central is the evolution of Microsoft Dynamics NAV, conceived and designed for the cloud.

At the time of writing, Microsoft Dynamics NAV's installation base is 120,000 companies, and Microsoft Dynamics 365 Business Central licensed users are growing; no other ERP software for the small and medium-sized market comes close in terms of numbers.

In addition, Microsoft Dynamics NAV has a wide range of add-on solutions available, and many applications are also appearing for Microsoft Dynamics 365 Business Central, although in this case, it will be apps instead of add-ons. Most of these add-ons are built directly within the Microsoft Dynamics NAV environment with the same user interface. So, by using these add-ons, your company will not need to learn any other new software.

One of the main selling points of Microsoft Dynamics NAV from the very outset was the ability to customize it exactly the way you run your business. Because of its flexibility, you can find a large number of tutorials and explanations on how to develop specific tasks, but not many on how to create a project from scratch.

The "excessive" flexibility of Microsoft Dynamics NAV

To take advantage of the flexibility that's built into Microsoft Dynamics NAV, a deep understanding of the standard application is required. Just because you're able to completely rewrite Dynamics NAV does not mean you should. Without knowing what you have out of the box, you may end up creating a function that's already part of the standard system, thereby wasting valuable time and resources.

The new rules for Microsoft Dynamics 365 Business Central

In this case, the philosophy is different. You no longer touch the standard product, which updates automatically. Instead, we use extensions (apps) that are installed on a parallel layer without touching the manufacturer's standard. This entails many advantages that we will discuss later in the book. In short, you can customize by keeping the product updated, while the app can be used in a repeatable way.

Who this book is for

This book is for Microsoft Dynamics NAV and Microsoft Dynamics 365 Business Central partners and end users who want to know everything about Microsoft Dynamics NAV and Microsoft Dynamics 365 Business Central implementations. It is aimed at those individuals who want to be project managers or get involved with these ERP systems, but who do not have the expertise to write code themselves.

What this book covers

Chapter 1, *Exploring Dynamics NAV and MSDYN365BC – Overview*, introduces you to what an ERP is and what you can expect from Microsoft Dynamics NAV and Microsoft Dynamics 365 Business Central. It introduces all the functional areas found in Microsoft Dynamics NAV 2018 and Microsoft Dynamics 365 Business Central, the different environments available, such as the Windows client, the Web client, and web services. For the nostalgic among you, we have also included details on the history of Microsoft Dynamics NAV.

Chapter 2, *Microsoft Dynamics NAV 2018 – An Overview*, provides an overview of the changes made within the application. Microsoft Dynamics NAV 2018 introduces a number of new functional and technical features. All the most important features of Microsoft Dynamics NAV 2018 are illustrated, both functional and technical, and some references to links have been added that are considered useful for understanding the product. This chapter also covers development and IT changes.

Chapter 3, *General Considerations*, introduces you to general considerations relating to these fantastic products. The differences between Microsoft Dynamics NAV, Microsoft Dynamics 365 Business Central on-premise, and Microsoft Dynamics 365 Business Central online (Saas) are explained, and the advantages and disadvantages of each are illustrated. This chapter could be useful in helping you to understand which solution to implement based on the project that must be realized.

Chapter 4, *Implementation Process – Partner's Perspective*, explains the meaning of implementation and covers different methodologies that can be applied while implementing Microsoft Dynamics NAV and Microsoft Dynamics 365 Business Central. Several individuals may get involved in an implementation process, each one playing their own role and performing different jobs. This chapter also covers the phases and tasks needed to complete a Microsoft Dynamics NAV or Microsoft Dynamics 365 Business Central implementation, from pre-sales through to deployment.

Chapter 5, Implementation Process – Customer's Perspective, explains what is expected from the company's team (users, key users, and project leader), and how to deal with the changes that the new ERP software will entail for everyone within the company. For a really successful implementation of Microsoft Dynamics NAV or Microsoft Dynamics 365 Business Central, the companies in relation to which this ERP software has been implemented must actively participate in the project.

Chapter 6, *Migrating Data*, covers the tools that can be used to import data into Microsoft Dynamics NAV or into Microsoft Dynamics 365 Business Central, such as RapidStart services or XMLports. Companies may be unfamiliar with Microsoft Dynamics NAV or Microsoft Dynamics 365 Business Central, but they are usually not new companies. They have been working for a while and they have all kinds of data at their disposal, such as customer, vendor, item, and accounting information.

This chapter also explains what types of data are commonly migrated to this ERP software and the strategies used to migrate this information. With a step-by-step example, the chapter enables you to migrate master data, open entries, historical data, and open documents.

Chapter 7, *Upgrading to Dynamics NAV and MSDYN365BC*, covers the main development considerations that should be taken into account when developing for Microsoft Dynamics NAV. This includes a detailed explanation of the data model principles in Microsoft Dynamics NAV and how the posting processes are designed. It also includes explanations about where and how to write customized code.

Almost every Microsoft Dynamics NAV implementation implies development. The customized code must fit inside the application's standard code and it should look as if it were part of the standard. This makes it easier for the user to understand how customized modules work and for partners to support them.

Chapter 8, *Development Considerations*, covers the main development considerations that should be taken into account when developing for Microsoft Dynamics NAV and Microsoft Dynamics 365 Business Central. This includes a detailed explanation of the data model principles and how the posting processes are designed. It also includes explanations about where and how to write customized code.

Almost every Microsoft Dynamics NAV implementation implies development. The customized code must fit inside the application's standard code and it should look as if it were part of the standard. This makes it easier for the user to understand how customized modules work and for partners to support them. In Microsoft Dynamics 365 Business Central (SaaS), it is not possible to change standard objects and the development mode is based only on the New Modern Development Environment.

Chapter 9, *Implementing Functional Changes*, demonstrates how Microsoft Dynamics NAV and Microsoft Dynamics 365 Business Central implementations are not just for companies that have never used this ERP software before and will now start doing so. Implementation can also be effected for companies already using Microsoft Dynamics NAV or Microsoft Dynamics 365 Business Central. They will not be complete implementations, of course; probably just the implementation of a new module or functionality. There are a number of things to take into account in these kinds of implementations.

Chapter 10, *Data Analysis and Reporting*, provides an overview of the tools available to analyze Microsoft Dynamics NAV and Microsoft Dynamics 365 Business Central data, both inside and outside the application, such as the use of filters and FlowFilters, statistics, charts, existing reports, analysis views, account schedules, or how to extract data from Microsoft Dynamics NAV and Microsoft Dynamics 365 Business Central. Data analysis and reporting are important parts of the management of a company.

This chapter also includes a report development section that is meant to explain the anatomy of reports, to show how to define your dataset, and to show how the visual layout is designed.

Chapter 11, *Debugging with Dynamics NAV and MSDYN365BC*, covers debugging in Microsoft Dynamics NAV and Microsoft Dynamics 365 Business Central, conditional breakpoints, debugging other user sessions, and debugging C/AL code in the Old Development Environment and AL code in the New Development Environment (Visual Studio Code plus Microsoft AL Language extension). All these features will ensure that the debugging experience is a happy one.

Chapter 12, *Popular Reporting Options*, outlines some of the reporting and analysis options that are included in Microsoft Dynamics NAV and Microsoft Dynamics 365 Business Central that extend their functionalities and are very useful to users and companies. Utilizing web services, the options for analyzing your data are endless, and we'll also cover third-party tools that can be useful for creating reports in a simple and convenient way for users.

Chapter 13, *Microsoft Dynamics 365 Business Central*, covers Microsoft Dynamics 365 Business Central in detail, how it originates on the Microsoft Dynamics NAV platform, and how it is integrated with several other Microsoft services. Microsoft Dynamics 365 Business Central is designed as a true multi-tenant public cloud service (SaaS) running on Microsoft Azure and sold through the Microsoft **Cloud Solution Provider** (**CSP**) program. Customers can access the service on the web, or by using apps for Windows, iOS, or Android devices.

This product can be integrated with the entire Microsoft Office 365 world using different tools, such as PowerApps, Azure Services, Microsoft Flow, and REST APIs. In practice, it is possible to do anything in the cloud with Microsoft Dynamics 365 Business Central.

Chapter 14, *Working and Developing with Docker and Sandboxes*, provides step-by-step information on how to install, configure, and activate Docker and Sandbox environments for test data, setups, and development in Microsoft Dynamics 365 Business Central and Microsoft Dynamics NAV. Sandbox environments are very useful for developing and testing data and applications before uploading to the Microsoft Dynamics 365 Business Central Online production environment.

Sandbox environments, online or in Docker containers, locally or in the cloud, are useful for everyone—customers, developers, and consultants—when studying and testing new product releases.

To get the most out of this book

To successfully follow the examples in this book, you will need to install Microsoft Dynamics NAV 2018, Microsoft Dynamics 365 Business Central on-premise, or buy a Microsoft Dynamics 365 Business Central cloud license.

Download the color images

We also provide a PDF file that has color images of the screenshots/diagrams used in this book. You can download it here `https://www.packtpub.com/sites/default/files/downloads/9781789133936_ColorImages.pdf`

Conventions used

There are a number of text conventions used throughout this book.

`CodeInText`: Indicates code words in text, database table names, folder names, filenames, file extensions, pathnames, dummy URLs, user input, and Twitter handles. Here is an example: "Rename `HelloWorld.al` to `PAGEEXT.50100.Item.al`."

A block of code is set as follows:

```
Trigger OnAfterGetRecord();
Begin
 Message('You are on record # ' + rec."No.");
End
```

When we wish to draw your attention to a particular part of a code block, the relevant lines or items are set in bold:

```
Trigger OnAfterGetRecord();
Begin
 Message('You are on record # ' + rec."No.");
End
```

Any command-line input or output is written as follows:

```
> docker images
> docker pull
```

Bold: Indicates a new term, an important word, or words that you see on screen. For example, words in menus or dialog boxes appear in the text like this. Here is an example: "Select **Chart of Accounts**. "

Warnings or important notes appear like this.

 Tips and tricks appear like this.

Get in touch

Feedback from our readers is always welcome.

General feedback: Email `feedback@packtpub.com` and mention the book title in the subject of your message. If you have questions about any aspect of this book, please email us at `questions@packtpub.com`.

Errata: Although we have taken every care to ensure the accuracy of our content, mistakes do happen. If you have found a mistake in this book, we would be grateful if you would report this to us. Please visit `www.packtpub.com/submit-errata`, selecting your book, clicking on the Errata Submission Form link, and entering the details.

Piracy: If you come across any illegal copies of our works in any form on the internet, we would be grateful if you would provide us with the location address or website name. Please contact us at `copyright@packtpub.com` with a link to the material.

If you are interested in becoming an author: If there is a topic that you have expertise in, and you are interested in either writing or contributing to a book, please visit `authors.packtpub.com`.

Reviews

Please leave a review. Once you have read and used this book, why not leave a review on the site that you purchased it from? Potential readers can then see and use your unbiased opinion to make purchase decisions, we at Packt can understand what you think about our products, and our authors can see your feedback on their book. Thank you!

For more information about Packt, please visit `packtpub.com`.

1
Exploring Dynamics NAV and MSDYN365BC – Overview

Microsoft Dynamics NAV and **Microsoft Dynamics 365 Business Central** (which, as mentioned in the preface, is an evolution of Microsoft Dynamics NAV that maintains the same functionalities and will be available both in the on-premise and SaaS releases), are **Enterprise Resource Planning (ERP)** systems that are specifically made for growing small to mid-sized companies.

 This is, at least, what Microsoft's marketing department says. In reality, Microsoft Dynamics NAV is also being used by large and publicly-traded companies around the world.

An ERP is a piece of software that integrates internal and external management information across an entire organization. The purpose of an ERP is to facilitate the flow of information between all business functions within the confines of organizations. An ERP system is meant to handle all the functional areas within an organization on a single software system. This way, the output of an area can be used as the input of another area, without the need to duplicate data.

In this chapter, we will talk about Microsoft Dynamics NAV 2018, the last existing version with the name "NAV" and on-premise connected to Microsoft Dynamics 365 Business Central, which will disappear before the end of the year. We do this for reasons of continuity toward the past because this book was born to illustrate the implementation of Microsoft Dynamics NAV.

This chapter will give you an idea of what Microsoft Dynamics NAV is, and what you can expect from it. The topics covered in this chapter are the following:

- What is Microsoft Dynamics NAV?
- The functional areas found in Microsoft Dynamics NAV 2018
- A history of Microsoft Dynamics NAV, with a timeline of its features
- How to use Microsoft Dynamics NAV in different environments (Windows client, Web client, Universal App, SharePoint framework, Outlook integration, Web services, and so on)
- Development considerations: How Microsoft Dynamics NAV is developed

From the Business Central overview perspective, the following topics will be covered:

- From Microsoft Dynamics NAV to Microsoft Dynamics 365 Business Central (move from on-premise to cloud-based SaaS)
- The cloud model (ERP auto-updated system)
- Events and extensions
- The New Modern Development Environment
- Microsoft Azure services

Understanding Microsoft Dynamics NAV

Microsoft Dynamics NAV 2018 is a **role tailored ERP**. Traditionally, ERP software is built to provide a lot of functionalities where users will need to hunt down information. This is more of a passive approach to information, in which the user will need to go somewhere within the system to retrieve that information.

Microsoft Dynamics NAV works differently. The role tailored experience is based on individuals within an organization, their roles, and the tasks they perform. When users first enter Microsoft Dynamics NAV, they see the data required for the daily tasks they perform according to their role. Users belonging to different functions will have a different view of the system; each of them will see the functions they need to properly perform their daily tasks. Instead of users chasing down information, the information comes to them.

Here's an example of the main screen of the Microsoft Dynamics NAV 2018 Business Manager role. All the relevant information for business managers is displayed in activities and charts for fast reading.

The Microsoft Dynamics NAV 2018 (Windows client role) home page looks as follows:

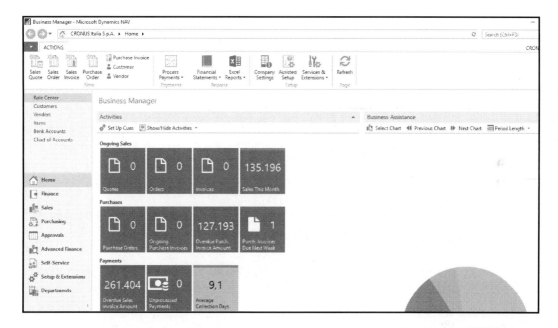

Note that for Microsoft Dynamics 365 Business Central, the pictures are taken from the current release at the time of writing; these could have since changed (pre- and post-October 2018 release).

The Microsoft Dynamics 365 Business Central W1 on-premise (Windows client role) home page looks as follows:

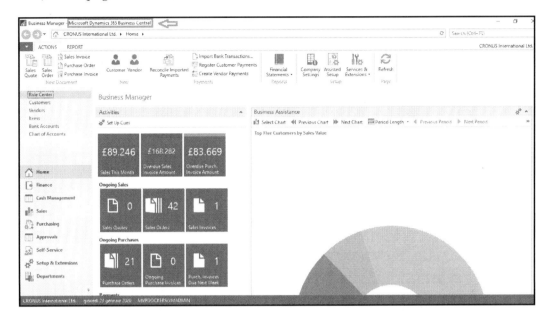

The Microsoft Dynamics 365 Business Central on-premise and SaaS (Web client role) home page looks as follows:

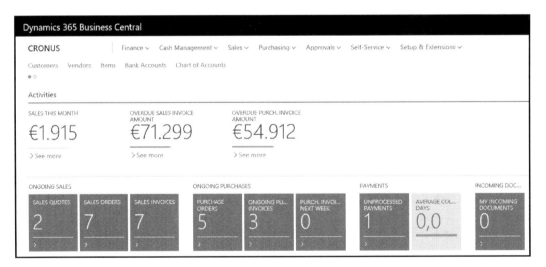

Functional areas in Microsoft Dynamics NAV

Microsoft Dynamics NAV covers the following functional areas inside an organization:

- **Financial management**: Most of the functionalities from "off-the-shelf" accounting software can be found in this module. These functionalities include, but are not limited to, G/L budgeting, financial reporting, cash management, receivables and payables, fixed assets, VAT and tax reporting, intercompany transactions, cost accounting, consolidation, multicurrency, and intrastate.
- **Sales and marketing**: This module concerns those companies that want to track customer orders and determine when the items can be promised to be delivered to the customer. This area covers customers, order processing, expected delivery, order promises, sales returns, pricing, contacts, marketing campaigns, and so on.
- **Purchasing**: This module is required when you buy goods and services, and you want to keep track of what you have ordered from your vendors and when the goods should be delivered to your door, so you can make the stuff or ship the stuff to your customers. This area includes vendors, order processing, approvals, planning, and costing.
- **Warehousing**: Where are your items in your warehouse? This functional area answers this question for you. Under the warehouse area, you will find inventory, shipping and receiving, locations, warehouse bin contents, picking, put-aways, assembly, and so on.
- **Manufacturing**: The manufacturing area includes product design, bills of materials, routing, capacities, forecast, production planning, production orders, costing, and subcontracting.
- **Job**: This module is typically used for companies that deal with long and drawn-out projects. Within this job area, you can create projects, phases and tasks, planning, time sheets, work in progress, and similar.
- **Resource planning**: If your company has internal resources for which you keep track of costs and/or revenues, this module is for you. This area includes resources, capacity, and other tools to keep track of costs and revenues associated with resources.

- **Service**: This functional area is designed for a company that sells items to their customers that need to be serviced periodically, with or without a warranty. In this service area, you can manage service items, contract management, order processing, planning and dispatching, service tasks, and so on.
- **Human resources**: This involves basic employee tracking. It allows you to manage employees, absences, and so on.

These areas are covered in more detail in the next section of this chapter.

One of the best-selling points about Microsoft Dynamics NAV is that it can be customized. A brand new functional area can be created from scratch, or new features added to an existing functional area. All development is undertaken using the **C/AL** (**Client-server Application Language**) programming language (in versions preceding Microsoft Dynamics NAV 2018); now it's a hybrid development system. You can use **C/SIDE (Client/Server Integrated Development Environment)** and C/AL, and/or VS Code with an AL extension, to develop in AL.

When someone creates a new functional area, a vertical (a wide range of functions for a specific industry) or a horizontal (a wide range of functions that can be applied across an industry), they usually create it as an add-on. An add-on can be registered with Microsoft, for an appropriate fee of course. If some features are added to an existing area, usually it is a customization that will only be used on the database of the customer who asked for the feature.

Making add-ons (and Apps) available greatly enhances the base Microsoft Dynamics NAV functionalities to fit the needs of every industry and every business. The mode of development has evolved over time.

One thing that is unique about Microsoft Dynamics NAV is that the entire code is located on a single layer. Therefore, if you customize an area, you had to do it by modifying the standard code and adding code to the middle of the standard object definition. This made it a little tough to upgrade in previous versions of Microsoft Dynamics NAV. However, with the release of Microsoft Dynamics NAV 2018, code upgrades can be effected automatically using PowerShell (this feature does not only exist in Microsoft Dynamics NAV 2018; it has been available since Microsoft Dynamics NAV 2013 R2 and was refined in Microsoft Dynamics NAV 2015). We will dive into PowerShell later.

This was the old and unique development philosophy existing up to Dynamics NAV 2015, from the introduction of the extensions (which took place in Dynamics NAV 2016) it is possible (and recommended) not to change the standard code anymore but to develop extensions (apps) that extend the functionality without touching the source code; in this way you can easily install updates.

Microsoft Dynamics NAV is built upon a three-tier architecture:

- Microsoft SQL Server and Microsoft Azure SQL are the data tier and are used to store the data in a database.
- The Microsoft Dynamics NAV Server service is the middle or server tier, managing the entire business logic and communication. It also provides an additional layer of security between clients and the database, and an additional layer for user authentication.
- On the client tier, we will find Windows clients and the Web client. Microsoft Dynamics NAV 2018 also supports other kinds of clients, including Web services (both SOAP and OData v4.0), mobile tablets and phones with Universal App, a SharePoint online integration, the Office 365 native integration, and the Microsoft Dynamics **NAV Application Server (NAS)** service.

You can install Microsoft Dynamics NAV in more complex scenarios, as you can have multiple instances of any of the core components.

In Microsoft Dynamics 365 Business Central SaaS, only the Web client and the native mobile app exist, the infrastructure is cloud-based, the development environment is not different to Microsoft Dynamics NAV 2018 (with Microsoft Dynamics NAV, you have a hybrid development, and you can choose to use C/SIDE or VS Code, or both); however, it is possible to design extensions (applications) with Microsoft Dynamics NAV 2018 using the **New Modern Development Environment**. This new development environment (composed by Visual Studio Code and the Microsoft AL language extension) is used instead of the C/SIDE and C/AL environment, which could be deprecated in the near future, as it is already with just Microsoft Dynamics 365 Business Central.

History of Microsoft Dynamics NAV and Microsoft Dynamics 365 Business Central

In this section, we will have a look at the transition from PC Plus to Microsoft Dynamics 365 Business Central.

We are not historians, but we thought that it would be important to know where we come from and where we are going. Some of the current restrictions or features can be better understood if we know a bit of the history of Microsoft Dynamics NAV. This is why we have added this section.

PC Plus (the father of Navision) was launched in Denmark and Norway in 1984 by the company PC & C A/S. PC-plus was a character-based (MS-DOS) accounting solution designed for the **SOHO** (short for **small office/home office**) market. Three years after its launch in 1984, the first version of **Navision A/S** was released.

In 2002, Microsoft bought Navision A/S and included it in the Microsoft Business Solution division. The product has gone through several name changes. The names Navision Financials, Navision Attain, and Microsoft Business Solutions—Navision, have been used to refer to the product that is currently called Microsoft Dynamics NAV. Note that all the previous names included the word **Navision**. This is why many people keep calling it Navision instead of NAV.

Prior to Microsoft Dynamics NAV 2009, the classic client was actually the primary end user interface before Microsoft revamped the user interface that we used to call **Role Tailored Client** (**RTC**) first, and currently Windows client.

One of the greatest technological breakthroughs with the original Navision was that the application programming objects, the user interface, and the database resided together, in a single file! Back in the late 1990s and early 2000s, no other software came close to having an efficient design like this.

This was the main menu for PC Plus 1.0:

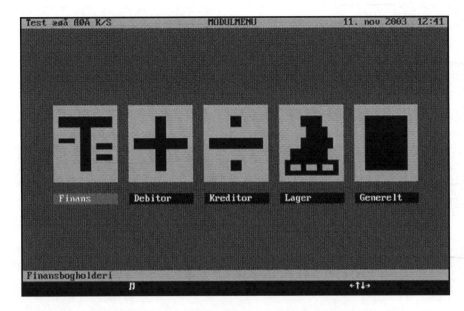

This was the main menu for Navision Financials version 2.0:

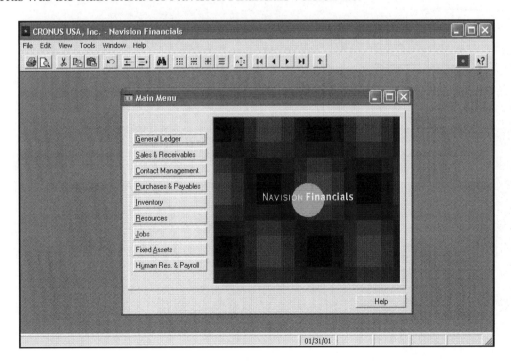

We're now close to two decades away from 2000 and technology has changed quite a bit. Microsoft Dynamics NAV has been kept very up to date, with the latest technology that has the best impact on businesses. However, most of these improvements and updates are in the backend. This is an important reason why Microsoft Dynamics NAV has never faded into history. There were a couple of user interface improvements; by and large, however, it mainly looks and feels very much the same as before.

This is the main menu for Microsoft Dynamics NAV 5.0:

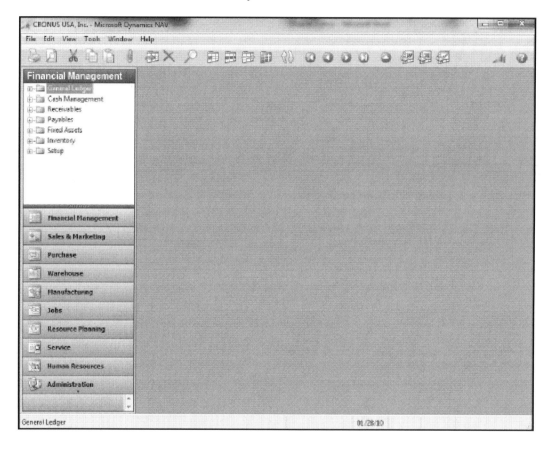

Then, something happened. With the rise of a company called Apple, people started paying more attention to the aesthetics and the overall interface of the technology they're using. People demanded not just powerful software with a strong backend, but they also wanted an elegant design with a simple and intuitive user interface.

Because of this shift in user perception, what was once the greatest innovation in accounting software since sliced bread had become not obsolete, but outdated.

When you put the old interface (called Classic Client) against some of the newer applications, even though the backend was light years ahead, the Classic Client was the ugly one. And we all know somebody who's made a terrible decision based only on looks, and not really what's inside.

So when Microsoft Dynamics NAV 2009 was introduced, the Role Tailored Client was released, which is the interface you see when you install Microsoft Dynamics NAV 2018 for end users. Microsoft Dynamics NAV 2009 was unique in that it allowed both Classic Client and RTC to coexist. This is mostly to appease the existing Microsoft Dynamics NAV gurus and users who did not want to learn the new interface.

In addition, in Microsoft Dynamics NAV 2009, classic reporting coexisted alongside **report definition language client-side** (**RDLC**) reporting. RDLC reports brought in a big change because the layout of the report had to be designed in Microsoft Visual Studio, outside Microsoft Dynamics NAV, in order to assimilate the advantages of SQL Server Reporting Services technology, while pages changed the way of developing the user interface.

This is what Microsoft Dynamics NAV 2009 in the RTC looked like:

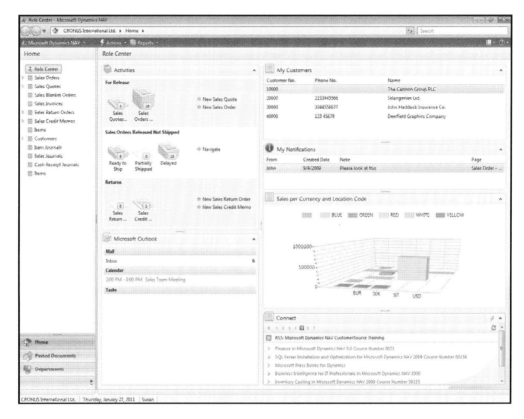

Screenshot showing Microsoft Dynamics NAV 2009 in the RTC

At first glance, Microsoft Dynamics NAV 2009 and Microsoft Dynamics NAV 2015 do not look too different. You will have to understand, however, that there were significant user interface and usability changes. We can list these changes, but if you're not already familiar with Microsoft Dynamics NAV (or Navision), you will find this of little or no interest.

When Microsoft Dynamics NAV 2013 was released, the Classic Client user interface was completely removed. Microsoft basically renamed the Classic Client as Development Environment. For the foreseeable future, it looks like the Development Environment and the Windows Client environment will remain separate.

Now, we are at Microsoft Dynamics NAV 2018 and Microsoft Dynamics 365 Business Central, with tons of performance and usability enhancements, and the aspect is a bit different.

This is what the Microsoft Dynamics NAV 2018 Windows Client looks like:

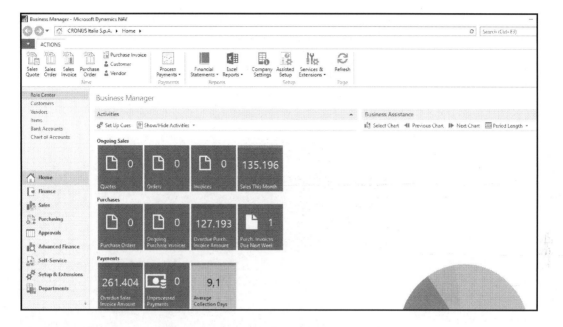

And here are the Microsoft Dynamics NAV 2018 Web client and phone client:

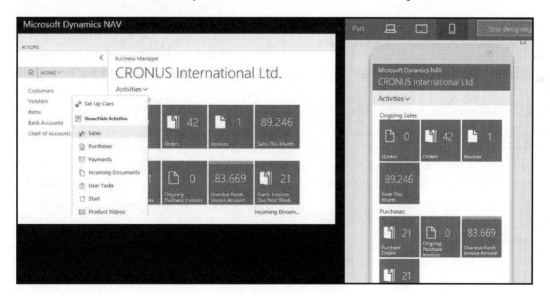

A view of Microsoft Dynamics NAV 2018 Web client (left) and phone client (right)

Microsoft Dynamics 365 Business Central is the evolution of Microsoft Dynamics NAV (the name Microsoft Dynamics NAV might disappear shortly); it will be available in two versions: on-premises and SaaS. Microsoft Dynamics 365 Business Central is designed for the cloud.

The Microsoft Dynamics 365 Business Central web-based client appears as follows:

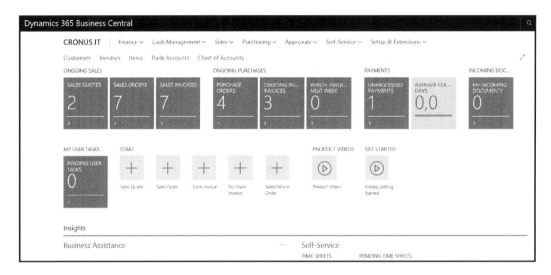

From Microsoft Dynamics NAV 2009 to Microsoft Dynamics 365 Business Central – a timeline of features

Recently, I went to some prospects who currently use old versions of Microsoft Dynamics NAV and want to upgrade to Microsoft Dynamics NAV 2018. I was asked to list and summarize the main features introduced in the various versions of Microsoft Dynamics NAV, starting with Microsoft Dynamics NAV 2009. Therefore, I decided to make a brief summary of the main features of Microsoft Dynamics NAV 2009, through to Microsoft Dynamics 365 Business Central.

The following diagram shows the Microsoft Dynamics NAV timeline with the best features of each NAV release, including Microsoft Dynamics 365 Business Central as is at the time of writing:

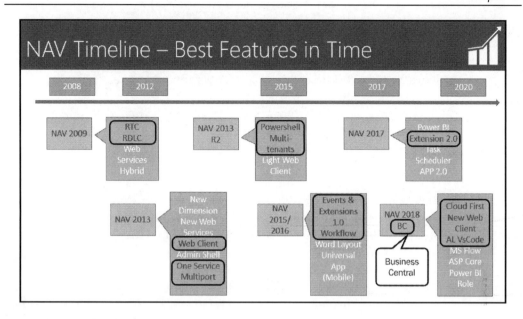

Let's have a quick look at the best technical and functional features:

- **Microsoft Dynamics NAV 2009 (and R2)**: RTC , multitier architecture (first three release levels), Web services (with separate service), Zeta Doc Express integration, online payment services, new CRM integration, and tree map visualization.

- **Microsoft Dynamics NAV 2013 (and R2)**: PowerShell, Admin Shell, multitenant, query, new model for dimensions, NAV Server multiport services configuration administration, NAV users (and multiple types of users), best charts, Web client, new NAS technology, SharePoint integration, single sign-on, rapid start services, .NET interoperability, help server, cash management, cost accounting, cache flow forecast, assembly management, SEPA v1.0, better service module integration, and inventory movements.

- **Microsoft Dynamics NAV 2015**: Print reports on job queue (On-Demand Scheduling), document reporting: Word layout, NAV Universal App, SEPA Direct, social listening support, Office 365 first full integration.

- **Microsoft Dynamics NAV 2016**: Workflow for developers (business and integration), Workflow for users, new approvals model (based on workflow), Events and Extensions, EDI (e-everything), Dynamics CRM native integration, Power BI, SQL Azure, deferrals, document management, incoming documents and OCR, currency exchange rates, new application test toolset.

- **Microsoft Dynamics NAV 2017**: Task Scheduler, Office 365 full integration, Embedded Power BI, Cortana Intelligence, setup and configuration (assisted by wizards), PowerApps and Microsoft Flow support, item workflow and item attributes and categories, Web client user experience, better SQL performance.
- **Microsoft Dynamics NAV 2018**: C/SIDE and VS Code development models, Microsoft Flow direct integration, Office 365 and contact interaction for Outlook, Extensions 2.0, API Library (for example, "Company" and so on), employee ledger entries, edit ledger entries in Excel, change global dimensions, IC (Intercompany)—automation of IC Outbox and IC Inbox, sales orders to purchase orders, direct transfer orders, user tasks, jobs improvements, Web client more customizable (design mode), Preview and Print from Web client, ODATA 4.0.
- **Microsoft Dynamics 365 Business Central**: This is the first release with a significant cloud impact! It facilitates utilization of all the features of Microsoft Dynamics NAV in the cloud, while still maintaining an on-premise version; currently available in two versions, on-premise and SaaS, with two licensing model; Essential and Premium. The SaaS version is exclusively used with a new Web client, an evolution of the Microsoft Dynamics NAV Web client, optimized for the user experience.

Functional areas

The core functionalities of Microsoft Dynamics NAV have not dramatically changed over the years. New functional areas have appeared and the existing ones still work as they did in the previous versions. In Microsoft Dynamics NAV 2009, Microsoft was focused on changing the entire architecture (for good), and Microsoft Dynamics NAV 2013 R2 is the consolidation of the new architecture, including multitenancy and Microsoft PowerShell support (a first step to the new cloud model). Microsoft Dynamics NAV 2016 is the first release with workflow and event integration. Microsoft Dynamics NAV 2018 enhances what was released with Microsoft Dynamics NAV 2016 and Microsoft Dynamics NAV 2017, including extension version 2.0 and the New Development Environment. All these architectural changes were made to bring Microsoft Dynamics NAV closer to existing Microsoft technologies, namely Microsoft Office 365, .NET, SQL Server, SQL Azure, Azure functions, Power Apps, Microsoft Flow, Microsoft Dynamics 365, Power BI, and Xamarin. In the meantime, the core functionality has not undergone a drastic facelift compared to the architecture.

Microsoft Dynamics 365 Business Central is the cloud evolution of Microsoft Dynamics NAV 2018, with the same core functionalities.

Microsoft has been adding small functional features and improving the existing functionalities with every new release. As you have seen earlier in this chapter, the basic Microsoft Dynamics NAV 2018 covers the following functional areas:

- Financial management
- Sales and marketing
- Purchasing
- Warehousing
- Manufacturing
- Jobs
- Resource planning
- Services
- Human resources

In Microsoft Dynamics NAV, the financial management area is the epicenter of the entire application. The other areas are optional, and their utilization depends on the organization's needs. The sales and purchase areas are also commonly used within a Microsoft Dynamics NAV implementation.

The screenshots will be based (where possible) on the Web client of Microsoft Dynamics NAV 2018, which is similar (only in appearance) to the Microsoft Dynamics 365 Business Central Web client. In reality, they are very different; Microsoft Dynamics NAV 2018 uses a first version of ASP.NET Core Web Client, while Business Central now supports an evolved **user experience** (**UX**) and has more capabilities than the Microsoft Dynamics NAV 2018 Web client (for example, headlines and breadcrumb, and many more).

The Microsoft Dynamics NAV 2018 Web client login page appears as follows:

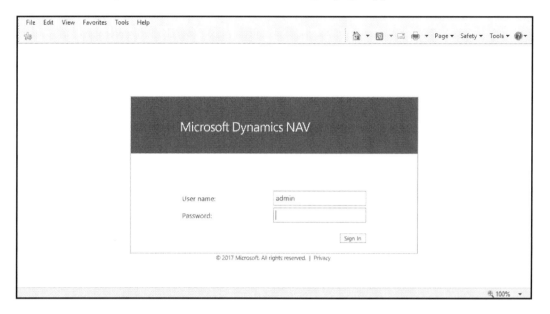

The **Sales Order Processor** role (Microsoft Dynamics NAV 2018 Web client) page appears as follows:

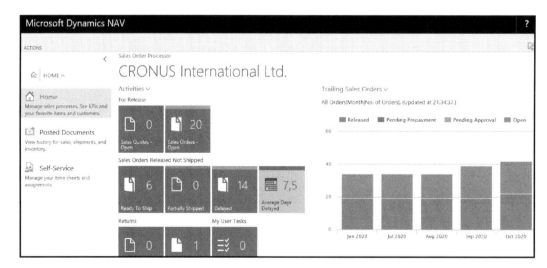

The **Departments** menu (Microsoft Dynamics NAV 2018 Window client) appears as follows:

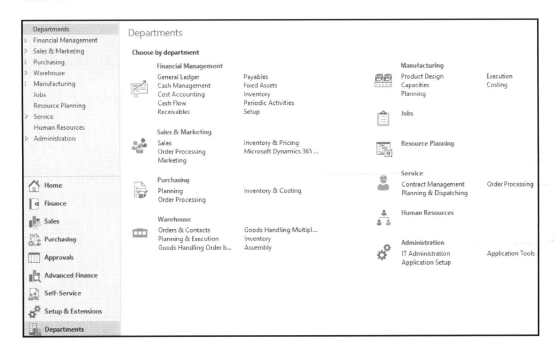

The Microsoft Dynamics 365 Business Central (on-premise in this case) login page appears as follows:

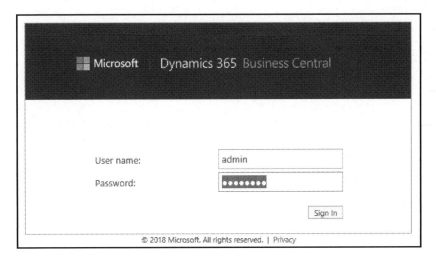

The **Sales Order Processor** role in Microsoft Dynamics 365 Business Central appears as follows:

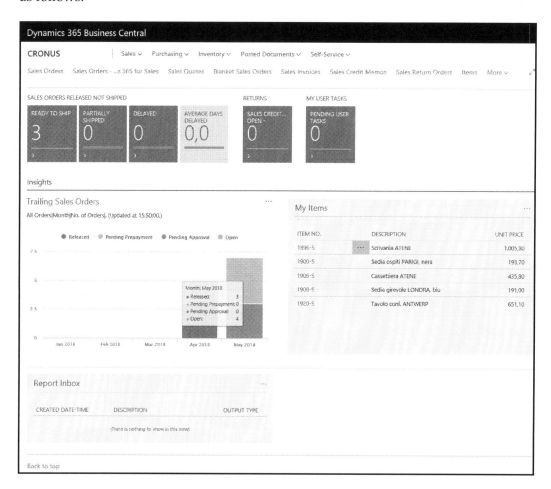

 Note: As already mentioned, the images of the pages are related to Microsoft Dynamics NAV 2018 Web client, albeit very similar in appearance to Microsoft Dynamics 365 Business Central (as you can see). A number of images of Microsoft Dynamics 365 Business Central are also shown, as they were at the time of writing (these may have changed as a result of updates).

Now, let's take a closer look at each area.

Financial management

As we said, financial management is the epicenter of Microsoft Dynamics NAV. Actually, accounting is the epicenter, and the general ledger is included inside the financial management area. What else can be found here? The following screenshot shows the main page of the **Financial Management** department:

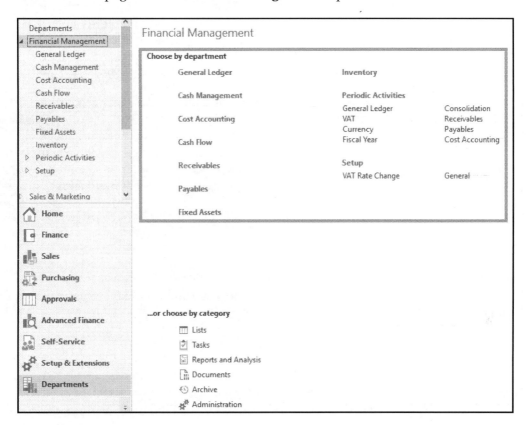

We'll provide a few details about each of these areas.

General ledger

Accountancy is the act of recording, classifying, and summarizing in terms of money and the transactions and events that take place in a company. Accountancy is thousands of years old; the earliest accounting records, dating back more than 7,000 years, were found in Mesopotamia. The fact that it has survived this long must mean that it's important.

Nowadays, of course, we don't use the same accounting system, but it is interesting that accounting is useful in every single company, no matter how different it is to any other company. Probably the fact that keeping accounting records is mandatory in almost all countries helps! For one thing, you need them to figure out how much money you made so that you can pay your taxes.

Accountancy has its own language: accounts, credit amounts, and debit amounts. This language is managed through strict and clear rules such as **generally accepted accounting principles (GAAP)**. Microsoft Dynamics NAV has implemented these rules using posting groups so that the system can translate everything to an accounting language and post it to the general ledger entries on the fly.

An important difference between Microsoft Dynamics NAV and other accounting systems is that you don't need to open an individual account for each customer, each vendor, each bank, or each fixed asset. Microsoft Dynamics NAV does not keep detailed information about them on the general ledger. Only one or a few accounts are needed for each group. This is something that shocks accountants when they use Microsoft Dynamics NAV for the first time. Then again, most accountants are easily shocked.

G/L budgets

The **general ledger** part also contains G/L budgets. This feature allows you to create accounting budgets with different levels of detail. You can break the budget down according to different periods (day, week, month, quarter, year, or any accounting period), accounts (on single posting accounts or heading accounts), business units, or dimensions.

The budget can be edited inside Microsoft Dynamics NAV or can be exported to Excel, edited there, and then imported back to Microsoft Dynamics NAV. You can do multiple imports from Excel and the new entries can be added to the existing ones.

You can also create distinct budgets inside Microsoft Dynamics NAV and then combine them in a single budget. The following screenshot shows the main **Budget Matrix** page:

After presenting the budget, you can find different ways of tracking it—either from the **G/L Balance/Budget Matrix** page, from the **Trial Balance/Budget** report, or from the account schedules defined by you.

The following screenshot shows the main **Budget Matrix** page in Microsoft Dynamics 365 Business Central:

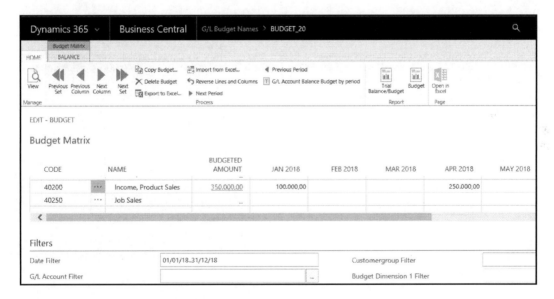

Account schedules

Account schedules are designed for the reporting and analysis of financial statements. If it were up to me, I would rename the function "Financial Statement Setup", but I'm sure someone higher up believes account schedules makes sense to the majority of the population.

Microsoft Dynamics NAV includes a number of standard statements, but the good thing about it is that you can modify the existing ones, or you can create new ones, in order to meet an organization's specific requirements.

Account schedules may consist of ledger entries, budget entries, or analysis view entries. Analysis view entries are used to summarize ledger entries by a period and a set of dimensions. You can also combine entries from these different sources into a single schedule.

You can also define what kind of information is shown in the rows and columns. Each column can show data from different periods so you can compare amounts over different periods. Account schedules are therefore a powerful tool that end users can use to create their own customized financial reports. The **ACC. SCHEDULE OVERVIEW** window is displayed in the following screenshot:

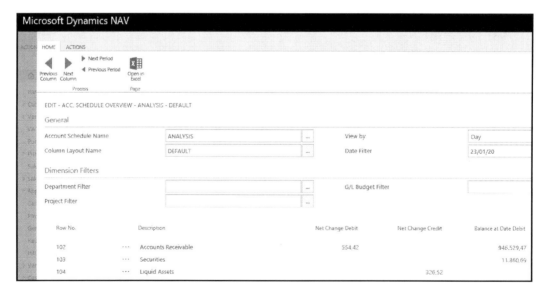

The **ACC. SCHEDULE OVERVIEW** in Microsoft Dynamics 365 Business Central page is displayed in the following screenshot:

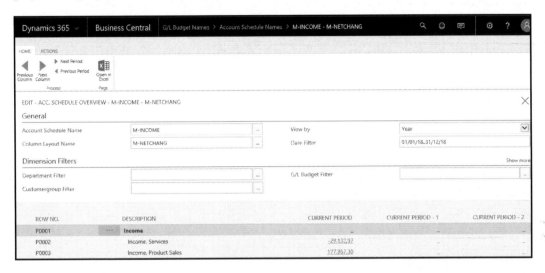

Cash management

The cash management feature is used to manage a company's bank accounts. You can process the payments received from customers, payments to vendors, and bank reconciliation.

You can create a bank account card for each bank account the company has. Whenever a transaction is made in Microsoft Dynamics NAV using a bank account, the system will post an entry in the bank account entry, plus a related G/L entry according to the bank posting group. The posting of bank entries is done from the cash receipt journal or from the payment journal. Other journals, including the general journals, may also be used.

 It's recommended that you only set up bank accounts for the banks on which you do a full bank reconciliation. For banks that you don't reconcile, such as your money market account or investment accounts, you can just make the transaction on the G/L level.

The payment journal includes a **Suggest Vendor Payments** action to help you decide what is to be paid.

Fixed assets

The **fixed assets** functionality is used to manage a company's assets, their cost, and depreciation, and it's also related to maintenance and insurances.

Fixed assets have unlimited depreciation books that track depreciation expenses reliably. All the ordinary methods of depreciation are available, plus the ability to create custom depreciation methods is also available.

Fixed assets include two different journals: the FA G/L journal, and the FA journal. The FA G/L journal is used to post entries on the FA ledger entry and also a corresponding entry on the G/L entry. The FA journal is used only to create entries on the FA ledger entry. This means that, depending on your configuration, you may not be posting anything related to FA in the G/L entry. You therefore need to be careful and know exactly when to post on the G/L and when not to, but keep everything synchronized.

VAT reporting and intrastat

Value Added Tax (**VAT**) doesn't really apply to people doing business in those countries where VAT is not required, such as the United States. It is a transaction that is paid by the end consumer and business. In Microsoft Dynamics NAV, you can find a table called **VAT Entry**, where all VAT transactions are recorded, mainly through purchase and sale invoices. In addition, the corresponding amounts are also posted on the accounts determined by its posting groups.

As in many other areas, VAT processes are mainly based on their own entries, not on the amounts found in the accounting areas.

A process named **Calculate and Post VAT Settlement** helps you to post the G/L transactions for a VAT settlement. Dynamics NAV also includes VAT statements that are pretty similar to account schedules we discussed before. Therefore, you can define your own VAT statements that will help you to submit them to the tax authorities.

Intrastat is a mandatory reporting process for all **European Union** (**EU**) companies that trade with other EU countries/regions. Each company within the EU is responsible for reporting the movement of goods to their statistics authorities every month and delivering the report to the tax authority. In Microsoft Dynamics NAV, the intrastat journal is used to complete periodic intrastat reports.

The intrastat journal requires item entries to contain information related to tariff numbers, transaction types, and transport methods. The tariff numbers are assigned to each item card, while transaction types and transport methods are assigned to sales and purchase documents.

Sales tax

Sales tax is a tax that is only calculated and paid in relation to the sale of certain goods and purchases. Since the tax is applied during the point of sale, the seller will be the responsible party calculating and collecting this tax. Then, either monthly or quarterly, the seller gives the collected sales tax to the government.

There are four major components in sales tax that you will need to set up:

- **Tax groups**: This is the classification of goods and services that you sell to your customers.
- **Tax jurisdictions**: These are the different jurisdictions that you need to report sales tax to. In the United States, depending on where you sold the product, there may be up to seven jurisdictions you need to report your sales tax to.
- **Tax area**: This allows you to group the jurisdictions together so that it's a lumped percentage for all the jurisdictions you report to.
- **Tax details**: This is where you define to which jurisdiction you sell certain types of products and/or services, whether they are liable for sales tax or not, and at what percentage rate.

Intercompany transactions

Intercompany postings are used to buy/sell goods and services between companies that are set up in your database. This function eliminates the need to enter purchase and sales orders manually in each of the companies where you buy and sell.

When company A creates a document that needs to be sent to company B, the following flow occurs:

1. Company A creates the document and sends it to their IC outbox
2. Company A sends all the transactions from their IC outbox
3. Company B receives the transactions in their IC inbox
4. Company B converts the IC inbox transactions to a document and processes it

A transaction can be sent to the partner's inbox directly if both companies coexist in the same database, or you can also send transactions by email or through XML files.

Consolidation

Consolidation is the process of adding up general ledger entries of two or more separate companies (subsidiaries) into a new company, called the **consolidated company**. Each individual company involved in a consolidation is called a **business unit**.

Note that we have only talked about adding up general ledger entries; no other entries on the system are used for consolidation purposes. In the chart of accounts of each business unit, you can indicate which accounts are to be included in the consolidation.

The consolidation process creates a summarized G/L entry on the consolidated company for the period you have selected while running the process, and for each account and combination of dimensions, if you choose to copy dimensions on the consolidated company. The consolidation functionality contains a process to help you register the consolidation eliminations.

Multicurrency

Multicurrency can be used if you buy or sell in other currencies besides your local currency. You can assign currency codes to bank accounts and also to customers and vendors. You can also use multicurrency to record general ledger transactions in an additional currency (besides your local currency). The additional currency feature is very useful for international companies that need to report in a different currency to the one they use in their daily transactions. You can register exchange rates for each foreign currency and specify from which dates the exchange rates are valid. Each time you post a transaction in a different currency, a conversion is made to translate that currency amount into the local currency amount. All entries in Microsoft Dynamics NAV keep all the amounts in the transaction currency and the local currency in separate fields.

The adjust exchange rates process will help you to update the amounts of posted transactions to the new assigned rates. The following screenshot shows how the currency exchange rates are defined for the EUR currency:

To date, this functionality is the same in both Microsoft Dynamics NAV and Microsoft Dynamics 365 Business Central.

Sales and marketing

The sales area can be used to manage all common sales process information, such as quotes, orders, and returns. There are also tools to plan and manage different types of customer information and transaction data.

The following screenshot shows the main page of the **Sales & Marketing** area:

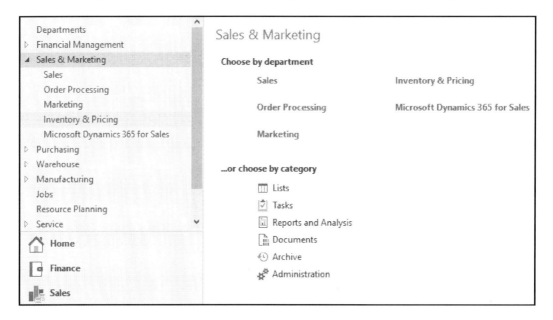

Customers

In the **Sales & Marketing** area, everything revolves around customers. The customer card contains a lot of information, but only a few fields are mandatory in order to be used by the customer on transactions; they are the ones that correspond to the posting groups. All other fields can be filled or not, depending on how you want the sales area to work, as demonstrated in the following screenshot:

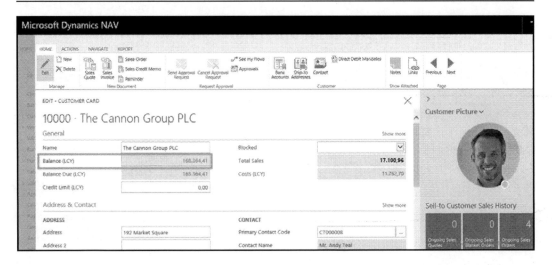

You can define a salesperson for the customer, to track the sales of each salesperson. You can set a credit limit for each customer so that you get a warning when you try to create a new order for the customer and the credit limit is exceeded. You can group your customers by price and discount groups to help you define prices. You can define different payment terms and methods. You can indicate how you are going to ship the goods to each customer, and you can also indicate a currency and language for the customer. Besides this, you can also create multiple bank accounts and credit cards.

Many times, a company establishes criteria to fill in all of this information. As an example, the company could have a norm that high-value customers will be part of a particular price group, will use specific posting groups, and will have particular payment terms. In this case, you can create as many customer templates as the defined criteria and apply a template each time a new customer is introduced to the system.

In the following screenshot, you can see all the fields that can be included in a **CUSTOMER TEMPLATE CARD**:

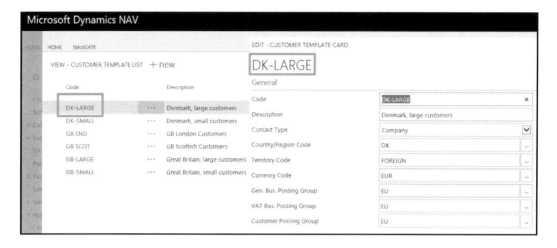

Order processing

The order processing part is all about documents. Microsoft Dynamics NAV allows you to create quotes, blanket orders, orders, return orders, invoices, and credit memos.

The sales process can start with any of the previously mentioned documents, depending on the company's needs. In the following diagram, you can see the information flow through the documents. The documents with a gray background are the ones from where the process can start:

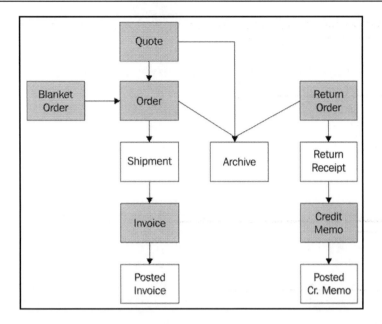

All the data from one document is carried forward to the next document. In addition, you can also create new documents by copying the data from any other sales document on the system.

In the previous diagram, the documents with a gray background are passed to the documents with the white background through a posting process, but posting routines can take a while to process.

Microsoft Dynamics NAV 2018 has a feature called **background posting**. If background posting is enabled, then data is put in a queue and posted later in the background. This allows users to keep working while the system posts their documents.

When you select a customer in a document, many fields from the customer card are copied to the document header. This is considered default data from that customer. You can change most of that data on a particular document.

Approvals

The approval system (in Microsoft Dynamics NAV 2018, it is a part of workflow) allows a user to **submit a document for approval** according to a predefined hierarchy of approval managers, with certain approval amount limits. The approval of a document can be initiated by an email notification sent to the user. Similarly, reminders of overdue approvals can be also sent. Pending approvals can also be viewed from the **Order Processing** menu.

The system allows you to create several approval templates where you can choose the document types to be included in an approval process and which approval and limit type are to be used for each document. Document amounts are the main criteria for including a document in an approval process. The different limit types that can be used are as follows:

- **No limits**: The document is included in the approval process, no matter how small or big the total amount is. It will then depend on the user setup.
- **Approval limits**: The document is included in the approval process if the total amount is greater than the amount limit.
- **Credit limits**: If a sales document that will put a customer over their credit limit is created, the document is sent for credit limit approvals. After this, amount approvals may also have to approve the document.

The following screenshot shows the **Sales Order Approval Workflow** page:

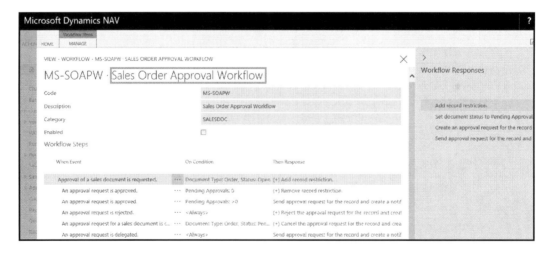

The following screenshot shows how the **Approval User Setup** and **NOTIFICATION SETUP** pages appear:

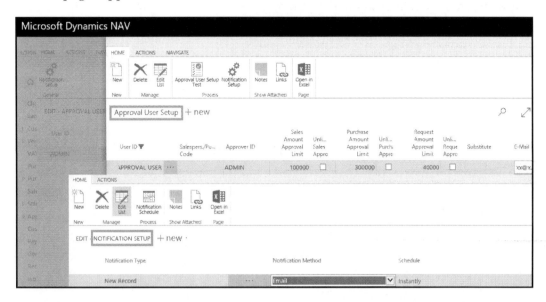

To date, the functionality is the same in both Microsoft Dynamics NAV and Microsoft Dynamics 365 Business Central.

Pricing

The pricing option allows you to specify how you want to set up sales price agreements. You can specify prices and discounts. Both prices and discounts can be for an individual customer, a group of customers, all customers, and for a campaign. You need to specify one price for each item. If no price is found, the last sales price of the item will be used. When a price agreement is created, you can specify whether or not VAT is included in the price. Sales prices and sales discounts are introduced in separate tables.

Microsoft Dynamics NAV always retrieves the best price. The best price is the lowest permissible price with the highest permissible line discount on a particular date.

In addition to specific item prices and discounts, you can also indicate invoice discounts or service charges. This can only be set up for individual customers, and not for a group of customers or a campaign.

When you create a sales document, a **Sales Line Details FactBox** indicates how many **Sales Price** and **Sales Line Discounts** can be applied to the document.

You can see the details by clicking on each blue number found in the FactBox. The sales price worksheet will help you change and update your current prices.

Marketing

The marketing functionality revolves around contacts. A contact can be a prospect that is not yet your customer, or your existing customer. Your company most likely does business with another company. And you're probably not the only person working at your company; the same can be said of the other company.

A contact is a way for you to keep track of all the people working at a particular company so you know who is working in what department.

You can create a contact and indicate their business relations. A contact can be related to customers, vendors, or bank accounts. You can categorize your contacts based on their industry groups or job responsibilities, or you can create your own profile criteria, for example, educational level, marital status, or hobbies.

The task management feature allows you to create and organize marketing campaigns. You can create to-do lists and link them to contacts and/or campaigns.

The opportunity management area allows you to keep track of sales opportunities, have an overview of what is in the pipeline, and plan ahead accordingly.

All of the interactions you do with your contacts are kept in the **Interaction Log**. This is where you can see a history of all the interactions you've had with your contacts.

The **CONTACT LIST** page looks like the following:

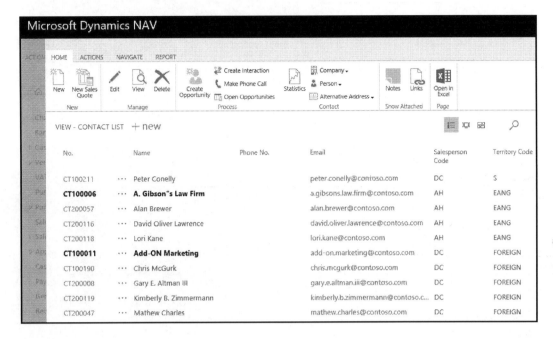

Purchasing

The purchasing area can be used to manage all the common purchase process information, such as quotes, orders, and returns. There are also tools to plan your purchases according to your company's needs.

The main page of the **Purchasing** area is shown in the following screenshot:

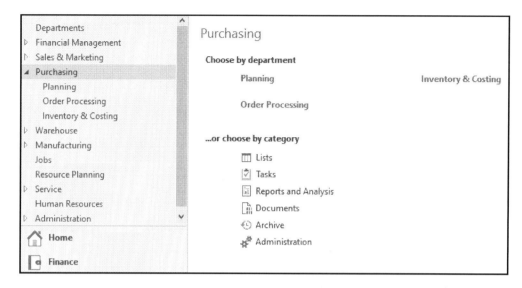

We'll provide a few details about each of these areas, although most processes are similar to the ones we have discussed in the *Sales and marketing* section.

Vendors

In the **Purchasing** area, everything revolves around vendors. Vendors' cards are pretty similar to customers' cards. Please refer to the *Customers* section of this chapter to see what you can expect from vendors.

Order processing

The order processing part is all about documents. Microsoft Dynamics NAV allows you to create quotes, blanket orders, orders, return orders, invoices, and credit memos.

Please refer to the *Order processing* subsection of the *Sales and marketing* section in this chapter to see what you can expect from order processing.

Approvals

The approval system (which is a part of Workflow), as seen for sales, allows the user to submit a document for approval according to a predefined hierarchy of approval managers with certain approval amount limits. The approval system works as explained in the *Approvals* subsection of the *Sales and marketing* section of this chapter.

Besides the different limits explained before, the purchase approval system includes a new type of limit, **request limits**. By using the request limit in combination with the request amount approval limit, a purchase request process can be set up for internal purchases in the company.

Pricing

The pricing option allows you to define purchase price agreements. It works similar to the pricing model of the *Sales and marketing* section of this chapter, with one difference. In the *Sales and marketing* section, we said that both prices and discounts could be set for an individual customer, a group of customers, for all customers, and for a campaign. In the *Purchasing* section, it can only be set for individual vendors.

Planning

If you purchase goods, the requisition worksheet can help to plan your purchases. You can manually enter items on the worksheet and fill in the relevant fields, or you can also run the **Calculate Plan Batch** process. This calculates a replenishment plan for the items that have been set up with the replenishment system of purchase or transfer; for example, the program will automatically suggest an action you should take to replenish the item. It could be increasing the item quantity on an existing order or creating a new order.

You can also use the **Drop Shipment** function to fill in the requisition worksheet lines. This function retrieves the sales orders that you want to designate for a drop shipment. You use **Drop Shipment** when an item is shipped directly from your vendor to your customer. The system may sometimes suggest planning lines that need extra attention by the planner before they can be accepted.

The **Calculate Plan Batch** job investigates the demand and supply situation of the item and calculates the projected available balance. The balance is defined as follows:

Balance = Inventory + Scheduled receipts + Planned receipts - Gross requirements

This also respects the minimum order quantity, the maximum order quantity, and the order multiple of each item.

The following screenshot shows how the **REQ. WORKSHEET** page appears after you have run the **Calculate Plan Batch** job:

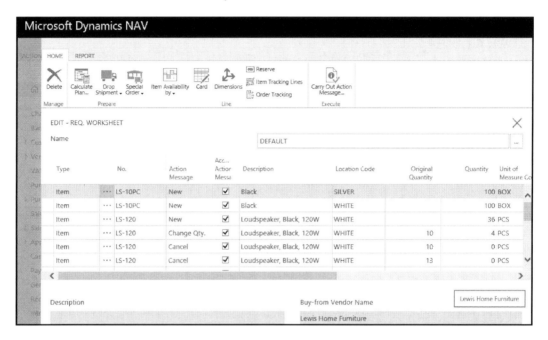

When you have finished reviewing the suggested purchases, you can use the **Carry Out Action Message** option to create new purchase orders and modify or cancel existing ones.

Warehouse

After the goods have been received and before they are shipped, a series of internal warehouse activities takes place to ensure an effective flow through the warehouse and to organize and maintain company inventories. Typical warehouse activities include putting items away, moving items inside or between warehouses, and picking items for assembly, production, or shipment.

The following screenshot shows the main page of the **Warehouse** area:

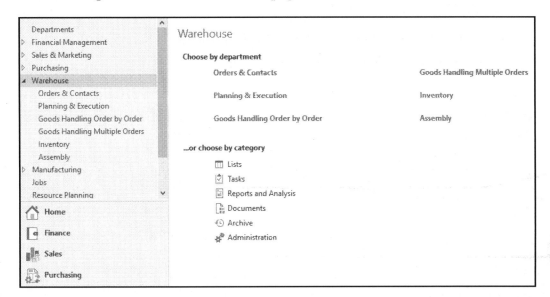

Items

In the **Warehouse** area, everything revolves around items. The item card contains a lot of information, but only a few fields are mandatory in order to be able to use the item on transactions: the base unit of a measure, and the fields corresponding to the posting groups.

All the other fields can be filled or unfilled depending on how you want the **Warehouse** area to work.

You can create multiple units of measure. You can categorize your item using the item category code and the product group code. You can indicate a shelf number for the item. You can use different costing methods, namely FIFO, LIFO, average, and standard. You can indicate how the replenishment of a product is going to be done (we have seen it in the *Purchasing* section of this chapter). You can also set up a lot of other information about the item such as cross-references and substitutes.

One item can have multiple variants. This is useful if you have a large number of almost identical items, for example, items that vary only in color. Instead of setting up each variant as a separate item, you can set up one item and then specify the various colors as variants of the item.

As part of your warehouse management, you may need to use multiple locations. We will cover locations in the next section. If you use multiple locations, you can create stock-keeping units for your items. Stock-keeping units allow you to differentiate between information concerning an item at different locations. As an example, the replenishment system of an item may be different at different locations. Stock-keeping units also allow you to differentiate between information concerning two variants of the same item. Information on the stock-keeping unit has priority over the item card.

One interesting feature about the item property is item tracking. You can track an item by serial number, lot number, expiration date, or a combination of all of them. You can create different tracking codes and set them up with different tracking policies.

The following screenshot shows an **ITEM TRACKING CARD** page:

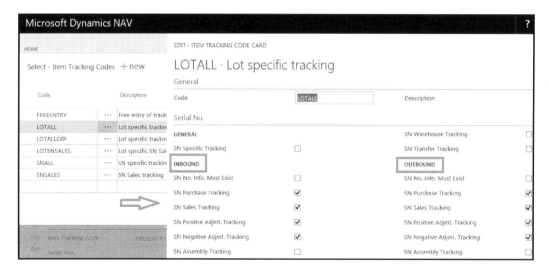

These policies reflect where it is mandatory to track the item; for example, you may only need to track a lot of purchases, but not sales.

Locations

You must set up a location in Microsoft Dynamics NAV for each warehouse location or distribution center. Even if you only have one warehouse or one location, you should still set this up.

You can specify the location elsewhere in the program, for example, on purchase and sales documents. This will then record the transactions for the location when you post, and you will be able to track the item inventory and item value on each location.

You can specify an unlimited number of bins in each location. A bin denotes a physical storage unit. You can then use bins on put-away and pick operations so that you can know where a specific item is stored.

Transfer orders

Transfer orders are used to transfer items between locations. The transfer order is a document similar to a sales order or a purchase order. The transfer order contains information about the source location, the destination location, and the date connected to the shipping and receiving of the order. An in-transit location must be used when working with transfer orders. The posting process of transfer orders is done in two separate steps, shipping and receiving.

Assembly

Assembly is used to create a new item, for example, a kit combining components in simple processes. This can be seen as a small manufacturing functionality, but does not require the complexity of full manufacturing.

To use this feature, you need to define assembly items. An assembly item is an item defined as **sellable** that contains an assembly **bill of materials** (**BOMs**). Items can be assembled to order, or assembled to stock.

You can create assembly orders that are used to manage the assembly process and to connect the sales requirements with the warehouse activities involved. Assembly orders differ from the other order types because they involve both output and consumption when posting.

Pick and put-away

Inventory can be organized and handled on the locations at the bin level. Multiple variables can be defined per bin as follows:

- Their type
- The type of actions that can be performed on the bin: pick, put-away, ship, and receive
- Their maximum capacity
- Their desired minimum capacity

With all this information, you can create pick and put-away documents that will tell you the following:

- Where to pick your inventory for shipment purposes
- Where to store your inventory when it is received

There are also documents to manage internal inventory movements, move inventory from one bin to another, and calculate the replenishment of pick bins.

Inventory

Each single item card contains a field called **Inventory** that specifies how many units of the item are in a location. Units are counted using the base unit of measure indicated on the item card. Microsoft Dynamics NAV automatically calculates the content of the field using the **Quantity** field in the **Item Ledger Entry** table. This means that every time a new **Item Ledger Entry** record is created, for example, after posting a sales order, the inventory of the item is updated.

You can filter the **Inventory** field so that its contents are calculated only on the basis of one or any combination of global dimension values, locations, variants, lots, or serial numbers.

An inventory is used in combination with other fields to know the availability of an item. Item availability can be shown by an event, a period, a variant, a location, the BOM level, and timeline. The following screenshot shows the **Item Availability by BOM Level** page:

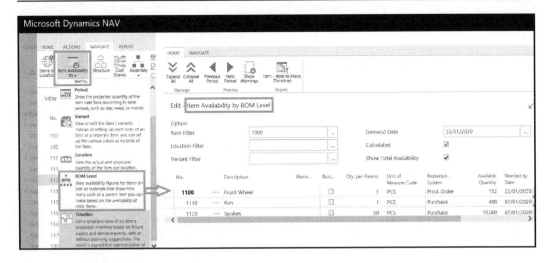

At least once in every fiscal year, you must take a physical inventory to see whether the quantity registered is the same as the physical quantity in stock. The physical inventory journals have been designed to help you during such a task, but an inventory is not only about units; it is also about the value of those units and their cost.

You can indicate different costing methods for an item. The choice determines the way a program calculates the unit cost. You can select any of the following costing methods: FIFO, LIFO, specific, average, and standard.

The system uses value entries to keep track of each item ledger entry's cost. One or more value entries can exist per item ledger entry. Every time you post an order, invoice, credit memo, and so on, the program creates value entries because all of these operations affect the item value. In addition, you can use the revaluation journal to change any item ledger entry cost. Some other concepts, such as freight or handling charges, may also affect the item value. You can use item charges to assign those charges to item ledger entries.

Manufacturing

The **Manufacturing** area is used to manage production. This involves the design and engineering work that will specify how and when items are handled, the components and resources that go into creating an end item, and the routing that define the process requirements of a given item that has been produced.

The **Manufacturing** area also provides tools to schedule production activities, manually or automatically pull production components for consumption, record time consumption, post finished operations that do not qualify as finished output but as scrapped material, and so on.

The following screenshot shows the main page of the **Manufacturing** area:

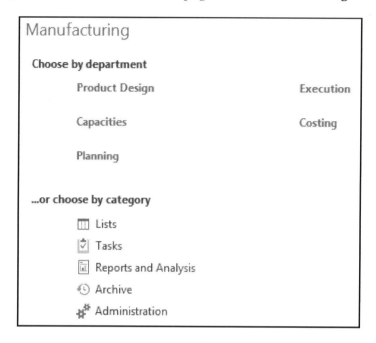

Product design

Product design starts on the item card. You need to create one item card for each end item that you want to produce, and also one item card for each component that you need to consume to obtain the end product.

For each component, you have to specify whether you purchase it, assemble it, or produce it. You also need to specify whether you need to stock the component or whether you just need it when an order is made. You can specify all of this information on the **Replenishment** tab of the item card, as shown in the following screenshot:

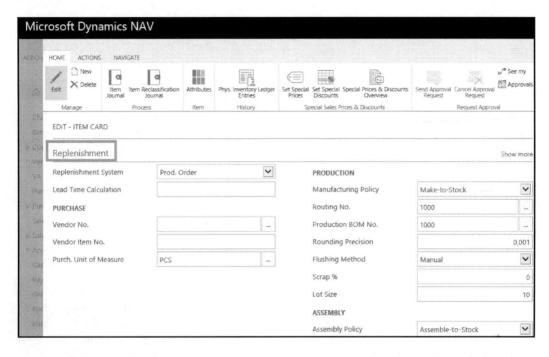

For items that need to be produced, you have to create a BOM. It is a listing of all the sub-assemblies, intermediates, parts, and raw materials that go into a parent item, along with the quantities of each component that is required.

Production BOMs may consist of several levels. You can use up to 50 levels. One production BOM always corresponds to one level. You have the option to copy the existing BOMs in order to create a new one.

The following screenshot shows the **PRODUCTION BOM** for item number **1000**:

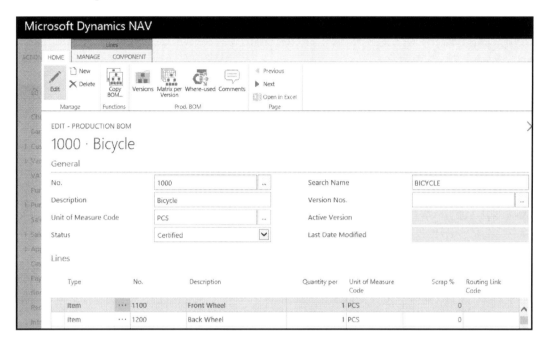

You also need to define routings to show the production process. The routings form the basis for production planning and control. Routings include detailed information about the method of manufacturing of a particular item. It includes the operations to be performed and sequenced. You can also include information about tools, resources, and personnel and quality measures.

Routing is the basis of process scheduling, capacity scheduling, material requirement scheduling, and the production documents.

The program also supports the production of parts families, that is, the same or similar item can be manufactured with a single routing. A production family is a group of individual items whose relationship is based on the similarity of their manufacturing processes. Forming production families can optimize material consumption.

Capacities

The program distinguishes between three types of capacities:

- Work centers
- Machine centers
- Resources

These are arranged hierarchically and each level contains subordinate levels. You can assign various machine centers to each work center. A machine center may only belong to one work center.

The planned capacity of a work center consists of the availability of the corresponding machine centers and the additional planned availability of the work center.

The planned availability of the work center group is thus the sum of all the corresponding availabilities of the machine centers and work centers. The availability is stored in calendar entries. To work with capacities, you need to create several calendars as follows:

- **Shop calendar**: This calendar defines a standard work week according to the start and end time of each working day and the work-ship relation. It also defines fixed holidays during a year.
- **Work center calendar**: This calendar specifies the working days and hours, shifts, holidays, and absences that determine the work center's gross available capacity measured in time according to its defined efficiency and capacity values.
- **Machine center's availability**: In this calendar, you can define the time periods when machine centers cannot be used. The machine centers are not assigned their own shop calendar; the work center shop calendar is used. The calendar for the machine center is calculated from the entries of the assigned shop calendar and the calendar absence entries of the machine center.
- **Resource capacities**: Resources, such as technicians, have their own capacity. You can use work-hour templates that contain the typical working hours in your company; for example, you can create templates for full-time technicians and part-time technicians. You can use work-hour templates when you add capacity to resources.

Planning

The planning system takes all the demand and supply data into account, nets the results, and creates suggestions to facilitate the balancing of supply and demand. Another goal of the planning system is to ensure that the inventory does not grow unnecessarily.

The terms running the planning worksheet, or running MRP, refer to the calculation of the master production schedule and material requirements based on the actual and forecasted demands. The planning system can calculate either the **Master Planning Schedule** (**MPS**) or **Material Requirements Planning** (**MRP**) on request, or it can calculate both at the same time. MPS and MRP can be explained as follows:

- **MPS**: This is the calculation of a master production schedule based on actual demand and the production forecast. The MPS calculation is used for end items that have a forecast or a sales order line. These items are called MPS items and are identified dynamically when the calculation starts.
- **MRP**: This is the calculation of material requirements based on the actual demand for components and the production forecast of the component level. MRP is calculated only for items that are not MPS items. The purpose of MRP is to provide time-phased formal plans, by item, and to supply the appropriate item at the appropriate time in the appropriate location and in the appropriate quantity.

Several planning parameters have to be filled in for the item, or the stock-keeping unit and the manufacturing set up, in order to tell the system how you want to plan your supply. The planning parameters control when, how much, and how to replenish, based on all the settings. Some of the planning parameters are as follows: the dampener period and quantity, the quantity reorder policy and reorder point, the maximum inventory, and the manufacturing policy or combined MPS/MRP calculation.

Planning is affected by numerous additional factors, such as the planning horizon defined by the order and the end dates specified when you run MPS/MRP from the **Planning Worksheet** or **Order Planning** page.

The forecasting functionality is used to create anticipated demand; it allows your company to create what-if scenarios in order to plan for, and meet, demand. Accurate forecasting can make a critical difference to the custom levels with regard to promised order dates and on-time delivery.

The sales forecast is the sales department's best guess at what will be sold in the future, and the production forecast is the production planner's projection of how many end items and derived sub-assemblies will have to be produced during specific periods in order to meet forecasted sales.

Execution

When materials have been issued, the actual production operations can start and then be executed in the sequence defined by the production order routing.

An important part of executing production is to post the production output to a progress report and to update the inventory with the finished items. Output posting can be done manually, or it can be done automatically with the use of backward flushing. In this case, material consumption is automatically posted along with the output when the production order changes to finished.

You also have to post the scrapped materials and consumed capacities that are not assigned to a production order, such as maintenance work. You can use the output journal and the capacity journal respectively to perform these operations.

Finally, you need to put away the output of the production. You will perform your put-away task according to how your warehouse is set up as a location. The inbound warehouse request will inform the warehouse that the production order is ready for put-away.

In basic warehousing, where your warehouse location requires put-away processing, but does not receive processing, you use the put-away inventory document to organize and record the put-away of the output. In advanced warehousing, where your location requires both put-away and reception processing, you create either an internal put-away document or a movement document to put away the output.

Costing

Many manufacturing companies select a valuation base of standard cost. This also applies to companies that perform light manufacturing, such as assembly and kitting. A standard cost system determines an inventory unit cost based on some reasonable historical or expected cost. Studies of past and estimated future cost data can then provide the basis for standard costs. These costs are frozen until a decision is made to change them. The actual cost to produce a product may differ from the estimated standard costs.

Standard costs of the manufactured item may entail direct material costs, labor costs, subcontractor costs, and overhead costs. A batch job can be run to create suggestions to change item costs as well as the standard cost on a work center, machine center, or resource cards. After revising the suggested changes, another batch job will help you to implement them.

Subcontracting

When a vendor performs one or more operational steps in production, subcontracting is a standard operational step in many manufacturing companies. Subcontracting may be a rare phenomenon, or an integral part of all production processes. Microsoft Dynamics NAV provides several tools to manage subcontract work:

- **Subcontract work center**: This is a work center with an assigned vendor (subcontractor). The subcontract work center can be used on a routing operation, which allows you to process the subcontracted activity. In addition, the cost of the operation can be designated at a routing or work center level.
- **Work center cost based on units or time**: This feature enables you to specify whether costs associated with the work center are based on the production time or a flat charge per unit. Although subcontractors commonly use a flat charge per unit to charge for their services, the program can handle both options: production time and flat charge per unit.
- **Subcontracting worksheet**: This feature allows you to find the production orders with the material ready to be sent to a subcontractor and also allows you to automatically create purchase orders for subcontract operations from the production order routings. The program then automatically posts the purchase order charges to the production order during the posting of the purchase order. Only production orders with a released status can be accessed and used from a subcontracting worksheet.

Job

The **Job** area supports common project management tasks, such as configuring a job and scheduling a resource, as well as providing the information needed to manage budgets and monitor progress. The jobs feature is meant to manage long-term projects that involve the use of man hours, machine hours, inventory items, and other types of usage that you need to keep track of.

Job cards

The **Job Card** page shows information about the job, such as the job number, job name, and information about job posting. There is one card for each job. In the old version of Microsoft Dynamics NAV, job tasks are showed on a separate page; now, the **Job Card** page includes the **Job Tasks** subpage as it happens, and an example for every sales and purchase document (with a header/lines page structure).

The following screenshot shows a **JOB CARD** page:

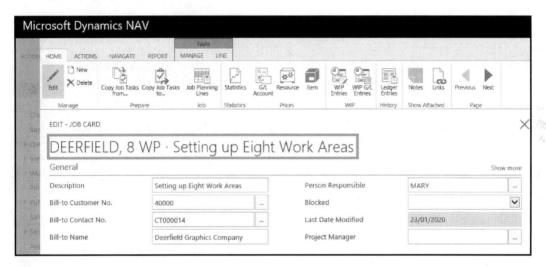

Job tasks subpage

A key part of setting up a new job is to specify the various **tasks** involved in the job. Every job must have a minimum of one task. In this way, it is possible to define a complex project structure

You create tasks by adding job task lines, as shown in the following screenshot:

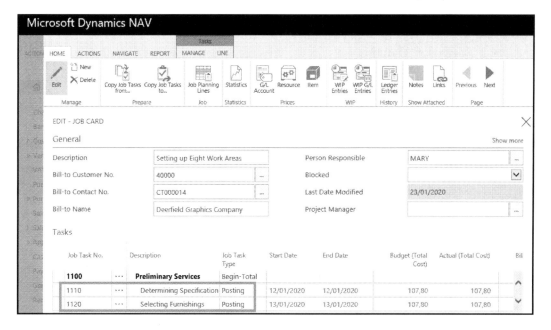

You have additional tools that help you to copy task lines from one job task to another. You can copy from a job task in the job you are working with, or from a job task linked to a different job.

The following screenshot shows an example of a job task's structure:

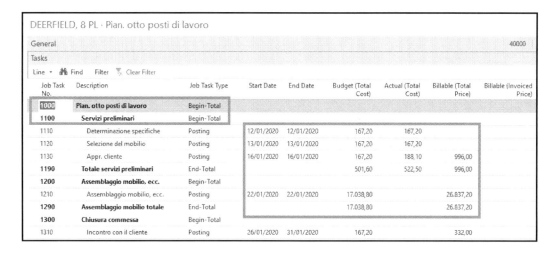

Planning lines

You can define each task that you have created for a job into planning lines. A planning line can be used to capture any information that you want to track for a job. You can use planning lines to add information such as which resources are required, or to capture which items are needed to fulfill the job.

For example, you may create a task to obtain customer approval. You can associate that task with planning lines for items such as meeting with the customer and creating a services contract.

For each planning line, you must define a line type, which can be **Budget**, **Billable**, or **Both Budget and Billable**. This is explained as follows:

- **Budget (schedule)**: This line type provides the estimated usage and costs of the job, typically in a time and materials-type contract. Planning lines of this type cannot be invoiced.
- **Billable (contract)**: This line type provides an estimated invoice to the customer, typically in a fixed price contract.
- **Budget and billable (both schedule and contract)**: This line type provides a scheduled usage equal to what you want to invoice.

In addition, you can specify an account type and fill in information such as quantity. As you add information, cost information is automatically filled in; for example, when you enter a new line, the cost, price, and discount for resources and items are initially based on the information that is defined on the resource and item cards.

The **JOB PLANNING LINES** page appears as follows:

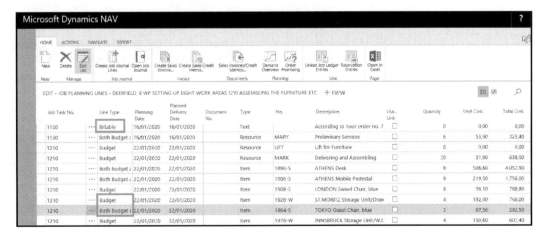

Time sheet

You can track machine and employee hours on the project using time sheets. Using the jobs functionality will provide a good overview, not only of individual jobs, but also of the allocation of employees, machinery, and other resources being used in all projects. You can also use this functionality for many types of services and consultancy tasks.

Time sheets in Microsoft Dynamics NAV handle time registration in weekly increments of seven days. You use them to track the time used on a job, service orders, and assembly orders. In addition, you can use them to record simple resource time registration and employee absences. Time sheets can be set up, so an approval is required before you can post them to the relevant job journal.

To date, the functionality is the same in both Microsoft Dynamics NAV and Microsoft Dynamics 365 Business Central.

Invoice jobs

During a job's development, job costs such as resource usage, materials, and job-related purchases can accumulate. As the job progresses, these transactions get posted to the job journal. It is important that all costs are recorded in the job journal before you invoice the customer.

You may invoice the job as a whole, or invoice just the selected billable lines. Invoicing can be done after the job is finished or at certain intervals during the job's progress, based on an invoicing schedule.

Work in process (WIP)

If a job runs over an extended period, you may want to transfer these costs to a **Work in Process** (**WIP**) account on the balance sheet while the job is being completed. You can then recognize the costs and sales in your income statement accounts when it is appropriate.

You can also calculate the WIP evaluation for each task within the job, or for the job as a whole, using different calculation methods. Microsoft Dynamics NAV allows you to calculate the value of the WIP of your jobs. The calculation is based on the **WIP method** selected for the individual jobs.

The WIP process creates WIP entries in connection with the jobs. This function only calculates WIP; it does not post it to the general ledger. To do so, another batch job must be run; the job posts WIP to G/L. There are several WIP methods that you can use on your jobs:

- **Cost value**: This begins by calculating the value of what has been provided by taking a proportion of the estimated total costs, based on the percentage of completion. Invoiced costs are subtracted by taking a proportion of the estimated total costs, based on the invoiced percentage.
- **Cost of sales**: This begins by calculating the recognized costs. Costs are recognized proportionally based on the scheduled total costs.
- **Sales value**: This recognizes revenue proportionally, based on the total usage costs and the expected cost recovery ratio.
- **Percentage of completion**: This recognizes revenue proportionally, based on the percentage of completion, that is, the total usage costs against schedule costs.
- **Completed contract**: A completed contract does not recognize revenue and costs until the job is completed. You may want to do this when there is significant uncertainty about the cost and revenue estimates for the job.

The system also allows you to create your own job WIP method that reflects the needs of your organization.

Resource planning

Many companies use resource management to track the time and effort that is involved in providing services; for example, an employee may visit a site to talk with a customer about a project. This time and effort can be charged to the customer on a sales order.

Resource planning is integrated with jobs, services, and assembly orders. When resources are used or sold in a job, for example, the prices and costs associated with them are retrieved from the information set up in the resource planning area.

But before you can start selling services and jobs, or assigning resources to assembly projects, you must set up information about policy and pricing, which can be used in resource transactions. All pricing information is adjustable.

Resource card

The resource card is used to specify resources, which can be employees, machinery, or other company resources.

 A lot of companies use the resource card to capture the **sale of non-stock items and services**. This will allow the data entry clerk to select from a list of predefined resources when they are entering a sales document, instead of going to and selecting from the **Chart of Accounts**.

For most companies, an optimal assignment of resources is an important part of the planning and production process. The following screenshot shows the **RESOURCE CARD** page:

You can base production and project planning on the availability and capacity of resources. Resources can also be included in bills of materials, job planning, and job costing. Resources can be integrated with the general ledger. Resources can also be posted using the documents in sales and receivables. Global dimensions can be used with resources.

You can invoice customers for sales that are composed of various resources. Resource costs can be calculated. You can use general ledger integration to post costs and revenues that are related to the sale of resources.

You can set up alternative costs for resources; for example, if you pay an employee a higher hourly rate for overtime, you can set up a resource cost for the overtime rate. The alternative cost that you set up for the resource will override the cost on the resource card when you use the resource in the resource journal.

Pricing

You can specify the default amount per hour when the resource is created. For example, if you use a specific machine on a job for 5 hours, the job would be calculated based on the amount per hour.

To correctly manage resource activities, you must set up your resources and the related costs and prices. The job-related prices, discounts, and cost factor rules are set up on the job card. You can specify the costs and prices for individual resources, resource groups, or all the available resources of the company. For services, you can adjust pricing in the **Service Item** worksheet.

A few batch jobs allow you to obtain resource price suggestions based on standard prices, or on alternative prices. You can then implement the price changes.

Service

Providing an ongoing service to customers is an important part of any business and can be a source of customer satisfaction and loyalty, in addition to revenue. Managing and tracking a service is not always easy, but Microsoft Dynamics NAV provides a set of tools to help. These tools are designed to support repair shop and field service operations and can be used in business scenarios such as complex customer service distribution systems, industrial service environments with bills of materials, and high-volume dispatching of service technicians with requirements for spare parts management.

With these tools, you can accomplish the following tasks:

- Schedule service calls and set up service orders
- Track repair parts and supplies
- Assign service personnel based on skill and availability
- Provide service estimates and service invoices

In addition, you can standardize coding, set up contracts, implement a discounting policy, and create route maps for service employees.

In general, there are two aspects of service management:

- Configuring and setting up your system
- Using it for pricing, contracts, orders, service personnel dispatch, and job scheduling

The following screenshot shows the main page of the **Service** area:

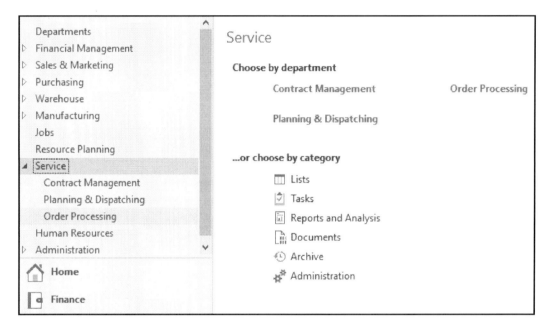

Service items

A service item is an item that has been sold to a customer and then registered for a service. A service item has a unique identification number and can be linked to an item. You can assign a warranty to service items and specify the response time for their service. Service items may consist of many components.

Service items can be created automatically when you ship sold items, or you can create them manually. The following screenshot shows the **SERVICE ITEM CARD** page:

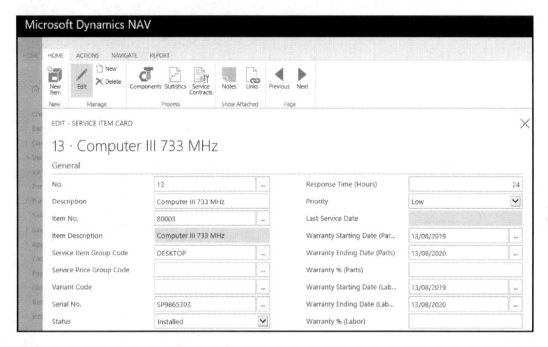

When you have set up service items, you can register them in service orders and service contracts.

Servicing some service items may require specific skills. If this is the case, you can assign skill codes to the items to which these service items are linked, or to these service items directly. This way, when a service is scheduled for the item, you will be able to assign the proper resources to do the job.

Sometimes, you cannot repair a service item, but you can choose to replace it instead. Microsoft Dynamics NAV offers you a chance to replace it either temporarily or permanently.

Contracts

One way to set up a service management business is to have standard contractual agreements between you and your customers that describe the level of service and the service expectations. You can set up contract templates, which you can then use to create standardized contracts for your business. In addition, you can set up a system to create quotes for services and to turn these quotes into contracts.

After you have set up the template, you can customize the resulting contract to keep track of service hours, or other items that may vary from customer to customer.

Contracts specify general information, which includes information about the serviced customer, the starting date of the contract, the service period, the response time, the bill-to customer, the invoice period, the annual amount, the prepaid and income accounts, price update specifications, and so on. A contract may include more than one service item.

You can also set up a system to keep track of contract status and view how gain and loss information about your contracts is being posted.

Price management

The price management feature allows you to apply the best price to service orders and to set up personalized service price agreements for customers. You can set up different service price groups, so you can consider the service item or service item group, in addition to the type of fault that the service task involves. You can set up these groups for a limited period of time, or for a specific customer or currency. You can use price calculation structures as templates to assign a specific price to a specific service task.

For instance, this makes it possible to assign specific items included in the service price in addition to the type of work included. This also makes it possible to use different VAT and discount amounts for different service price groups. To make sure that the correct prices are applied, you can assign fixed, minimum, or maximum prices depending on the agreements that you have with your customers.

Before adjusting the price of a service item on a service order, you are provided with an overview of what the results of the price adjustment will be. You can approve these results, or you can make additional changes if you want to have a different result. The entire adjustment is performed line by line, which means that there are no additional lines created.

The service price adjustment groups are also used to set up the different types of price adjustments. For example, you can set up a service price adjustment group that adjusts prices for spare parts, one that adjust prices for labor, another that adjusts prices for costs, and so on. You can also specify whether the service price adjustment should be applied to just one specific item or resource, or to all items or resources.

Each service price adjustment group holds information about the adjustments that you want to make to the service lines, as you can see in the following screenshot:

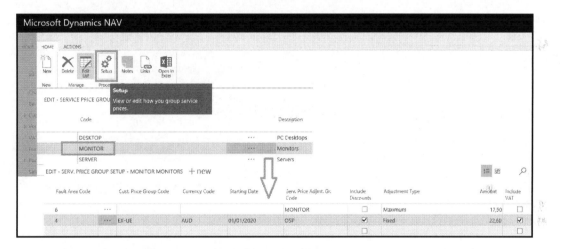

The service price adjustment function does not apply to service items that belong to service contracts. You can only adjust the service prices of items that are part of a service order. You cannot adjust the price of a service item if it has a warranty. You cannot adjust the price of a service item on a service order if the service line linked to it has been posted as an invoice, either in full or in part.

Service orders

Service orders are the documents in the Microsoft Dynamics NAV Service Management application area in which you can enter information about services (repair and maintenance) on service items.

Service orders are created in the following instances:

- When a customer requests a service.
- Automatically by the program at the intervals defined in service contracts.
- When you convert a service quote to a service order. A service quote can be used as a preliminary draft for a service order.

Service orders and service quotes are composed of the following instances:

- **Service header**: This contains general information about the service, such as the customer, the contract related to the order, the service order status, or the start and finish dates.
- **Service item lines**: These contain information related to the service item, such as the service item number, its description, the serial number, or the response time.
- **Service lines**: These contain information about the service costs, such as spare parts (items) used on the order, resource hours, G/L account payments, and general costs.

You may lend customers loaner items to temporarily replace the service items that you have received for servicing.

Service tasks

After you have created a service order or service quote, registered service item lines, and allocated resources to the service items in the order or quote, you can start repairing and maintaining the service items.

The service task page gives you an overview of the service items that need servicing. You can update the information on the service items for each task, such as the repair status, or enter service lines for that service item.

Fault reporting

When a customer brings in a service item for repair, you can assign a fault code to indicate the nature of the fault. The fault code can be used with the resolution code to determine the possible repair method to use. In the following screenshot, you can see an example of **FAULT CODES** and **RESOLUTION CODES**:

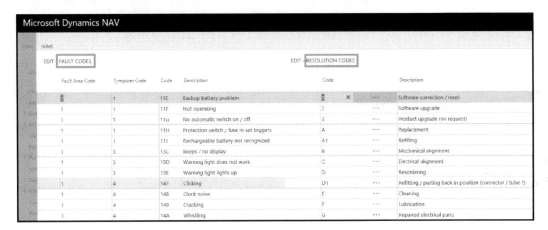

Depending on the level of fault reporting in a company, you might also need to register **Fault Area Codes** and **Symptom Codes**.

Human resources

The human resources feature lets you keep detailed records of your employees. You can register and maintain employee information, such as employment contracts, confidential information, qualifications, and employee contacts. You can also use the human resources feature to register employee absence.

To start using **Human Resources**, you must set up employees and other basic information. You can also associate various codes with an employee, which allows you to filter information and view specific employees.

Employees

To use the human resources feature, you need to create employee cards. From the employee card, you can enter basic information about the employee. The following screenshot shows the **EMPLOYEE CARD** page:

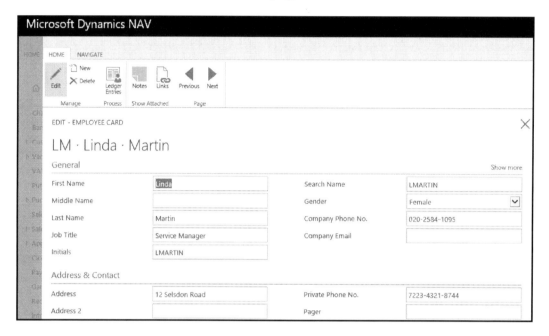

Linked to the employee card, you can set up alternative addresses, relatives, qualifications, and miscellaneous information where you can keep track of any information you want, for example, if the employee uses a company car. You can create as many miscellaneous articles as you need and link them to the employees.

The human resources application area is linked to the resources application area. So, when you update certain basic information about the employee (such as name, address, social security number, employment date, and other relevant information related to the employee), the program automatically updates the resource card for the employee.

Absence registration

You can register employee absences and assign different causes of absences. You can then see the information in various ways throughout the program and analyze employee absences. For example, you can compare your company's rate of absenteeism to national or industry-related averages for absenteeism.

A sudden increase in an employee's absences may reflect personal problems on the employee's part. With the **Employee Absence** table, you can take note of these problems at an early stage.

Country localizations

Microsoft Dynamics NAV comes with some country/region local functionalities to address specific needs. Most of these local functionalities are related to tax registering and tax reporting, or are legal requirements for the country.

You will find a complete list of local functionalities for Microsoft Dynamics NAV at `https://docs.microsoft.com/en-us/previous-versions/dynamicsnav-2016/hh922908(v=nav.90)`.

You will find a complete list of local functionalities for Microsoft Dynamics 365 Business Central at `https://docs.microsoft.com/en-us/dynamics365/business-central/about-localization`.

Microsoft Dynamics NAV Workflow

The workflow feature has been implemented in the application since Microsoft Dynamics NAV 2016. It enables you to model real-life business processes. It is defined as the movement of documents or tasks through a work process. Adopting workflow as a developer requires a move from functional code to "when-then" thinking.

The workflow topics are as follows: Workflow Templates and Designer, Workflow Model and Architecture, Approval and Notification Model, and Workflow User Group.

At present, it is also possible to create a workflow using Microsoft Flow, a new cloud platform dedicated to this management. In practice, it's possible to use both solutions; the Microsoft Dynamics 365 Business Central system works in the same way as Microsoft Dynamics NAV.

Vertical and horizontal solutions

As we said earlier in this chapter, one of the benefits of Microsoft Dynamics NAV is that it can be customized. A brand new functional area can be created from scratch, or new features added to an existing area.

Many people and companies have developed new functional areas, or have expanded the existing ones, and have registered their solution as an add-on. This means that the standard functionality of Microsoft Dynamics NAV is much more extensive than the functional areas we have covered in this chapter.

Actually, you can find almost 2,000 registered add-ons or third-party solutions that cover all kinds of functional areas. To ensure the quality of the add-ons released for Microsoft Dynamics NAV, Microsoft has introduced the Certified for Microsoft Dynamics NAV logo for all add-on partners who have passed rigorous tests through a third-party testing company.

If a customer asks you for a major modification of their Microsoft Dynamics NAV, the best solution will probably be to look for an existing add-on that already covers your customer's needs. Implementing this solution usually consists of configuration and some limited custom development. On the other hand, if you choose to develop it all from scratch, you might find yourself with a lengthy, high-cost, and high-risk project.

Accessing Microsoft Dynamics NAV

In the past, Microsoft Dynamics NAV had a single client access. But technology has changed and evolved, and so has Microsoft Dynamics NAV. The release of Microsoft Dynamics NAV 2009 already brought two new ways of accessing the application: the RTC and SOAP Web services. Microsoft Dynamics NAV 2018 also brings new accessibility options: the Web client and Universal App, and several other types of integration clients. It has also removed the accessibility option, the Classic Client, although it has been maintained and converted for development purposes.

In this section, we will explain the different environments in which you can access the Microsoft Dynamics NAV 2018 application.

Windows client

The Windows client is also known as the **RoleTailored Client**, or the **RTC** client. That was its name when the client was first released on Microsoft Dynamics NAV 2009. But Microsoft Dynamics NAV 2018 has the Web client, which is also a RoleTailored Client. So, we cannot call it the RoleTailored Client any more.

The Windows client is based on the individuals within an organization, their roles, and the tasks they perform. When users first enter Microsoft Dynamics NAV, they see the data needed for the daily tasks they do according to their role. Users belonging to different roles will have a different view of the system, each of them seeing only those functions they need to be able to perform their daily tasks.

For those of you who haven't used Microsoft Dynamics NAV 2009 yet, but who have had the opportunity to work with Microsoft Business Solutions NAV 4.0 or 5.0, you might remember how difficult it was at times to locate a specific feature in the jungle of the navigation pane. Switching back and forth between the specific menus in search of a menu item was a frustrating experience, especially for users performing tasks in several functional areas of the application. Unless you used shortcuts, accessing any feature required three or four clicks, provided you knew exactly where it was. The system also didn't do much to help users focus on what was needed to be done, and after you found the feature you needed, you typically had to spend extra time searching for documents or tasks that needed your attention. With the RoleTailored Client, the feature jungle was gone.

The Windows client allows users to widely customize the data they see on each page. They have the ability to personalize the pages according to their requirements by hiding, moving, and configuring parts contained on the pages, and also by saving queries, adding filters, and adding or removing fields. The ribbon can also be customized; you can add, remove, and rename actions, menus, and tabs.

The following screenshot shows what the **Role Center** of the Windows client looks like. **Role Center** is the main page of the client, and it is the first page a user sees when entering Microsoft Dynamics NAV (in this case, it is shown as the **Sales Order Processor** role):

The Windows client supports many methods for authenticating users who try to access the Dynamics NAV Web client:

- **Windows**: This credential type authenticates users using their Windows credentials (Active Directory, local workgroup, or the local computer's users). Because they are authenticated through Windows, Windows users are not prompted for credentials when they start the Windows client.
- **Username**: This setting prompts the user for username/password credentials when starting the client. These credentials are then validated against Windows authentication by the Microsoft Dynamics NAV Server.
- **NavUserPassword**: This setting manages authentication by the Microsoft Dynamics NAV Server, but is not based on Windows users or Active Directory. The user is prompted for username/password credentials when they start the client. The credentials are then validated by an external mechanism.

- **AccessControlService**: Using this setting, NAV uses the Microsoft Azure **Access Control Service** (**ACS**, this feature will be superseded after November 2018) or **Azure Active Directory** (**Azure AD**) for user authentication services.

Web client

The Microsoft Dynamics NAV Web client gives users access to Microsoft Dynamics NAV data over a network, such as the internet. From a web browser, users can view and modify data from a user-friendly interface that resembles the Windows client where the starting point is **Role Center**. The **Role Center** page can be customized according to a user's individual needs based on their role, company, and daily tasks. The Web client does not replace the Windows client, but complements it by enabling scenarios that are not possible with the Windows client.

The following screenshot shows what the role center of the Web client looks like:

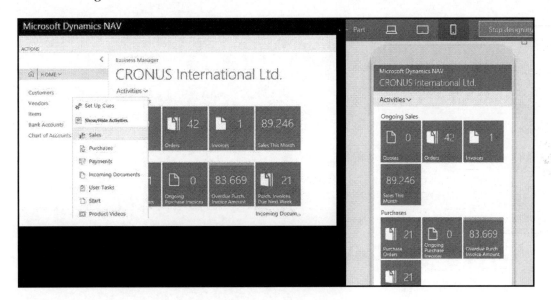

The Microsoft Dynamics 365 Business Central Web client (Business Manager role) dashboard looks as follows:

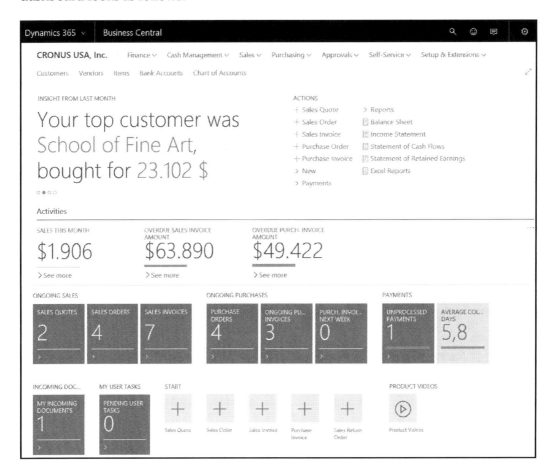

Web client – "In-Client" Designer and User Personalization

Personalize your workspace directly in the browser. Today, it is actually possible to configure the Web client as you want (configured by the browser); it has become a desktop interactive whiteboard where you can customize almost everything.

Nowadays, it is possible to perform the following actions:

- Reposition the freeze pane
- Move and hide page parts
- Reposition or hide Cues and Cue Groups
- Use list parts on Role Centers

The Microsoft Dynamics NAV Web client shown here supports most of the features that the Microsoft Dynamics NAV Windows client supports; however, there are a number of exceptions and limitations:

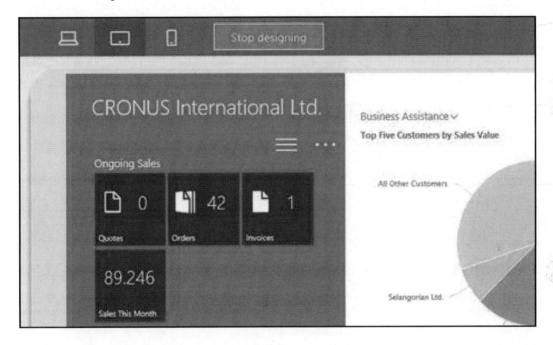

The full list of the limitations can be found at `https://docs.microsoft.com/en-us/dynamics-nav/feature-limitations-of-the-microsoft-dynamics-nav-web-client`.

Personalization in Microsoft Dynamics 365 Business Central SaaS is not possible in production environments, only in Sandbox environments, as can be seen in the following screenshot:

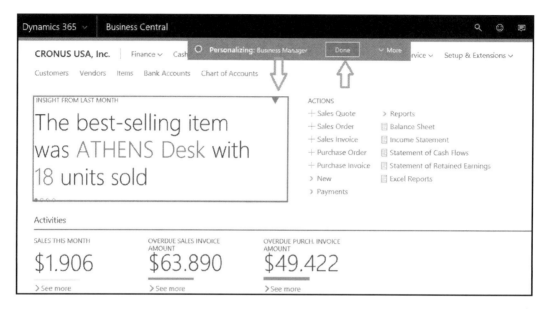

Tablet client, phone client, and Universal App

Let's first talk about the tablet client. With Microsoft Dynamics NAV 2015, the tablet client has been introduced. This means that you can download an app to connect to a web server on your iOS, Android, and Microsoft tablet devices. The design of the tablet client is focused on how you usually hold the tablet—using both hands and holding it like a steering wheel. The design has been done so that you can navigate between screens in an easy way.

The tablet functionalities are based on the Web client. So, this means that whenever you modify something in a page, it will translate into the Web client and the tablet client. The following image shows Microsoft Dynamics NAV on three devices:

Image showing Microsoft Dynamics NAV can be used on three different devices

With Microsoft Dynamics NAV 2016, the Universal App has been introduced. This is a new product. With Microsoft Dynamics NAV 2016, the same app released for tablet has been enhanced to also support the phone experience. It could then be downloaded and deployed in tablet and phone devices in a universal way. Universal means that it supports most of the device universe, covering iOS, Android, and Microsoft tablets and phones; an app for every device, with Windows continuum technology supported.

When we talk about Universal App, we mean that it works on different devices, but that behaviors are different depending on the device, OS, and so on.

If we run the Universal App on a Windows computer with a keyboard attached, then it will show the Web client interface where print preview is available, and from preview direct printing too.

If we run the Universal App on a computer without a keyboard (in tablet mode), then print preview and the option to direct print are not available. Universal Apps only save as PDFs and print using the available viewer and printer; the same is true if we use other OSes or devices instead of Windows.

Where can I download the apps? The apps can be downloaded from some marketplaces (Microsoft Windows Store, Google Play Store, and Apple Store), as demonstrated in the following screenshot:

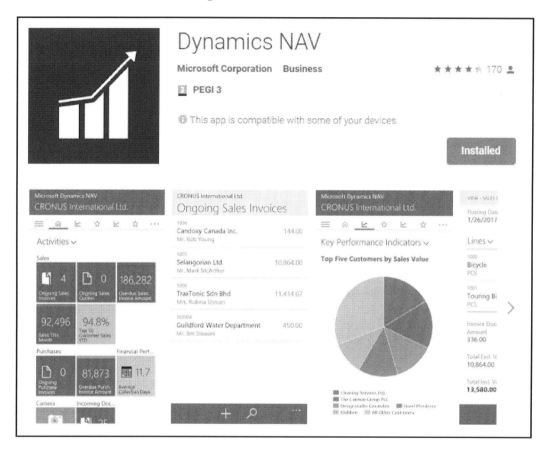

Downloading the Dynamics NAV app

SharePoint integration (remote client)

Microsoft Dynamics NAV SharePoint integration (remote client) enables you to interact with Microsoft Dynamics NAV data from a Microsoft SharePoint website. By integrating with SharePoint, the Microsoft Dynamics NAV SharePoint client can use the business and administration features available in Microsoft SharePoint, including workflows, business connectivity services, workspaces, SharePoint authentication, and scalability.

Working with Microsoft Dynamics NAV pages and reports in the SharePoint remote client is very similar to working with pages and reports in Microsoft Dynamics NAV Windows client, or Microsoft Dynamics NAV Web client. The Microsoft Dynamics NAV SharePoint client is designed for occasional users who typically need an overview of their daily work status and perform relatively straightforward or light data entries:

The Cronus Company Team Site dashboard view

Web services

Microsoft Dynamics NAV provides Web services, which makes it easy for other systems to integrate with Microsoft Dynamics NAV. Web services allow you to expose the business logic of Microsoft Dynamics NAV to other environments.

Web services are a lightweight, industry-standard means of making an application's functionality available to a wide range of external systems and users. Microsoft Dynamics NAV 2018 supports the creation and publishing of Microsoft Dynamics NAV functionality as Web services. You can expose pages, code units, or queries as Web services and even enhance a Web service page with an extension code unit. When you publish Microsoft Dynamics NAV objects as Web services, they are immediately available on the network.

Developers can publish two types of Web services from Microsoft Dynamics NAV objects:

- **SOAP Web services**: You can publish either Microsoft Dynamics NAV pages or code units as SOAP services.
- **OData Web services**: You can publish either pages or queries as OData services. The OData protocol offers new and flexible opportunities for interacting with Microsoft Dynamics NAV data. For example, you can use OData Web services to publish a refreshable link to Microsoft Dynamics NAV data that can be displayed in Microsoft Excel using Power Pivot or in SharePoint.

Three different objects can be exposed as Web services:

- **Page Web services**: When you expose a page as an OData Web service, you can query that data to return a service metadata (EDMX) document or an AtomPub document. When you expose a page as a SOAP Web service, you expose a default set of operations that you can use to manage common operations such as create, read, update, and delete. For SOAP services, you can also use extension code units to extend the default set of operations that are available on a page.
- **Code unit Web services**: Currently available only for SOAP Web services, code unit Web services provide you with maximum control and flexibility. When a code unit is exposed as a Web service, all the functions defined in the code unit are exposed as operations.
- **Query Web services**: When you expose a Microsoft Dynamics NAV query as an OData Web service, you can query that data to return a service metadata (EDMX) document or an AtomPub document.

Dynamics NAV Development Environments

In Microsoft Dynamics NAV 2018, you can use the Microsoft Dynamics NAV Development Environment (C/SIDE plus C/AL) or the New Modern Development Environment (VS Code plus the AL Language Extension) to develop Microsoft Dynamics NAV applications. The Microsoft Dynamics NAV Development Environment, which was also an end user client in the earlier versions of Microsoft Dynamics NAV, was formerly known as the Classic Client. The New Modern Development Environment is a completely different system—modern and open source, based on VS Code (Visual Studio Code).

The Old Development Environment (C/SIDE)

When you open the Old Development Environment, the **Object Designer** opens, which gives you access to Microsoft Dynamics NAV objects. You can use the Object Designer to modify the application or to create new application areas.

The following screenshot displays how the C/SIDE appears:

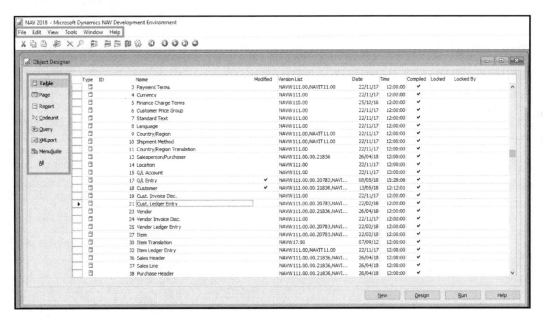

Screen showing the appearance of C/SIDE

Events and extensions

Events and extensions are the core of the new development model for Microsoft Dynamics NAV 2018 and, overall, Microsoft Dynamics 365 Business Central:

- **Events**: This is a new model to help you create safe, upgraded extensions to Microsoft Dynamics NAV and in Microsoft Dynamics 365 Business Central. It is designed for cloud, multitenancy, and repeatability, which will enable developers to change behavior and add functionality without explicitly modifying source code (Microsoft gives developers a pre-built way to add customizations). It's a modern programming style in terms of C/AL Style; an event is like an integration point, or "hook", into Microsoft Dynamics NAV.
- **Extensions**: This is the correct way for you to think about developing, packaging, and delivering, and is a modern development approach. An extension is put together using the code the developer has written using the events. The extension wraps up all of that code and puts it into a package that you could just click on and install. Only code that has been written in one of the events can be part of the extension; we are currently at extensions version 2.0.

You can extend and customize a Microsoft Dynamics NAV deployment without modifying the original application objects. With extension packages, you install, upgrade, and uninstall functionalities in on-premise or SaaS deployments. Customers can easily add or remove horizontal or customized functionality to/from their solution that upgrades much easier than past solutions.

For more information, you can visit the following URLs:

- **Events**:
  - https://blogs.msdn.microsoft.com/nav/2015/10/15/integration-events-in-microsoft-dynamics-nav-2016/
  - https://docs.microsoft.com/en-us/previous-versions/dynamicsnav-2016/mt299398(v=nav.90)
- **Extensions**:
  - https://blogs.msdn.microsoft.com/nav/2015/10/12/introducing-extensions-in-microsoft-dynamics-nav-2016/
  - https://docs.microsoft.com/en-us/dynamics-nav/microsoft-dynamics-nav-extention-packages
  - https://docs.microsoft.com/en-us/dynamics-nav/how-to--develop-an-extension

The New Modern Development Environment

The New Modern Development Environment is made up of VS Code and a Microsoft AL Language extension. The New Modern Development Environment has become necessary to modernize the system and allows the creation of applications in a parallel layer, so that the system can update itself since the standard is not modified. The Microsoft AL Language extension is the new tool to develop extensions. You can learn more at `https://github.com/Microsoft/AL`.

The following screenshot shows how the New Modern Development Environment appears:

New Modern Development Environment screen

Microsoft AL is the new language based on Extension 2.0 and is itself an extension. It can be installed from the Microsoft Dynamics NAV 2018 DVD or directly from the Microsoft Store.

The installation is different for the two technologies. In practice, it is installed in different ways:

- For Microsoft Dynamics NAV 2018, it is installed from the DVD. You can take a look at this post for more details: `https://saurav-nav.blogspot.com/2018/03/al-installing-al-with-microsoft.html`.

- For Microsoft Dynamics 365 Business Central, it is installed from the Microsoft Store or directly from VS Code. You can take a look at these posts for more details: `https://marketplace.visualstudio.com/items?itemName=ms-dynamics-smb.al`, and `https://docs.microsoft.com/en-us/dynamics365/business-central/dev-itpro/developer/devenv-get-started`.

The following screenshot shows the Microsoft AL Language Extension installed from VS Code; search for `AL` in **EXTENSIONS: MARKETPLACE**:

Let's compare the two development environments—C/SIDE plus C/AL versus VS Code plus AL:

- **Old Development Environment:** C/SIDE, Object Designer, FOB, and TXT Objects
- **New Modern Development Environment:** VS Code, .APP Objects (extensions only)

The following diagram also demonstrates this comparison:

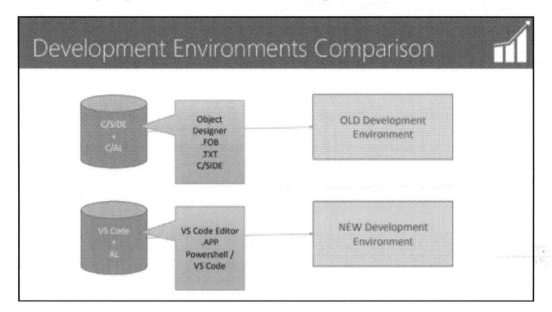

As previously mentioned, whatever you change in the development environment will be reflected in all of the different clients; this significantly reduces the development time to deploy changes to your clients.

The Microsoft cloud model

The Microsoft cloud model is composed of a series of services, designed specifically for the cloud. All these applications and services can interact with one another, creating a dense network of services and opportunities. Every year, new services are launched, and now the offer is very wide and diversified.

Microsoft cloud services – a suite of applications

Microsoft cloud services are as follows: Azure, Azure Services, Azure IoT, Power Apps, Office 365 Suite, Cognitive Services, Cortana Intelligence, SharePoint, Power BI, Microsoft Flow, Microsoft Dynamics 365, and Microsoft Dynamics 365 Business Central.

Dynamics 365 Business Central (on-premise, SaaS)

Microsoft Dynamics 365 Business Central is a modern solution for modern businesses.

Microsoft Dynamics 365 Business Central (DYN365BC) connects business processes to help SMBs grow sales, manage finances, and streamline operations. It is designed as a true multitenant public cloud service **(SaaS)** running on Microsoft Azure. Customers can access the service on the web using Web client, or apps for Windows, iOS, or Android devices (`https://www.microsoft.com/en-in/p/microsoft-dynamics-365-business-central/9nblggh4ql79?rtc=1activetab=pivot:overviewtab`).

Microsoft Dynamics 365 Business Central enables customers to upgrade their accounting software and legacy ERP systems with a single, comprehensive solution to manage core business processes across finances, operations, sales, and customer service. Along with its new capabilities, the application will include an all-new user experience so it is easy to get started with a familiar Microsoft Office 365 user interface, personalized feeds, and smart notifications.

Microsoft Dynamics 365 Business Central is based on the Microsoft Dynamics NAV platform and several other Microsoft services. Microsoft Dynamics 365 Business Central will present the full functionality of Microsoft Dynamics NAV under two different offerings (licensing model):

- **Essential**:
  - Financial management
  - Supply chain
  - CRM
  - Human resources
  - Project management
- **Premium (this covers essential, plus the following two additions)**:
  - Service management
  - Manufacturing

Microsoft Dynamics 365 Business Central's appearance is as follows:

Appearance of Microsoft Dynamics 365 Business Central

Summary

In this chapter, we have seen that Microsoft Dynamics NAV is an ERP system targeted at small and medium-sized companies; Microsoft Dynamics 365 Business Central is the on-premise and SaaS evolution of Microsoft Dynamics NAV. In the next version of Microsoft Dynamics NAV, it will be called Microsoft Dynamics 365 Business Central on-premise, or something connected to Microsoft Dynamics 365 Business Central, but no longer "NAV".

Microsoft Dynamics NAV is focused on roles and their daily tasks, and offers solutions in different functional areas including financial management, sales and marketing, purchasing, warehousing, manufacturing, job, resource planning, services, human resources, and add-ons created by partners. We have described each functional area so that you know what to expect.

Microsoft Dynamics NAV can be used in different environments, such as the Windows client, the Web client, the Tablet Client, the Universal App, the SharePoint integration feature, or an external application that connects to Microsoft Dynamics NAV via Web services. The development environments are used to develop new features on top of Microsoft Dynamics NAV.

In the next chapter, we will cover the new features released with Microsoft Dynamics NAV 2018 in detail.

2
Microsoft Dynamics NAV 2018 – An Overview

There are quite a few new things in Microsoft Dynamics NAV 2018. Releases prior to Microsoft Dynamics NAV 2013 mainly concentrated on application or architectural changes, while Microsoft Dynamics NAV 2013 incorporated changes in relation to both aspects at the same time, and Microsoft Dynamics NAV 2018 has made drastic improvements to what was originally built for Microsoft Dynamics NAV 2013.

In this chapter, we will get an overview of the new features included in Microsoft Dynamics NAV 2018. We will first go through the features that end users will appreciate in Microsoft Dynamics NAV 2018. After this, we will take a look at the features that developers and administrators will appreciate (the IT changes).

Microsoft Dynamics 365 Business Central, as mentioned in the previous chapter, is the evolution of Microsoft Dynamics NAV 2018, and contains all the features that will be illustrated shortly.

The Web client of Microsoft Dynamics NAV 2018 has been improved, while the Web client of Microsoft Dynamics 365 Business Central is completely different. It can be said that Microsoft Dynamics NAV has been **reborn** as Microsoft Dynamics 365 Business Central on-premise and SaaS.

We will look at Microsoft Dynamics 365 Business Central in detail in Chapter 13, *Microsoft Dynamics 365 Business Central*. In this chapter, we will cover Microsoft Dynamics NAV 2018 in depth, since this book was originally developed for Microsoft Dynamics NAV and there are still many users who will, sooner or later, want to migrate to Microsoft Dynamics 365 Business Central.

The main concepts that we will cover are as follows:

- Application changes
- Development changes
- IT changes
- Deprecated features

Microsoft Dynamics NAV 2018 – what's new

We will now talk about the features introduced in Microsoft Dynamics NAV 2018; some are completely new, while others are functional optimizations already present in previous releases.

There are many interesting features in Microsoft Dynamics NAV. I have decided to report some that I consider to be important and that need to be borne in mind with regard to projects. Anyone wanting to use Microsoft Dynamics NAV 2018 or Microsoft Dynamics 365 Business Central must be aware of these features in order to use them in projects. These features are outlined in the following diagram:

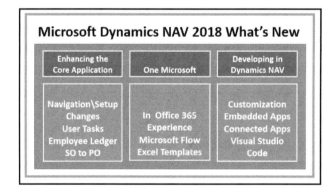

The product is really vast, so it is not possible to illustrate everything. The important thing is to provide **the pills** to remember what is, and what was, introduced over time, as illustrated in the project's timeline in the first chapter. For more information, you can refer to the Microsoft Dynamics NAV portal page on Microsoft docs at `https://docs.microsoft.com/en-us/dynamics-nav-app/`.

Application changes in Microsoft Dynamics NAV 2018

There are many things that have changed in the new release of Microsoft Dynamics NAV. A number of things have disappeared, some have changed, some have remained identical to Dynamics NAV 2016, seen in the previous edition of this book, and a bunch of new functionalities and improvements have been added.

The first thing that users will see is the new look and feel of Microsoft Dynamics NAV. Microsoft has implemented a metro-style design across all of their product lines. Microsoft Dynamics NAV is no different. The basic metro design is essentially focused on the content of the application, and not its graphics.

 This new look and feel of the Windows client is not all that different from its predecessors; it is different, however, to the Windows client of Microsoft Dynamics 365 Business Central. Microsoft Dynamics 365 Business Central does not have a dedicated Windows client; its Windows client is the same as that found in Microsoft Dynamics NAV 2018, apart from the fact that it opens a Microsoft Dynamics 365 Business Central instance. The Dynamics NAV 2018's Web client is, however, quite different to the Web client of Dynamics 365 Business Central, both in appearance and in technology. The Universal App has, however, remained more or less similar to the one introduced in Microsoft Dynamics NAV 2015.

Improvements made to clients for application users

Several improvements have been made to the Windows client and to the Web client with a view to improving user productivity, even if Microsoft suggests using the Web client (even though, as I recall, the Windows client also exists on Microsoft Dynamics 365 Business Central on-premises), since the Windows client will soon become obsolete and probably only the Web client will remain. Today, the Web client is regarded as a new modern user experience: faster, more navigable, more customizable, usable on every device, and user friendly.

Windows client – role center layout

The role center layout remained almost identical to that in Microsoft Dynamics NAV 2016. In the following screenshot, you can see the sales order role center:

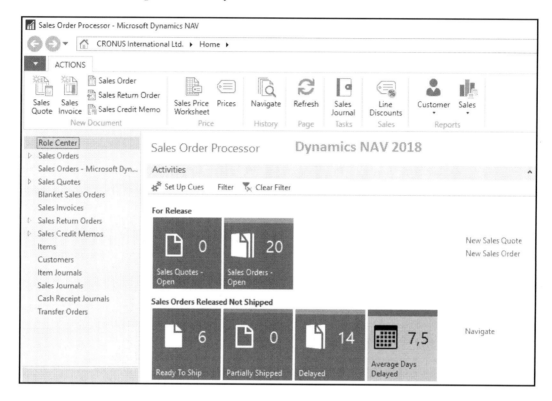

Some available parts and fact boxes that can be displayed in the role center have been added:

- **My Notification**
- **Report Inbox**
- **Power BI Reports**
- **My Job Queue**

Some of these items were already present in Microsoft Dynamics NAV 2016, but I am reporting them here in any case because they are certainly useful for users as they allow you to manage a sort of virtual desk by keeping several types of information under control from the same role center, as demonstrated in the following screenshot:

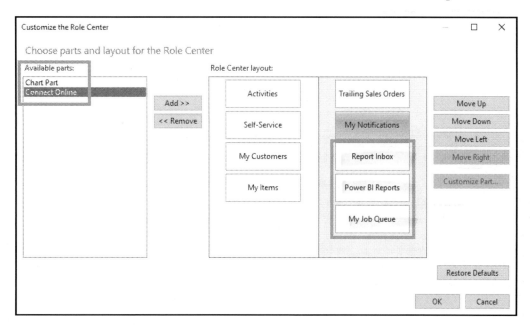

After customizing the role center page, it appears as it does in the following screenshot, with a lot of useful information available to users concerning role centers:

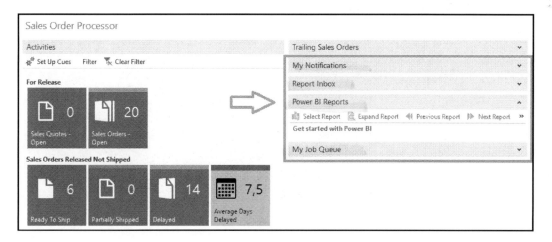

Web client for Microsoft Dynamics NAV 2018

The Web client is a bit different in respect to both Microsoft Dynamics NAV 2016 and NAV 2017, since a number of new features and improvements were introduced in this release.

These improvements include the following:

- The Print Preview function is available in any browser; it is now available in all non-Internet Explorer browsers (Google Chrome, Microsoft Edge, Mozilla Firefox, and Safari).
- You can use Web client as a tool for user personalization ("In-client" Designer).
- A faster, redesigned, and optimized layout (all line actions in the ribbon):

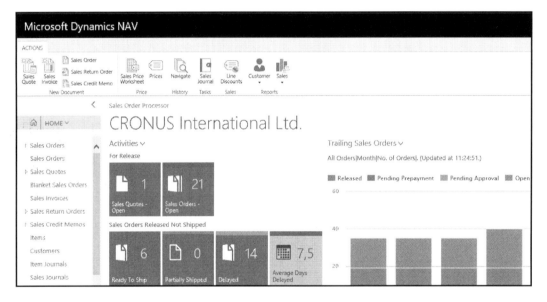

Web client for Microsoft Dynamics NAV 2018

You can see all the new features and improvements regarding the Web client at `https://totovic.com/2017/12/08/nav-2018-web-client-improvements/`. The limitations associated with the Web client are listed at the following link: `https://docs.microsoft.com/en-us/dynamics-nav/feature-limitations-of-the-microsoft-dynamics-nav-web-client`

Web client is more customizable (with "In-client" or "In-app" Designer)

You can personalize you workspace directly in your browser. This feature is referred to as "In-client" or "In-app" Designer. Nowadays, it is possible to reposition the freeze pane, move and hide page parts, reposition or hide cues and cue groups, and use `ListParts` on role centers.

Depending on the type of page and what it includes, you can do the following:

- Add, move, and remove fields.
- Add, move, and remove columns in a list.
- Change the freeze pane of columns in a list. The freeze pane locks one or more columns to the left-hand side of a list so that they are always present, even when you scroll horizontally.
- Move and remove cues (tiles).
- Move and remove parts. Parts are subdivisions or areas on a page that contain features such as multiple fields, another page, a chart, or tiles.

The Microsoft Dynamics NAV Web client "In-client" Designer is as shown in the following screenshot:

You can see how to use the "In-client" Designer feature at `https://robertostefanettinavblog.com/2017/12/23/all-about-nav-2018-web-client-personalization/`.

Preview and print from Web client

Now, you can preview a report in any web browser by choosing the **Preview** button. You can preview any report layout (RDLC plus word layout) with a responsive layout and support for picture and custom fonts.

Updated Universal App

Microsoft Dynamics NAV is also now a **Universal App**; basically, if you have this in a laptop, the application will be displayed in a regular Web client. If you turn your device into a tablet, then it will turn the application to tablet mode. Basically, any device will be able to display Microsoft Dynamics NAV, including your mobile phone; you can run also it on holographic devices such as Microsoft HoloLens.

In the Universal App, each screen that you see on the tablet is a direct translation of a page in a normal Windows client. Whenever you make a change in the **Page Designer**, it will be automatically reflected in the Web client, tablet client, or any user interface that connects to the Microsoft Dynamics NAV service tier, as can be seen in the following screenshot:

Universal App screenshot

Windows 10 Continuum

With this elegant feature, you can turn your phone into a desktop computer, project it on to your big screen, and control it using Bluetooth or wireless adapters:

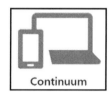

IT changes

Several IT-related changes have been introduced with the release of Microsoft Dynamics NAV 2018, including the following:

- Easier installation and deployment
- Easier administration
- New clients
- New services

Microsoft Dynamics NAV Server administration tool

Microsoft Dynamics NAV 2018 includes an updated server administration tool for administering Dynamics NAV Server.

It is a snap-in for the **Microsoft Management Console** (**MMC**). When installing the server option, the server administration tool is a default feature.

Once the server option is installed, you will find it on your Windows Start menu with all the other Microsoft Dynamics NAV components installed on the same machine.

From the server administration tool, we will have a clear picture of all the Microsoft Dynamics NAV instances running on the machine, their version, status, and configuration (name, the database to which the instance connects, ports for the different types of services, and so on).

From the server administration tool, we can add or remove instances (we can even add instances running on a different server), edit their settings, start or stop services, and so on.

There are numerous options and parameters to be set. All of them can also be set by PowerShell, with those features most commonly used indicated by the orange rectangles in the following screenshot:

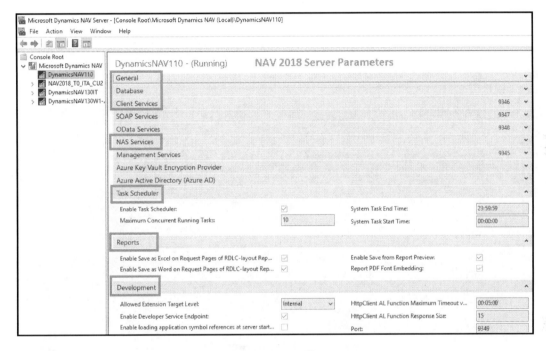

Microsoft Dynamics NAV 2018 Server administration console

 You can find more information at the following links: `https://docs.microsoft.com/en-us/dynamics-nav/configuring-microsoft-dynamics-nav-server` and `https://robertostefanettinavblog.com/2017/12/03/nav-2018-service-options-recap/`.

Windows PowerShell – new and updated cmdlets

Microsoft Dynamics NAV 2018 comes with a set of PowerShell cmdlets that allow us to perform administrative tasks on our Dynamics NAV installation.

You will also find it on your Windows Start menu with all the other Dynamics NAV components installed on the same machine.

You can run cmdlets from Microsoft Dynamics NAV 2018 Administration Shell, shown as follows:

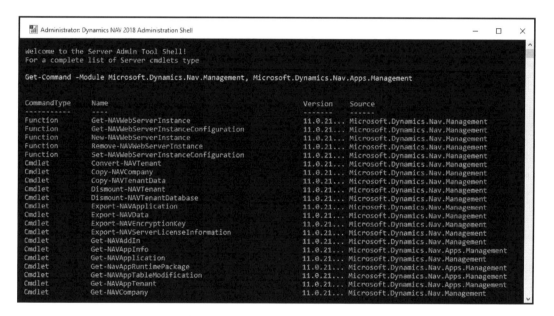

Run PowerShell cmdlets from Microsoft Dynamics NAV 2018 Administrator Shell

Or, run them from Windows PowerShell ISE mounting the Dynamics NAV
PowerShell libraries, shown as follows:

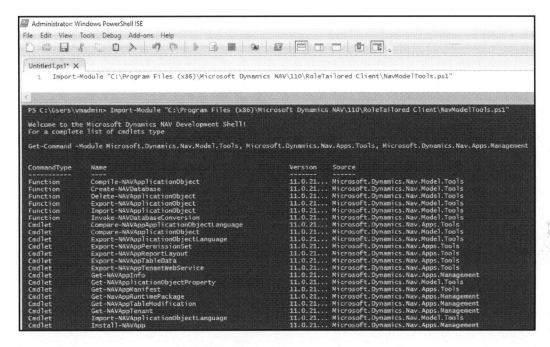

Run PowerShell cmdlets from the Windows PowerShell ISE shell

When you run the cmdlets, a list of all the available `cmdlet` command types for
Microsoft Dynamics NAV will be displayed.

Microsoft Dynamics NAV 2018 introduced some new cmdlets.
These cmdlets and their descriptions are taken from the Microsoft
MSDN website: `https://docs.microsoft.com/en-us/powershell/`
`dynamics-nav/overview?view=dynamicsnav-ps-2018`.

New and updated PowerShell cmdlets for server and development

A number of new PowerShell commands have been added. Let's examine some of them as follows.

Microsoft Dynamics NAV Server – start/stop

The following is a comparison between the old and new commands to start, stop, and restart the Microsoft Dynamics NAV Server:

Old	New
Set-NAVServerInstance – Start	Start-NAVServerInstance
Set-NAVServerInstance – Stop	Stop-NAVServerInstance
Set-NAVServerInstance – Restart	Restart-NAVServerInstance

Merging application objects

The following are the cmdlets for merging ***application objects*** for an upgrade, as described under the *Upgrade automation – an overview* section later in this chapter:

Cmdlets	Description
Compare-NAVApplicationObject	Compares text files with Microsoft Dynamics NAV application objects and then calculates the delta between the two versions. The result of the comparison is a number of text files with the calculated delta.
Get-NAVApplicationObjectProperty	Gets Microsoft Dynamics NAV application object properties from the specified application object text files.
Join-NAVApplicationObjectFile	Combines multiple application object files into a single text file.
Merge-NAVApplicationObject	Compares the changes that have been made to the application objects between two versions of Microsoft Dynamics NAV, and applies the difference to a third set of application objects. The result of the merge is a number of text files with the merged application objects. Any conflicts that the cmdlet cannot merge are identified in conflict files.
Set-NAVApplicationObjectProperty	Sets Microsoft Dynamics NAV application object properties in the specified application object text files.
Split-NAVApplicationObjectFile	Splits a text file that contains two or more application objects into separate text files for each application object.
Update-NAVApplicationObject	Applies a set of deltas to specified application objects. The files that describe the delta are generated by the Compare-NAVApplicationObject cmdlet.

Upgrading data

The following are the cmdlets to upgrade data, as described under the *Upgrade automation – an overview* section of this chapter:

Cmdlets	Description
Start-NAVDataUpgrade	Starts the data upgrade process for upgrading data in the business (tenant) database.
Resume-NAVDataUpgrade	Resumes a data upgrade process that has been suspended on account of an error.
Stop-NAVDataUpgrade	Stops a data upgrade process.
Get-NAVDataUpgrade	Gets information about the data upgrade process that is currently running or the last completed data upgrade process.

Updating captions in application object files

The following are the cmdlets to update captions in application object files. These are very useful when you are trying to put in (or take out) additional languages for your Microsoft Dynamics NAV software:

Cmdlets	Description
Export-NAVApplicationObjectLanguage	Exports captions from specified text files with Microsoft Dynamics NAV application objects. The captions are exported to text files.
Import-NAVApplicationObjectLanguage	Imports strings in a specified language into text files that contain Microsoft Dynamics NAV application objects.
Join-NAVApplicationObjectLanguageFile	Combines multiple text files with captions for Microsoft Dynamics NAV application objects into a single text file.
Remove-NAVApplicationObjectLanguage	Deletes captions in a specified language from Microsoft Dynamics NAV application objects.
Split-NAVApplicationObjectLanguageFile	Splits a text file that contains multi-language captions for two or more application objects into separate text files for each application object.
Test-NAVApplicationObjectLanguageFile	This cmdlet tests captions in Microsoft Dynamics NAV application objects to test and validate that the strings have been translated for the specified languages.

Office 365 Administration

The following are the cmdlets for an Office 365 Administration setup with Microsoft Dynamics NAV:

Cmdlets	Description
Set-NavSingleSignOnWithOffice365	Performs configuration changes to support a single sign-on with Office 365 for a Microsoft Dynamics NAV Windows client and a Microsoft Dynamics NAV Web client.
New-NavSelfSignedCertificate	Facilitates the creation of self-signed certificates that are used to protect communication between a NAV service and a Microsoft Dynamics NAV Web client.

Prior to Microsoft Dynamics NAV 2013 R2, you were allowed to back up data from a specific company, and then restore that data in a completely separate database in a completely separate environment. In Microsoft Dynamics NAV 2013 R2, with the introduction of multiple tenants, backups by company were no longer available.

This made it extremely hard for Microsoft Dynamics NAV partners or customers to move data from a specific company to another environment. You had to take the entire Microsoft SQL database and replace the database in your development environment. Testing based on scenario data became almost impossible. This is especially frustrating when you only want to replace the data, and not the application objects.

Importing and exporting NAV data

A lot of developers were relieved when these cmdlets were introduced in place of the company backups. The following are the cmdlets for importing and exporting Microsoft Dynamics NAV data:

Cmdlets	Description
Export-NAVData	Exports data from a Microsoft Dynamics NAV database. You can export company-specific data, and you can choose to include global data, application data, or application objects.
Import-NAVData	Imports data into a Microsoft Dynamics NAV database from a file. You can import the entire data in the file, or you can choose to include specific companies, global data, application data, or application objects. Note that you can only import an application into an empty database.
Get-NAVDataFile	Gets information from a file that has been exported from a Microsoft Dynamics NAV database. The extracted information includes the types of data that the file contains along with company names.

 You can find more information at `https://docs.microsoft.com/en-us/dynamics-nav/changes-to-microsoft-dynamics-nav-cmdlets-from-previous-release`.

Development changes (new and updated)

Microsoft Dynamics NAV 2018 has introduced a number of development changes (also used in Microsoft Dynamics 365 Business Central), and updated some existing ones. The following are the changes relating to the development environment, with new ways of developing document type reports and changes in the standard C/AL code, which has been redesigned in a number of areas.

Essential C/AL functions available

Although there are more than 100 functions in C/AL, there are several functions that you will use more frequently than others; the table in this section describes the most common C/AL functions.

The following functions are the essential C/AL functions for Microsoft Dynamics NAV:

Operations	Functions
Operations on tables	The GET, FIND, and NEXT functions The SETCURRENTKEY, SETRANGE, SETFILTER, GETRANGEMIN, and GETRANGEMAX functions The LOCKTABLE, INSERT, MODIFY, MODIFYALL, DELETE, and DELETEALL functions
Calculation	The CALCFIELDS, CALCSUMS, FIELDERROR, FIELDNAME, INIT, TESTFIELD, and VALIDATE functions
Messaging	The ProgressWindow, MESSAGE, ERROR, and CONFIRM functions
Menu	The STRMENU function

> You can find more info at this link: https://docs.microsoft.com/en-us/dynamics-nav/essential-c-al-functions.

Triggers

Triggers are available for the different objects in Microsoft Dynamics NAV 2018. They activate a function when a certain event occurs. When C/AL functions are executed as a result of a predefined event on either an object or a control, the event triggers the function. Together, the event and function make a trigger; you edit triggers in the C/AL editor.

The following are different types of triggers:

- Report and data item triggers
- Table and field triggers
- XMLport triggers
- Page and action triggers
- Codeunit triggers
- Query triggers

You can find more information at the following links: `https://docs.microsoft.com/en-us/dynamics-nav/triggers` and `https://docs.microsoft.com/en-us/dynamics-nav/triggers-overview`.

Extensions 2.0

Instead of defining customizations in the original source code (you don't need more to modify the standard code of a product), extensions are written alongside the solution source, where the integration with the source is handled by events. An extension can add new objects and extend existing objects that are present in the solution; Microsoft Dynamics NAV 2018 and Microsoft Dynamics 365 Business Central now support extensions 2.0.

You can find more info at this link: `https://docs.microsoft.com/en-us/dynamics365/business-central/dev-itpro/developer/devenv-how-publish-and-install-an-extension-v2`.

The New Modern Development Environment (Visual Studio Code plus AL Language extension)

Now, you can use the New Modern Development Environment to develop, as it happens also for Microsoft Dynamics 365 Business Central on-premises, it's possible to develop with both technologies, C/Side with C/AL, and Visual Studio Code with Microsoft A/L:

Now, it's possible to develop customizations both with the old development environment and with the New Modern Development Environment using a hybrid development system (although, in this way (not recommended), `finsql.exe` must be run with the `generatesymbolreference` parameter). You can see how to use the New Modern Development Environment at `https://robertostefanettinavblog.com/2017/11/18/c-sidec-al-vs-vs-codeal/`.

APIs for Microsoft Dynamics NAV

Let's have a look at different concepts related to APIs in Microsoft Dynamics NAV:

- **API library**: Microsoft Dynamics NAV 2018 contains 44 ready-to-go APIs (application programming interfaces) to create apps connected to Microsoft Dynamics NAV. It is also possible to create your own APIs.
- **API page type**: You can design web service API endpoints directly from the following page:

Available APIs

COMPANY	FINANCE	SALES	PURCHASING	REPORTS
company	accounts	customers	irs1099Codes (US only)	agedAccountsPayable
companyInformation	dimensions	customerPayments	purchaseInvoices	agedAccountsReceivable
countriesRegions	dimensionLines	customerPaymentJournals	purchaseInvoiceLines	balanceSheet
currencies	dimensionValues	salesInvoices	vendors	cashFlowStatement
employees	generalLedgerEntries	salesInvoiceLines		incomeStatement
items	journals	salesOrders		retainedEarningsStatement
itemCategories	journalLines	salesOrderLines		customerSales
paymentMethods		salesQuotes		vendorPurchases
paymentTerms		salesQuoteLines		trialBalance
shipmentMethods		salesCreditMemos		
taxAreas		salesCreditMemoLines		
taxGroups				
unitsOfMeasure				

Connected apps

You can use connected apps (connected apps are just extensions that use APIs or web services for interacting with external systems) in Microsoft Dynamics NAV 2018, for example, to connect with third-party services, as demonstrated in the following diagram:

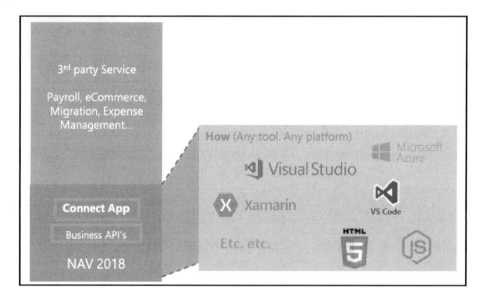

New service connections and extensions pages

The new service connections and extensions management pages provide a great places for accessing various setups and settings, and also for managing extensions. Service connections, such as OCR, SMTP, currency exchange services, and CRM connections, can also be managed from the **SERVICE CONNECTIONS** page.

In the following screenshot, you can see all setups available in the **SERVICE CONNECTIONS** page:

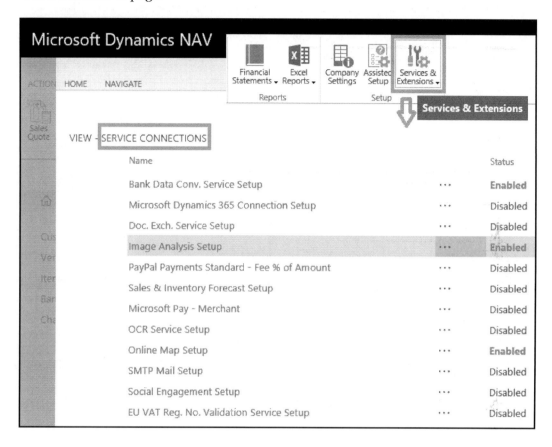

In the following screenshot, you can see all the extensions installed in
the **EXTENSIONS MANAGEMENT** page:

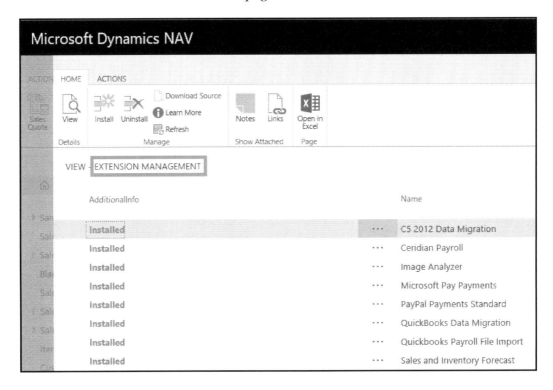

Image Analyzer - contact person and item

The Azure Cognitive services for Microsoft Dynamics NAV can be used with contacts
and items:

- **Contact person**: While attaching images to the contact
  card, automatically detects a person's age and gender.
- **Item**: You can identify attributes of an item from a diagram, including type
  and color, and create suggested attributes, as can be seen from the
  following screenshot:

Detected Attribute Name	Confidence Score (%)	Action to Perform	Details	Add to the Item Description
Table	83.60	Use as category	Category: 'TABLE'	Add to the item description
Indoor	85.04	Ignore		Add to the item description
Furniture	88.32	Use as attribute	Item attribute: 'Color' = 'Furniture'	Add to the item description

Image Analyzer is an API based on the Computer Vision API, h is available on
Microsoft Cognitive services for Azure:

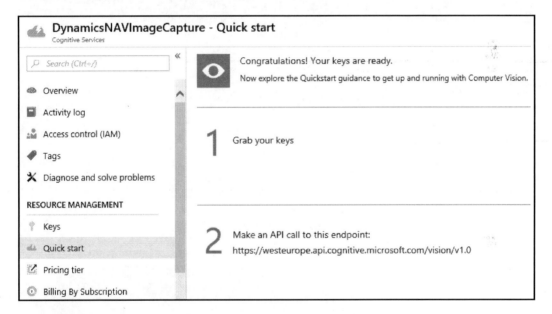

You can see how to use the Image Analyzer at `https://blogs.msdn.`
`microsoft.com/nav/2017/12/13/smart-solutions-2-programming-`
`computer-vision-in-cal-code/`.

Functional changes

We will now illustrate some functional changes included in Microsoft Dynamics NAV 2018 that I considered interesting from the perspective of the realization of a project.

Sales order to purchase order

You can create a **purchase order (PO)** from a **sales order (SO)** instantly in Microsoft Dynamics NAV; this feature, introduced in Microsoft Dynamics NAV 2017, has been improved in the NAV 2018 release:

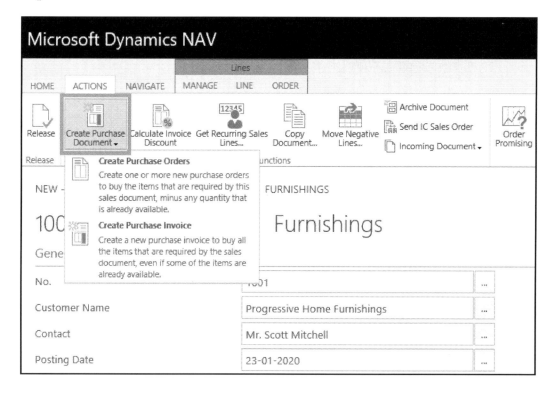

Assisted setup by wizards and manual setup

Commonly required configuration tasks have assisted setup (wizards), which aid in the process. All of these can now be accessed in one place. Sublists allow for filtering to settings within an area, such as finance, inventory, and manufacturing:

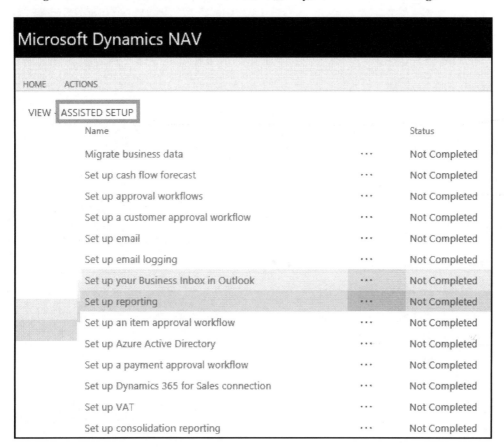

User tasks

User tasks are a new feature with which you can create tasks to remind you of work to be done, or to assign tasks to yourself or other users.

A **Pending User Tasks** cue is added to all roles (a "to-do" list for each user in their role). You can manage system-wide tasks, assign tasks to any user, track a task's due date, create recurrence for tasks, and show a user task list:

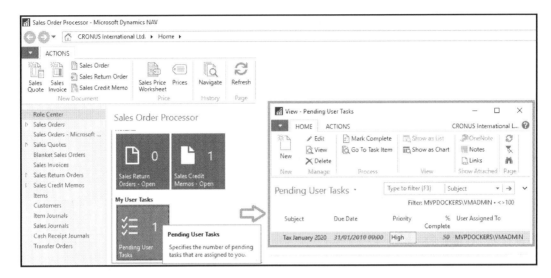

You can also define recurring user tasks:

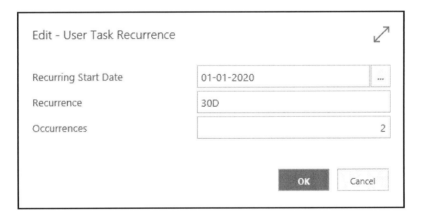

Direct transfer orders

Now that you can create a direct transfer order, you no longer need to use an in transit location to generate a transfer order.

Employee ledger entries

You can create journal entries for employees directly. There is no longer a need to create vendors for employees; you can also make payments to the employee in payments journal.

Preconfigured Excel reports

The Business Manager and Accounting Role Center has a new option in the ribbon for **Excel Reports**. Users may select from a drop-down menu of preconfigured reports that are ready to print from Excel. These reports include ones that are broadly useful, such as **Balance Sheet**, **Cash Flow Statement**, and **Trial Balance**:

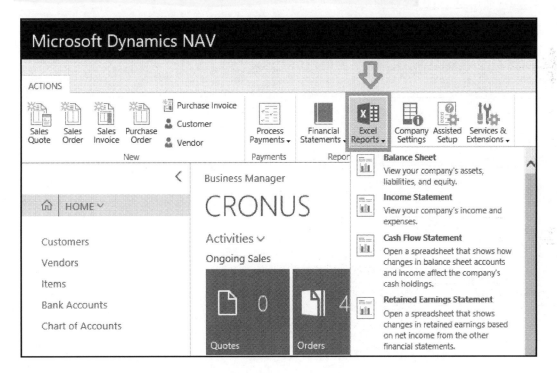

Edit in Excel feature

The edit in Excel feature is added to many journal pages in Microsoft Dynamics NAV, enabling you to create, edit, and publish journals to Microsoft Dynamics NAV from Microsoft Excel, as demonstrated in the following screenshot:

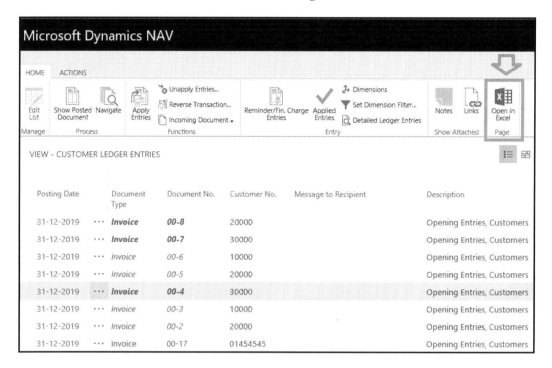

 You can see how to edit in Excel at this link: `https://docs.microsoft.com/en-us/dynamics-nav/configuring-dynamics-nav-excel-addin`.

Change Global Dimensions

The **Change Global Dimensions** feature was improved, and now runs as follows:

- Change Routine is parallelized and executed per table in separate independent background jobs.

- Other users can work with read all data in tables that are not involved in the updating of global dimensions. However, any changes to tables in the list are blocked until all of them are completely updated.
- Any failed task can be rerun from the place of failure (start from the failure point and complete)

The following screenshot shows the **Change Global Dimensions** feature:

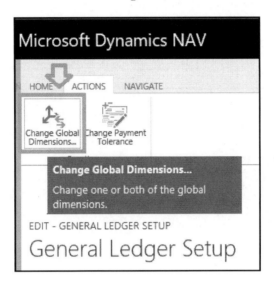

You can see how to change global dimensions at this link: `https://robertostefanettinavblog.com/2018/02/28/change-global-dimensions-in-nav-2018/`.

IC (intercompany) – automation of IC outbox and IC inbox

Many improvements related to the automation of intercompany transactions were introduced. For example, when two companies are engaged in sales and purchase transactions (intercompany transactions), the update feature ensures that both parties receive the appropriate invoices every time a transaction is made.

You can see how to use the updated intercompany feature at this link: `https://docs.microsoft.com/en-us/dynamics-nav-app/` `intercompany-manage`.

Item charges – volume and weight

You can also now distribute item charges according to volume and weight.

EU GDPR support and data classification

Since Microsoft Dynamics NAV 2018 Cumulative Update 4, EU GDPR support for Microsoft Dynamics NAV has been introduced. Now, it is possible to manage data classification directly from Microsoft Dynamics NAV and manage user data in respect of GDPR regulations:

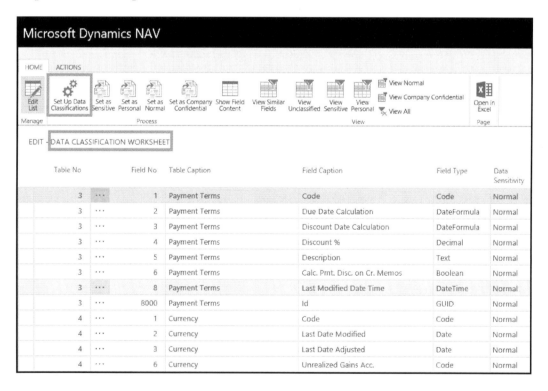

You can see how to use the GDPR feature at this link: `https://robertostefanettinavblog.com/2018/04/13/nav-gdpr-tools-in-action-nav-2018-cu4/`.

Microsoft Dynamics 365 for sales integration

Sales orders from Microsoft Dynamics 365 for Sales can be automatically converted to sales orders in Microsoft Dynamics NAV 2018 without the need for manual intervention.

Microsoft Flow integration

Microsoft Flow is embedded in Microsoft Dynamics NAV 2018. You can create, edit, and manage your flows from within Microsoft Dynamics NAV, as demonstrated in the following screenshot:

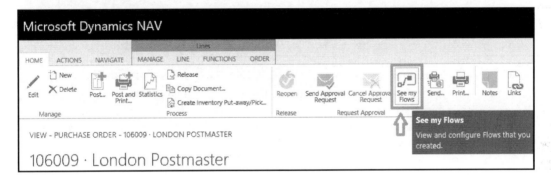

Power BI reporting integration

With the introduction of Microsoft Office 365, Microsoft included something called **Power BI** (short for **Power Business Intelligence**). What used to cost a lot of money for a BI solution, Microsoft is now essentially including as part of the Office 365 package. This means that you can utilize Power BI to have a graphical dashboard for your business using live data from Microsoft Dynamics NAV.

The best way to send data to Power BI is to utilize a new object type called Query. The Query object type was actually introduced in Microsoft Dynamics NAV 2013. So, as long as you can publish the query as a web service, Power BI utilized with Excel will suck the data up!

Technically speaking, you do not need Microsoft Dynamics NAV 2018 to use Power BI. If you're using at least Microsoft Dynamics NAV 2009, you can use Power BI as your business intelligence tool.

In Microsoft Dynamics NAV 2018, you can use reports created in Power BI from the role center directly, with a dedicated part allowing direct access to the reports:

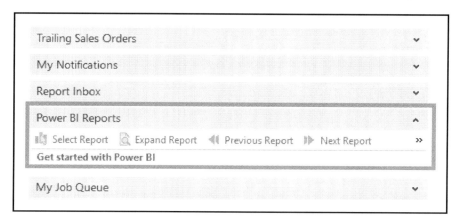

An updated Microsoft Dynamics NAV Power BI connector is available, so now you can configure all the necessary connection information from a single page. With the new Power BI reporting control, you can gain awareness of your Power BI reports by making them visible from within the most highly-used lists in Microsoft Dynamics NAV, and you can also interact and filter the reports by simply selecting records from the associated list page. You can show Power BI reports in the dedicated Power BI fact box in Microsoft Dynamics NAV:

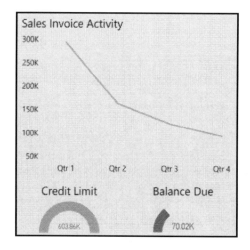

Contact iterations in Microsoft Outlook

You can use Microsoft Dynamics NAV templates to create emails in Microsoft Outlook. You can also track the interactions on the Microsoft Dynamics NAV contact record, as demonstrated in the following screenshot:

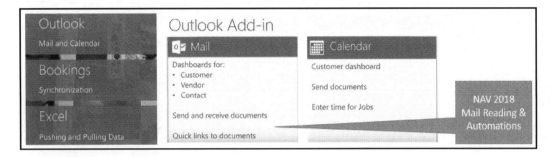

 You can see how to use the contact integration feature at this link: `https://docs.microsoft.com/en-us/dynamics-nav/ integrating%20dynamics%20nav%20and%20office.`

Upgrade automation – an overview

Upgrading your Microsoft Dynamics NAV basically entails three principal elements:

- Converting the database to the new version
- Upgrading the application code to the new version
- Upgrading the data to the new version

Of the three processes, upgrading the application code and the data take up the most time. This can cause companies to shy away from upgrading to the latest version of Microsoft Dynamics NAV.

Upgrade automation – the application code

The first problem associated with upgrading is upgrading the application code. Prior to NAV 2016, to upgrade the application code, you had to export the objects of the previous version, and the next version, into text files. Then, you would use any off-the-shelf software or freeware to assimilate the modifications done on the older version with the new version.

To remedy this, Microsoft introduced a PowerShell script called `Merge-NAVApplicationObject`. When you run this command using PowerShell, it will automatically merge the code for you. If the process detects a conflict or a problem that it cannot resolve on its own, it will place the conflicts in a separate area for you to resolve it manually.

What used to take hundreds of hours for a version upgrade can now be done in a fraction of the time!

 To learn more about upgrading the application code using PowerShell, please visit `https://msdn.microsoft.com/en-us/library/dn271652(v=nav.90).aspx`.

Upgrade automation – data

The second time-consuming portion of the upgrade is upgrading the data. Initially, after you're done with modifying the application, you had to run an upgrade toolkit that converted the data from the prior version to the new version. Depending on the size of the database file, the processes would take hours, even days, per company!

To remedy this problem, Microsoft included four PowerShell commands (called cmdlets) in Dynamics NAV 2016 Administration Shell:

- `Start-NAVDataUpgrade`: This starts the process of the data upgrade
- `Stop-NAVDataUpgrade`: This stops the upgrade process that's currently running
- `Resume-NAVDataUpgrade`: This resumes the upgrade process that was stopped
- `Get-NAVDataUpgrade`: This gets the status of the upgrade that's currently running

With these new commands and PowerShell, you can complete the upgrade of data in a fraction of the time that it used to take.

 To learn more about upgrading data through the Administration Shell, please visit the following link: `https://msdn.microsoft.com/en-us/library/dn762348(v=nav.90).aspx`.

Enhancement in security and encryption

Microsoft's strategy to move from desktop computing to cloud computing is no secret; the release of Microsoft Office 365 reinforces their cloud- and subscription-based strategy.

Microsoft introduced OAuth Authentication for OData and SOAP endpoints. This allows for more secure connections between custom apps, Microsoft Dynamics NAV, and Microsoft Office 365.

Native integrations

For Microsoft Dynamics NAV 2018, direct integrations are available with almost all Microsoft applications. There are native connectors available for the following:

- Microsoft Power Bi
- Microsoft Flow
- Dynamics 365 Sales (CRM)
- SharePoint Online
- Microsoft Booking

Best features from previous releases of Microsoft Dynamics NAV

Microsoft Dynamics NAV 2018 has introduced many architectural changes, but also a number of updated application functionalities. As already mentioned, since they are interesting, I decided to report on them in this edition of the book as well.

Best and updated application features

Some of the features in Microsoft Dynamics NAV 2018 that are new or improved from previous versions will now be illustrated. Users who will use Microsoft Dynamics NAV 2018 should be aware that they exist.

RapidStart services improved

If you're migrating from your legacy system to Microsoft Dynamics NAV, one of the most important steps is to migrate the data from your legacy system to Microsoft Dynamics NAV. Using the **RapidStart** service, you can now map the data from your old legacy software to Microsoft Dynamics NAV directly.

This will eliminate the need for a developer to write custom import processes that are only used once (for example, for a new company start-up or for a new go-live with Microsoft Dynamics NAV).

The operation of the RapidStart service will be explained, together with some examples, in a later chapter about Microsoft Dynamics 365 Business Central.

Let's take a look at the configuration package in Microsoft Dynamics NAV:

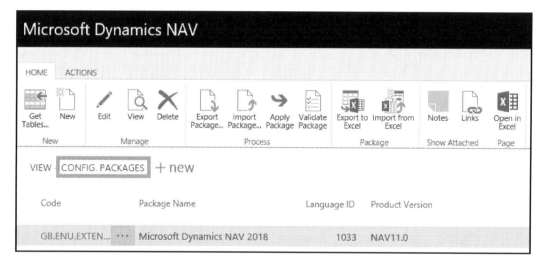

Each line of the configuration package represents a table in Microsoft Dynamics NAV.

The edit window appears as shown in the following screenshot:

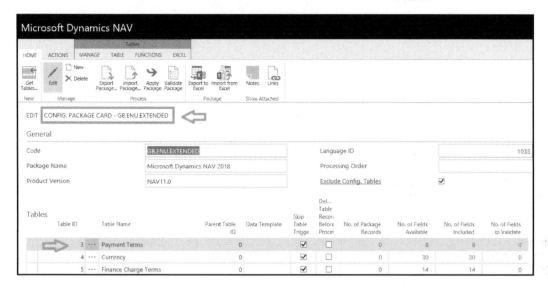

The edit window

To specify the fields within a table, click on the line of the table you wish to map the fields for:

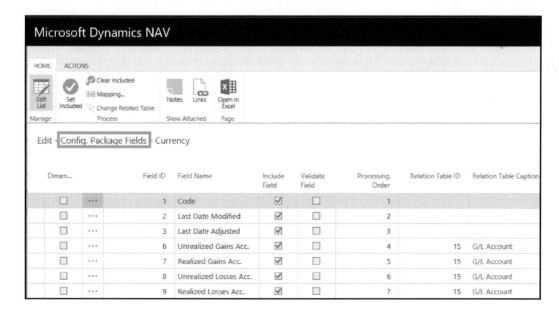

A few key functions of the configuration package to keep in mind are as follows:

- Data can be imported with or without validating against business rules that are built into the tables
- You can create import/export options for all the tables within Microsoft Dynamics NAV
- You can specify fields you want to import/export within each table
- You can export the data format that you have configured in Microsoft Excel so that your legacy system adheres to the format you specify
- After the data is imported, you can manage conflicts and duplicate data in a worksheet

Schedule reports

One of the major drawbacks of the base Microsoft Dynamics NAV product is the ability to schedule reports, or the lack thereof. With the release of Microsoft Dynamics NAV 2018, you can now schedule any reports to be run on a certain date and at a certain time using **Job Queue**.

Job Queue is a feature in Microsoft Dynamics NAV that was introduced in version 4.0. It basically allows you to schedule processes to run at a certain time on a specific day. Reports are scheduled using Job Queue. Job Queue should run in the background while using **NAS** (short for **Navision Application Server**) for a report to be scheduled properly.

It is possible to schedule a report On-Demand, and decide when it must be executed and in what format it must be created; once the report has been processed, it appears in the processed reports window of the Role Center.

When you run a report in Microsoft Dynamics NAV 2018, you will now see a new option called **Schedule;** try to launch the **Customer - Top 10 List** report.

When you click on **Schedule** (step 3, shown in the following screenshot), it will prompt you for a description, output type, and when to start and end:

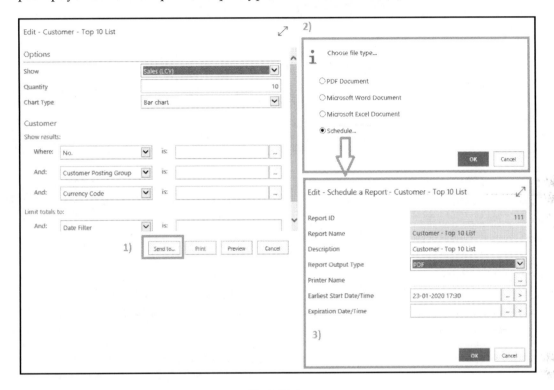

The schedule view

Once you click on **OK**, the report will be sent to Job Queue entries to be processed with the Job Queue. The following screenshot shows the **Edit – Job Queue Entry Card** report for ID 111:

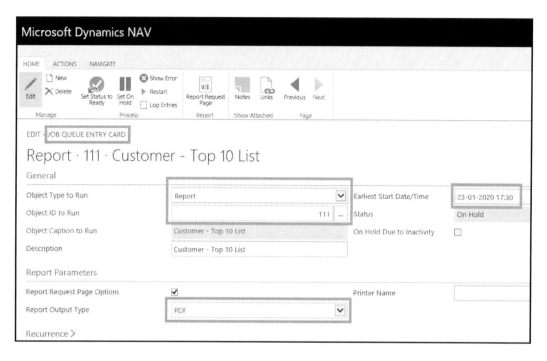

Once the report is run, it will be automatically removed from the **Job Queue Entries** (I recall that this is On-Demand scheduling) and put into the **Report Inbox**. In your **Role Center**, you will see a new fact box called **Report Inbox**. This will be where all of the scheduled reports will be placed after execution:

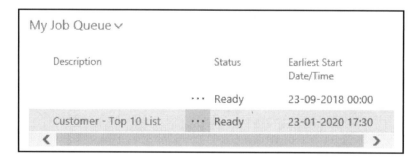

When the report is ready, click on **Show/Unread Reports** and it will show the report based on the output type you have defined:

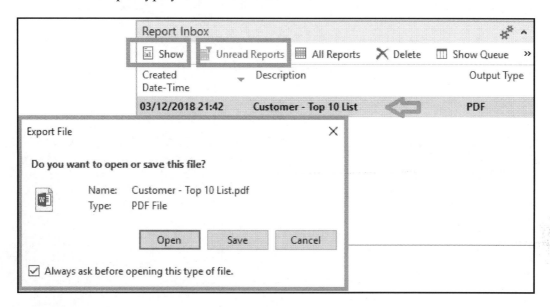

 For more information on schedule reports, visit `https://docs.`
`microsoft.com/en-us/dynamics-nav-app/ui-work-report.`

Emailing documents

Automatic emailing of invoices is probably one of the top requests we get from our customers. With Microsoft Dynamics NAV 2018, you're now allowed, for example, to send out invoices as you post them.

On the sales order, you'll see a new icon called **Post and Email**. After the invoice is posted, a prompt will be displayed with the customer's email address defined on the customer card. In addition, you can add custom messages to the email, as shown in the following screenshot:

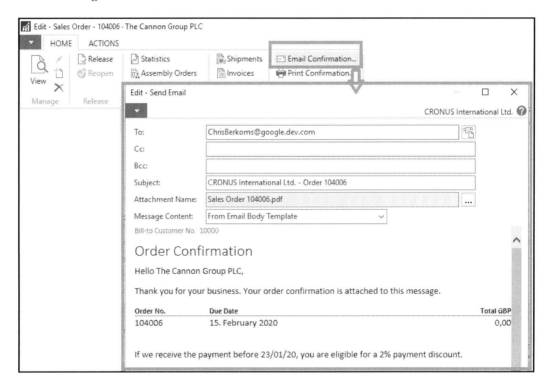

If you want to continue to edit the document in Outlook, check the **Edit in Outlook** checkbox, and it will open the message in Outlook with the PDF attachment:

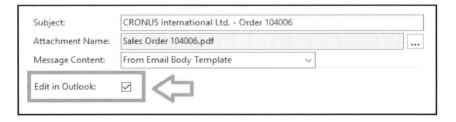

Assisted setup

Assisted setup is a new feature useful for guiding your users through setup scenarios, which is composed of a lot of wizards that are ready to use. We can consider these to be like a setup kit for configurations.

With assisted setup, the following is possible:

- To use a predefined set of data to set up main features (for selected areas)
- To have a great initial setup configuration for your new company (enhanced first-time experience)

The following is a list of some assisted setup wizards that are ready to use: migrate business data, approval workflows, item and customer approval, set up Dynamics 365 for sales, set up reporting, setting up VAT, and set up email:

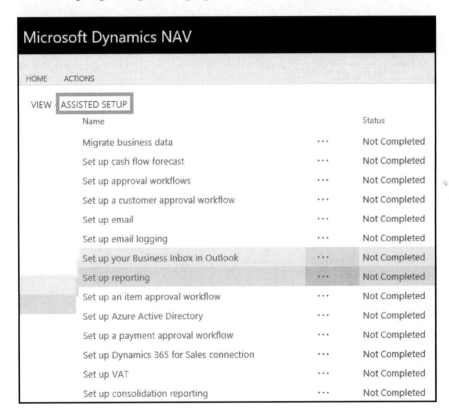

For more information on assisted setup, please visit the following link: `https://robertostefanettinavblog.com/2016/11/04/nav-2017-assisted-setup/`.

Item attributes

You can use the item attributes feature to create and add different types of attributes to the items in Microsoft Dynamics NAV. For example, you can define attributes such as length, width, color, and size, whatever you want basically; those attributes could then be used when searching for items or in reports, as demonstrated in the following screenshot:

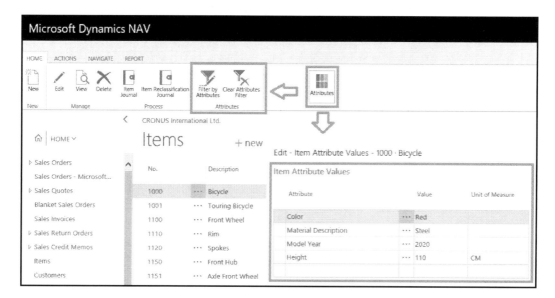

 For more information on item attributes, please visit the following link: `https://www.olofsimren.com/functionality-improvements-in-nav-2017/`.

Job improvements

We have now a new layout and project manager assignment in Microsoft Dynamics NAV's jobs. The project manager role center have been changed to show information specific to the jobs the user is managing, and each job has a project manager defined; this should get the project managers going on the jobs that are not doing that well:

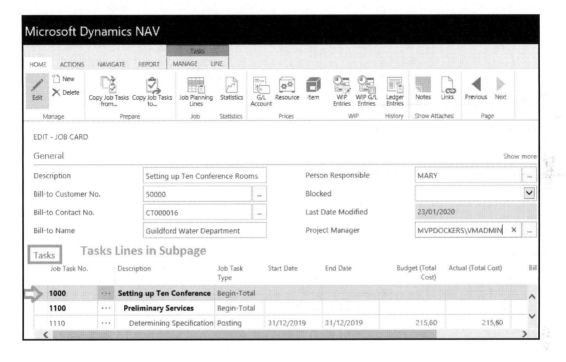

Task scheduler

The task scheduler enables you to control when certain operations or processes (tasks) are run. Basically, a task is a code unit or report that is scheduled to run at a specific date and time. Tasks run in a background session between the Microsoft Dynamics NAV Server instance and database. Behind the scenes, the task scheduler is used by the job queue to process job queue entries that are created and managed from the clients, as demonstrated in the following screenshot:

Task scheduler NAV server option

TaskScheduler data type

The `TaskScheduler` data type is a complex data type for creating and managing tasks in the task scheduler, which runs code units at scheduled times:

Function	Description
CREATETASK	Adds a task to run a codeunit at a specified date and time.
SETTASKASREADY	Sets a task to the Ready state. A task cannot run until it is Ready.
TASKEXISTS	Checks whether a specific task exists.
CANCELTASK	Cancels a scheduled task.

Task scheduler functions

In the following screenshot, you can see the task scheduler in action:

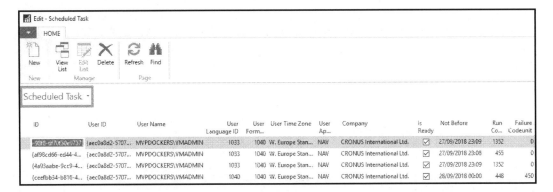

Task scheduler in action

For more information on task scheduler, please visit the following links: `https://robertostefanettinavblog.com/2016/11/04/nav-2017-task-scheduler/` and `https://msdn.microsoft.com/en-us/dynamics-nav/createtask-function`.

Cortana Intelligence

Cortana Intelligence takes advantage of historical data and improves your insight into your predicted sales, helping you manage your stock and respond to your customers' needs. Based on the forecast, the sales and inventory extension helps to create replenishment requests for vendors, saving you time. In following screenshot, **Sales & Inventory Forecast Setup**, you can see Cortana AI (Artificial Intelligence) for predictions connected to Microsoft Dynamics NAV.

The following screenshot shows the **Sales & Inventory Forecast Setup** for Cortana Intelligence:

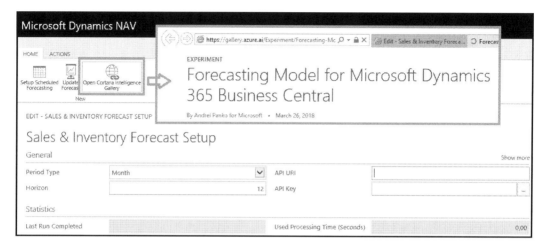

Document exchange service (OCR services)

Microsoft has teamed up with a company called Lexmark that allows you to scan incoming documents and automatically create the relevant purchase documents.

 For step-by-step information on setting up the document exchange service, please visit the following site: `https://docs.microsoft.com/en-us/dynamics-nav-app/across-how-to-set-up-a-document-exchange-service`.

Exchange rate update

This should've been there a while ago, but Microsoft has released an out-of-the-box functionality that will update the exchange rates based on whatever foreign exchange website that provides a web service data feed. In the standard Microsoft Dynamics NAV demo company, it hooks up to Yahoo.

 For more information on exchange rate updates, please visit the following link: `https://www.encorebusiness.com/blog/dynamics-nav-currency-exchange-rate-services`.

Native integration with Microsoft Dynamics 365 (CRM)

This is really more of an upgrade from the previous integration tools. The previous version of the Microsoft Dynamics CRM connector was not really flexible about what data you want to send from and to Microsoft Dynamics CRM. As a result, partners had to purchase a connector created by a third party.

The latest release of the connector for Microsoft Dynamics 365 (CRM) allows you to have flexibility regarding what table and what fields you want to integrate with Microsoft Dynamics 365. In addition, the pages in Microsoft Dynamics NAV allow you to drill down to Microsoft Dynamics 365 information.

 For information on setting up the connector for Microsoft Dynamics NAV 2018, please visit the following link: `https://docs.` `microsoft.com/en-us/dynamics-nav/setting-up-dynamics-crm-` `integration.`

Workflow management

As organizations grow more complex and the orders that come in become more challenging, having a system-managed workflow is a must. Microsoft Dynamics NAV 2016 introduced the ability to set up workflow processes when processing orders through an organization.

You're allowed to set up workflow processes when certain conditions are met. It allows you to notify the proper personnel, set up approval requests and approvals, and archive a workflow process for a specific order.

In Microsoft Dynamics NAV 2018, the workflow has been improved, and other models that are ready to use have been added; it is also possible to extend its operation by creating new custom workflows through development.

The following screenshot shows the Microsoft Dynamics NAV ready-to-go **Workflow Templates**:

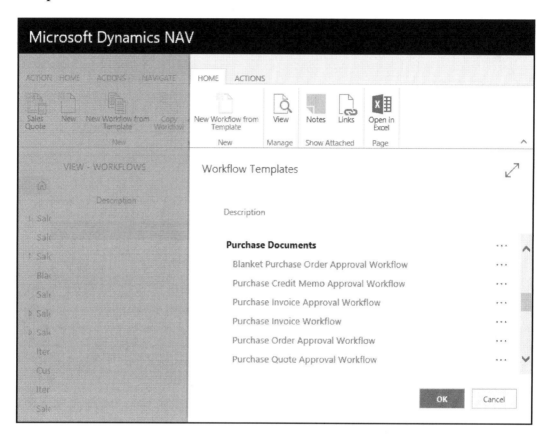

Some nice ready-to-go workflows templates are the following:

- Item Approval
- Customer Approval
- Vendor Approval
- Sales Order Approval
- Sales Invoice Approval
- Purchase Order Approval
- Purchase Invoice Approval
- General Journal Approval

For more information on setting up a workflow for your Dynamics NAV implementation, please visit the following link: `https://docs.microsoft.com/en-us/dynamics-nav-app/across-how-to-create-workflows` and also my blog at: `https://robertostefanettinavblog.com/2015/10/11/nav-2016-testing-workflow/`.

Posting preview

Prior to posting a journal, you will now be able to preview the impact of the transaction before you actually commit it to the financial ledger.

Prior to this feature, users needed to ask IT to create a test database using the latest data. Depending on how large your database is, it may take a long time. In addition, this is a time waster as far as your IT staff are concerned. This process is horribly inefficient.

The **Preview Posting** function can be found throughout Microsoft Dynamics NAV, as demonstrated in the following screenshot:

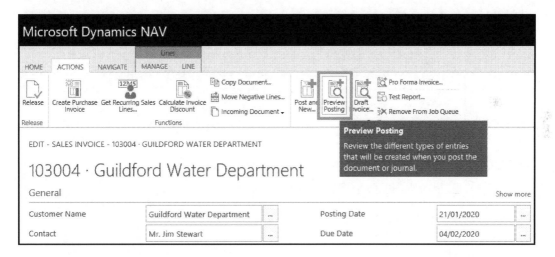

For more information on Preview Posting, please visit the following link: `https://docs.microsoft.com/en-us/dynamics-nav-app/ui-how-preview-post-results`.

Deferrals

If you have revenues or expenses that are recognized over a period of time, you can now use deferral posting. You may use functionality to automatically defer revenues and expenses over a specified schedule.

To distribute revenues or expenses across the accounting periods involved, you have to set up a deferral template for the resource, item, or G/L account that the revenue or expense will be posted for.

When you post the related sales or purchase document, the revenue or expense is deferred to the accounting periods involved, according to a deferral schedule that is governed by settings in the deferral template and the posting date.

For more information on deferrals, please visit https://docs. microsoft.com/en-us/dynamics-nav-app/finance-how-defer-revenue-expenses.

Document reporting

When Microsoft introduced **Report Definition Language Client-side (RDLC)** as its main report writing tool, a lot of Microsoft Dynamics NAV developers cried foul. Why? Because programming Microsoft Dynamics NAV reports using RDLC was like pulling teeth! Add to this the complexity of creating an actual report, and what you get when you preview a report is very often not what gets printed out on PDF or paper. This is especially true when creating document-type reports such as a sales order or sales invoice.

With the horrendous feedback associated with the development of RDLC reports, Microsoft got to work and released a tool to develop document-type reports using Word for layout purposes. This means you can use the pre-made templates for invoices using Microsoft Word.

There are some pre-made reports with Word document layouts in Microsoft Dynamics NAV 2018. These are as follows:

- 1302—Standard Sales - Pro Forma Invoice
- 1303—Standard Sales - Draft Invoice
- 1304—Standard Sales - Quote

- 1305—Standard Sales – Order Conf.
- 1306—Standard Sales – Invoice
- 1307—Standard Sales – Credit Memo
- 1322—Standard Purchase – Order

These reports can only be accessed using the SMALL BUSINESS role center.

To see and configure the **Word Layout** designer, let's perform the following steps:

1. First, start the Development Environment for Microsoft Dynamics NAV 2018. Find report 1305 and click on **Design**:

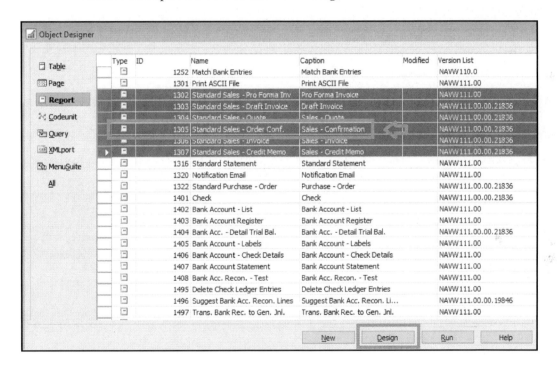

2. Next, navigate to **Tools** | **Word Layout** | **Export**:

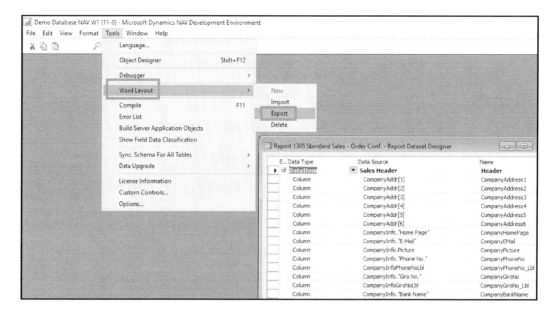

3. Next, from the Web client navigate to **Search Menu** | **Report Layout** | **Custom Report Layout**. The following screenshot shows the **EDIT – REPORT LAYOUT SELECTION** window:

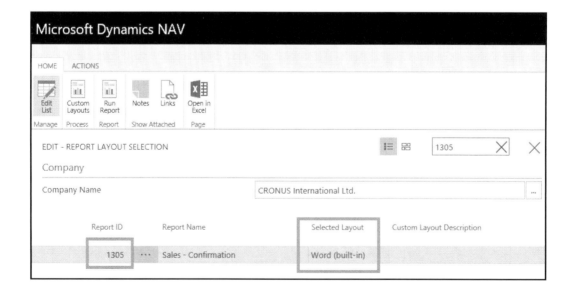

4. From here, Microsoft Dynamics NAV will prompt you for a place to save the **Word (built-in)** layout. Open the Word document and apply any pre-formatted templates from Word.

5. When you're done with editing the layout, import it back into the Microsoft Dynamics NAV 2018 Development Environment, go into the designer mode for report `1305`, and then navigate to **Tools** | **Word Layout** | **Import Layout**. Please note that you're allowed to keep the RDLC layout or the Word layout. However, you will need to tell Microsoft Dynamics NAV which layout to use. This can be controlled by going to **CUSTOM REPORT LAYOUTS**, as demonstrated in the following screenshot:

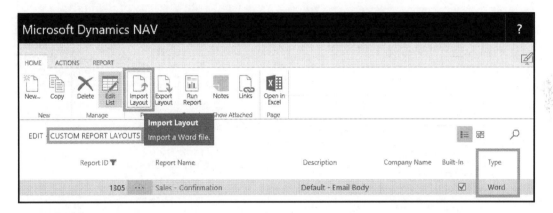

For a step-by-step tutorial on how to edit the **Word Layout** for Microsoft Dynamics NAV 2018, please visit the following link: `https://docs.microsoft.com/it-it/dynamics-nav/how-to--create-a-word-report-layout-for-a-report.`

.NET interoperability

Microsoft Dynamics NAV can be extended with the .NET Framework assemblies. We can reference assemblies and call types directly from the C/AL code of Microsoft Dynamics NAV objects, such as pages and code units. Microsoft Dynamics NAV objects can also subscribe to events that are published by the .NET Framework types:

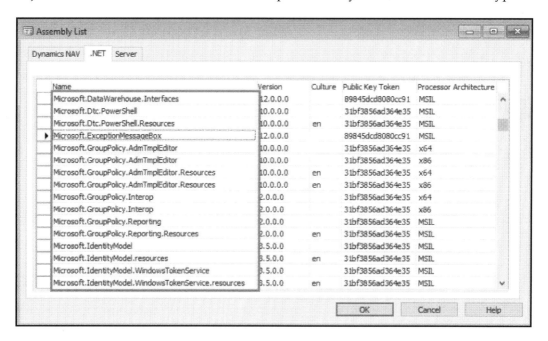

For more information on .NET interoperability, please visit the following link: `https://docs.microsoft.com/en-us/dynamics-nav/ extending-microsoft-dynamics-nav-using-microsoft-.net- framework-interoperability.`

Enhancements in RoleTailored client control add-ins

Control add-ins have been enhanced with the following features:

- **Additional data types are supported with database binding**: Dynamics NAV 2018 now supports data types, such as `DateTime`, `Boolean`, `Char`, `Decimal`, `Int32`, `Int64`, and `Guid`. Data binding and firing of the `OnControlAddIn` C/AL trigger is enabled by implementing the respective interfaces.
- **Methods and properties can be exposed to C/AL code**: To extend user interface controls on a page, methods and properties can be exposed in a control add-in assembly so that they can be called by the C/AL code on page triggers.
- **Control add-ins can be sized**: We can now specify an area of a page that a control add-in occupies, both with a fixed size or by setting the control add-in to resize as the page window resizes in the Microsoft Dynamics NAV Windows client.

Summary

Microsoft Dynamics NAV 2018 introduces a number of changes compared with the previous versions of the application. These changes are applicable to all the application areas; there have been changes to the client in the way it accesses the application, to the functionality, to the way development is executed, and there have also been IT-related changes.

In this chapter, we went through most of the relevant changes concerning an implementation introduced in Microsoft Dynamics NAV 2018 and some interesting features from the previous releases.

In the next chapter, we will examine a number of general considerations relating to Microsoft Dynamics NAV and Microsoft Dynamics 365 Business Central, such as the data model used in the application, the way posting routines are developed, and the SIFT technology.

General Considerations 3

Knowing the Microsoft Dynamics NAV philosophy of how things are done is an important aspect of successfully implementing Microsoft Dynamics NAV for any organization.

This is also important for users and people working in a company that uses, or will use, Microsoft Dynamics NAV as their ERP. They have to know how to do their job in Microsoft Dynamics NAV and be especially aware of the consequences of what they do.

Everyone involved in implementation needs to fully understand the way Microsoft Dynamics NAV works; not only because they are the people responsible for transmitting that knowledge to users, but also because they will most likely be designing and developing new functionalities and modifying existing ones. Therefore, it is important to use the same philosophy Microsoft Dynamics NAV uses in all of its standard functionalities. Breaking away from the core philosophies of Microsoft Dynamics NAV will confuse end users.

In this chapter, we will cover the following topics:

- The structure of Microsoft Dynamics NAV 2018
- The way information flows in Microsoft Dynamics NAV 2018
- Other general considerations
- Why to upgrade or move to Microsoft Dynamics 365 Business Central
- The structure of Microsoft Dynamics 365 Business Central

As a principle, the considerations that apply to Microsoft Dynamics NAV are also valid for Microsoft Dynamics 365 Business Central, but care must be taken because, in the cloud, not everything is possible (or it could be more complex to manage) and there might be limitations caused by the infrastructure (that is not on-premise!). However, it is possible to use workarounds to manage situations that seem simple in on-premise systems but seem more complex in the cloud.

The data model

If you have never worked with Microsoft Dynamics NAV before and have only started started playing around with it, there are a few words you will see over and over again, including setup, journal, posting group, post, document, entry, dimension, among others. You may not have a clue what all of these mean or what they are used for, but don't worry—we will explain it all!

Microsoft Dynamics NAV is structured into different functional areas, namely, financial management, sales and marketing, purchase, warehouse, manufacturing, jobs, resource planning, service, and human resources.

Each of the functional areas has its own setup, where the behavior of each of the areas is defined. A general setup also exists in the **Administration** menu.

As discussed earlier, Microsoft Dynamics 365 Business Central is the evolution of Microsoft Dynamics NAV and, to date, it maintains the same features of Microsoft Dynamics NAV 2018. It is used only with a Web client, which makes it slightly different from Microsoft Dynamics NAV.

To date, Microsoft Dynamics 365 Business Central SaaS does not have a Windows client and can only be accessed through web browsers. Microsoft Dynamics NAV 2018 and Microsoft Dynamics 365 Business Central web clients are different, and the latter has far more features than its equivalent on-premise version. The on-premise version of Microsoft Dynamics 365 Business Central could still have a Windows client, something we'll talk about in a later chapter.

Master data

Each of the functional areas has a master data table. The `Customer` table is the master data table for the **Sales & Marketing** area. The `G/L Account` table is the master data table for the Financial Management area. There are also other master tables and secondary master tables, which relate to the main master table in a functional area. For instance, the `Customer` table has quite a few secondary master data tables, such as **Bank Accounts**, **Ship-to Addresses**, and **Contact**. They are defined in this way because a single customer may have multiple contacts, bank accounts, ship-to addresses, or cross-references.

The secondary master data of a main master data register can be found in the **NAVIGATE** tab (although not all items in the **NAVIGATE** tab are secondary master data):

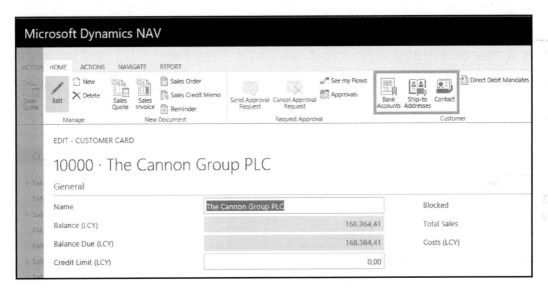

So far, we've seen what we could call core master data tables, which hold the basic information in a functional area, and we've seen that these tables may have some secondary master data tables associated with them.

A different kind of master data also exists in Microsoft Dynamics NAV. We could call it information helper master data tables. A few examples of this kind of data are locations, currencies, payment terms, payment methods, units of measure, and item-tracking codes.

Some helper master data may have its own secondary master data. For example, locations have zones and bins, and currencies have exchange rates.

Documents

Several documents exist in Microsoft Dynamics NAV, such as sales documents (quotes, orders, invoices, return orders, and credit memos); purchase documents (quotes, orders, invoices, return orders, and credit memos); warehouse documents (transfer orders, receipts, put-aways, shipments, internal movements, and picks); and manufacturing documents (production orders and component picking). A document combines information from different master data tables and is one of the entry points to a transaction.

For example, a **SALES ORDER** document combines information from the `Customer` table (the customer making the purchase), the `Item` table (the items that are being sold), the `Resources` table (the resources that will provide the services the company offers), and other information related to a sales order.

When the sales order is processed, it will lead to one or more transactions, such as `Item` transactions (the amount of stock of the item will be reduced by the quantity being sold) and **General Ledger** transactions (accounting entries will be created when the sales invoice is posted).

A document always has a header-lines structure presented on a single screen. In the **Header** section, you will find general information that applies to the entire document, such as **Sell-to Customer No**. In a `Sales Order` document, you will find the status of the document or the shipment date. In the **Lines** section, you will find detailed information about the document, such as a list of all of the items being sold in a sales order.

A Microsoft Dynamics NAV document is normally composed of three sections:

- **Header** information
- **Lines** information
- **Header Totals** information

The following screenshot shows the **Header**, **Lines**, and **Header Totals** sections (a complete Microsoft Dynamics NAV document):

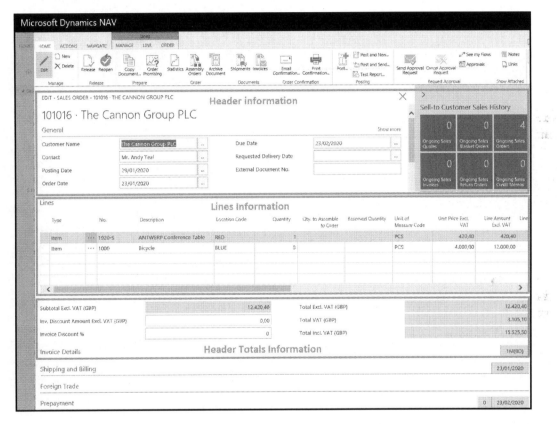

The Header, Lines, and Header Totals sections

The following is a part of the same screenshot, taken from Microsoft Dynamics 365 Business Central:

The Header and Line sections in Microsoft Dynamics 365 Business Central

Under the **ACTIONS** tab, you will always find one or more printing options to print the currently selected document. A printed document in Microsoft Dynamics NAV looks something like the following screenshot (in this case, it is in **Preview Report** mode):

Order Confirmation 6002

Oktober 12, 2020
Page 1 / 1

Beef House
Frau Karin Fleischer
Südermarkt 6

DE-40593 Dusseldorf
Germany

CRONUS International Ltd.
5 The Ring
Westminster
W2 8HG London

External Document No.	Salesperson	Quote No.	Shipment Method
	John Roberts		Ex Warehouse

No.	Description	Quantity		Unit Price Excl. VAT	VAT %	Line Amount Excl. VAT
1964-S	TOKYO Gastestuhl, Blau	34	stück	193.713	0	6,586.24
1996-S	ATLANTA Whiteboard, base	11	stück	1,403.995	0	15,443.95
80100	Printing Paper	14	Pack	1.765	0	24.71

				Total EUR Incl. VAT		22,054.90

Printed documents in Microsoft Dynamics NAV have all of the information that is commonly needed. Most companies that implement Microsoft Dynamics NAV ask their partners to modify the layout of printed documents; at least those that are sent (either as a PDF file or as a printed paper copy) to their customers or vendors.

Besides the **Print** option, you will also find the **Post** action in a document; both are in the **HOME** tab (where the most common posting actions are found) and in the **ACTIONS** tab (where all posting actions can be found):

A non-posted document is a document for which the action that is supposed to be done, has not been done yet. That is, a non-posted **SALES ORDER** document is an order for which the items that were ordered have not yet been shipped or the services that have been requested by the customer have not been provided. You can see non-posted documents as a work area in which the user can enter the required information and post it when it is ready.

When you post a document, you are telling Microsoft Dynamics NAV that the actions for the document have been completed (a sales order has been shipped, the items of a production order have been produced, a purchase order has been received, a sales invoice has been accounted for, and so on).

The posting action modifies the original document (to state that it has been posted) and creates new documents, that is, posted documents. For example, when a sales order is posted with the **Ship** option selected, `Posted Sales Shipment` is created and, when a sales invoice is posted, `Posted Sales Invoice` is created.

You will find posted documents from a Microsoft Dynamics NAV functional area under the **Posted Documents** section:

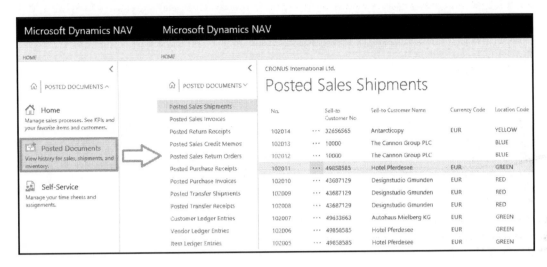

The Posted Documents section

The following is a screenshot from Microsoft Dynamics 365 Business Central showing the **POSTED SALES SHIPMENTS**:

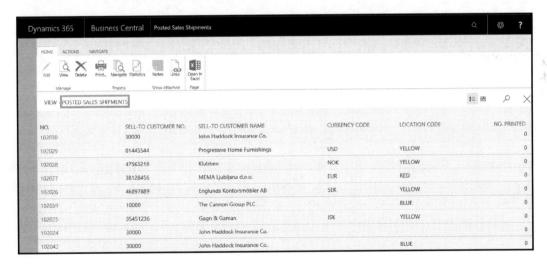

The POSTED SALES SHIPMENTS view in Microsoft Dynamics 365 Business Central

Journals

In Microsoft Dynamics NAV, you will see journals all over the place, in every single functional area. Just to name a few, if you move around the **Departments** menu, you will find a lot of different types of journals, such as **General Journal**, **Payment Journal**, **Item Journal**.

The following screenshot shows an example of **Item Journals**:

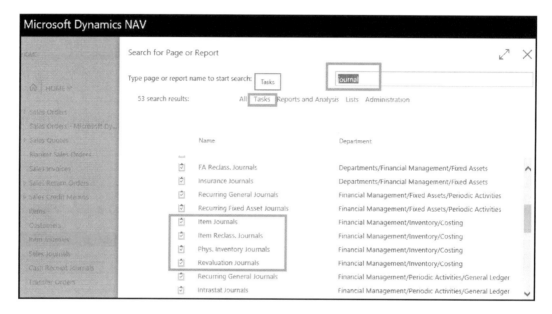

Journals are where all kinds of transactions in Microsoft Dynamics NAV, such as accounting transactions, sales transactions, and item transactions, take place. When you post a document, such as a sales order, Microsoft Dynamics NAV will use the journals internally to post to the appropriate ledger tables.

You can actually write down all of the company transactions in journals and post them there (journals also have a posting action) without using any kind of document. In fact, some companies follow this method, although we would not recommend it.

Imagine you want to post a sales invoice for an item you have sold, a resource, and a fixed asset. Using the appropriate G/L accounts, you have to perform the following steps:

1. Post all of the transactions by going to **Item Journals** and posting the necessary movements to reduce the amount of stock
2. Go to **Resource Journal** and post the necessary services associated with the order
3. Go to **FA Journal** and post the reduction of the fixed assets associated with the order
4. Go to **General Journal** and post the accounting transaction of the sale and accounts to be received

That's quite a lot of work to just make a sale and would surely make your accounting department angrier and grumpier.

This is one of the benefits of having documents in Microsoft Dynamics NAV. It goes to the appropriate journals, depending on the document and concepts used in the document. This creates necessary journal lines and posts these various journals.

So, why are journals important to users if all of the important transactions are done using documents? The reason is there are always transactions that do not have a document, so a journal will have to be used.

Among the journals, the one that is the most used in Microsoft Dynamics NAV is probably **GENERAL JOURNAL**. It is mainly used to post accounting transactions. There are many accounting transactions, such as salary payments to employees, that a company has to make and the company does not have a document to make them (not in Microsoft Dynamics NAV, at least).

In the next screenshot, you can see the **GENERAL JOURNAL**:

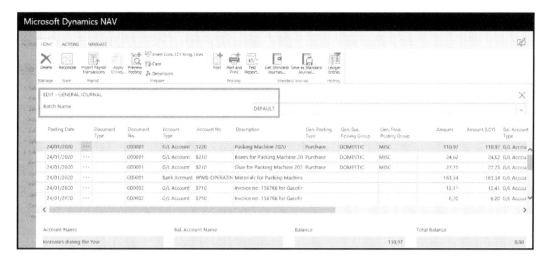

The GENERAL JOURNAL view

Another journal that is commonly used is **Item Journal**, where stock increases and decreases not associated with a document can be registered. What happens if an item is broken and thrown away? There is no document in Microsoft Dynamics NAV to enter such a transaction. Well, the place to actually do this is **Item Journal**, where the user can post a stock decrease for the item that has been broken.

Many journals that we've seen on the Microsoft Dynamics NAV menu are actually the same journals, but they show, and let the user enter, different information and have preselected options and built-in functionalities, depending on what the journal is meant for. For example, **Item Journal**, **Phys. Inventory journal**, and **Output Journal** actually rely on the same real journal, that is, **Item Journal**.

PYHS. INVENTORY JOURNAL is meant to register the system inventory differences when a physical count is completed. It's an item transaction; that's why it's built on top of **Item Journal** but has some differences.

In a **physical inventory**, we count how many units we have in the warehouse. We know how many units we've counted, but we do not know how many units are registered in Microsoft Dynamics NAV. That's why, in **PHYS. INVENTORY JOURNAL**, we enter the real quantity we've counted, in the **Qty. (Phys. Inventory)** field, and the functionality of the journal decides whether to positively or negatively adjust the inventory in the warehouse:

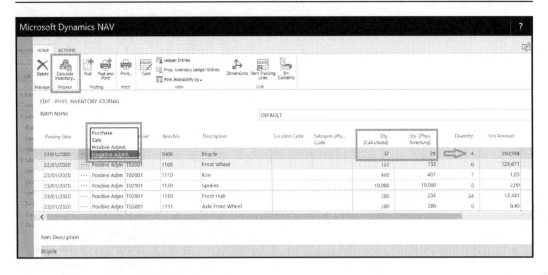

OUTPUT JOURNAL is meant to register the stock increase of a manufactured item in the system when a production order is finished. It is again an item transaction and that's why it is built on top of **Item Journal**. However, the user will have to provide some extra information that is not usually entered in other kinds of item transactions, such as the **Production Order** that is being posted, **Operation** in **Production Order**, or **Scrap Quantity**. The **Output Journal** line shows the user the fields that they have to fill in to post this transaction. These fields are not shown in other item journals:

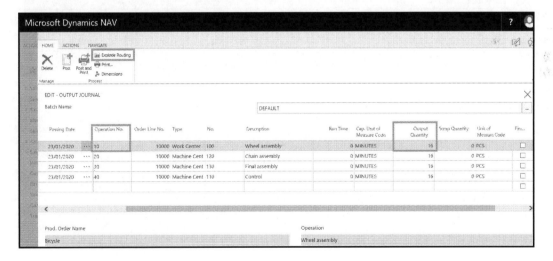

Once a journal is filled in with all of the necessary transactions, it has to be posted. Once it is posted, entries will be created and the journal lines will disappear (except for those that belong to **Recurring Journal**).

Ledger entries

Entries are the result of a posted transaction and they are always related to a master record.

In the following table, you will find the most important entries in Microsoft Dynamics NAV. You will also see the master tables they are related to:

Entry table	Related master table
G/L Entry	G/L Account
Cust. Ledger Entry	Customer
Vendor Ledger Entry	Vendor
Item Ledger Entry	Item
Res. Ledger Entry	Resource
Bank Account Ledger Entry	Bank Account
VAT Entry	Customer or Vendor
Job Ledger Entry	Job

Entries are created by a journal. **G/L Entries** are created by **General Journal**, which can also create **Cust. Ledger Entries**, **Vendor Ledger Entries**, **Bank Account Ledger Entries**, and **VAT Entries**. **Item Ledger Entries** are created by **Item Journal**.

In the following diagram, you can see which journal is responsible for creating which entry:

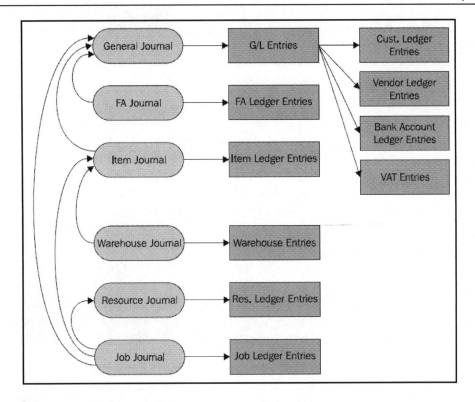

The preceding diagram also shows that some journals, if needed, can call other journals. So, the final result of the transaction will not only be the corresponding ledger entries for the journal that is being posted, but also ledger entries corresponding to a different journal.

For example, when posting an **Item Journal** transaction, Microsoft Dynamics NAV will automatically post costs (depending on the entry type) to the Inventory account, the Inventory Adjustment account, or the **Cost of Goods Sold** (**COGS**) account. The **General Journal** lines will be created and their posting route will be called from the **Item Journal**.

Ledger entries in Microsoft Dynamics NAV are the result of transactions. They are the final stage of a transaction. In general, once a ledger entry has been created, it cannot be modified or deleted.

However, there is some information that must be updated on the posted ledger entries. For example, after you post a sales invoice, at some point, the invoice will be paid if you want to stay in business. Therefore, **Cust. Ledger Entry** will have to be updated to reflect the new remaining amount for the invoice.

This is managed in Microsoft Dynamics NAV using detailed ledger entries. Most entry tables in Microsoft Dynamics NAV have a related detailed entry. Some information in the entry table is actually a calculation of the related detailed entries. So, there is no need to modify the original entry or even the related detailed entry. Changes are resolved by adding new detailed ledger entries. This will allow the accounting department to have full traceability of the number of times the invoice is paid and/or any credits that have been applied to the invoice.

You will find only two exceptions to the norm:

- The first are fields used for the system's internal purposes (such as the **Open** field found on some entry tables).
- The second are some specific fields that the user can modify manually, such as the **Due Date** field in customer and vendor entries or the **Shipment Agent Code** field in the shipment's header. Changes in these fields are handled in special codeunits.

Creating ledger entries

Let's see how this actually works step by step:

1. Using the **CRONUS International demonstration company**, create a new sales invoice for customer number `10000`, with the name `The Cannon Group PLC`. Create a line on the invoice for the item and enter `1000` and `Bicycle`. The quantity of the line will be `1 PCS`. You will find this in the following path:

   `Departments/Sales & Marketing/Order Processing/Sales Invoices`

The following screenshot shows what it should look like:

2. Post the **Sales Invoice**. After the posting process, the system will ask whether you want to open the posted document. Click on **No**:

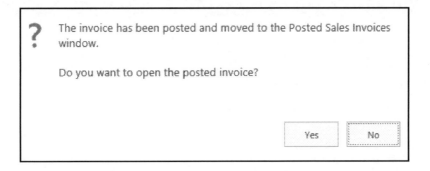

3. Open the **Customer Card** for customer number 10000, The Cannon Group PLC.

4. Click on the **NAVIGATE** tab and then on **Ledger Entries** (or press *Ctrl + F7*):

5. Locate the **Cust. Ledger Entry** value that corresponds to the invoice that has been posted. The **Original Amount** for this entry is **4,000.00** with **1,000 sales tax**. The total of **5,000** is the same as the actual **Remaining Amount**. Yes, CRONUS sells expensive bicycles:

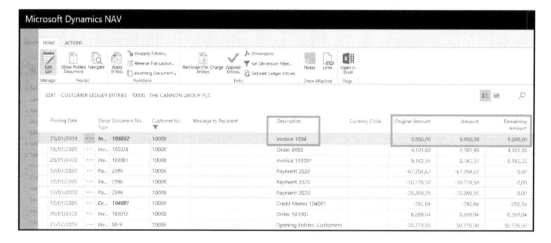

6. Open the **Cash Receipt Journal**. You will find it at the following path:

```
Departments/Financial Management/Cash Management/Cash Receipt
Journals
```

7. Create a line in the invoice to indicate that a partial payment of 2,000 was made on February 16, 2020, using the following steps:

   1. Select **Payment** as the **Document Type**
   2. Select **Customer** as the **Account Type**
   3. Select customer number **10000** as the **Account No**
   4. Select **Invoice** as the **Applies-to Doc. Type**
   5. Select the invoice that has been posted in the **Applies-to Doc. No** field

   In this example, it is invoice **103032**.

   Note that, since the amount of the original invoice was **5,000**, the system has automatically set up the **Amount** field of the payment to -5,000. Change it to **-2,000** to *partially* pay the invoice. The **Amount** value in the **Cash Receipt Journal** field is negative because the payment of a sales invoice is, in accounting language, a credit amount and is translated in Microsoft Dynamics NAV as a negative amount:

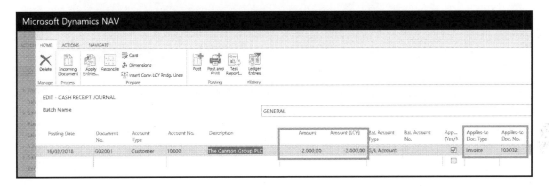

8. Post the **Cash Receipt Journal**.
9. Open **Customer Card** for customer number 10000, The Cannon Group PLC.

10. Click on the **Navigate** tab and then on **Ledger Entries** (or press *Ctrl + F7*). Locate the **Cust. Ledger Entry** value that corresponds to the invoice that has been posted in the previous steps. You will also see a **Cust. Ledger Entry** that corresponds to the **Payment** we have just posted:

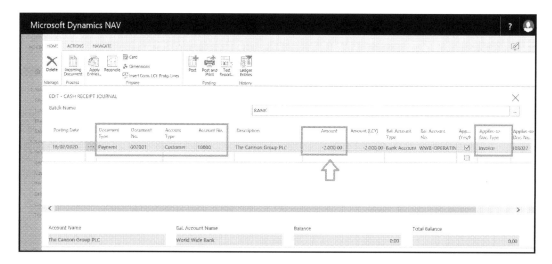

Note that the **Remaining Amount** for the **Invoice** was updated after we posted the partial payment. The **Remaining Amount** now shows **3,000**:

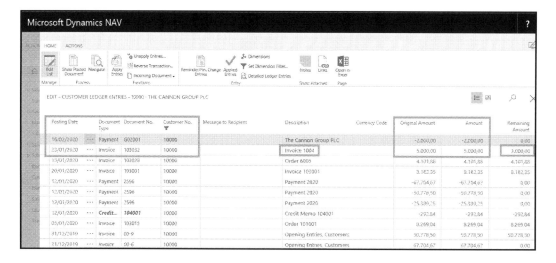

11. Click on the **Remaining Amount** field for the invoice. The **View - Detailed Cust. Ledger Entries** page is opened. There are two detailed entries for our **Invoice entry**:

  - The first one is the initial entry that corresponds to the **Invoice** entry with **Document No. 103035**
  - The second one is the entry that corresponds to the **Payment** entry that has **Document No. G02004**, which has been applied to the invoice

The **Remaining Amount** for the invoice entry is the sum of these two detailed entries: **5,000** + **(-2,000)** = **3,000**:

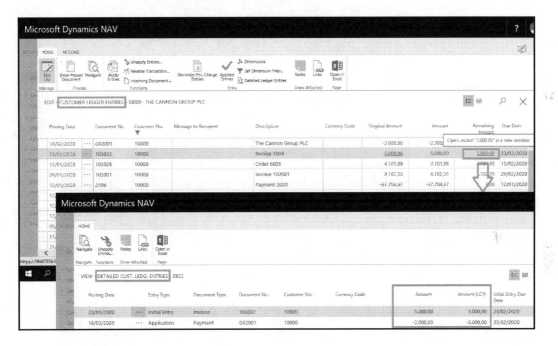

Not all **CUSTOMER LEDGER ENTRIES** tables have a **DETAILED CUST. LEDGER ENTRIES** table.

In the following diagram, you can see which ledger entry tables have a detailed ledger entry table and the names of those detailed ledger entry tables:

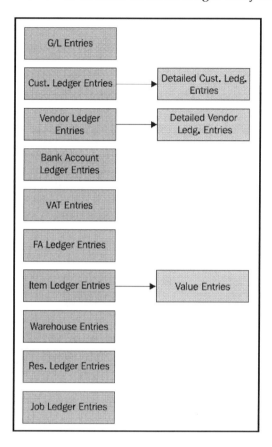

Combining all concepts

So far, we've covered master data, documents, journals, and entries. As we covered each of these concepts, we explained a little bit about how they were connected to each other. Now, we will see the general model that combines all four concepts.

The general data model looks something like the following diagram:

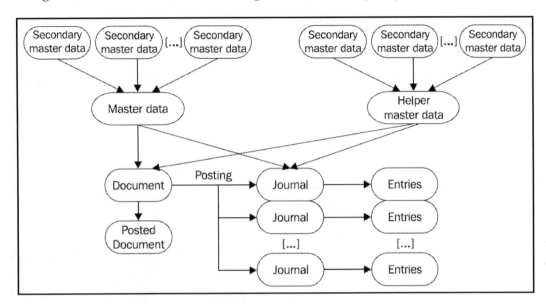

Master data and **Helper master data** are combined in **Document**. When a **Document** is posted, its corresponding **Posted Document** is created. Also, **Journal** lines are created and posted. The **Journal** lines will end up in different **Entries**.

Master data and **Helper master data** can also be combined directly on **Journal** without using a document. These **Journal** lines will also end up in different **Entries**.

No save button

Microsoft Dynamics NAV does not have any kind of save button anywhere in the application. So, data is saved into the database as soon as the user leaves a field.

Likewise, a record is inserted in its table right after the field (or fields) of the primary key. Some pages, such as **Sales Line** and the different journals have the `DelayedInsert` property set to `Yes`, which means that the record won't be inserted until the user moves the cursor to the next line or the next record.

The major advantage is that users can create any card (for instance, **Customer Card**), any document (for instance, **Sales Order**), or any other kind of data without knowing all of the information that is needed. Let's explain this with an example.

A new customer has to be inserted into the database. For Microsoft Dynamics NAV, it is mandatory to fill in some information to actually be able to post any transaction with the customer. The mandatory fields are **Gen. Bus. Posting Group** and **Customer Posting Group**:

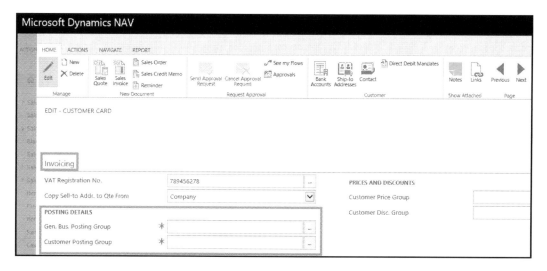

As you can see in the previous screenshot, the **Customer Posting Group** field has not been filled in for this customer. It doesn't matter right now; you can leave the card without losing the rest of the information that was introduced and come back to it when you have figured out the **Customer Posting Group** that should be used with this customer. The not-losing-the-rest-of-the-information part is important.

Imagine that there actually was a **Save** button; you would spend a few minutes filling in all of the information and, once you've done that, hit the **Save** button. The system then carries out some checks and finds out that one field is missing. It throws you a message saying that the customer card cannot be saved. So you basically have two options:

- Lose the information introduced up until that point, find out the posting group for the customer, and start all over again.
- Cheat. Complete the field with an incorrect value so that the system actually lets you save the data. Of course, you can come back to the card and change the data once you've found the right information.

Nothing will prevent any other user from posting a transaction with that customer in the meantime.

When is the data verified?

How does Microsoft Dynamics NAV verify the data that the user enters? Certainly not by someone looking over their shoulder. The data is verified when it is needed. In most cases, information in the master tables is needed when selecting a record either in a document, in a journal line, or when the posting routines are run.

Since customer number **61000** has a relevant field missing on its card, if you try to select this customer in **Sales Order**, you will get a runtime error that will say the **Customer Posting Group** must have a value in **Customer No.=61000**. It cannot be zero or empty.

Some other data, such as the posting dates, will be checked when posting a transaction. You can set up your Microsoft Dynamics NAV solution so that you only allow your user to post transactions using a specific range of dates. Posting dates can be restricted for the whole company or only for certain users.

Posting dates are an example of data that the system checks when posting a transaction. If posting dates are not allowed, an error message will be thrown saying: **Posting Date is not within your range of allowed posting dates**.

The main drawback

There is one main drawback of validating data this way. The problem will not occur until you try to post. An example would be when we have to post a shipment; the shipping agent is waiting with their truck and Microsoft Dynamics NAV throws an error message because someone up the chain didn't do their job properly.

Problems like this can be mitigated by setting default values for the mandatory fields through modifications or through templates. However, the company should have the proper process or guideline in place for people to follow; users should be responsible for their work. Basically, accountability is required.

In a way, this drawback is a benefit because there's no place for people to hide. Mistakes will be reflected in a relatively short time frame within your organization, and you will be able to weed out who's good and who's not.

In our case, if the truck leaves and the person in the warehouse has to fill in the documents manually, you can go and get in touch with the person responsible for configuring the data.

The Edit button

The **Edit** button is used to enter pages in edit mode, as well as in view mode. This feature is present both in lists and on card pages; this mode prevents inadvertent changes to the data.

The following screenshot shows the **Edit** button on the **Items** page:

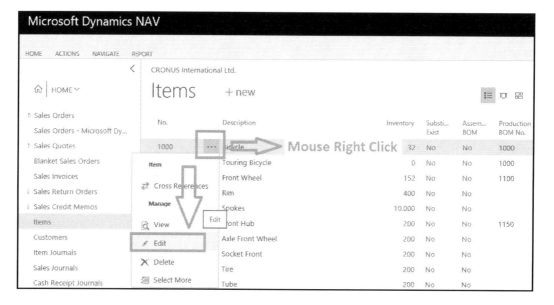

The following screenshot shows the **Edit** button on the **ITEM Card** page:

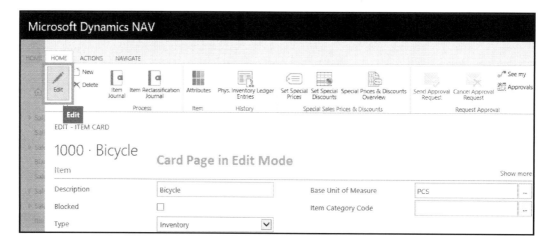

The posting routines

Microsoft Dynamics NAV has a big keyword (among others), called **Post**. If you read the word **Post** anywhere in an application or see the following icon, it means that, if you click on the button, a routine will be run and this will lead to posted documents and posted entries that are on their last stage; it is trusted data that won't change anymore. This is important for many IT and accounting audits:

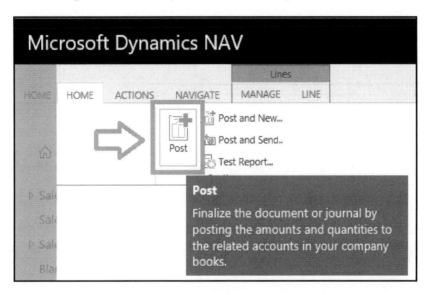

As explained in *The data model* section of this chapter, Microsoft Dynamics NAV has some tables called Entries (G/L Entries, Cust. Ledger Entries, Vendor Ledger Entries, Item Ledger Entries, and so on) that correspond to transactions related to master data. The only way to insert data into entry tables is through the posting routines. Numerous validations are carried out during posting routines, as the system has to check whether all of the data is correct and that no inconsistencies exist.

One unique posting process usually creates multiple entries, and all of the entries are related and consistent with each other. For instance, when you post a sales invoice, the system needs to create the following entries (depending on what the invoice includes):

- **Customer entries**: Used to track all of the transactions related to the customer.

- **Item entries**: Used if an invoice contains items for which you need to reduce the stock levels of. Plus, it is used if, in the future, you need to track all of the transactions related to one particular item.
- **VAT (tax) entries**: You will need to report to tax authorities all VAT (tax) charged to your customers. Therefore, the VAT (tax) amount charged on every invoice has to be tracked.
- **General ledger entries**: Accounting rules say that, when you issue an invoice, you have to record the related amounts on certain accounts. Microsoft Dynamics NAV does this for you by creating G/L entries.

As explained in *The data model* section of this chapter, entries are created by reading information from a **Journal** line. Therefore, if you choose to post a document, the first step that the system must follow is to create all of the related journal lines. Then, all of the related entries have to be created. The following diagram shows the general schema:

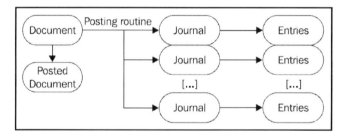

Posted data cannot be modified (or deleted)

Out of the box, posted data cannot be modified or deleted. Posted documents can be deleted, but only after a paper copy has been printed for manual archiving.

Not being able to modify or delete ledger entry data is one of the most basic requirements of any legitimate accounting software.

> Frankly, no software would allow you to modify ledger entry data. Think about how trustworthy your financial data would be if your auditors found out you can modify the financial ledger!

This may cause some frustration for Microsoft Dynamics NAV users who are used to a home-grown system or other off-the-shelf accounting software, where they can just void data without any repercussions. This is usually not an issue when you only have one person using the system, because they know exactly why a transaction needed to be voided. When your business grows to a certain size, just voiding transactions will not only raise a slew of questions from your auditors, but will also lead to inconsistent financial statements.

As mentioned earlier, there are a few exceptions where posted documents can be deleted or fields can be changed:

- Posted documents can be deleted after you have printed a paper copy for your ever-hungry filing cabinet. This feature cannot be used as a way to undo a document, as only the document is deleted but the corresponding ledger entries remain in the database.

 This feature was introduced back when database size was an issue. Document records were deleted to keep the size of a database small. However, with current technology, this is not really an issue. Typically, I advise companies not to delete posted documents.

- Some specific fields can be modified by a user manually, such as the **Due Date** field in customer and vendor entries or **Shipment Agent Code** in the **Shipments** header. Changes to these fields are handled by special codeunits.

You'll notice that none of the preceding exceptions deal with any dollar values or transaction dates. This is strictly implemented to maintain the integrity of your financial data!

As we saw in earlier sections of this chapter, when one document is posted, the result consists of several entries that are all consistent with each other and to the rest of the application data.

If data cannot be changed, how can users correct a mistake in data? The solution is to post reversed documents or entries so that the net effect of the transaction is zero. This will give you a complete paper trail of what happened to a transaction and what actions are done to "void" that transaction.

Navigating through your data

In Microsoft Dynamics NAV, it is extremely easy to navigate through data, remove default filters set by the system, and set your own filters to find or analyze your own data.

The Navigate functionality

You have probably seen the following **Navigate** button in many places in Microsoft Dynamics NAV:

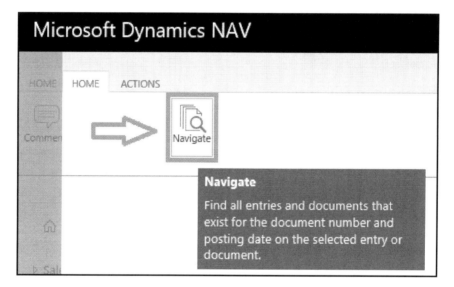

You can actually see it on every single page that shows posted transactions, either in **Posted Documents** and/or in ledger entry pages.

When you click on the **Navigate** button, a page will be displayed, magically showing all of the posted documents and entries related to the record from where you hit the **Navigate** button. This means that, if you are ever wondering which transactions are related to an entry, Microsoft Dynamics NAV will do the hard work for you and find anything related to that particular document number.

Earlier in this chapter, we created and posted a **Sales Invoice**. If we open **Posted Sales Invoice** and hit **Navigate**, the following navigation page will be opened:

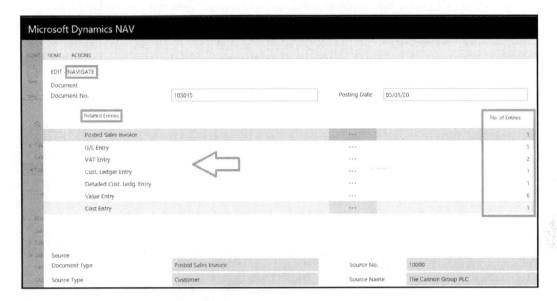

The navigation page is telling us that we can find a **Posted Sales Invoice** document, five **G/L Entry** records, three **VAT Entry** records, one **Cust. Ledger Entry**, one **Detailed Cust. Ledg. Entry**, and one **Value Entry** table related to the **Document No.** field with the value of **103035** in the **Posting Date** field with the value **05/01/20**.

Basically, when you posted this invoice, all of these documents and entries were created.

If we want to take a look at any of the documents or entries, we have to select the information we want to look at and click the **Show** button.

 The **Navigate** feature is used within **Document No.** and **Posting Date**. The **Navigate** feature will show all of the posted documents and entries that have used the same **Document No.** and **Posting Date**. If you use the same numbering rules for, let's say, sales invoices and purchase invoices, the **Navigate** functionality may show you information about all of the **Sales Invoice** and **Purchase Invoice** tables that have the same **Document No.** and **Posting Date**, although they may have no relation to each other at all.

Note that there are three different ways in which you can navigate for information: **Find by Document**, **Find by Business Contact**, and **Find by Item Reference**. By default, the **Find by Document** method is used. This navigates using internal document numbers. You can use the **Find by Business Contact** method to navigate using **External Document No.** (the **Customer PO** number or the vendor invoice number, for example) or the **Find by Item Reference** method to navigate using serial or lot numbers.

> If you develop customized ledger entries or documents, do not forget to modify the **Navigate** functionality so that it also considers customized tables. You will have to add code in the FindRecords and ShowRecords functions found on the Page object that has the number 344.

Other ways to browse data

The **Navigate** functionality is extremely useful and is extended all over the application; it is used to drill down to detailed transactions of a specified entry. Instead of drilling down to specific entries, sometimes, you just want to bring up a specific table related to the record you're looking at. For example, what if you want to bring up the customer card to check for some information when you're on the posted invoice document?

There is no need to close **Posted Sales Invoice** and exit out of whatever you're doing. The reason is a relation exists; in the case of **Posted Sales Invoice**, this is between **Posted Sales Invoice** and the customer.

You can browse directly on a document by clicking on the number of occurrences field:

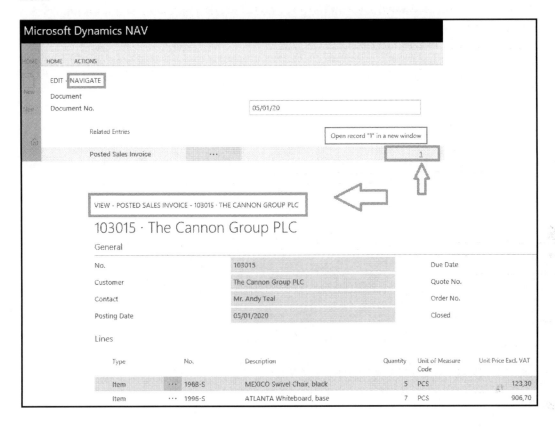

Hyperlinks

Take a look at the **General** fast tab of the **ITEM CARD**. The value of the **Qty. on Sales Order** field is shown as a hyperlink. If you click on it, a drop-down list is shown with the **Sales Order** list, as follows:

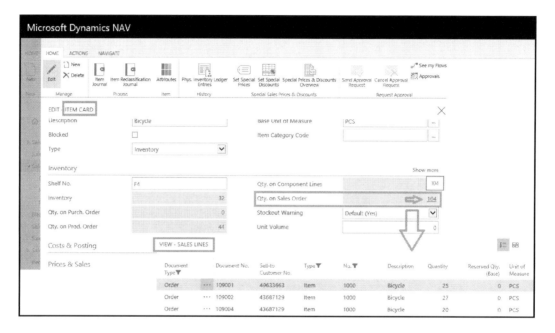

Hyperlinks are also shown when a value in a field is the result of a calculation (calculated FlowFields). In this case, clicking on the hyperlink will open a page where the records taken into account during the calculation are shown.

The following screenshot shows the sales order list page and, from there, you can access the sales order card (show document):

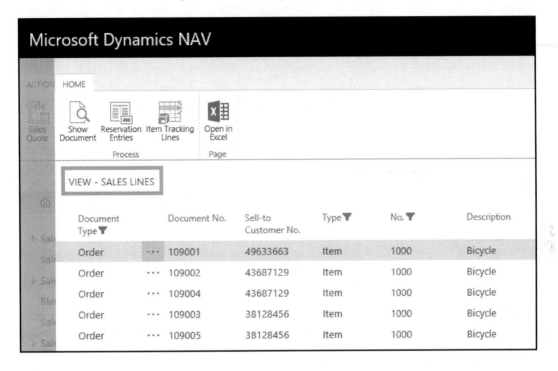

Sorting on list pages

When you pull up a list page, you can dynamically sort it based on any of the columns that are displayed. To sort a specific column of the list page, just click on the column header. Pull up the **CUSTOMERS** list and click on the **Name** column header:

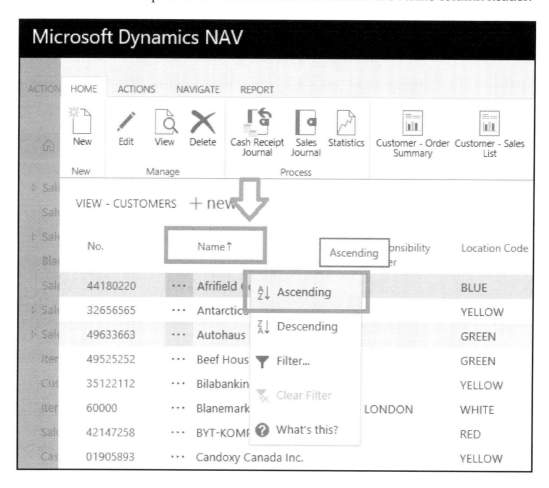

When the arrow on the column header points upward, it means that the list is sorted in ascending order. Now, if you click on the column header again, the arrow will point downward. This means that the records are sorted in descending order. You can also click on the ellipses (...) to open the order/filtering drop-down list.

You can click on any of the columns and the records will be sorted dynamically.

Filtering for the data you need (advanced filters)

Sometimes you need to look for a set of information but you do not want to print it into a report; you just want to extract the data and perform your own manipulations.

Fortunately, there are other ways to find data in Microsoft Dynamics NAV. Applying your own filters to a page to display only the information you're looking for is a powerful tool that will save you thousands of consulting hours per year.

Imagine you're a brand new customer service representative and just want to get a list of all of the customers in your territory. You want to find all the **DOMESTIC** customers that are to be shipped to from the **YELLOW** location.

 Note: advanced filters and saved views are actually only usable by the Windows client of Microsoft Dynamics NAV, not in the Web client and Universal App. They are not managed in Microsoft Dynamics 365 Business Central either.

You might examine all of the reports that exist in Microsoft Dynamics NAV and end up finding the one you need. But if you don't find it, don't worry; the following are the steps for doing so:

1. Open the **Customer** page (**Departments/Sales & Marketing/Order Processing/Customers**).

2. Display the **Advanced filter** by navigating to **Customer | Advanced Filter**:

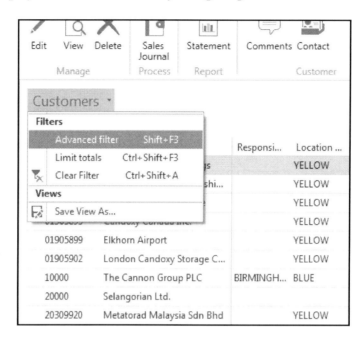

3. Click on **Add Filter** to add your own filters. A **Where** field is shown.

4. Select the field for which you want to apply a filter. In our case, we want to apply the filter to **Location Code** and **Customer Posting Group**:

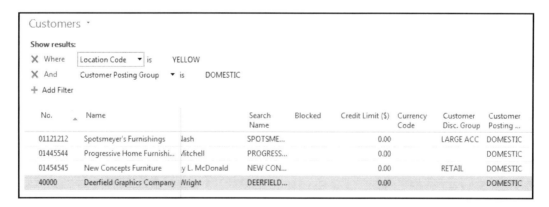

5. The information we were looking for is now displayed, that is, all of the customers that are to be shipped to from the **YELLOW** location and are **DOMESTIC** customers.

At this point, you can copy and paste to Excel or simply click on **Microsoft Excel** on the ribbon and the data will be exported to Microsoft Excel.

Saved views

Note that a saved view in Microsoft Dynamics NAV is like a database query in other systems; it is a very powerful tool for filtering and showing data with a pre-configured and reusable structure. Saved views can be embedded in a user's role or distributed to other users.

> *In Microsoft Dynamics NAV, it is possible to save and publish filtered pages as views. This feature was introduced some years ago and is a very useful feature, with this feature users can extract a lot of information, you can retrieve filtered data in simple way (...reducing reporting effort).*
>
> *– Roberto Stefanetti*

For more information, you can refer to `https://robertostefanettinavblog.com/2018/06/08/how-to-distribute-nav-views-and-user-personalizations/`.

Let's consider a simple scenario: a saved view on a **Customers** list. Assume that you need to frequently access the information based on the same filters that you set on the list. You can save the filters that you set, represented by a small icon on the **Role Center** home page:

1. Go back to the **Customers** list, set the filters, and display the list of the information you want.

2. Navigate to **Customers | Save View As**:

3. A popup will be displayed to allow you to change the description of your **View** and where you want to save it to. In our case, we can just save it to the **Home** page:

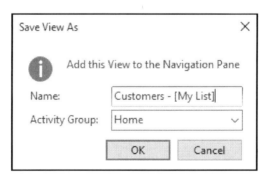

4. A message will be displayed, asking you to restart the application. Once restarted, the **Customers - My List** view will be on your **Home** page:

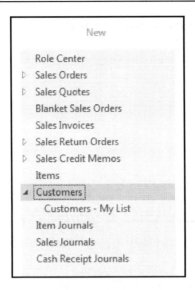

Other examples of a filtered view

An example of a filtered view is the **Purchase Orders** page, which we can list as a filtered view. For example, a dynamic data filter can be used:

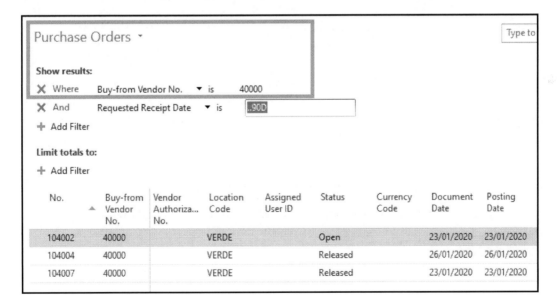

Note that saved views are actually usable only by the Windows client of Microsoft Dynamics NAV, not in the Web client, Universal App, or Microsoft Dynamics 365 Business Central (at the time of writing this book, but Microsoft is working on it and it should be included in the next updates of Microsoft Dynamics 365 Business Central). These are already set to be released with the fall 2018 update.

You can check Microsoft Dynamics 365 Business Central updates at `https://docs.microsoft.com/en-us/business-applications-release-notes/october18/dynamics365-business-central/`.

For more details and to understand how to best use filtered views, take a look at my blog post about this topic: `https://robertostefanettinavblog.com/2018/06/08/how-to-distribute-nav-views-and-user-personalizations/`.

Real-time data gathering – SIFT technology

Sum Index Field Technology (**SIFT**) is a built-in technology that exists in Microsoft Dynamics NAV and is used for totaling. It seems that Microsoft bought Navision for FlowFields, which are considered to be a brilliant feature.

In other ERP systems, totals, subtotals, and balances are calculated and stored somewhere. This calculation has to be redone over and over so that numbers are up-to-date.

In Microsoft Dynamics NAV, if you're a developer, you don't have to worry about calculating subtotals, as it can be done through SIFT. Creating a new **Subtotals** field is as easy as indicating in the field properties that it is FlowField and specifying the formula in the field. After this, you will not have to worry about keeping it up-to-date.

As a user, you know that the balances for your G/L accounts, customers, vendors, and bank accounts always display real-time information, similar to the other calculations done using SIFT. A few examples are the quantity on hand of an item or all of the customer statistics that are shown on the right-hand side of the screen when looking for or creating sales orders.

Everything leads to accounting

Accounting rules teach you how to translate everything that happens in a company into accounting language, that is, debits and credits.

Microsoft Dynamics NAV implemens these rules using posting groups, so the system can translate everything into the accounting language and post it to general ledger entries on the fly. Posting groups are related to master data. When you create a new record in the master data (for instance, you create a new customer), you need to specify which posting group it belongs to:

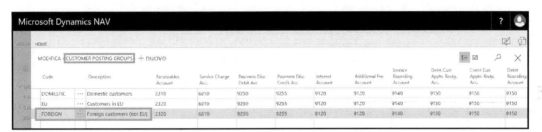

In the previous screenshot, you can see the existing posting groups for customers. For each posting group, all of the columns are filled with an account value. Microsoft Dynamics NAV uses these accounts to post general ledger entries any time a transaction is carried out with a customer.

You can create as many posting groups as the amount of detailed information you need. In Europe, for example, you have to separate domestic customers, customers from the European Union, and foreign customers. This is why three customer posting groups exist on the CRONUS International demo company.

The following posting groups exist, and each master data is related to at least one of these:

- Customer Posting Group
- Vendor Posting Group
- Job Posting Group
- General Posting Setup
- Bank Account Posting Group
- VAT (Tax) Posting Setup
- FA Posting Group
- Inventory Posting Setup
- Service Contract Account Group

Every time you post a transaction related to any master data record, general ledger entries will be created. This way, accountants only have to bother about transactions that no other area in the company posts.

On some special occasions, integration with accounting can be disabled. We can find an example of this in the **Fixed Assets** module. If integration is disabled, it is the user's responsibility to ensure that **Fixed Assets** entries are consistent with the amounts posted on the fixed assets accounts from the charts of accounts.

The Date Compression toolkit

If your database is too large—you have too many historical data and some tables with millions of records—it is possible in Microsoft Dynamics NAV to use some tools dedicated to data compression (the Date Compression feature).

Microsoft Dynamics NAV does not have a real data archive procedure, but it is possible to use these tools to optimize databases and tables. These tools delete data only after having created historical data that represents them; you can use data filters to achieve this. It can be useful to use data filters if you have been using Microsoft Dynamics NAV for several years with very large databases.

What are these tools?

There are several, and with different functional modes. I'll list a few, but note that these features are not actually available on the Web client; only in the Windows client. It will be necessary to understand if they are to be inserted successively:

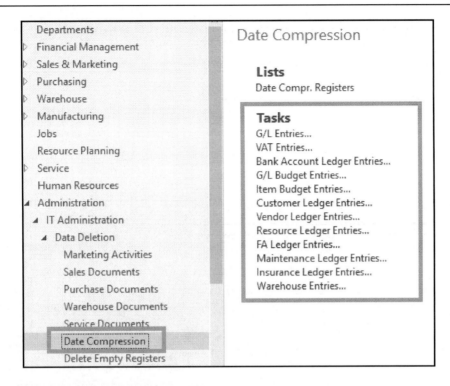

These tools are also available in the Windows client of Microsoft Dynamics 365 Business Central on-premise system.

The Date Compression toolkit is available for the following:

- Customer Ledger Entries
- Vendor Ledger Entries
- Resource Ledger Entries
- VAT Entries
- G/L Entries
- G/L Budget Entries
- Fixed Assets Ledger Entries
- Maintenance Ledger Entries
- Warehouse Entries

An example of Date Compression for warehouse entries is shown in the following screenshot:

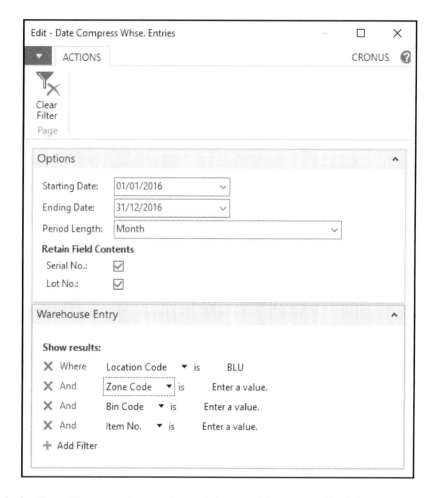

Through the Date Compression register, it is possible to see all of the compression operations performed.

The Microsoft Dynamics NAV and Microsoft Dynamics 365 Business Central database

Microsoft Dynamics NAV 2018 stores its data in a Microsoft SQL Server database or a Microsoft Azure SQL database. Microsoft Dynamics NAV 2009 and earlier versions of Microsoft Dynamics NAV used either a Microsoft SQL database or a native database for Microsoft Dynamics NAV. The native database has been discontinued and is no longer available.

Now let's talk about the databases for Microsoft Dynamics 365 Business Central. Microsoft Dynamics 365 Business Central SaaS is only deployed using Microsoft Azure SQL databases for both tenant and application databases. The on-premise fall 2018 update release for Microsoft Dynamics 365 Business Central will have the same database version support it currently has Microsoft Dynamics NAV 2018. Therefore, it will support Microsoft SQL Server—whether on-premises, virtualized, or hosted in Azure IaaS—and Microsoft Azure SQL Database.

The database topology used by Microsoft Dynamics NAV is a relational database, and referential integrity within the database is respected (where implemented). Currently, Microsoft Dynamics NAV rarely implements that at database level. Consistency is guaranteed through the application. Why? Because the base application was originally developed for the native database (deprecated since Microsoft Dynamics NAV 2013). In Microsoft Dynamics NAV, data integrity is maintained partially by the database engine itself but mainly by code.

When developing new Microsoft Dynamics NAV functionalities, consider data integrity in your analysis and design work.

The TableRelation property

The Microsoft Dynamics NAV Server service uses the `TableRelation` property of fields in tables to maintain data integrity.

There are plenty of fields in Microsoft Dynamics NAV tables that are related to other tables. In a sales invoice, for instance, the **Sell-to Customer No.** field is related to the **Customer** table:

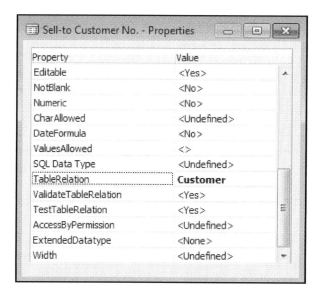

The relationship is stated in the `TableRelation` property of the field. **Sell-to Customer No.** is related to the primary key field of the **Customer** table.

A relation is established for three important purposes, and two of them are related to data integrity:

- **To establish data integrity**: If `TableRelation` is defined, only the values existing in the related table will be allowed to be written to the field. That is, you cannot create a sales invoice for a customer that does not exist. This rule can be omitted if `ValidateTableRelation` is set to `No`.
- **To maintain data integrity**: If a value is changed in the primary key fields of a related table, the change will be propagated to all the tables that have `TableRelation` with the first table. This means that, if you rename a customer, all of the existing sales invoices will change their **Sell-to Customer No.** field value so that the sales invoice points to the renamed customer (and not to the old value of **Customer No.**).
- **To enable the lookup functionality**: If `TableRelation` is defined for a field in a table whenever you are editing the value of that field, the system will allow you to pick up one of the possible values by showing a drop-down list.

`TableRelation` properties can be as simple as the one shown for the **Sell-to Customer No.** field in the **Sales Header** table, but they can also be more complicated. Conditional `TableRelation` properties can be defined, or you can apply filters to the relationship.

`TableRelation` of the **No.** field in the **Sales Line** table is an example of a conditional `TableRelation` property:

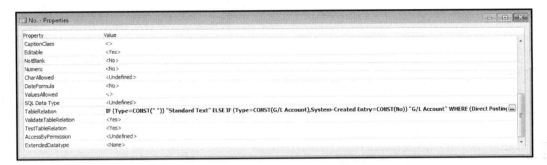

It's such a long `TableRelation` value that it is difficult to even read and understand in the `TableRelation` property. To take a better look at it, click on the **Assist Edit** button that appears at the rightmost part of the **Value** column for the `TableRelation` property.

An example of `TableRelation` with a filter can be found in the **Ship-to Code** field from the **Sales Header** table:

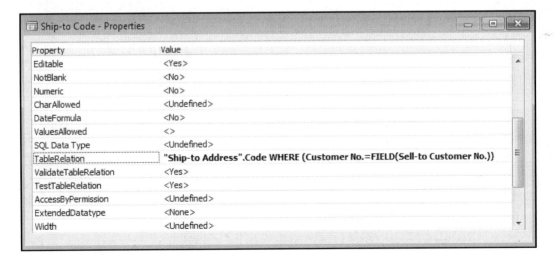

In this `TableRelation` table, a filter is applied, so we can only select **Ship-to Addresses** belonging to the customer for whom the sales document was created.

Coded data rules

Coded data rules are written in table and field triggers. They are used to enforce data integrity when it cannot be obtained with simple mechanisms, such as field types or table relations.

One of these data rules that you can see all over the application can be found in the `OnDelete()` trigger of most tables. In this trigger, conditions are usually checked to prevent the user from deleting certain information.

The following screenshot shows an example of C/AL code existing in the `OnDelete` trigger for **Table 14 - Location - C/AL Editor**:

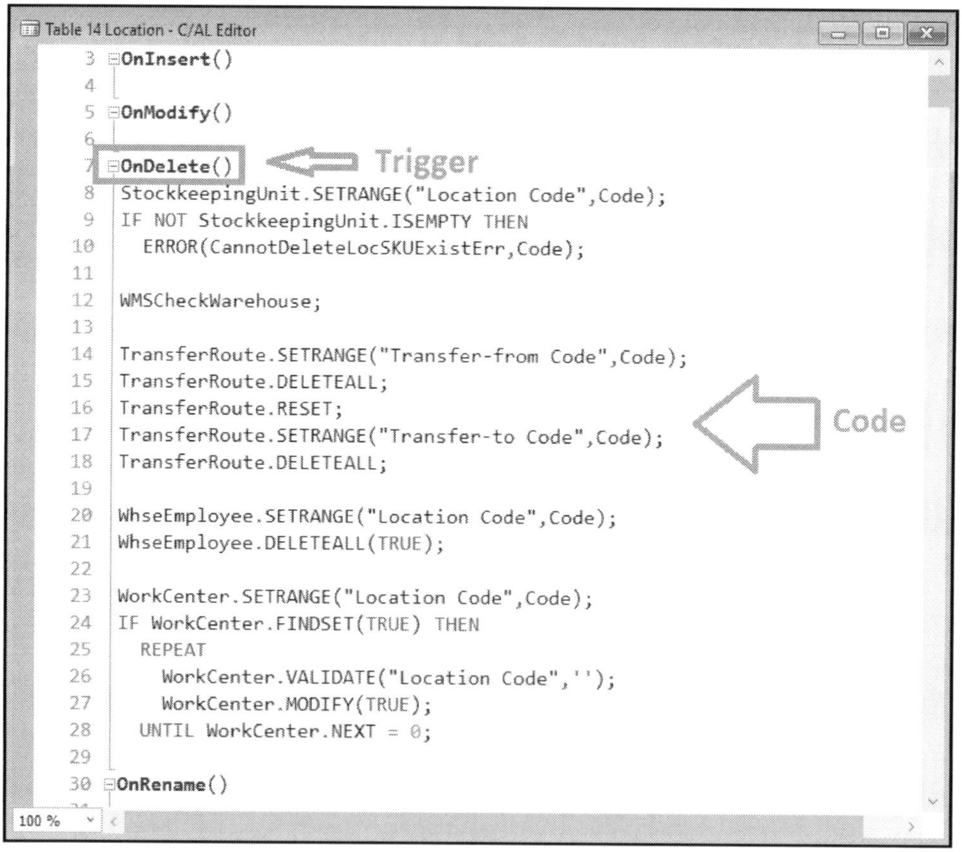

In the `OnDelete()` trigger of the **Location** table, some conditions are checked using the `WMSCheckWarehouse` function. If some conditions make it impossible to delete the location, an error message will be shown and the action will not be taken.

In the `OnDelete()` trigger of tables, code also exists to ensure that related information is deleted as well. In the example, transfer routes for the location that is being deleted are deleted as well. The `WMSCheckWarehouse` function also deletes the zones, bins, and bin contents of the location that was deleted.

If you're interested in learning more programming related aspects of Microsoft Dynamics NAV, please refer to *Programming Microsoft Dynamics NAV*, also published by Packt.

Microsoft Dynamics 365 Business Central – why upgrade to or adopt it?

Why upgrade to or buy Microsoft Dynamics 365 Business Central? There are several reasons, which I will try to list in the following.

Certainly, today, it is impossible not to have a product in the cloud; although there is still a hard core of on-premise installations (and Microsoft Dynamics 365 Business Central will also be maintained in on-premise format), the cloud is the present and Microsoft is investing a lot in it.

As a cloud-first product, Microsoft Dynamics 365 Business Central will be seeing frequent updates from Microsoft, a notable difference from the typical Microsoft Dynamics NAV solution ownership experience of the past. Microsoft Dynamics 365 Business Central's emphasis on newness comes with many strengths, but also drawbacks. I will offer a short comparison of the strengths and limitations of Microsoft Dynamics 365 Business Central, compared with Microsoft Dynamics NAV 2018.

History of Microsoft Dynamics 365 Business Central

The product was born to enter and attack the cloud market. For some years, Microsoft has been making changes to Microsoft Dynamics NAV to make it more versatile and open to the cloud; Microsoft Dynamics 365 Business Central is the evolution of Microsoft Dynamics NAV, which adopts its functionalities, with cloud-oriented and cloud-based technology.

The product has been improved during the transformation from Microsoft Project Madeira (the first release of the product) to Microsoft Dynamics 365 for Financials and to the correct Microsoft Dynamics 365 Business Central. The product now contains all of the existing features in Microsoft Dynamics NAV 2018, with the remaining constraint that it is possible to use only the web client or the Universal App instead of the Microsoft Dynamics NAV Windows client.

The strengths of Microsoft Dynamics 365 Business Central

What are the strengths of Microsoft Dynamics 365 Business Central? As mentioned previously, there are many, so let's look at some. We will discuss them in the following subsections.

Documentation

With Microsoft Dynamics 365 Business Central, even the documentation has changed. There is a lot of documentation available compared to the past (and in multiple languages). For partners, there are courses and videos available. A forum dedicated to the product has already been activated.

Some useful links include the following:

- https://docs.microsoft.com/en-us/dynamics365/business-central/
- https://community.dynamics.com/business/
- https://github.com/Microsoft/AL/wiki/Frequently-Asked-Questions
- http://aka.ms/ReadyToGoOnlineLearning

Cloud first and automatic upgrades by design

Yes, the product has now become cloud by design. This means that Microsoft will update cloud systems first, then on-premises ones later. Using an ERP in the cloud means always being up-to-date with the latest version of the product.

The New Modern Development Environment

The new modern development environment, born first for Microsoft Dynamics 365 Business Central, then used for Microsoft Dynamics NAV 2018, is innovative, allowing you to develop extensions (and to certify them—or not). It is useful for customizing the product in a much less invasive way than in the past.

The new modern development environment is composed of Visual Studio Code and the Microsoft AL language extension and allows the development of extensions in a professional way, updated to the market standard. This new environment is a significant change from the past.

Microsoft cloud services and the Virtual Cloud Desktop

Microsoft commercial cloud services are constantly evolving. Many already integrate natively or have connectors available for Microsoft Dynamics 365 Business Central. Others will connect soon, and we can now say that the cloud world offers a complete package of solutions (which I refer to as the Business Cloud Package).

Through native integration with Microsoft Office 365, Outlook, Microsoft Dynamics 365, Flow, and Power BI, to name but a few, it is possible to have a real virtual desk on the cloud. In fact, Virtual Cloud Desk is a suggestion for a new role in Microsoft Dynamics 365 Business Central. In practice, you never leave the cloud because all of the necessary information is there, including the ERP.

Scalability

Microsoft Dynamics 365 Business Central is hosted by Microsoft on Azure. The environment is composed of the following:

- A Multitenant database
- Architecture based on events
- An extensions model for development
- AppSource to distribute apps

With this model, it is possible to manage the philosophy: create, repeat, and scale. That is the basis of the extension development model.

Sandboxes and Docker for testing and development

We can't have separate development environments; only those purchased by the tenant. However, with sandbox and Docker containers, it is possible to have test environments to test both products and extensions (useful for customers, consultants, and developers). In this way, only tested apps are installed in the production environment, with less risk of compromising the solution in use.

Demo environments can also be created in instances of customers. Microsoft reserves the right to clean and delete these environments as needed.

Costs and pricing

I'm not commercial, I do not want to talk about costs and prices, but what I can say is that you will certainly save money in the end. Some reasons include: you pay if you use it, the system is self-updating, it is always online if necessary, and it is always under backup. If you need some more reasons: it also has a modern development environment, it's scalable, it can be used without installing anything, and it's easy to use.

As already anticipated in the first chapter, we have two licensing models, Essentials and Premium, and you can buy a monthly subscription license; a monthly subscription license includes application, hosting, and maintenance.

The following is the pricing (at the time of writing):

Microsoft Dynamics 365 Business Central is only available in the public cloud

For now, Microsoft Dynamics 365 Business Central is only available in the public cloud. Microsoft Dynamics 365 Business Central on-premise or in a private cloud will become available in Fall 2018. Using the public cloud brings benefits and limitations. Let's have a look at them.

Benefits of the public cloud

With the license, you are entitled to use the product and updates, as already mentioned, and integration with other products is guaranteed.

Limitations of the public cloud

The system is closed (but secure). You can't access the data tier. Only the environment-specific tenant that you have purchased exists. You can't create development environments; only sandboxes in the same tenant for the purpose of testing data. Therefore, the modality of the approach is very different from the on-premises world.

It is not possible to download a backup because, as mentioned, you do not have access to the data tier. The system does not go down but it is possible to restore data if necessary. The backup is managed by Microsoft, with no way to schedule an auto-backup. Therefore, a backup cannot be launched by the end user but, if necessary, it is possible to open an issue with Microsoft and they can provide a restore.

You can use RapidStart Services package to export data, but that isn't a real backup system (you can't restore your database after a crash failure) like an on-premises system. Rather, this tool allows you to export, for example, the setup data for master tables and secondary tables (a copy of the setup).

Web client limitations

Microsoft Dynamics 365 Business Central is a good offering, but more work is needed in my opinion. The client is very nice, more convenient, and has more features than the previous ones, but it is missing some features used by Microsoft Dynamics NAV customers through the Windows client. Examples include advanced filters and filtered views, which will probably be added in the fall 2018 update. However, it is usable and is in line with expectations.

In the coming releases, these missing features will surely be added, making it almost the same as the old Windows client, and other innovative features are sure to be added as well.

Summary

In this chapter, we looked at general considerations for Microsoft Dynamics NAV and Microsoft Dynamics 365 Business Central, and learned their philosophies. It is important for everybody to learn to work together, since every part of Microsoft Dynamics NAV and Microsoft Dynamics 365 Business Central is tied together in one way or another. The implementation of these systems could be used to re-engineer a company's processes. Applications aside, implementing Microsoft Dynamics NAV and Microsoft Dynamics 365 Business Central will give your employees an opportunity to understand exactly how your company operations work, resulting in more productivity.

So far, we have introduced Microsoft Dynamics NAV 2018, in Chapter 1, *Exploring Dynamics NAV and MSDYN365BC – Overview*; we talked about the new features that the current version has introduced in Chapter 2, *Microsoft Dynamics NAV 2018 - An Overview*; and we have now talked about the general philosophy of Microsoft Dynamics NAV.

In the coming chapters, we will talk about how you can implement this ERP in your company!

4
Implementation Process – Partner's Perspective

In this chapter, we will learn about the Microsoft Dynamics NAV 2018 and Microsoft Dynamics 365 Business Central implementation process from the perspective of a reseller. This chapter will explain the meaning of implementation and show that there are different methodologies that you can apply.

In an implementation process, several actors may get involved, each one playing their own role. We will learn what kind of roles can be found in a Microsoft Dynamics NAV or Microsoft Dynamics 365 Business Central implementation and the job that can be expected from each role.

We will also see that the implementation process can be broken down into phases, and we will learn about the tasks included in each phase.

The main topics discussed in this chapter are as follows:

- Defining what an implementation is
- Using methodology
- Roles involved in an implementation project
- The phases of the project
- Considerations for an implementation of Microsoft Dynamics 365 Business Central

What is an implementation?

What is an implementation? To implement means performing a series of steps that usually includes the following:

- Requirements analysis
- Project scope analysis
- Customizations
- Integrations
- Key user training
- Product delivery

These steps are often supervised by a project manager who uses different project management methodologies. Through the **plan-do-check-act** (**PDCA**) steps typical of project management (the Deming Cycle), it is possible to keep the project under control.

To implement a system successfully, a large number of interrelated tasks need to be carried out in an appropriate sequence. That is what needs to be done in a Microsoft Dynamics NAV or Microsoft Dynamics 365 Business Central implementation process to get the software (Microsoft Dynamics NAV, Microsoft Dynamics 365 Business Central, be it on-premise or SaaS) to operate properly in its environment (the company that will use these programs as their business management software).

An advantage of Microsoft Dynamics NAV is the ability to set it up any way you like; oftentimes, people take this flexibility to the point of diminishing (or negative) return.

Companies are completely different from one another. They work completely differently, as they have different processes and ways of doing business. Microsoft Dynamics NAV, just like individual companies, can work in many different ways. Each company has to find its own way. And that is actually what will be done in the implementation process where you choose the way in which you want Microsoft Dynamics NAV to work.

Microsoft Dynamics NAV is a software product that requires you to set it up properly before you can start working with it. There are some areas that have to be configured and many decisions that have to be taken, master data that has to be introduced into the system, and a host of other decisions that have to be taken before a company can start using Microsoft Dynamics NAV as their business software. Taking shortcuts in order to "save" on implementation cost is guaranteed to cost the customer more in the long run.

Microsoft Dynamics NAV, as with many other business software products, provides a large stack of what are called horizontal functionalities that may be useful for any company, regardless of the business sector in which they work. It also provides the needed flexibility to adapt to any specific vertical requirements.

> **Vertical and horizontal solutions**: A **vertical solution** is a stack of functionalities thought of and developed to cover the industry-specific requirements of a business sector. Manufacturing companies need software solutions different from what a health care company needs, for example. A **horizontal solution** is a stack of functionalities that every single company needs or can use, such as word processing or spreadsheet applications. In Microsoft Dynamics NAV and Microsoft Dynamics 365 Business Central, application modules such as Financial Management are part of the horizontal solution, as they are useful and necessary for every single company.

Apart from a host of horizontal functionalities, Microsoft Dynamics NAV offers some out-of-the-box vertical application modules, such as the Manufacturing module, that will probably be used by manufacturing companies, but not by retail companies, for instance.

All of the out-of-the box application modules and functionalities that Microsoft Dynamics NAV offers can be put together in what is called the **standard solution** or **standard software**. Don't take the word standard as something standardized by an international standards authority. That is not what standard means in this context. It is actually refers to how Microsoft, based on the feedback of how companies use an ERP application, the necessary functionalities that can be applied across most of the companies that use Microsoft Dynamics NAV.

If the standard Microsoft Dynamics NAV does not meet the specific requirements that a company needs, a large channel of Microsoft Dynamics NAV partners exists, who may have developed a vertical solution. The solution probably complies with many of the requirements of what client's industry.

You will find vertical solutions for as many business sectors as you may think of—retail, real estate, educational, health care, and non-profit, to name just a few. Custom development can also be done for a specific company to modify or extend Microsoft Dynamics NAV functionality to meet the unique demands of your customer's requirements.

In an implementation process of Microsoft Dynamics NAV, you have to choose whether you will implement the standard Microsoft Dynamics NAV, and/or a vertical solution offered by yourself or by any other company. You will have to choose which functionalities will be used and how they will be used; you will have to know if development will be required, and then you will have to implement all of this by installing the product, developing what needs to be developed, and configuring what's required.

After figuring out the framework that's needed for an implementation, you also need to load the initial data the company needs to start working with (primarily, their master data, such as their database consisting of customers, vendors, or items). Finally, you have to train the end users who will use Microsoft Dynamics NAV, as they have to know how everything works and which tasks they are expected to perform in the system.

For Microsoft Dynamics 365 Business Central, the implementation is not very different but we must take into account some aspects of the product.

Some pros and cons for Microsoft Dynamics 365 Business Central SaaS include the following:

- It is cloud-based and exists on the Web client only, not on the Windows client
- The source code of the standard product cannot be changed
- You can only use extensions to develop and install customizations
- The system updates itself
- The old horizontal platforms no longer exist as monoliths, and will be implemented as extensions

From the perspective of a new implementation, for those coming from Microsoft Dynamics NAV (although it applies to everyone), it is necessary to keep in mind these rules of use of this product that is a novelty compared to the past. We will discuss this extensively in Chapter 13, *Microsoft Dynamics Business Central*.

Methodology

Each implementation of Microsoft Dynamics NAV is completely different from the others. The reason is because each company, no matter how similar the industry, is run differently. The company that is going to use the ERP software (usually called **the customer**) is different, the requirements are different, the scope is different, and even the team implementing it might be different. This brings a lot of uncertainty to the process and is the main reason why methodology has to be used.

Implementing Microsoft Dynamics NAV is considered as working in a project environment. By definition, a project is a temporary endeavor undertaken to meet unique goals. The company implementing Microsoft Dynamics NAV (usually called **the consultant**) is probably used to this kind of environment. On the other hand, the customer is probably used to working in an operational environment, where the same processes are repeated over and over. For the customer, implementing a new ERP system is like running in the jungle, with dozens of options to take at each step but no idea about where to go. Therefore, methodology is not only going to help the consultant, but also the customer, understand exactly what's going on.

Methodology is not only applicable to the development and the implementation, but also to stuff such as how the project is going to be billed or how the project team is going to transfer knowledge to the support department at the end of the project. You have to define some aspects before starting any project:

- **Billing**: A Microsoft Dynamics NAV project means investment of time and work before the go-live date. Usually, projects do not show results until the end. Even on agile methodologies, you will need several iterations before the go-live date. Both the partner and the customer must be balanced in order to have the best relationship possible. This can only be achieved by billing the project as it moves forward.
- **Estimating time and cost**: At the beginning of the project you will have to estimate the project, either in cost or time. Use templates to help you estimate and ensure that you don't forget any task. It is normal to think about the development time of a certain requirement, and forget the time it takes to design or implement it. It is also normal to forget the tasks related to managing the project, which are time-consuming.

For each requirement, you can use a template similar to the following one:

	Analysis	Development	Test	Implementation
Requirement 1	3h	10h	2h	2h
Requirement 2	1h	4h	1h	0.5h

Use this template to estimate all the requirements, even the ones that are going to be accomplished with standard functionality, because they will take up implementation time. Also, use this template (or a similar one) to estimate migration requirements.

Use another template for the remainder of the implementation tasks. Write down all the tasks required for implementation and make sure to check them all when estimating a new project.

Some tasks that you should not forget include project management, software installation, training, and support. To estimate the project management tasks, we use a percentage of the entire project estimation. It is up to you to fix this percentage, but it could be something like 10 percent. In a complex implementation, you can also break down this task and perform the estimation from there.

- **Planning**: Determine how you will plan the project, in terms of all the phases and the everyday work. Visibility is important; therefore, the whole team and other stakeholders in your company have to be aware of the project plan. You might also need to use a tool such as Microsoft Project or Microsoft Excel to plan the whole project. You could then print the plan of the whole project and distribute it to the people who are going to be involved in its implementation.

 Using Microsoft Project versus Microsoft Excel: Both tools are great for planning. However, I find Microsoft Excel a much better tool because it's something the customer is familiar with. Instead of teaching the customer Microsoft Project, we can focus on determining which dates are important for which milestones.

The project plan should be shared with the customer as early as possible. This helps everyone plan their vacation and time off to ensure they are around when they need to be around.

- **Purchases**: Your project will, at least, involve the purchase of the customer's Microsoft Dynamics NAV license. In some projects, you will also have to buy other things, such as hardware, if you are in charge of providing it. Determine when and how you are going to do all of your purchasing, and do it the same way in all of your implementations.

- **Communication with the customer**: Communication is a very important part of any project. Determine how, who, and when you are going to communicate with your customers:
  - It can be through meetings, emails, phone calls, or shared documents. Also, decide on the single point of contact from the partner's side, as well as the customer's side.
  - If too many people from the partner's side talk with too many people from the customer's side, it can be chaotic and you will probably end up with inconsistencies.

- **Communication between the team**: This is also very important, especially if the team is placed in different locations. If someone has talked to the customer and has decided on something, the rest of the team must be made aware of it. One of the best ways to keep a tab on everything is to immediately follow up with an email on what was decided, to both the customer and the parties involved as partners.

- **Development and testing**: Determine the strategy the company is going to use when developing and testing, in terms of how the code will be written and marked. If you have not defined this, you could end up with everybody developing on a local machine, marking their code in a completely different way, and having to invest a lot of time to put everything together.

- **Acceptance of the developments**: Your implementation methodology has to ensure that the customer accepts the developments as the project progresses. This involves delivering the bits and pieces of the project as soon as they're completed. Don't wait to show everything in the last week before the go-live date. If you do so, prepare yourself for a tough support phase with an unhappy customer.

- **Documentation**: Determine what has to be documented, the structure each document will have, and how it will be named:

  - It may seem that this is a very bureaucratic process, but it can really be as simple as you want. By documentation we don't mean that each project has to generate a thousand pages of documentation, but that the few documents that are generated follow the same structure and are archived in the same place.

  - Even on smaller projects where only one person is involved, plan ahead so another person can come in and pick up where that one person left off if they goes on vacation.

- **Reporting and control**: Think about what kinds of reports you will have to generate and the kind of control that the project will have. You may want to control the project advance, time, cost consumption, and so on. Invest time in your project to this area, even if the project seems to be okay, or you won't see the diversions until it's too late. To control the project advance, we recommend you plan demo/training sessions, so that each developer can show their work to the rest of the team. These demo/training sessions have two purposes. One, the project gains visibility and becomes part of the communication between the team members that we talked about earlier. Two, it allows feedback from the team members on improvements needed in a project or whether a project is being done completely wrong.

In project management, there are different kinds of methodologies. The main ones are waterfall and agile. The waterfall approach is the most used approach while implementing Microsoft Dynamics NAV, but agile gives better results, especially on software requirements. This is why agile approaches have been gaining ground for the past few years.

In the next sections, we will cover both approaches and learn how to use the best of both.

The waterfall approach

The waterfall model is a design process in which progress is seen as flowing steadily downward (like a waterfall) through the phases.

The following diagram shows the typical representation of a waterfall approach:

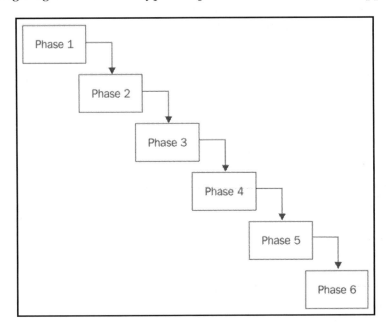

As you can see in the diagram, one phase does not start until the last one has finished. In the next section of this chapter, we'll talk about the phases of a Microsoft Dynamics NAV or Microsoft Dynamics 365 Business Central implementation, which are presales, getting the requirements, analysis, development, deployment, and support.

In our case, the analysis phase cannot start until all of the requirements have been taken care of, and the development phase cannot start until all of the requirements have been analyzed.

Companies have chosen this approach because it is the one that, theoretically, brings more certainty. Using this approach, the whole scope of the project is defined after getting the requirements, so it is easy to fix a cost for the project and fix an ending date. But, as we said, this is just theoretical. In reality, the requirements that are gathered at the beginning of the project may not be what you end up going live with. The reason is because in the earlier stages, the customer does not know Microsoft Dynamics NAV or Microsoft Dynamics 365 Business Central, but once they realize the potential of these systems, they will certainly want to change how they work for the better.

This is very similar to building or remodeling a house. In most cases, the owners want to make changes to what the architect drew because they see something that can totally make their house a lot better.

When it comes to Microsoft Dynamics 365 Business Central projects, the waterfall approach is obviously also usable, as it's a methodology.

The most common problems encountered in waterfall projects are often linked to bad commercial agreements that could sink a project: fixed price requirements, limited availability/access to the key users on the customer's side, limited flexibility in the scope of the contract to remove unneeded line items from the gap analysis, and misunderstanding of the requirements and problems with the solutions could sink a project.

The agile approach

The agile approach is based originally on the agile manifesto and on agile principles (`http://agilemanifesto.org/principles.html`).

The agile approach is based on iterative and incremental development. It is typically represented as in the following diagram:

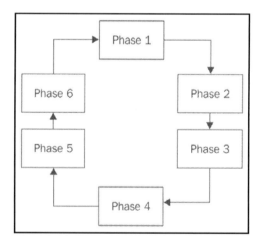

In this approach, you perform several iterations through all of the phases before you reach the end of the project. With this approach, the customer needs to be more involved in the project and work more closely with the partner team.

The agile approach is the best to meet the requirements and is able to more closely fit the customers' needs. It is an approach that adds more value. However, it is hard to estimate time and costs at an early stage. And for the company implementing Microsoft Dynamics NAV or Microsoft Dynamics 365 Business Central, not exceeding their budget may also be very important; in some cases, even more important than the value added.

This is usually solved by establishing a win-win/lose-lose relationship between the customer and the partner. Both parties agree on a desired cost. If the project ends up with less cost than expected, then both sides win. If the project ends up costing more than expected, then both sides lose.

We have worked for many years on projects implemented by following the waterfall approach. The cost of the project is set up at the beginning of the project, and sometimes it can be tough to ask the customer for a revised budget.

With the cost already fixed, the customer always tries to get more value for the same price and the partner ends up lowering the quality for the same price. Fights between both happen when one party says that this is not what we agreed upon in the first place, and the other party argues that this was implicit in the requirements.

The win-win/lose-lose relationship balances the equation between the value added and the final cost. Agile is obviously also usable for Microsoft Dynamics 365 Business Central projects; it's a methodology.

The most common problems encountered in agile projects are few collaborations (these are critical to a successful project, including members of both the partner and the customer organisations); a lot of new incoming requirements, which are difficult to manage on a schedule; and too many changes that could sink the project.

The best choice – waterfall or agile?

Which is better—the waterfall or agile approach for Microsoft Dynamics NAV or Microsoft Dynamics 365 Business Central implementations? My opinion is that it depends on the project. If it's a consultancy project: waterfall, and if it's a development project: agile (agile Scrum methodology, in this case). If it's a complex project: waterfall.

Inside agile – Scrum overview

What is Scrum? Scrum is an agile methodology, a simple powerful set of principles and practices that helps teams deliver products in short cycles, enabling fast feedback, continual improvement, and rapid adaptation to change; you can use Scrum to continuously improve and deliver early.

Where does this word come from? The term "Scrum" comes from a 1986 *Harvard Business Review* article in which authors Hirotaka Takeuchi and Ikujiro Nonaka made an analogy comparing high-performing, cross-functional teams to the Scrum formation used by rugby teams.

Why do we talk about Scrum? Because Microsoft also uses it for many projects—it is currently used for the development of Microsoft Dynamics NAV and Microsoft Dynamics 365 Business Central.

What is the Scrum Guide? The Scrum Guide contains the definition of Scrum. Ken Schwaber and Jeff Sutherland developed Scrum, and the Scrum Guide is written and provided by them. For more information, you can refer to `http://www.scrumguides.org/`. The following figure shows the **SCRUM** methodology:

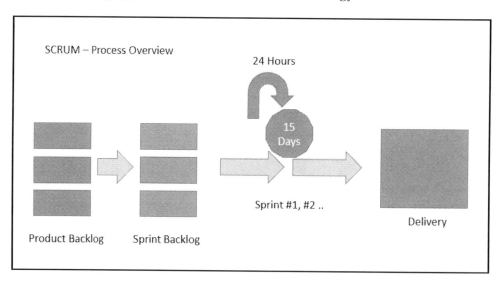

The Scrum core model consists of the following:

- **Actors in Scrum**: The Scrum Master, the product owner, and the development team
- **Activities in Scrum**: Sprints and product backlog

The most important concepts are inspection and adaption. Scrum prescribes four formal events for inspection and adaptation:

- Sprint planning
- Daily scrum
- Sprint review
- Sprint retrospective

 For more details, you can visit `http://www.scrumguides.org/scrum-guide.html#uses`.

Now, we will discuss the advantages and disadvantages.

Let's first have a look at some advantages:

- **Small projects**: Scrum is nice for small, fast moving projects with small teams
- **Fast documentation**: Documentation for agile projects is faster than for waterfall projects
- **Multiple iterations**: Continuous feedback from users
- **Daily meetings**: The individual productivity of each team member can be measured
- **Continuous WIP check**: Progress in work is clear through regular meetings
- **Issue resolution**: Issues are identified well in advance through the daily meetings and hence can be resolved speedily, with fast mistake resolution
- **Delivery**: You can always deliver products within a scheduled time

Some disadvantages are as follows:

- **Tasks are not detailed**: If a task is not well defined, project cost and time estimates will not be accurate, with the risk of not completing them.
- **Weak Scrum Master**: Scrum works well for project management when the Scrum Master trusts the team they are managing. If they do not work well and do not check carefully, it can lead to failure of the project.
- **Weak teams**: If the team is weak, the project will either never be completed, or will fail. If any of the team members leave during development, it can have a hugely negative effect on project development.

- **Lack of experience**: This methodology requires experienced team members only. If the team consists of people who are novices, the project cannot be completed in time.
- **Poor quality**: Project quality is hard to implement and there is no step-by-step quality check of the project.

 For a nice comparison between agile Scrum and waterfall project management approaches, you can visit `https://www.scrumstudy.com/whyscrum/scrum-vs-traditional-pm`.

Using the best of both

To use the best of both approaches, you can have an initial "getting the requirements" phase, but with less detail than in the waterfall approach. In this first phase, the requirements of all areas are covered, so it helps the partner team to make an approximate estimation of the project cost and time. This helps the customer identify whether the project fits their needs, and also their budget. After that, you loop through all the phases, focusing on a few requirements at a time. Of course, using this approach, the cost of the project is only an approximation; it may cost less or more.

If the project is finished with less cost than estimated, both the customer and the partner win, because they share the benefits of the savings. On the other hand, if the project costs more than expected, both have to share the cost overrun. This can be achieved by returning part of the savings to the customer, and compromising on the cost of the underestimated projects.

This kind of relation between the customer and the partner is new in the Microsoft Dynamics NAV world and several cultural aspects must change inside the organizations that use it, but we are sure that the results will be worth it.

Microsoft Dynamics Sure Step

Microsoft Dynamics Sure Step is a methodology designed by Microsoft, focused specifically on the implementation of all the stacks of Microsoft Dynamics ERP and Microsoft Dynamics 365 (CRM) products, in which Microsoft Dynamics NAV is included. The Sure Step process is available for both **on-premise** and **cloud** deployments.

This methodology is not just a set of methods and a knowledge base about implementation projects. It consists of the following:

- Best practices that let the consultant know how an implementation task or a set of tasks should be performed to achieve the best possible result, or to avoid mistakes that have already been made by someone in the past.
- Tools that make it easier to perform the tasks by automating or streamlining time-consuming and error-prone tasks, such as organization and business process mapping.
- Templates that boost productivity by providing a documentation framework. Preparing documentation using these templates ensures that every important aspect of the documentation has been touched, and that nothing important has been missed.

The Sure Step methodology provides the two distinct implementation approaches we have been discussing, namely, the waterfall approach and the agile approach. We will define them in the following sections.

The Microsoft Dynamics Sure Step home page appears as follows:

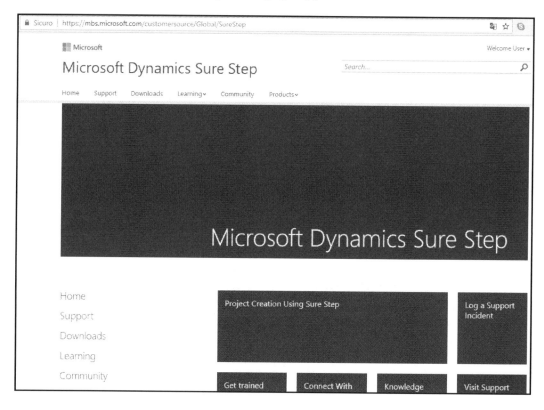

Source: https://mbs.microsoft.com/customersource/Global/SureStep

Next, we will talk about the on-premise version of Sure Step. You can find the link to download it in the Sure Step portal. Once installed, the software should look as shown in the following screenshot:

Dynamics Sure Step on-premise—welcome page

The Sure Step Methodology section is the startup page. From this page, through the **Reference** tab, you can access all existing resources in Sure Step. With the **Documents** tab, you can access all existing documents. It's possible to manage **SOLUTION IMPLEMENTATION & UPGRADE** and **Project Types** by directly clicking on the icons. Once clicked, the icons will open a section dedicated to what we are doing:

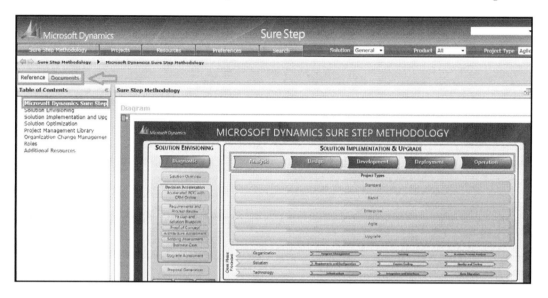

The SOLUTION IMPLEMENTATION & UPGRADE options

The **SOLUTION IMPLEMENTATION & UPGRADE** options are as follows:

- **Analysis**
- **Design**
- **Development**
- **Deployment**
- **Operation**

Project Types are as follows:

- **Standard**
- **Rapid**
- **Enterprise**
- **Agile**
- **Upgrade**

Another solution – Microsoft Azure DevOps (VSTS)

Even though Dynamics Sure Step is still recommended and used, you can also use other products. One of those products is **Visual Studio Team Services** (**VSTS**). With this tool, you can manage projects, both in waterfall and agile mode, including Scrum. It is possible to manage a project, its documentation, and the release of the software by version. It can also be integrated with Sure Step. Visual Studio can be also integrated with Git for source code control, which is a great resource.

 Microsoft is changing and improving this technology, at the time of writing this book the name was VSTS, it has recently been changed to Azure DevOps, the screenshots may have changed.

The following screenshot shows an example of a **Scrum Project** in VSTS:

Project types based on the waterfall approach

There are three types of waterfall-based implementation project types. In addition, there is one waterfall-based upgrade project type. Hence, in total there are four types of waterfall-based project types. They are as follows:

- The Rapid Project Type
- The Standard Project Type
- The Enterprise Project Type
- The Upgrade Project Type

The Rapid Project Type

This is, in theory, the fastest and most straightforward approach. The Rapid Project Type is designed for out-of-the-box implementations of Microsoft Dynamics NAV solutions. This means that when you choose this method, you use Microsoft Dynamics NAV as is, without any customizations. It prescribes 14 activities from solution to "go-live."

In my personal experience, this is a terrible approach to Microsoft Dynamics NAV and I would never recommend any company to use this implementation method. Taking away customization from Microsoft Dynamics NAV is taking away one of the most powerful tools Microsoft Dynamics NAV has to offer. It's like taking the balloons away from a clown. Without the balloons, the clown will just be scary.

The following is a screenshot of the **Rapid Project Type**, including the activities shown in the left navigation tree:

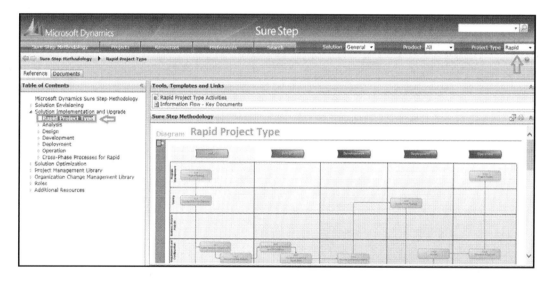

The Rapid Project Type view

The Standard Project Type

This is typically used in most Microsoft Dynamics NAV implementations for fixed-price implementations. Using this method allows the Microsoft Dynamics NAV partner to know and understand your business. It allows all of your users to know your Dynamics partner as well, so an accurate estimate can be established.

The following screenshot is of the **Standard Project Type** in Sure Step:

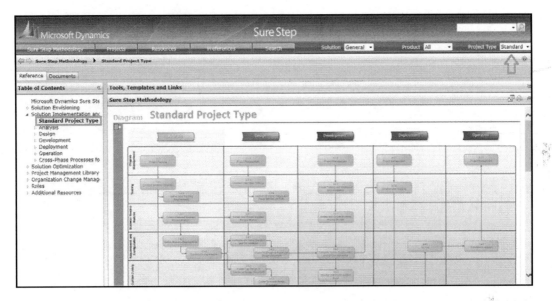

The Standard Project Type view

The Enterprise Project Type

This is the most detailed of all the Sure Step project types. This project type is typically used in large organizations where multiple departments with multiple heads of departments in multiple locations need to be involved in the project. Basically, you should use this project plan if all of the hands in the world need to be in the cookie jar.

The following is a screenshot of the **Enterprise Project Type** in Sure Step:

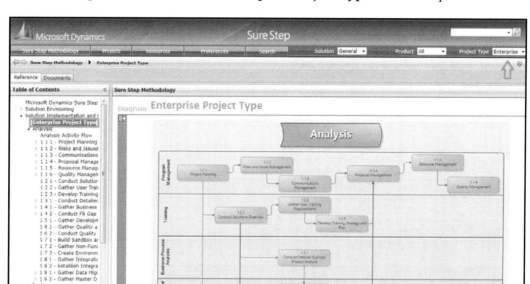

The Enterprise Project Type view

The Upgrade Project Type

This is a project type specially designed to address upgrade projects. It differentiates between technical upgrades and functional upgrades. A technical upgrade is meant to port an existing solution to a new product version. A functional upgrade is meant to not only port an existing solution to a new product version, but also to add new functionalities to the new product version.

The following is a screenshot of the **Upgrade Project Type** in Sure Step:

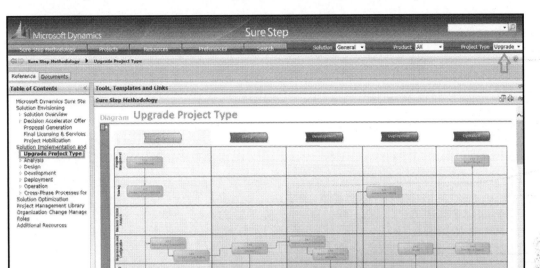

The Upgrade Project Type view

The Agile Project Type

This type is used to manage the Microsoft Dynamics NAV implementations where the solution needs to fit very specific needs of the customer, for whatever reason. These customers are typically very involved with their partner, from specification design to development to testing.

The next screenshot shows the **Agile Project Type** in Sure Step:

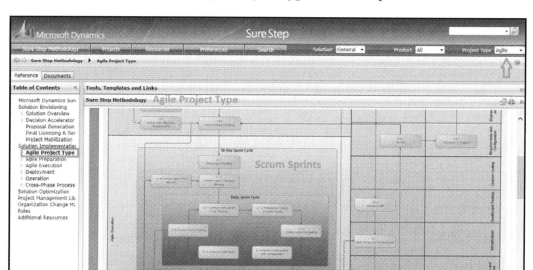

The Agile Project Type view

The Sure Step Agile Project Type is based on Scrum technology and has sprint cycles to include the analysis, design, and development phases.

A sprint cycle is a set period of time during which specific work has to be completed and made ready for review. At the end of each sprint, you are adding value to the project by adding finished portions of the product. Usually, sprints last from one week to one month.

The Agile Project Type has two phases, **deployment** and **operation**, at the culmination of the Sprint cycles. So, in this context, the Agile Project Type deviates from a strict agile approach, and is fashioned as a blended approach for ERP/CRM deployments.

Ready-to-go scenarios – the Microsoft Dynamics NAV optimization offering

There are some scenarios ready to be used (ready-to-go scenarios) for all types of Microsoft ERP and there are some optimized for Microsoft Dynamics NAV, also usable for Microsoft Dynamics 365 Business Central.

The following is an example of a ready-to-go solution for Microsoft Dynamics NAV's optimization offering, **Performance Review**:

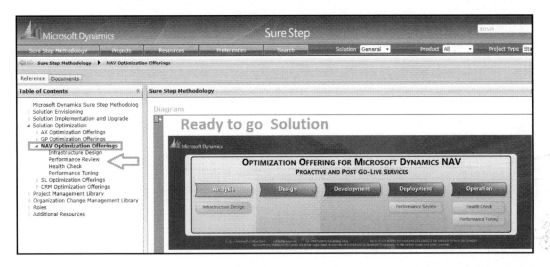

Ready to go Solution

Roles

Implementing an ERP solution, such as Microsoft Dynamics NAV 2018 or Microsoft Dynamics 365 Business Central, in a company is not a trivial task. A lot of things have to be taken into account and a lot of things have to be done. That's why a lot of people have to get involved in the project, both in the company implementing Microsoft Dynamics NAV, that is, the partner, and in the company that will use Microsoft Dynamics NAV as their management software, that is, the customer.

Everyone will have a different and well-defined role in the project. In this section, we will try to explain who should get involved in the project and the tasks that they will be performing.

In the partner team, the following roles exist:

- Salesperson
- Project manager
- Business consultant
- Analyst

- Developer
- Implementer

In the customer team, we find the following roles:

- Project manager
- Key users
- End users

Note that one person can have multiple roles. It's not uncommon for a Microsoft Dynamics NAV partner to have one person that takes on all the roles mentioned earlier! It's also not uncommon for the customer to have one person who is the project manager, the key user, and the end user as well.

Salesperson

The salesperson acts even before the implementation project begins, but it is an important role, as they are the one who defines the big lines of the project requirements and who creates the expectations of the customer about what Microsoft Dynamics NAV is and will be. We will discuss this in detail later on in this chapter.

Project manager

The most important role in the project is that of the project manager. Two project managers exist in an implementation project, one on the partner's side and another one on the customer's side. They have the most responsibility for the whole process of implementing Microsoft Dynamics NAV.

The project managers define the scope of the project, the functionalities that will be implemented, the management of resources, and the timeline.

Business consultant

The first roles that come into play in the project are those of the business consultants from the partner's team and the key users from the customer's team. These two roles define the business processes used by the customer, which of these processes will be done in Microsoft Dynamics NAV, and how the system should behave.

While defining the business processes, the business consultant explains to the customer's key users whether these processes can be done in standard Microsoft Dynamics NAV, whether the processes exist in Microsoft Dynamics NAV but are slightly different from those required by the customer (in which case, the customer may change their process to adapt to the Microsoft Dynamics NAV process, or the Microsoft Dynamics NAV process may be changed to adapt to the customer's process), or that the process doesn't exist at all in Microsoft Dynamics NAV and will have to be developed.

The business consultant writes down a document (the **Project Requirements Document (PRD)** or the **Implementation Specifications**) in which all of the business processes that have to be included in Microsoft Dynamics NAV are explained. The document points out which business processes are covered by standard Microsoft Dynamics NAV and which require development. When development is needed, the document has to explain the expected behavior of the development.

The PRD is the main document of the project. Once the business consultant has written it, the key users who defined the processes will have to read it and make sure everything important to their business is covered in the document.

The business consultant and the key users, with the aid of their respective project managers, have to agree on a final PRD, as this is the document that describes the project and that will be used later on by the analyst and the implementer to get to a final solution.

The business consultant should be someone who knows about business, as they must be able to understand the customer's business processes and needs. The business consultant should also be someone who knows standard Microsoft Dynamics NAV behavior and capabilities, as they must be able to distinguish whether a specific business process is covered by Microsoft Dynamics NAV or not.

Often, there are specialized business consultants in a specific area or functionality. For example, we can find financial business consultants and warehouse business consultants. Financial business consultants know about the business processes related to financial management and how the financial management functionality works in Microsoft Dynamics NAV 2018, but they know nothing (or not too much) about warehouse management or any other business area. Warehouse business consultants know about the business processes related to warehouse management and how the warehouse is handled in Microsoft Dynamics NAV 2018, but they know nothing (or not too much) about financial management or any other business area.

In some instances, several business consultants may be involved in a Microsoft Dynamics NAV implementation project when several and completely different business areas are implemented.

Business consultants are often brought into the presales stage by the salesperson in order to help the customer define what is achievable within the customer's budget and time frame.

Key users

The key users from the customer's side should be those who know the processes currently being followed in the company. They should be aware of the problems or inefficiencies the current processes have and be willing to actively participate in the project.

In the same way that more than one business consultant may get involved in the project, with each one handling a specific business area, several key users may also participate in the definition of the project requirements, each one also handling a specific business area.

A common error regarding key users is to pick the heads of departments as the key users without analyzing whether they are the right people to play this role. Having good key users, just as having good business consultants, is vital to the deployment of the project, as they are the ones who will define the project, the needs, and the processes.

The key users have to be good communicators and should know their own processes. Sometimes, the heads of departments may know the *theory* of their own processes, but since they are not the ones doing them on a daily basis, they may not know the real processes (which may differ from the *theoretical* processes).

The heads of departments may or may not be good key users. We will discuss this in more detail in the next chapter, which will be dedicated to the implementation process on the customer's side.

Once the PRD is written and the project requirements are clear, both the analyst and the business consultant continue with the deployment of the project.

The business consultant will focus on all of the standard functionalities of Microsoft Dynamics NAV that the customer will use. The analyst will focus on all of the functionalities of Microsoft Dynamics NAV that have to be modified somehow or developed from scratch.

Some functionalities in Microsoft Dynamics NAV can behave in multiple ways, depending on how they have been configured. The business consultant is the person who defines the way in which the system has to be configured to meet the business process requirements reflected in the PRD.

Analyst

The analyst is the person who defines the way in which the standard functionalities of Microsoft Dynamics NAV will be configured to meet the business process requirements defined in the PRD. The analyst also defines the way in which new functionalities will be developed and the way the customer's data will be migrated into the system.

To achieve this task, the analyst must be someone who knows the standard design of Microsoft Dynamics NAV and the development capabilities of the system. Modifications have to be carefully designed because the right modification in the wrong area may cause inconsistencies in other areas or functionalities. It may also disable the future use of a standard functionality. In addition, new functionalities should be implemented using the same design philosophy as behind Microsoft Dynamics NAV.

Developer

Developers are basically the coders, but not only: it is not enough to know a language; a knowledge of ERP systems would also be useful (my opinion is based on experience).

Once the developments required to be done in the project are defined, the developer comes onto the scene. The developer is the person who will develop the modifications and new functionalities defined by the analyst.

Once the developments are finished, the business consultant should test them to validate that they definitely meet the business process requirements defined in the PRD.

Implementer

At this point, everything is ready for the implementer to start working on the project. The implementer will configure the system as defined by the business consultant and will perform the data migration processes in test environments, using standard Microsoft Dynamics NAV 2018 tools (defined later on in this book) or using tools defined by the analyst and developed by the developer.

Before going live, the implementer will validate all the business processes that will be running inside the system with the customer's key users, namely, the standard Microsoft Dynamics NAV processes that have been configured, the processes that have been modified to meet the customer's requirements, and the processes that have been developed completely from scratch.

The implementer will be in charge of training the customer's end users about the usage of the system before the chosen go-live date.

The day the customer goes live, the implementer is the one who performs the data migration processes and, for a defined period of time, supports the customer's end users from the day they begin using Microsoft Dynamics NAV.

End users

The end user uses, on a daily basis, the final solution defined by the key users and the business consultants, developed by the developers, and implemented by the implementer.

The entire system is designed so that the end users can do their job, using Microsoft Dynamics NAV as their main tool. Usually, the end users get involved towards the end when the software is about to be rolled out, but they are the ones most affected since it affects their daily work.

Summarizing the roles

To summarize, the roles that are played in the implementer's game and the tasks these roles perform are categorized as follows:

- In the partner's team, there are the following roles:
    - **Project manager**: Defines the scope of the project and the timeline. The project manager has the most responsibility for implementing the project.

- **Business consultant**: Defines the business processes, gets the project requirements, and writes the main document of the project, the PRD, in which the customer's business processes to be covered by Microsoft Dynamics NAV are explained, especially those that will require development. The business consultant also defines the way in which standard functionality has to be configured to meet the customer's business process requirements and validates the developments done by the developer.
- **Analyst**: Defines the way in which the standard Microsoft Dynamics NAV functionality will be modified, the way new functionalities will be developed, and the way the customer's data will be migrated into the system.
- **Developer**: Develops the modifications and new functionalities defined by the analyst.
- **Implementer**: Configures the system, validates the data migration processes, validates all the processes with the customer's key users, trains the end users on the usage of the system, performs the data migration tasks on the go-live date, and supports the end users for a defined period of time when the system is live.
- In the customer's team, there are the following roles:
    - **Project manager**: Defines the scope of the project and the timeline. The project manager has the most responsibility for implementing the project.
    - **Key users**: Defines the business processes, defines the project requirements, and reads the PRD document written by the business consultant.
    - **The end users**: Uses, on a daily basis, the final solution defined by the key users and the business consultants, developed by the developers, and implemented by the implementer.

As we have defined, different roles exist both on the partner's side and the customer's side. Each role performs a specific set of tasks. The same person, though, may play different roles in the same project. The business consultant in the partner's team may also be the implementer, for example.

Phases

The following section of this chapter will describe each phase in a Microsoft Dynamics NAV implementation, and the tasks each phase includes. In a waterfall environment, you can do one thing after another. In an agile environment, don't forget to loop through all of the phases, especially those of getting the project requirements, analysis, development, and part of the task from the deployment phase.

It's especially important to define how information will flow through all the phases to ensure that important information does not get lost.

Presales

This is the first contact between the partner and the customer—the big lines on which the project will be drawn.

This phase is usually executed by the sales or marketing teams, with the help of a business consultant. Many companies think that at this stage, the project hasn't started yet, so they don't think that this job is part of the project. But it actually plays a very important role.

Selling a project like a Microsoft Dynamics NAV implementation is not just selling the software itself. It is not enough just to be aware of what the product can or cannot do. Part of successfully selling Microsoft Dynamics NAV is instilling confidence in how you will approach the project.

Therefore, the salespeople need to sell not only the product, but also the methodology the company is using, and the amount of work the customer will face in the next months. In addition, a good salesperson will discuss how the partner will help the customer face this challenge.

As the salespeople are part of the project, they have to identify fundamental aspects that will help the other members to do their job. A salesperson can help by identifying some of the risks of the project, for instance, mentioning the departments that have asked for a new ERP system or someone from the customer's side who is not convinced about the need to change the ERP. They also have to identify whether the customer processes are mature enough or need to be rethought. They are also responsible for properly identifying the key people in the customer's organization capable of doing this rethinking, or figure out if they are expecting the partner to do it for them.

All of this may completely change how the project will be approached. So it is important to identify this at the earlier stages. At the end of this stage, a first cost and duration estimation must be done. It is important to be as close to reality as possible.

Getting the project requirements

This is the time for discussion between the partner and the customer. I mean a real deep discussion, almost like a husband and a wife would. The business consultants and the key users will hold a series of meetings in which the key users will explain to the business consultants the way they do business, the information they have to handle through their business processes, the reports they run, the users that are involved in the different stages of each process, the problems they have with their actual business processes, and, most importantly, how they expect the new system to help them solve their daily pains.

The business consultants will need to listen carefully to the key users and understand their pain points from their current operation. Only after understanding the customer's needs will they be able to design the right solution for the customer.

In order to do that, they not only have to be active listeners, but should also actively participate in the definition of the processes by asking all kinds of questions to the key users, namely, periodicity of the process, volume, amount of people involved, how automated it should be, how to handle exceptions to the process, how strict the process is, how important it is, and any other questions you may think of.

As they listen to the explanations of the customer's processes, they should point out how this process is handled in Microsoft Dynamics NAV to identify and mention as an evidence to everyone the differences between the customer's actual business process and the way it is handled in Microsoft Dynamics NAV. This way, the customer may decide to change or re-engineer their own processes or may ask to modify the behavior of Microsoft Dynamics NAV to adapt to their predefined process.

With all of the information gathered in the project requirements meetings, the business consultants should write a document in which the processes are explained and defined in as much detail as possible. This document should be reviewed by the key users so that everyone agrees that what was explained is what has been understood, and that all of the decisions made in the project requirements meetings are reflected in the document.

As part of the project requirements, data migrations will also have to be handled and will include questions such as what kind of data will be migrated into Microsoft Dynamics NAV, what volume of information this means, from where the data will be extracted and in which format, and so on.

To make sure everything has been talked through and defined, it is important for the business consultants to have a checklist of things to ask to the customer and use it in the project requirements meetings.

In this checklist, all Microsoft Dynamics NAV functional areas should appear and have their own questions. Let's see an example of a checklist:

- **Financial management**:
    - What are the tasks of the financial department?
    - Which chart of accounts is used? Is it sector specific?
    - How are posting accounts created?
    - Which kinds of transactions are posted? Can they be predefined or established as recurring transactions?
    - Which kinds of analytical information will have to be reported?
    - Does the company create accounting budgets? How often? Are they created over the chart of accounts or over analytical concepts?
    - What legal reporting does the company have to do? How often?
    - Does the company consolidate the accounting information with some other company in the same group?
    - Are additional currencies used?
    - How are banks managed?
    - Are fixed assets managed in the ERP system?
    - How many fixed assets has the company got?
    - Which depreciation method is used?
    - Do you keep maintenance track of your fixed assets?
    - Will the fixed assets have to be automatically imported in Microsoft Dynamics NAV?
- **Marketing and sales**:
    - Do you create your contacts in the ERP system?
    - Do you use a CRM system?

- **Customers and sales processes**:
    - How many customers do you have?
    - Is extra information about the customers needed in the customer card?
    - Do your customers have different shipment directions?
    - How do you classify your customers?
    - What is your sales process?
    - Do you invoice your customers per sales order or do you make a single invoice with multiple sales orders?
    - When do you invoice your customers?
    - Which documents are sent to the customers?
    - How are the sales prices established?
    - Are discounts applied to the customers?
    - Who introduces new sales orders in the system?
    - Do the sales orders require some kind of approval?
    - Which payment terms are applied to the customers?
    - Which payment methods are used to get the payments from the customers?
    - Do you ask your customers for prepayments of the sales orders?
- **Vendors and purchase processes**
- **Items and stock management**
- **Warehouse management**
- **Jobs and resources**
- **Manufacturing**
- **Service**
- **Human resources**
- **Others**:
    - Will Microsoft Dynamics NAV receive information from some external application? A website, maybe?
    - Will Microsoft Dynamics NAV have to send information to some external application?
    - On how many different devices will Microsoft Dynamics NAV be used?

We have just written the functional areas of Microsoft Dynamics NAV and a few examples of questions that can be asked for some of them. A complete checklist should be written for all of the functional areas and all of those questions should be answered in the project requirements meetings.

Designing the solution

The solution design includes the configuration needed in standard Microsoft Dynamics NAV functionality for it to meet the customer's requirements. It also includes the technical analysis and design of modifications, the development of new functionalities, and the data migration tools that will be used to get the data into the system. Different things have to be taken into account for each type of design.

Configuration

All kinds of configurations have to be established in a Microsoft Dynamics NAV implementation process:

- Posting groups will determinate how the documents and transactions will end up in an accounting transaction. There are several posting groups that have to be configured, such as the following:
    - General Posting Setup
    - Customer Posting Group
    - Vendor Posting Group
    - Fixed Assets Posting Group
    - Bank Account Posting Group
    - Inventory Posting Group
    - Inventory Posting Setup
    - VAT (Tax) Posting Setup
    - Currencies
    - Job Posting Group
- Series of numbers to be used in all of the documents and the master data registers.
- The dimensions that will be used for analytical purposes.
- The allowed dimensions' combinations and the dimension priorities.
- The default dimension values for G/L accounts, customers, vendors, items, and so on.

- The following is the setup of all functional areas:
  - **General ledger setup**:
    - Permitted posting dates
    - The way addresses appear in printouts
    - The invoice rounding precision
    - The global and shortcut dimension codes
    - The payment tolerance
  - **Sales and receivables setup**:
    - The series of numbers to be used in the customers, and sales documents
    - Whether it is mandatory to inform about an external document number in the sales documents
    - Whether stock-out and customer credit warnings should be prompted to the user
    - Whether the posted invoices and credit memos should also create shipments and return receipts
  - **Purchases and payables setup**:
    - The series of numbers to be used in the vendors and purchase documents
    - Whether it is mandatory to include an external document number in the purchase documents
    - Whether the posted invoices and credit memos should also create receipts and return shipments
  - **Inventory setup**:
    - The series of numbers to be used in the items and item documents, such as transfer orders
    - Whether the cost and expected cost should automatically be posted to the general ledger
    - Whether it is mandatory to use locations in item movements
  - **Warehouse setup**:
    - The series of numbers to be used in the warehouse documents
    - Whether receipt, put-away, shipment, and pick documents are required

- **Manufacturing setup**:
    - The series of numbers to be used in the manufacturing documents and resources, such as work centers

- **Jobs setup**:
    - The series of numbers to be used in jobs
    - Whether the job item costs should automatically be updated

- **Resources setup**:
    - The series of numbers to be used in resources
    - Work types
    - Resource units of measure

- Item tracking codes, if they are required.
- Payment terms for the customers and vendors.
- Payment methods for the customers and vendors.
- Configurations that will be used at the customer or vendor level, such as whether prices for a certain customer or vendor are VAT-included or not.
- Configurations that will be used at the item level, such as the costing method to be used or replenishment parameters.
- Approval workflows for the sales and purchases documents.

This is a list of typical and common configurations that have to be established in Microsoft Dynamics NAV. But that's not all. There is a bunch of things that can be achieved in Microsoft Dynamics NAV through configuration. Not only do those configurations have to be established in the implementation, but they also have to be documented so that the users apply the same configurations to items, customers, vendors, and so on, that are created in the future.

Modifying standard Microsoft Dynamics NAV functionality

Modification of the standard Microsoft Dynamics NAV functionality may be as simple as showing extra existing fields in some pages, or as complex as altering the way in which the item costs or posting routines are managed.

All modifications have to be designed carefully so that they do not cause inconsistencies in other areas or functionalities and do not disable the future use of a standard functionality.

For example, if a modification is done regarding items, even if item variants are not used, make sure you take them into account so as to not disable the item variant functionality. Why? That's because you never know if the customer's business will change in the future and will require item variants.

We will discuss development in depth in Chapter 8, *Development Considerations*.

New functionalities

New functionalities should be designed in compliance with the design philosophy behind Microsoft Dynamics NAV, as explained in Chapter 3, *General Considerations*.

These functionalities include using a master data table, using series of numbers to number your master data registers and your documents, writing a posting routine for your functionality, using non-modifiable ledger entry tables, and using posting groups if the new functionality has to end up in accounting transactions.

Data migration

For each kind of data that will be migrated into the system, we will have to define the tool to be used to achieve this task. In Chapter 6, *Migrating Data*, all kinds of details regarding data migration are explained.

Development

Once the analyst has defined the developments that have to be done, it's time for the developer to do their job.

The development should follow the standard course of development in Microsoft Dynamics NAV, using the appropriate naming convention for tables, captions, fields, pages, and all of the other Microsoft Dynamics NAV objects.

All kinds of developments should be clearly identified using the Documentation trigger than can be found in every single Microsoft Dynamics NAV object (this is strictly related to C/AL, not so valid for AL extensions), and also by using the comment lines in the code itself to identify where the developed code begins and where it ends.

Don't wait until the development has finished to validate it and show it to the customer. Use prototypes for complex functionality development and show it to the customer as it gets developed. This way, the design and development misunderstandings or mistakes can be identified in the early stages and corrected so that no-one's time is lost.

For development, from Microsoft Dynamics NAV 2018 onward, it is possible to use two development models: the hybrid mode with C/AL and AL extension, or the AL extension development only. For Microsoft Dynamics 365 Business Central SaaS, you can develop only with the AL extension.

Automatic testing with the Application Test Toolkit

An interesting feature of Microsoft Dynamics NAV (named the "Application Test Toolkit") is the ability to perform automatic tests. These tests can be very useful before the tests to be done with the customer. It is possible to create real test scenarios and have them run automatically, hence speeding up the user test as a pre-test is performed first. This is very useful after a release upgrade to test all features (including old features if they are maintained, and new features). The first Test Toolkit was implemented a long time ago with Microsoft Dynamics NAV 2013.

The Automatic Test Toolkit – how does it work?

You can write application tests in C/AL and run them individually or collectively. The Microsoft Dynamics NAV distribution includes NAV objects, a library of application tests ready to go, helper functions, and test runners so you can automate your application tests; you can also run tests from PowerShell.

You can also generate random data for your application tests: `https://docs.microsoft.com/en-us/dynamics-nav/random-test-data`. For example, use the application test libraries to verify your application after upgrading to the latest release of Microsoft Dynamics NAV (more at `https://docs.microsoft.com/en-us/dynamics-nav/how-to--run-automated-applicationtests`).

For Microsoft Dynamics 365 Business Central with the AL extension, the process is a bit different (and this is not a development manual), however, you can look here: `https://docs.microsoft.com/en-us/dynamics365/business-central/dev-itpro/compliance/apptest-testingyourextension`.

Deployment

The deployment phase ends with the go-live day. A lot of work must be done before the system is ready to start being used, and it is time to synchronize the entire job done in the previous phases. The best way to face this synchronization is to actually have some of the tasks done in the previous stages as provisional work. This way, major inconsistencies can be found and fixed.

The deployment phase includes the following tasks:

- Software and hardware installation
- Configuration
- Data migration
- User acceptance testing
- End users training
- Go-live!

Software and hardware installation

This task is all about installing the Microsoft Dynamics NAV components on the server side and installing the Microsoft Dynamics NAV client on the required machines. Also, we need to make sure that Microsoft Dynamics NAV is accessible from all of the required devices.

In big implementations, with lots of users using Microsoft Dynamics NAV from different locations, a load test must be performed. A load test simulates the amount of transactional operations and concurrent pressure that the system will face. The load test will help you determine whether the hardware was properly sized and configured or not.

We recommend you install the Microsoft Dynamics NAV test environment at an earlier stage in the project, so that you can release functionality to the customer as it gets developed. It will help you with the final user acceptance test and will allow you to improve your development.

Configuration

Microsoft Dynamics NAV includes many tables with the word "setup" in their names. They are the base with which to define how each module will behave, so they need to be properly configured. There are also all sorts of supplementary setups, including posting groups, payment methods, dimensions, security roles, and so on.

If you are going to release your developments to the customer periodically, not just at the end of the project, then you will have to execute the configuration task at the beginning of the project. This way the customer can see and test the development with an environment that is similar to the one they will find once they start using the system. If you do so, you will also help the people doing the development. It's easier to develop using a development environment similar to the production one.

Don't think that if you do it at the beginning of the project, you will have to do the same job twice. The company you set up at the beginning cannot be used for production, since test transactions and documents will be posted during development and testing. However, you can always copy all of the tables, except entries, posted documents, and master data. There are more than 200 tables that can be considered as part of the Microsoft Dynamics NAV configuration.

We've done this dozens of times and it's something that really helped us in our implementation, so we encourage you to try it.

Data migration

Chapter 6, *Migrating Data*, explains in detail what has to be taken into account to perform data migration. In many cases, the data will have to be transformed or adapted in order to use it in Microsoft Dynamics NAV.

The data migration task should be performed twice. The first time should be done in the test environment, so that the user acceptance test can be performed using real data. The second data migration is done the day before the go-live day. You can also do the first data migration at the beginning of the project. This way you will help the developers do their job with real data, which will help them understand the company they are developing for.

Since data migration requires the partner to work closely with the customer, an early data migration will help both the partner and the customer to get used to working together. It will also help the customer to get more involved with the project right from the beginning.

User-acceptance test

All of the work is done and the system is ready to go live. During development, each individual functionality has been tested several times and, on every release, the users test the system. One more test is required—the one that tests the whole system. All of the processes have to be tested, from the initial input, going through all the stages, to the last output. You also need to test whether the data generated during each process fits their analysis and reporting requirements.

This test is the last chance to find out if something is wrong and needs to be adjusted. Detecting an issue during the acceptance test and fixing it before going live may save a lot of money.

It's after this test that both the partner and the customer have to agree that everything is ready to go in production. Do not go live if anyone is not comfortable after the test.

End users' training

Last but not the least, the end users have to be trained. They are the ones who are actually going to use the system, so they need to know how it works. Many of them will see Microsoft Dynamics NAV for the first time during the training. If possible, make them practice with the system during the training.

The training shouldn't be taken too early or they will easily forget what they have been told.

Go-live!

Finally, the go-live is here. We need to perform the final data migration, validate this data, and start working!

Post-implementation support

As you can probably guess by now, Microsoft Dynamics NAV is not like installing Microsoft Office. It's not a static software where the vendor installs it and then leaves. It's a constantly evolving organism that must be maintained, because the customer's business will always face new challenges that require more out of Microsoft Dynamics NAV.

The support phase starts on the go-live day when Microsoft Dynamics NAV is ready and all of the users start to intensively use the system.

No matter how hard you try during the training (but try hard anyway), the users will have a lot of doubts and they need someone by their side. So, for the first couple of weeks, depending on the size of the implementation, someone from the partner side is going to be at the customer's office to help them resolve issues as they come up.

But this is not only about functional questions and problems. It would be easy if it was only about this. Actually, the support phase is the hardest one! During this phase you will also have to handle the following issues:

- **Old tasks from previous phases**: You will be carrying over a few tasks from the previous phases that weren't important enough to stop the go-live. But the day you start, those tasks become very important all of a sudden. Those tasks become important because the users don't feel comfortable with the new process. They may have a hard time adapting to the new way of doing things. The rate at which the users adapt to the new processes varies depending on the individual. Not only does extreme patience have to be practiced, but empathy from the support person will need to be observed as well.
- **System stabilization**: Even if testing had been done before the go-live day, you can expect the users to find bugs in your developments once they intensively start using the system. Some setups may be wrong as well. You will have to handle and fix all these kinds of issues.
- **Data stabilization**: A massive data migration will have been done right before the go-live day and a lot of other data will have been configured or entered by hand. Although the data will have been checked before going live, issues with the data will also appear. For the next few weeks, you will have to spend time stabilizing that data.

Dynamics 365 Business Central implementation considerations

It is possible to use the same tools discussed here for Microsoft Dynamics 365 Business Central as well. The project's effort could be different if it is a new project, or a migration project from old versions of Microsoft Dynamics NAV.

Remember that on-premise is different from SaaS, in the case of a new project, it is important to immediately explain that, in the cloud, there are pros and cons. The cons are some limitations considering the on-premise Business Central version, sometimes it is better to use what is already there, automatic updates are an excellent point in favor of providing added value. In the case of upgrades and use of the Web client only, it is necessary to understand whether there could be limitations before users accept the new cloud-based solution.

Development of a Microsoft Dynamics 365 Business Central solution should also consider the dependencies problem. You should avoid monolithic extension and should split the implementations into "functional modules" that have dependencies. This must be carefully planned for future upgrades as well.

Summary

In this chapter, we saw that an implementation is a process that gets software operating properly in a company. To do so, we need to use a methodology that will take us from the beginning to the end of the project, not only on the technical part of the project, but also regarding other aspects, such as billing the project, effort estimation, planning, and communication.

We saw different methodological approaches, such as the waterfall approach and the agile approach (with Scrum), and how they are addressed in Microsoft Dynamics Sure Step.

We also saw the phases and the activities included in typical Microsoft Dynamics NAV and Microsoft Dynamics 365 Business Central implementation projects.

In the next chapter, we will learn some tips about the implementation process on the customer's side.

5
Implementation Process – Customer's Perspective

In order to have a successful implementation of Microsoft Dynamics NAV or Microsoft Dynamics 365 Business Central, the company for which these ERP systems are implemented has to actively participate in the project.

In this chapter, we will cover the following aspects of the work a company should carry out to implement an ERP system such as Microsoft Dynamics NAV or Microsoft Dynamics 365 Business Central:

- Defining goals
- Defining internal processes and key users
- Defining requirements for the new ERP system
- Defining acceptable gaps and workarounds for a standard product
- Collecting all "nice-to-have features" from key users for the next steps in the projects
- Involving end users
- Following up on the entire process of implementation

We will explain the theory of all of these points, and we will also follow up on the entire process with a very specific example from a real-world implementation.

Definition of goals

Implementing Microsoft Dynamics NAV or Microsoft Dynamics 365 Business Central as your ERP system is not a turnkey project. Purchasing and implementing an ERP system is not like installing Microsoft Office, for which you run the `Setup.exe` file and are done with it (based on "next-next-end" philosophy). Implementing an EPR is a process and, with such a process, you need the people that are involved to actively participate in all phases of the implementation. How involved the client's team is will affect the final result of the implementation:

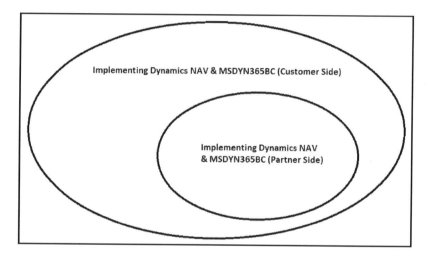

In the preceding diagram, you can see that implementing Microsoft Dynamics NAV or Microsoft Dynamics 365 Business Central on the partner side is a project that can be framed within a larger project, the implementation on the customer side. Depending on the scope of the project, the amount of work on each side may differ.

As in any project, defining goals is essential, to measure whether the project succeeds or not. Goals have to be clearly defined at the beginning of the project and all parties must agree on them. If you don't define clear goals, you may find yourself working as hard as you possibly can and still never able to satisfy your boss or end users.

It not uncommon to define goals such as "improve the sales process." The question is, by how much does it have to be improved? How is the improvement going to be measured? When are you going to measure it? Honestly, most of these questions take more time than they're worth. Most of the time, the measurement of these goals is just a gut feeling.

However, if they are defined clearly by your customer, measurements can be achieved:

Measuring goals

Before defining goals that are measurable, you and your partners should clearly agree on how the goals are to be measured, before and after. For example, if a goal is to reduce the number of chargebacks from a customer within six months, then it could be as simple as looking at the G/L accounts to which you post chargebacks.

Some goals are tougher to measure, for example, if the goal is to increase the productivity of the workforce, it may not be as simple as running some financial reports. For goals like these, it's recommended to define what "increase productivity" means. Is it to reduce printed documents? Is it to reduce the time between customer service calls? Once that's defined, the next question would be how to quantify and measure the goal.

When defining a goal, it should be **SMART**, as shown in the following definition:

Specific
Measurable
Achievable
Relevant
Time bound

Define different goals for your company and partners that are going to implement your Microsoft Dynamics NAV or Microsoft Dynamics 365 Business Central. Each party will be responsible for different parts of projects and their goals must be specific to the area they are responsible for. If the definition of goals is clear enough, it will help everybody to focus on the tasks that will help to accomplish them. This is something that will benefit any party involved in the project.

Let's now take a specific example from a real-world Microsoft Dynamics NAV or Microsoft Dynamics 365 Business Central implementation. The example is from a company that provides public and private health care services. This company uses a specific health care software and accounting software. With the explosive growth this company has experienced, they need something more robust to accommodate changes in the company for now and the future.

They want to start out by replacing the accounting software, which only keeps track of accounting information. Through careful software selection, they made the right choice and selected Microsoft Dynamics NAV or Microsoft Dynamics 365 Business Central. As we described in an earlier chapter, Microsoft Dynamics NAV is not just an accounting application—it is actually an ERP system that can perform several business functions within an organization.

The main goal that this company wants to accomplish with Microsoft Dynamics NAV is to make their departments stick to a budget. This budget will be established at the beginning of the year for each service that the company's departments offer. Currently, they do not have a detailed budget per service and they do not keep track of costs per service.

Making departments stick to a budget is not actually a goal. It's not something specific or time-bound; it is a general vision of where to go. To accomplish this vision, several goals that point in the same direction will have to be accomplished, one at a time.

The goals to accomplish that vision could be as follows:

- Being able to define budgets per service
- Determining the service to which each cost applies
- Being able to compare budgets and real costs
- Getting a report of costs for a specific service

Let's take that last goal—getting a report of costs for a specific service. It is still a goal but it is not a SMART goal. It is specific, measurable, achievable, and relevant; however, there is no timing for the goal. Let's write down the goal in a different way: getting a report of costs for a specific service at the end of each month. This is definitely a much better goal.

Defining internal processes and key users

Once the goals of the project are clear, and when the company knows what they want to accomplish with their brand new ERP, it's time to go into details and write down all of the company processes one by one that will have to be performed or supported by Microsoft Dynamics NAV.

When you think about your processes, don't just expose what they should theoretically be. Ask the people who are actually carrying out those processes about what they really do. Also, ask about the exceptions to the processes, as handling exceptions for a normal process usually requires more time from end users.

You may want to take this opportunity to eliminate exceptions for a normal process by changing how the process works. Exceptions are basically processes that are created to do something that a normal process does not accommodate. So, essentially, the user has to pay special attention and spend extra time handling these exceptions. What's worse is if they start building exception processes on top of exception processes—that's when we really talk about wasting time.

If an exception happens a lot, then it should be incorporated into a normal process. If not, then I would try my best to eliminate that exception, either by changing the process or by setting up company policies so that those exceptions do not occur:

Questions to be asked

For each process, the following questions, at least, have to be answered:

- Who is the key user of the process?
- What is the desired outcome of the process?
- What are the start and end points?
- What activities are performed?
- What is the order of the activities?
- Who performs the activities?
- What information is required (documents)?
- How often is this process done?
- What is the importance of the process?

Identify the key user

The first thing to do is define the key user of the process (they could also be your sponsor). The key user will be responsible for the whole process and will respond to management. Then, the key user exposes themselves to risks, without being able to know the outcome of the project. Sometimes (in small companies), there are no key users. In that case, it is necessary to understand which of the company management or delegates will follow the process; sometimes, an external consultant is hired just to follow a client-side project (for example, with a temporary management contract).

The key user is the one who validates the initial process (As-Is) and the final process (To-Be) through functional testing and is a key figure as the word itself (key user).

Questions about processes

Take the example of your sales process. What is the start point for your sales orders? Customers pick up the phone, call you, and tell you exactly which items they want in what quantities. Or maybe you receive orders by email, customers submit them through a website, or orders are submitted through EDI. Or maybe your salesperson visits your customers and gets sales orders, customers ask you for sales quotes that finally get accepted (and hence converted into a sales order) or rejected, or you have blanket sales orders for a certain period of time, after which you do not receive any further sales orders.

In reality, it may be a combination of all of these and other methods to get sales orders into the system. It's your responsibility, not your consultant's, to know and understand how you receive sales orders and to properly document them so that an 8-year-old can read your documents and know exactly how you receive orders into your system.

After sales orders are received, you will probably check them for the following: do you have a minimum sales order amount? Do you sell your items per unit or per box? If you sell per box, you probably have to check whether the quantities asked for by customers are multiples of quantities per box. Do you establish a credit limit for your customers? If so, before processing an order, you may want to check whether the customer's limit has been exceeded. You may also want to check the requested delivery date. Is it possible to serve the customer in time or should you talk to them and negotiate a different delivery date?

Once the sales order has been revised and accepted, it has to be executed. What does this mean? How do you prepare your shipments? Do you group orders per customer so that multiple orders are prepared and served together? Do you pick items from all of the orders of the day together and then pack them separately per order or per customer in the preparation area? Do you attach sales shipment documents to packaging? Which carriers do you use? Do you primarily ship LTL or small parcels?

And finally, in the sales invoice document, how do you process your invoices: do you post an invoice per sales shipment at the same time the sales shipment is done, a sales invoice per sales order, or a single sales invoice per customer at the end of the month including all of the sales orders served in that month?

Now that we have a bunch of questions and their answers, it is time to write it all down. While writing down your processes, you may come across new questions that have to be asked and answered. For example, you may know that your process has two sequential activities, but you may not have a clear picture of what triggers the beginning of the second activity. This is probably a good question to ask people involved in the process.

Writing your processes in a structured way—preferably using any kind of business process modeling diagrams or workflows—will help you and other people to understand them and will also allow you to rapidly measure how simple or complex a process is and identify bottlenecks and redundant work, and, basically, where the weakness of the process lies so that it can be improved.

Let's go back to our example of getting a report of costs for a specific service. This process was done in the company before the implementation of Microsoft Dynamics NAV. It wasn't done monthly though, as it took too long, and it was done manually. By asking the people involved in the process, we found out the following:

- **Desired outcome**: The cost of a specific service in a specific year.
- **Start point**: The service contract has reached its end.
- **End point**: The cost of a specific service in a specific year.
- **Activities and their order**: The following is a list of the activities performed:
  1. Prepare a list of the vendors that provide goods for this service.
  2. Go through all of the purchase invoices of the vendors in the list prepared in the first activity.
  3. Determine whether the purchase invoice is complete or in a high percentage, attributable to the service that is being analyzed.
  4. If it is attributable to the service that is being analyzed, write down the purchase invoice amount on a spreadsheet.
  5. Ask the head of the department providing the service who (and for what percentage of their time) works for the service.
  6. Calculate the cost of human resources attributable to the service. Write down the calculated amount on a spreadsheet.
  7. Get the total purchase invoice amount corresponding to general supplies or costs (water supply, energy supply, phone, general insurances, and so on). Because of actual accounting practices, this amount can be found in a specific general ledger account.
  8. To the service being analyzed, attribute a percentage of the total amount obtained in the previous activity. The percentage attributable to the service will be calculated based on the human resources spent on it and the surface the service uses from the entire company's surface.
  9. Add up all the amounts on a spreadsheet:

     - **People who perform the activities**: All of the activities are performed by a person in the administration department.
     - **How often are they done**: They are done each time for a different service.

- **Importance**: It is a very important process, as this report will be used when negotiating with public authorities the income that the company will receive to perform this public service in subsequent years.

We can write down the activities, their order, and relation to other activities using a flow chart. It will look similar to the following diagram:

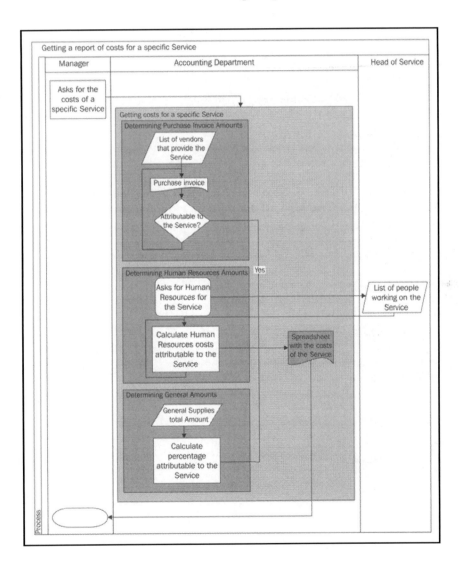

Improve before automating

IT tools allow us to automate all kinds of tasks with the aim of reducing time and errors. But not everything should be automated. An inefficient and complex process can be sped up using some kind of automation but it will still be an inefficient and complex process. Because of its complexity, the cost (in terms of time, validation, and money) of automating the process will probably be greater than expected.

In addition, trying to automate an already messed up process will only make your process more messy. It is much better to improve your business processes and think about automation once they are good and efficient.

You should also think about the importance of a process and about how often that process is done. A process that is done dozens of times per day is probably worth automating, while a process that is done once a year may not be the best candidate for automation.

The process in our example has to be clearly improved before any kind of automation is applied to it. We cannot just take it as it is and automate only some of the activities.

The longest task is the process of going through all the purchase invoices and determining whether they are attributable to a specific service. The human decision part probably cannot be automated now or in the near future.

Getting the requirements

How do I know what my requirements are? Well, if internal processes have been defined, this should be an easy question to answer. You should start with the most important and frequent processes, and move on to the least important or infrequent processes. The important and frequent ones should be handled by the ERP, while the least important and infrequent processes may or may not be handled by the ERP, depending on your goals and the budget for the implementation.

General considerations for Microsoft Dynamics NAV and Microsoft Dynamics 365 Business Central

Talk to the consultants who will be implementing Microsoft Dynamics NAV or Microsoft Dynamics 365 Business Central for your organization. Tell them what your process looks like, who is involved in it, what information is required, and so on. They will tell you how this specific process is resolved in these ERP systems.

If the way these ERP systems handle the process matches the way you handle the process, you've struck gold! You will be able to keep on doing what you're already doing without any kind of modification to the behavior of the application. This is a requirement that may not need any work at all or, at most, may need some tweaking.

If the way these ERP systems handle the process does not match the way you handle the process, two possible options exist: modify the behavior of the system to meet your requirements, or *change the way* you handle your process to meet Microsoft Dynamics NAV's or Microsoft Dynamics 365 Business Central's way of doing things. You may even consider an option that combines the best of both options.

Is it OK to switch to the way these ERP systems handle the process? What will this involve? Will a different kind of information be needed? Who will have to be responsible for the process? Will it be the same people or different people? Will the steps or activities of the process be done in the same order or in a different order than before? Will all of this fit with the other processes? What will the cost of changing the way we handle a specific business process be?

On the other hand, is it possible to modify Microsoft Dynamics NAV or Microsoft Dynamics 365 Business Central to handle the process in a different way? What would such a modification imply? How much development work would be needed to modify the behavior of the system? What would be the cost of changing the way these ERP systems handle a unique business process?

By doing this exercise with all of your processes, one by one, you will end up with your list of requirements.

Considerations for Microsoft Dynamics 365 Business Central

Microsoft Dynamics 365 Business Central Online is an **SaaS** (short for, **Software as a Service**) with monthly fee offerings and there are very different things to consider compared to on-premise systems. This ERP system runs in the cloud, in a controlled environment directly governed by Microsoft, and updates, upgrades, and patches are included in the fee; with on-premise ERP systems, you need to pay to apply patches and to have upgrades performed. Further details can be found in `Chapter 13`, *Microsoft Dynamics 365 Business Central*. Customizing and extending a product are two very different things.

In Microsoft Dynamics 365 Business Central Online, the system is updated by itself, customizations can be done directly from the browser (In-client Designer), and functional changes can be made only through extensions applied to events.

It's not possible to change the standard product; only extensions can be used to modify the functionalities of the system. In this way, the system is more stable, more safe, and does not reach a declination of the standard product creating "brand new products," as sometimes happened with Microsoft Dynamics NAV projects.

So, with Microsoft Dynamics 365 Business Central, it's necessary to adapt to the standard product more than was done with Microsoft Dynamics NAV in the past.

Define acceptable gaps and workarounds

The standard product is a great product, but obviously it cannot contain all the functionalities necessary for the company. It is necessary to try to adapt to it or use workarounds to manage what may seem unmanageable.

In addition to the work of consultants, already seen in the previous chapter, the customer must play their part in trying to adapt as much as possible to the standard and accept any unmanageable gaps that can be bypassed by workarounds proposed by the consultant. The customer (the key user of the process in general) must always be the sponsor of the project and of the product.

If, instead, new gaps/requirements emerge that cannot be managed through workarounds (during the project or after the go-live date), it is necessary to classify them so as not to alter the course of the project, under an example of classification. For example, we can classify the new requirements/gaps that are detected in this way:

- Need to start
- Need after starting
- Nice to have

In this way, we can better schedule what will have to be done based on real needs that emerge:

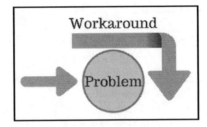

Workaround in action – using standard dimensions instead of customizing

Let's go back to our example of reporting the costs of a specific service. There are things in Microsoft Dynamics NAV and in Microsoft Dynamics 365 Business Central called **dimensions**. These are actually meant to be able to analyze any information according to a specific value of a dimension.

One way to resolve the reporting goal in our example is to set up a dimension that will be called **service**. The values of this dimension will be all the different services the company provides.

The service dimension can then be set up as mandatory in all the general ledger accounts that are used to post expenses. This means that, before an expense is posted, whether it is a purchase invoice or any other expense such as salaries, insurances, and so on, someone has to determine the service to which the expense is attributed. If this is not determined prior to the posting of the expense, an error message will be raised. That is, you will not be able to account your expense if you do not attribute it to a service.

This completely changes the process. At the moment, assignment to services is determined a while after the expenses have been accounted, or are never determined if no one asks for the costs of a specific service. But having all this information can automate the process of getting an amount for a specific service in a specific period of time. If the information is in the system, a report can be automated using the appropriate reporting tools.

Once you have the whole explanation of the standard functionality provided in Microsoft Dynamics NAV or in Microsoft Dynamics 365 Business Central, the best option in the example is to change the way the process is handled and use the standard way proposed by the products.

Two requirements will come up, as follows:

- Set up a dimension called `service` and make it mandatory in all general ledger accounts that are used to post expenses
- Develop a report to get the total expenses amount for a specific dimension value in a specific period of time

The first requirement will only require configuration work. The second one can be addressed through configuration (setting up the appropriate analysis view is a feature in Microsoft Dynamics NAV and in Microsoft Dynamics 365 Business Central to report the general ledger amounts based on the dimension values) or a custom report can be developed.

Change management

This does not meanchanging your company's management team!

Implementing a brand new ERP means a lot of changes within an organization. The first change is the software the company is using. This will affect the people that use the ERP intensively, and they will probably be worried about the project and how it will affect their daily tasks.

But this is not the only change that the company will face. While changing the ERP, you will probably change some processes, or you could even change who is responsible for doing certain tasks. Usually, these changes are not easy to make. You will have to take action in order to reassure people and help them during the change process.

For example, on an implementation project I was involved in recently, the company had an employee whose major task was to post all the sales invoices in the system after the user "checked" whether everything was correct with the invoice before posting.

With the implementation of Microsoft Dynamics NAV or Microsoft Dynamics 365 Business Central, it was proposed that it made more sense that the warehouse staff post the invoice along with the shipment so that the invoice could go along with the shipment. Now, that particular employee probably felt that they were going to lose their job, so they perhaps started to avoid the project instead of helping with the implementation.

We had to assure the employee that their position would evolve. Instead of checking each order for pricing, address information, and so on, one by one, the employee would now be responsible for setting up accurate pricing in the **Customer Sales Price** field, maintaining the different addresses in the **Ship-to Address** field, and keep their credit up-to-date. This meant that, instead of checking each order one by one (sometimes up to a thousand orders a day), they would be managing the setup data for customers. This was a much better use of their time and it definitely increased their productivity. The checking is done beforehand, not at the time of posting.

The first thing you need to do to face a change in management is to identify all the stakeholders of the project. After that, you need to analyze their needs and their expectations of the project. You will also have to determine whether they support the project or not, and what action you can take to change their position, if they don't.

Usually, communication is the easiest way to face change. Keep all of the stakeholders informed about what the project is all about, why the company has decided to implement Microsoft Dynamics NAV or Microsoft Dynamics 365 Business Central, how will it affect them, and how the project is advancing.

If communication is not enough for some stakeholders, you will need to take other action. Getting them involved is usually a good way to change their vision of the project. Think carefully about how you are going to handle all those changes. People are the most valuable asset you have to make a project a success.

Get involved in testing the system

When a project starts, a consultant will take all the requirements needed to implement Microsoft Dynamics NAV or Microsoft Dynamics 365 Business Central and determine which of those requirements will be covered with the standard application and which ones will be developed for you.

Implementing Microsoft Dynamics NAV or Microsoft Dynamics 365 Business Central for a company is a unique process, since it will cover the specific needs of your company. Even for similar companies, there will be many differences between processes, making their implementation unique. No matter how much experience the implementer has in the companies of your sector, you and the people in your organization are the best testers to verify that everything works as defined.

Usually, the implementer will set up a second Microsoft Dynamics NAV server (or a Microsoft Dynamics 365 Business Central Sandbox instance, as explained in a later chapter) for you, so that you can test the system before it goes to production. The consultants and developers will conduct their own tests before delivering the solution, but it is also important that you invest time in testing whatever you have received. Any issue found before the go-live day is much easier to solve than when it's used in a production environment.

Ask different people with different tasks within your organization to test the system. This way, every area will be covered by different people and the more eyes you can have over on the application, the more issues you will usually find than if just one person was testing every area.

Testing with real data is one of most accurate types of testing you can do. Before you start testing, you may want to insist that your Microsoft partner creates an environment loaded with your data first. That way, when users are performing testing, it's more "real".

Regarding Microsoft Dynamics 365 Business Central, to load data into the production environment, in a copy of the production company or in a sandbox environment (to test customer data before importing it into production environments, as an example), you can use the RapidStart Services tools, explained in Chapter 6, *Migrating Data*. Chapter 14, *Working and Developing with Dockers and Sandboxes*, will explain how to operate in sandbox environments.

Involve end users

End users are the people who will actually be using Microsoft Dynamics NAV or Microsoft Dynamics 365 Business Central on a daily basis. The project will truly succeed if they fully utilize the system. And they will only fully utilize the system if they believe it's reliable and find that it makes their jobs easier.

For all of this to happen, it is important that they get involved in every step of the implementation, from the very beginning. They may not have a high position within the company, and they may not have the power to make certain decisions, but they will definitely have a lot to say.

When we talked about the definition of internal processes, we said that you had to ask yourself and your people what your processes were, the activities inside each process, and the information used by the process. We also said that real processes should be considered and not just *theoretical* processes. The ones who actually know real processes and activities are end users. If their input is not taken into consideration, and you do not involve them, you will not be working with complete information, thus, you will not be able to define your real requirements.

Even if the final solution really meets all the requirements defined in the project, if those are requirements are not well-defined, the project will fail as end users will not find it useful. Instead, they will keep doing their extra processes and keep their own information in spreadsheet files. In fact, it will make your existing processes even worse.

The definition of processes and requirements is the most important part in which end users should get involved. If they get involved in defining how they work and how the system should behave, they will really find the system useful and actually embrace it.

But that's not the only part of the implementation process in which they should get involved. It is also important that they participate in the testing process, especially for those functionalities that have been either modified or completely developed. If they participate in the testing process, they might find errors or other kinds of improvements that could be made to make everything easier. If they bring these to your attention, the Microsoft Dynamics NAV or Microsoft Dynamics 365 Business Central implementers will be able to fix or improve the relevant processes. If they do not get involved in the testing process, they may find errors or improvements once the functionalities are live but they might never tell you. Instead, they will create exception processes for their daily job that will make everything less efficient and more chaotic.

Continuous follow-up

To maintain precise control of a project, to manage problems that emerge during the project, and to provide an estimate of when the project will be completed, it is also necessary for the customer to perform continuous follow-up. If this is not done, functional testing will be difficult to validate. There is also the risk of not verifying something that could be critical, which may lead to non-satisfaction of the project.

For example, the atomic bomb was the first project managed using real project management; the countdown of NASA is considered the most perfect instrument of analysis and control in the world. Managing an ERP project does not involve any of this, just common sense and continuous follow-up.

It is always necessary to keep a project under control, to avoid the emergence of unexpected deviations from the original guidelines that could increase the risk of failure of the project itself.

In particular, it is useful to request the following:

- A follow-up during go-live time
- A follow-up after go-live time
- A follow-up to check internal customer satisfaction levels(before and after go-live time)

Summary

In this chapter, we looked at how to handle the implementation of Microsoft Dynamics NAV or Microsoft Dynamics 365 Business Central from a customer's perspective. We covered a few areas but the whole idea is that you, as a customer, have to manage the implementation as a project. The implementer cannot do all the work for you. People within your organization will have tasks and responsibilities assigned to them, and you will have to monitor and control all of those tasks.

Get involved with the project management and with the project's progress; in order to make the project successful, continuous follow-up is needed to check the project's progress step by step. The customer must work hand in hand with the consultant to get good results (a mixed team is the best).

In the following chapter, you will see how a company may have data in other applications (their old ERP system, spreadsheet files, and so on) and how it can be massively imported into Microsoft Dynamics NAV or Microsoft Dynamics 365 Business Central.

Migrating Data
6

Microsoft Dynamics NAV, since its 2013 release, is completely configured and tuned. A range of brand new functionalities have been developed and everything is ready for you to go live. There's only one thing missing in the database—the data. Microsoft Dynamics NAV 2018 and Microsoft Dynamics NAV 365 Business Central offer many ways and useful tools to import the data.

In this chapter, we'll see which tools can be used in Microsoft Dynamics NAV and Microsoft Dynamics 365 Business Central to migrate data into the system, and how to convert the data to meet Microsoft Dynamics NAV and Microsoft Dynamics 365 Business Central requirements. We'll look at tools including the following:

- RapidStart Services
- XMLport
- User-defined tools
- APIs

Not all of these tools are available on Microsoft Dynamics 365 Business Central SaaS. We'll also see what kind of data is commonly migrated to Microsoft Dynamics NAV or Microsoft Dynamics 365 Business Central, and which strategies can be used to migrate it. The kind of data and strategies are listed as follows:

- Master data
- Open entries
- Historical data
- Open documents

Tools for migrating data

There are several ways to migrate data into Microsoft Dynamics NAV or Microsoft Dynamics 365 Business Central. You choose the method depending on what is to be migrated and whether any additional processes need to be carried out on the provided data to meet the Microsoft Dynamics NAV and Business Central requirements.

We'll go through the different tools available to migrate the data. We'll also explain how to write our own tools if the ones provided out of the box don't meet our requirements or expectations.

RapidStart Services with configuration packages

RapidStart Services is a feature introduced in Microsoft Dynamics NAV 2013, and is available today in Microsoft Dynamics NAV and Microsoft Dynamics 365 Business Central. It allows you to import your company data by using a built-in data-import engine.

With RapidStart Services, you can set up the tables involved in the configuration process of new companies. You can create a questionnaire to guide you and your customers through the collection of setup information. Your customers have the option of using the questionnaire to set up application areas on their own or they can open the setup page directly and complete the setup there. Most importantly, RapidStart Services helps you, as a customer, to prepare the company with default setup data, which you can fine-tune and customize. Lastly, when you use RapidStart Services, you can configure and migrate existing customer data, such as a list of customers or items, into the new company.

On Windows client, the RapidStart Services tools can be found under **Department** | **Departments** | **Administration** | **Application Setup** | **RapidStart Services** for Microsoft Dynamics NAV or Microsoft Dynamics 365 Business Central on-premise.

The following screenshots are taken from Microsoft Dynamics 365 Business Central on-premise (from Windows and Web client). In this screenshot, you can see the **RapidStart Services** option:

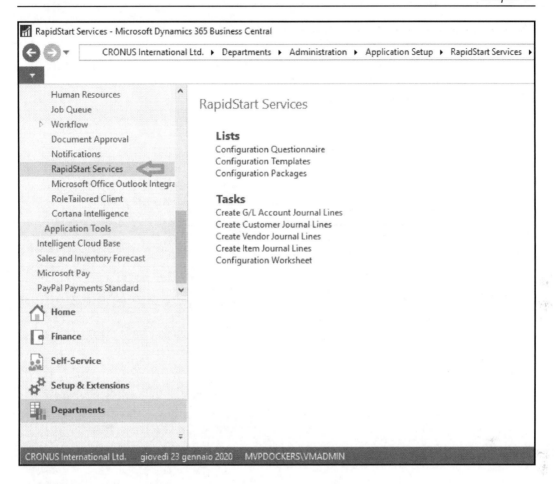

In the Web client, search for configuration packages in the **Search** menu. You'll see an extended configuration package, GB.ENU.EXTENDED, in this case, because we are using the setup for the GB localization:

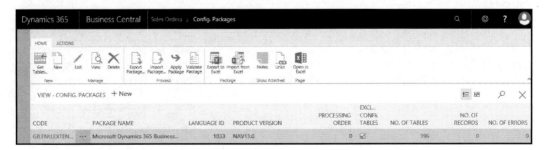

The following components can be used to set up a new company:

- Configuration wizard
- Configuration packages
- Configuration worksheet
- Configuration templates
- Configuration questionnaire

Let's work through these components by following a step-by-step example. Before starting the example, you need to create a new company, and you may have an easier time if you change your role to that of **RapidStart Services Implementer**.

In this example, we'll perform the following actions:

1. Create a new company using PowerShell
2. Change our profile to **RapidStart Services Implementer**
3. Use the configuration wizard
4. Create a data configuration package
5. Apply the configuration package

Let's discuss these steps in more detail.

 The screenshots shown are related to the Web client and were taken from the release before that of October 2018; they might be changed and layout may be different in the October 2018 release, be patient for this.

Creating a new company using PowerShell (in Microsoft Dynamics 365 Business Central on-premise)

The following steps will guide you through creating your new company within PowerShell. I'm using Microsoft Dynamics 365 Business Central on-premise in this case, but the steps will be the same for Microsoft Dynamics NAV 2018 (PowerShell features are not available in Dynamics 365 Business Central SaaS):

1. Start the Microsoft Dynamics 365 Business Central Administration Shell (make sure to right-click on the icon and select **Run as Administrator**).
2. Type `New-NAVCompany`.
3. Let's name the new company `DemoRapidStart`.

4. For **ServerInstance**, type in the same server instance you're using to connect to Microsoft Dynamics 365 Business Central. If you installed with the default settings, type `DynamicsNAV130`, otherwise, run the Microsoft Dynamics 365 Business Central Administration and check the services that are running.

5. Press *Enter* and wait for a few seconds until the system finishes creating the company. When the process is done, as shown in the following screenshot, it will bring you back to PowerShell Command Prompt:

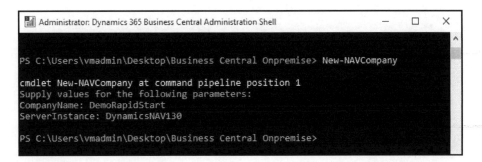

6. Open the Web client.

7. On the **MY SETTINGS** page, click on **Company**, shown in the following screenshot, and the **ALLOWED COMPANIES** page will be opened:

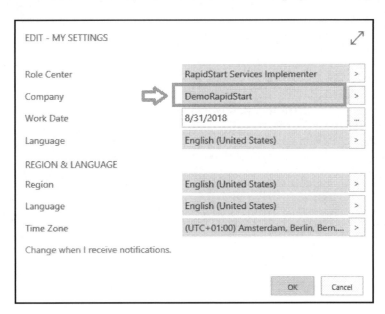

8. Select the `DemoRapidStart` company from the **ALLOWED COMPANIES** page. Then, click on **OK**:

You have now entered in the `DemoRapidStart` company.

Changing the profile to RapidStart Services Implementer

Perform the following steps to change the **User Personalizations**:

1. Open the **User Personalizations** page.
2. Double-click on the **User ID** field to bring up the card page.
3. Assign the **Profile ID** and **User ID**, as shown in the following screenshot:

4. Close the Web client and open it again. Your Role Center now looks like the following screenshot:

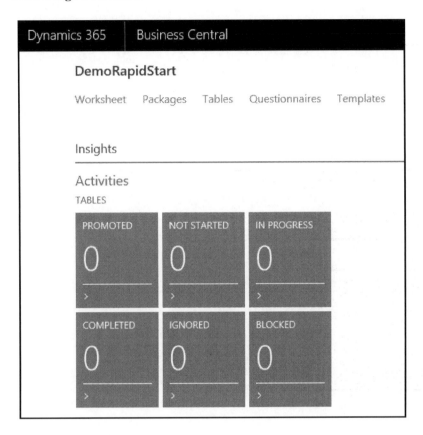

Now that we have a new company, `DemoRapidStart`, and we've selected the **RapidStart Services** role, we're ready to use all of the components of the RapidStart Services tool to set up our company.

Using the RapidStart Services Wizard

The RapidStart Services Wizard is used to quickly configure a new company. Click on the **RapidStart Services Wizard** option found on the ribbon bar:

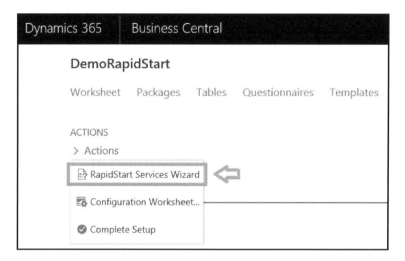

A new page will open where you'll be able to enter basic information about the new company. You can also load your company's logo by right-clicking on the **Picture** box:

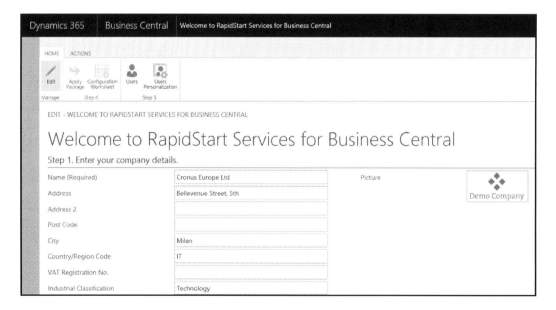

You can go through all of the tabs of the page, entering the required information. The **Select package** tab is mentioned in the *Applying a configuration package* section.

Working with configuration packages

In Microsoft Dynamics NAV 2018 and Microsoft Dynamics 365 Business Central on-premise, there are more than 200 tables that can be considered configuration tables. If you intend to utilize all of the features in Microsoft Dynamics NAV or Microsoft Dynamics 365 Business Central on-premise, you need to fill them in when you create a new company; the same does not apply to Microsoft Dynamics 365 Business Central SaaS, as there are fewer configurable tables available because the set of tables are limited.

You'll find almost 50 tables with the word *setup* as their description, but there are many other tables that can also be considered setup tables. Here you can see a list of some setup tables:

- **Posting Groups**: There are 10 tables located here
- **Journal Batch and Journal Template**: More than 20 tables are located here
- **G/L accounts and Account schedules**: Almost 10 tables are present here
- **Payment terms, Payment methods, Currencies, Languages, Countries and Regions, Post codes, and Series**: These are the other setup tables without the word *setup* in their description

Having to edit all of these tables manually on each implementation can take a long time. Fortunately, this is where the `RapidStart` package can help by speeding up the process.

The best approach is to create a configuration package for the data on the configuration tables and then apply it on each new implementation, like a template.

You can create one configuration package per functional area. For example, you can create one package for the manufacturing functionalities and one package for the finance functionalities. Another approach can be to create one package for each type of data. For example, you can create one package with the data related to all of the posting groups found in the application and one package for all of the master data.

In this section, we'll see how to create a configuration package and how to apply it to a new company.

Creating a new configuration package

In this section, we're going to create a new configuration package with all of the posting groups' tables found on the application. Since posting groups refer to general ledger accounts, we are also going to include the chart of accounts in our package.

Follow these steps to create the new configuration package:

1. Select a company containing the data that you want to include in your configuration package. Then, change the company back to our example company, CRONUS International.

2. From the **RapidStart Services Implementer** Role Center, click on the **Packages** option.

3. Click on the **New** button on the ribbon bar. The **Config. Package Card** page opens. Fill in the fields in the **General** tab, as shown in the following screenshot:

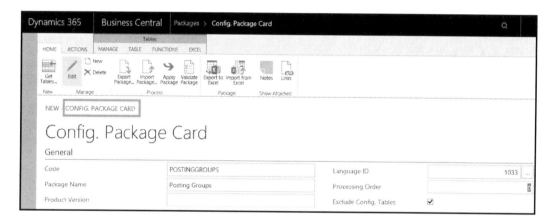

4. Add tables to the package by creating new lines on the **Tables** tab, as shown in the following screenshot. You'll only have to fill in the **TABLE ID** column:

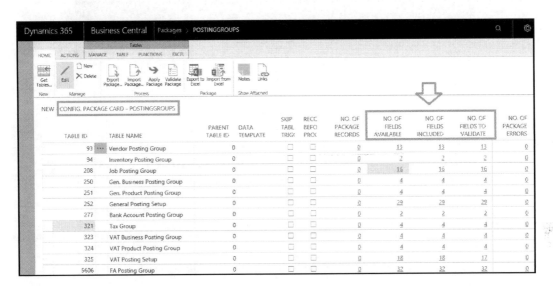

5. When you insert a table in the package, all of the table fields are included by default. In some cases, you may want to exclude certain fields from the package. Select the **G/L Account** line and click on **TABLE | Fields**. On the **CONFIG. PACKAGE FIELDS** page, uncheck the **INCLUDE FIELD** column for the **Global Dimension 1 Code** field and the **Global Dimension 2 Code** field. This will also remove the **VALIDATE FIELD** checkbox. Click on **OK** to close the page.

Position the mouse on the record related to **G/L Account** table, click on the **Fields** button and the **Config. Fields** page will be opened:

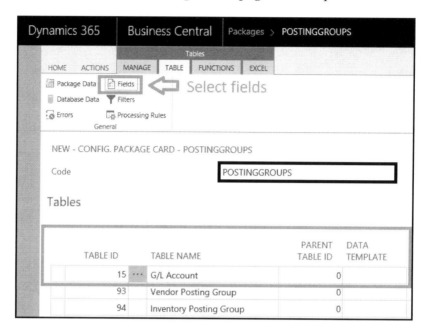

The following screenshot shows how to select the **CONFIG. PACKAGE FIELDS**.

With this page, it is possible to define which fields must be included in the **Export Package** (for the relative table in which we are placed), define the table relation for each field, and, if necessary, validate data:

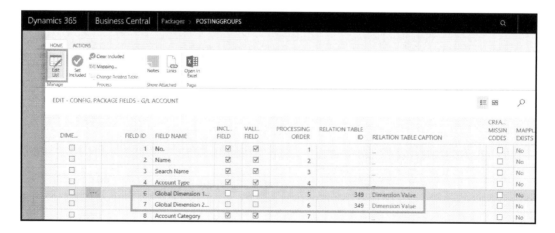

6. Click on the **Export Package** option on the ribbon bar. This will create a
   RAPIDSTART file that you can save. Go ahead and save the file somewhere
   on your computer so we can import it into the DemoRapidStart company:

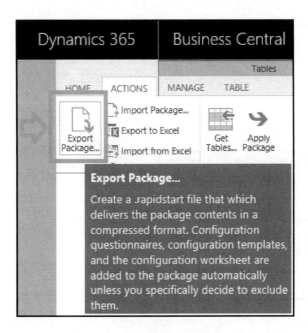

You'll see the following message on the screen:

Applying a configuration package

In the previous section, we created a new configuration package. In this section, we
are going to apply this package to the DemoRapidStart company, which is the new
company we created earlier in this chapter.

Follow these steps to apply the configuration package:

1. On the Web client, open the `DemoRapidStart` company.
2. From the **RapidStart Services Implementer** Role Center, click on the **RapidStart Services Wizard** option:

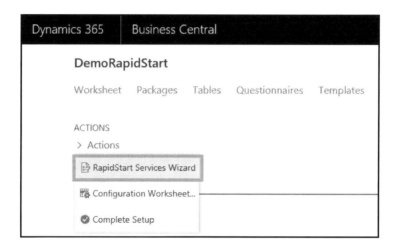

3. On the **Select package.** tab, select the configuration package that you created in the *Creating a new configuration package* section:

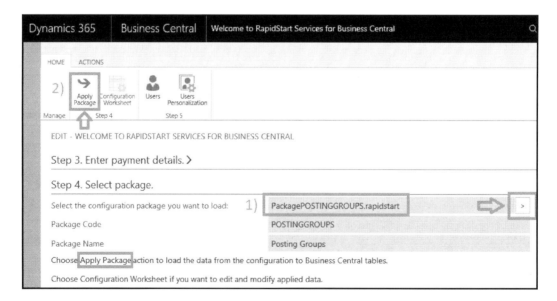

4. Click on the **Apply Package** option found on the ribbon bar. When the process is done, you'll get a confirmation message:

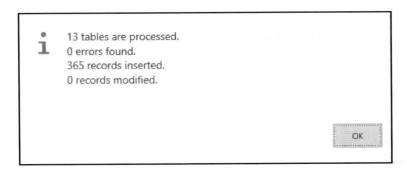

The data contained in the configuration package has now been imported to the `DemoRapidStart` company. You can also import packages from the packages page that we saw when we created the configuration package.

The configuration worksheet

In the previous section, we created a configuration package and imported all of the tables and fields that were within that package. But what if we want to migrate specific tables but use the same field setups in the package? For the purpose of eliminating the need to create a different configuration package for each table that we want to convert, this is where the configuration worksheet comes in; we can consider the configuration worksheet a kind of Data Migration wizard.

The configuration worksheet allows you to migrate specific tables using a specific configuration package that we set up in the previous step. You can plan, track, and perform your own data imports instead of asking developers to create XMLports to import data into Microsoft Dynamics NAV and Microsoft Dynamics 365 Business Central on-premise and SaaS.

For those of you who have used the previous versions of Microsoft Dynamics NAV, the configuration worksheet is the old migration tool with some new features.

The configuration worksheet is used to create the structure of tables that need to be imported with the company data. You'll be able to export this structure to Microsoft Office Excel, fill in the data, and then import it back into Microsoft Dynamics NAV. This makes it easy for companies to copy and paste information from another ERP system. This is also very handy if you're going to be importing data from existing Excel sheets that the users are working with.

Basically, the configuration worksheet allows you to select and choose specific tables to import/export using the configuration package.

Let's explore how the configuration worksheet works by importing the `Customer` table and all of the related tables into our new company.

Creating the data migration structure

Make sure you're currently working in the `RapidStartDemo` company. We must first open the configuration package and set up a new package:

1. Click on **Packages** from the home page or you can access it by going to **Departments** | **Administration** | **Application Setup** | **RapidStart Services** for Microsoft Dynamics NAV or Microsoft Dynamics 365 Business Central on-premise/configuration packages. In the Web client, search for `configuration packages` in the search menu.

2. Click on **New** to create a new package and name it `Customer`.

3. In the lines area, type `18` for the **Table ID** field.

4. Click on **TABLE** in the lines area and select the **Fields**. Doing so will automatically populate the fields that are defined in the table, which can be seen in the following screenshot:

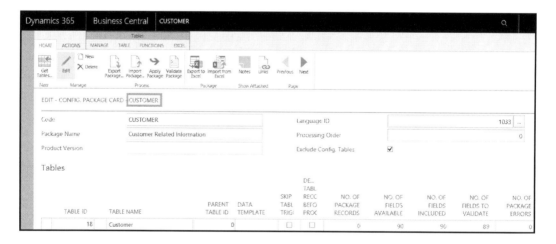

5. Once we've created the configuration package, we can assign it to a configuration worksheet.

Perform the following steps to define the tables in a configuration worksheet:

1. Change the user role to **RapidStart Implementer.**
2. Open the **Configuration Worksheet** from the **RapidStart Implementer** Role Center:

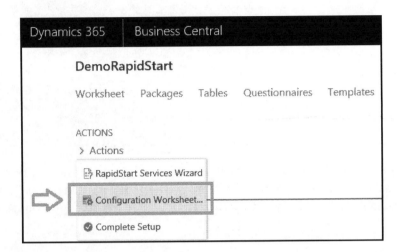

3. Create a line for table **18, Customer**. You only need to fill in the **LINE TYPE** and **TABLE ID** fields:

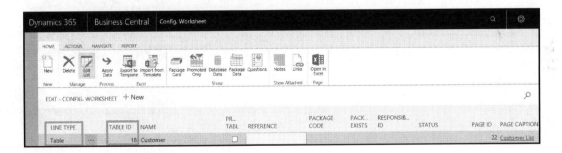

4. Click on **ACTIONS** and select **Assign Package**.

5. Select the **CUSTOMER** package and click on **OK**:

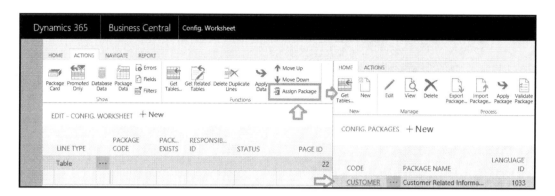

BOOM! We're done! You're now ready to use this configuration to copy the customer data from CRONUS International Ltd. to the RapidStartDemo company. All you need to do is click on the **Copy Data** button to copy the customer data over.

We proceed by performing the following steps:

1. Click on the **Copy Data** button under **HOME**.

2. Click on **Copy Data** from the prompt.

3. Click on **Yes** on the confirmation message:

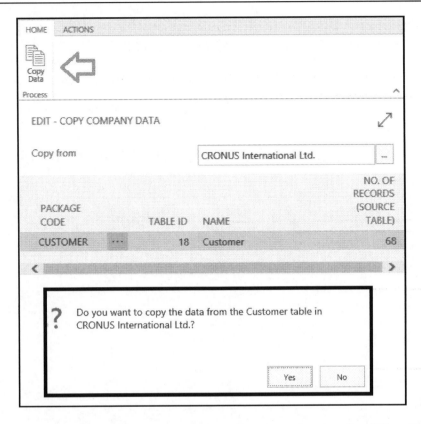

4. After the data is copied over, you can click on the **Database Data** from the **Config. Worksheet,** or go to **Customer List** to see the customer information that has been copied over.

Copying related tables

Microsoft Dynamics NAV and Microsoft Dynamics 365 Business Central are built based on a relational database. In the case of the Customer table, there are a lot of tables that are related, for example, Payment Terms Code. Just copying over the Customer table enable it to function properly in our new company.

Prior to RapidStart, you would've had to find out all of the tables that the `Customer` table is related to by going into the Development Environment. Fortunately, there's a function called **Get Related Tables** in the **Config. Worksheet** and the configuration package that takes care of this for us.

Select the `Customer` record from the **Config. Worksheet** and click on **Get Related Tables**. This will populate all of the related tables onto our worksheet:

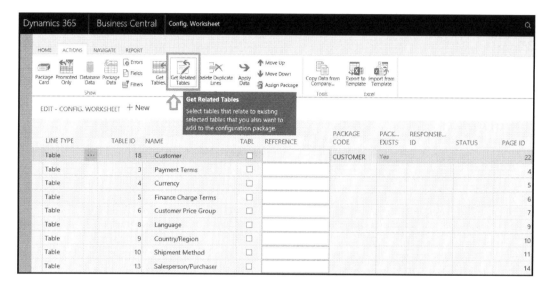

One thing you'll notice after you get the related tables is that **PACKAGE CODE** is all blank. To assign a package to all of the records, do the following:

1. Highlight all of the lines.
2. Click on **Assign Package**.
3. Select the `CUSTOMER` package.
4. Click on **OK**:

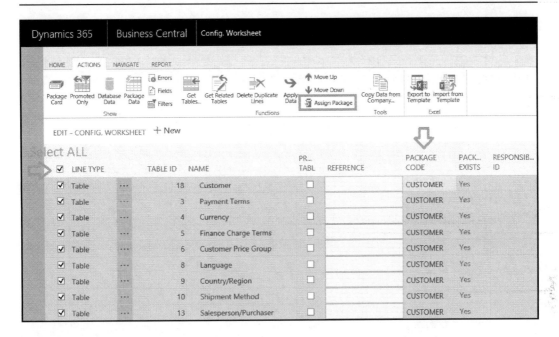

Assigning the package to the tables on the worksheet will also populate the fields that are related to the tables.

Using Excel templates

We used the **Copy Data** option to copy the data from a company that's set up within Microsoft Dynamics NAV or Microsoft Dynamics 365 Business Central. Suppose we want to migrate the data from an external source. We wouldn't want to use the copy data functionality because that data isn't even in Microsoft Dynamics NAV yet!

We can utilize Microsoft Dynamics NAV to export the structure that we've defined on the configuration package and configuration worksheet into Microsoft Excel. Then, you can either copy/paste the data or manually enter the data into Excel and import it back in to Microsoft Dynamics NAV. To do so, perform the following steps:

1. Go to the **Config. Worksheet**.
2. Highlight `Payment Terms` (you can highlight more lines if you want to export them into the same Excel sheet).

3. Click on **Export to Template**:

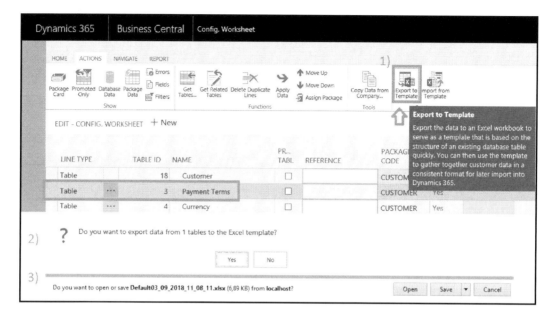

4. Give the file a name and save it somewhere on your computer.
5. After the file is saved, open the Microsoft Excel file and fill in the information without modifying the column structure.

> If you need to modify the column structure, make sure to update the **Processing Order** field in the **Config. Package** field. This will change the order in which the fields are read.

6. Fill in the Microsoft Excel sheet as shown in the following screenshot:

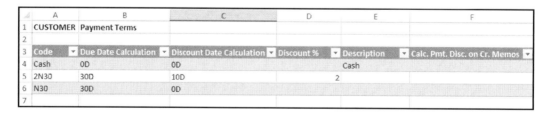

7. Save and close the Microsoft Excel sheet and go back to the configuration worksheet. We'll import what we've filled in into the RapidStartDemo company.

8. Click on **Import from Template**. Select **Yes** from the prompt and choose the Microsoft Excel sheet that you saved in the preceding step:

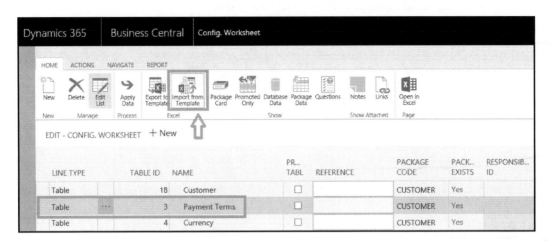

9. When the data is imported from Microsoft Excel, Microsoft Dynamics NAV will put it in the holding spot, called **Package Data**. Click on the **Package Data** from the configuration worksheet to check what was imported. The following screenshot shows the Payment Terms package data:

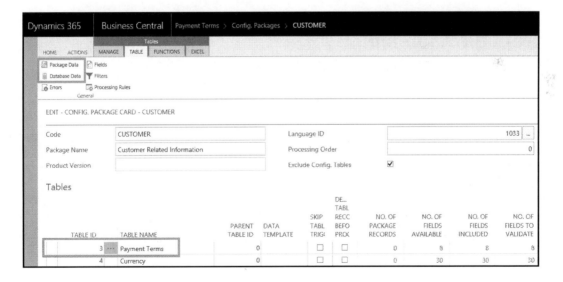

10. Once you've confirmed that this is indeed what you want, click on **Apply Data**. This will create the records in our database. If we open the PAYMENT TERMS table, we'll see the records created in the RapidStartDemo company:

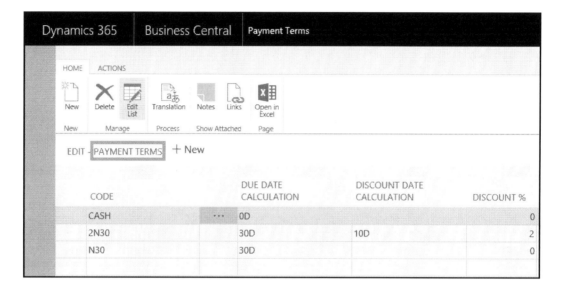

Configuration templates

Templates are used to default data on some fields when we import data into Microsoft Dynamics NAV or Microsoft Dynamics 365 Business Central. There are some mandatory fields that don't exist on the dataset that you're importing the data from, using the configuration templates; we'll be able to default these mandatory fields.

It is possible to use this tool for any table for which it is necessary to define a model, the defined model will be used to pre-fill the necessary/mandatory fields and guide the user to a correct data entry.

You usually create templates for the master data, such as customers, vendors, and items master data.

> You can also use data templates for daily operations to create records that are based on templates.

In this section, we are going to see how to create a configuration template and how to use it while importing data into Microsoft Dynamics NAV or Microsoft Dynamics 365 Business Central.

Creating a configuration template

Each template consists of a header and lines. On the header, you specify the table related to the template. On the lines, you specify which fields are included in the template and their default values.

You can find **Configuration Templates** in the **Search** menu:

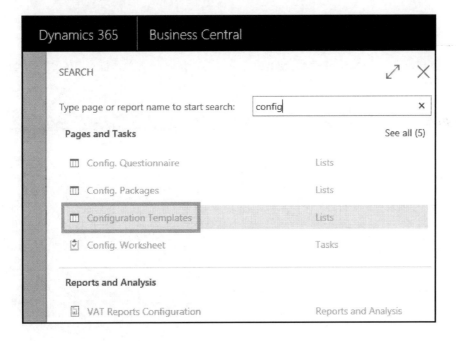

Once open, you can already find a list of ready-to-use templates (ready to go!); there are different types for items, customers, and both domestic and foreign customers and vendors:

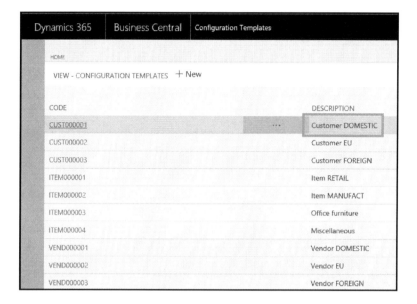

The following is an example of a template setup for DOMESTIC customer in CRONUS International:

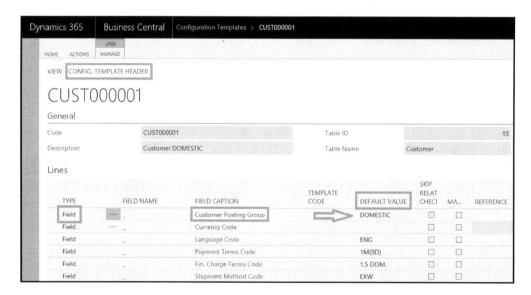

Let's create a new template and apply it to an existing configuration package. While you're in the `DemoRapidStart` company, do the following:

1. Open the **Configuration Templates** page and click on the **New** button.
2. In the **Code** field, enter a unique ID for the template. Let's name it `CUSTTERM`. In the **Description** field, enter a description.
3. In the **Table ID** field, enter the table to which this template has been applied. In our case, it will be table `18`.
4. Create a new line and select the **FIELD NAME** field. The **Field List** window displays the list of fields in the table. Since we want to default `Payment Terms Code` to `N30`, select the `Payment Terms Code` field and then click on the **OK** button.
5. In the **DEFAULT VALUE** field, enter `N30`:

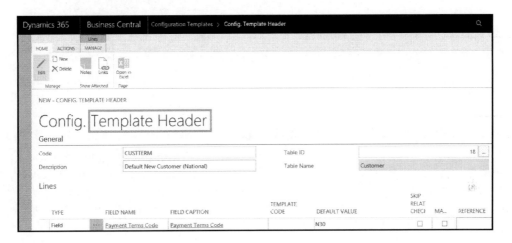

Using configuration templates

Using configuration templates with RapidStart Services is as simple as selecting *the template we want to use* on a line of a configuration package. The following steps will demonstrate this:

1. Open the **Packages** page.
2. From the list of packages, open the `Customer` package we created in *Creating the data migration structure* section.
3. Find the `Customer` table included in the package. In the **DATA TEMPLATE** field, select the template that we created in the previous section.

And we are done! When importing new customers using the package, the template will be applied, as seen in the following screenshot:

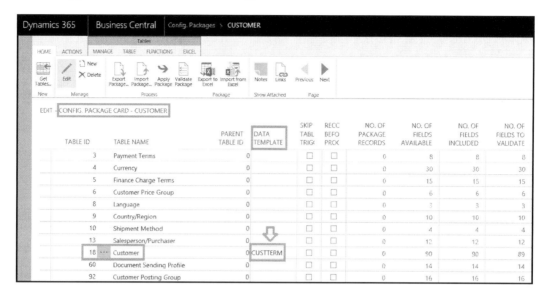

The configuration questionnaire

The configuration questionnaire is used to collect data from the users to help configure a new company. You can create a list of questions and provide it to users as a Microsoft Excel or an XML file. When the user completes the questionnaire, you import the file into the new Microsoft Dynamics NAV or Microsoft Dynamics 365 Business Central company and then apply it to the database.

The idea behind the configuration questionnaire is to allow the Microsoft Dynamics NAV partner to bypass speaking to customers directly and automate the setup. Why on earth would any partner do this to a customer? Simple if your Microsoft Dynamics NAV solution is so vertical that you can practically set it up blindfolded, you can probably write down all of your knowledge and have the system set itself up.

There are already a series of questionnaires ready to be used, which are very useful to understand how they are made and used as examples; they are of various kinds, from sales to inventory:

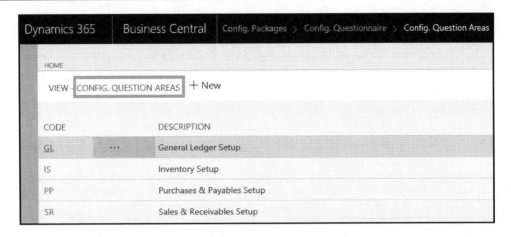

Follow the steps described in the next section to create and complete a configuration questionnaire.

Creating a configuration questionnaire

Follow the steps listed here to create a configuration questionnaire:

1. Open the **Config. Questionnaire** page and click on the **New** option:

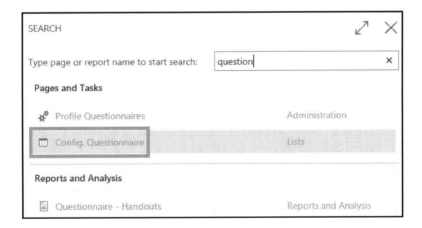

2. Provide a code and a description.
3. Click on the **Config. Questions Areas** option found on the ribbon bar.
4. In the **Code** field, enter a code for the question area.
5. In the **Table ID** field, choose the ID of the table for which you want to collect information.

6. Click on the **Update Questions** option found on the ribbon bar. Each field in the table is added to the questionnaire with a question mark following its label. You can rephrase the label to make it clear how the question should be answered. For example, if a field is called **Name**, you can edit it to state `What is the name of <data being collected>`. As needed, you can also delete the questions that you don't want to include in the questionnaire.

7. Repeat these steps to add additional question areas.

In the following screenshot taken from CRONUS International, you can see an example of a questionnaire for the inventory setup area:

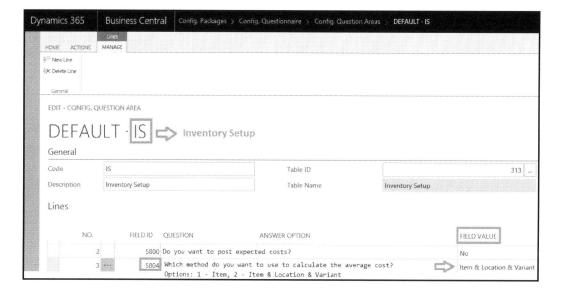

Completing the configuration questionnaire

Once you have the configuration questionnaire figured out, you can export it to Microsoft Excel and send it off to the customers to fill in. Change to the CRONUS International company to see a list of the pre-made questions:

1. Open the CRONUS International company.

2. Open the **Config. Questionnaire** page, click on the **Export to Excel** option found on the ribbon bar, and save the file:

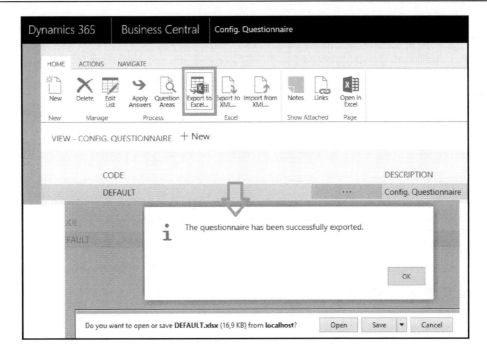

3. Complete the configuration questionnaire by entering the answers in the Excel workbook. There are worksheets for each of the question areas that have been created for the questionnaire. Save the file. Here is an example of a Microsoft Excel file with questions:

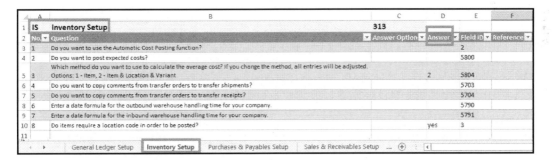

4. Back in the questionnaire, click on the **Import from Excel** option. Select the XLSX file that you have saved.

5. Click on the **Config. Question Areas** option and select one question area to begin the process of validating and applying the answers to the setup questionnaire.

6. After the validating process is complete and the answers to the whole questionnaire are applied, click on the **Apply Answers** option of the **Config. Questionnaire** page.
7. To apply answers for a specific question area, click on the **Apply Answers** option from the **Config. Question Areas** page.

Using RapidStart Services from PowerShell

For Microsoft Dynamics NAV and Microsoft Dynamics 365 Business Central on-premise, an interesting operating mode, useful in the case of environments with multiple databases and many companies to be configured, is the possibility to recall RapidStart Services from PowerShell.

In this way, it is possible to launch batch imports without user intervention—previously saved packages are retrieved and executed by PowerShell cmdlets in silent mode.

Powershell cmdLets for RapidStart Services

As mentioned, it is possible to deploy a configuration package using a PowerShell cmdlet; it's possible to use PowerShell cmdlets for the following:

- Performing data import across multiple Microsoft Dynamics NAV or Microsoft Dynamics 365 Business Central on-premise installations without opening each of installation manually
- Configuring additional application areas for multiple customers

You can achieve this goal by using Microsoft Dynamics NAV 2018 or Microsoft Dynamics 365 Business Central on-premise Administration Shell using InvokeNAVCodeUnit PowerShell cmdlet, as in the following example of utilization:

```
Invoke-NAVCodeunit –Tenant Default –CompanyName "CRONUS International
Ltd." –CodeunitId 8620 –MethodName ImportRapidStartPackage –Argument
C:\TEMP\RS_DEMO_CONFIG.rapidstart –ServerInstance DynamicsNAV130
```

 For more information, you can take a look at https://docs.microsoft.com/en-us/powershell/module/microsoft.dynamics.nav.management/import-navconfigurationpackagefile?view=businesscentral-ps.

Summarizing RapidStart Services

We have already covered RapidStart Services. Before moving to another tool to migrate, there are a few things you should know about RapidStart Services:

- RapidStart Services can be used both for importing and exporting data. It isn't a tool reserved just for importing data when you first start working with Microsoft Dynamics NAV or Microsoft Dynamics 365 Business Central.
- RapidStart Services doesn't only insert new data into the database; it can actually be used to modify the data as well. This functionality can be used as a "find and replace" substitute that was sorely missed by users using the classic client, to modify the data, export it to an Excel template, modify whatever needs to be modified, and import the data again. The tool will perform the following actions:
    - Create a new record in the corresponding table if no record exists with the same values on the primary key fields as the imported record.
    - Update a record in the corresponding table if the record imported already exists in the table. The record will be updated with all of the information coming from the imported record.
- RapidStart Services consumes a lot of time while importing and exporting data. It took us one minute to import 5,000 customers and some minutes to apply them. However, importing that exact same data using an XMLport (the next tool we'll explain) took us just a couple of seconds.

Using XMLports to migrate data

An XMLport is a Microsoft Dynamics NAV and Dynamics 365 Business Central object type; it's an object or can be declared as a data type (an instance of the object) used to import and export data encapsulated in XML format. Fixed text and variable text formats are also available on an XMLport to import and export data from a plain text file.

XMLports can be developed by the internal designer; you can also develop XMLports using AL language and these can be used in the online version of Microsoft Dynamics 365 Business Central.

XMLport Designer can be found in **Object Designer**, as shown in the following screenshot:

	Type	ID	Name	Modified	Version List
☐ Table		1225	Imp / Exp Data Exch Def & Map		NAVW 111.00
☐ Page		1230	Export Generic CSV		NAVW 111.00
☐ Report		1231	Export Generic Fixed Width		NAVW 111.00
		1232	Exp. Bank Data Conv. Serv.-CT		NAVW 19.00
✕ Codeunit		1501	Import / Export Workflow		NAVW 111.00.00.21836
☐ Query		1600	Sales Invoice - PEPPOL 2.1		NAVW 111.00
☐ XMLport		1601	Sales Credit Memo - PEPPOL 2.1		NAVW 111.00
		1602	Sales Invoice - PEPPOL 2.0		NAVW 111.00
☐ MenuSuite		1603	Sales Credit Memo - PEPPOL 2.0		NAVW 111.00
All		1660	Import Payroll		NAVW 110.00
		5050	Export Contact		NAVW 17.10
		5051	Export Segment Contact		NAVW 17.10
		5151	Integration Records		NAVW 111.00
		5801	Export Item Data		NAVW 111.00
		5900	Imp. IRIS to Area/Symptom Code		NAVW 18.00
		5901	Import IRIS to Fault Codes		NAVW 17.00
		5902	Import IRIS to Resol. Codes		NAVW 17.00
		8610	Config. Data Schema		NAVW 110.00

By using XMLport Designer, we specify all of the XML tag names and their types (element or attribute). We also map these tag names to data structures (tables, records, or fields) in the Microsoft Dynamics NAV and Microsoft Dynamics 365 Business Central database.

We'll create an XMLport to import customers, just as we did in the *Configuration worksheet* section. By performing the same example with both tools, we'll be able to compare them and have some elements to decide which one we should use in our migrations.

We'll be importing the following data into the Customers table:

- Name
- Address
- City
- Salesperson code
- Payment Terms Code

 XMLports works in every client. You could develop your own XMLports, if you like, for basic import/export functionality in the form of a per-tenant app. XML ports can also be used with Dynamics 365 Business Central and developed as Extension V2.

XMLport structure

To understand XMLport structure, we'll create a new XMLport as an example, using the following steps:

1. Open the Microsoft Dynamics NAV Development Environment or Microsoft Dynamics 365 Business Central Development Environment.
2. Navigate to **Tools** | **Object Designer** (or press *Shift + F12*).
3. Select **XMLport**.
4. Click on the **New** button (or press *Alt + N*).
5. XMLport Designer will open with an empty XMLport.
6. Create the structure shown in the following screenshot:

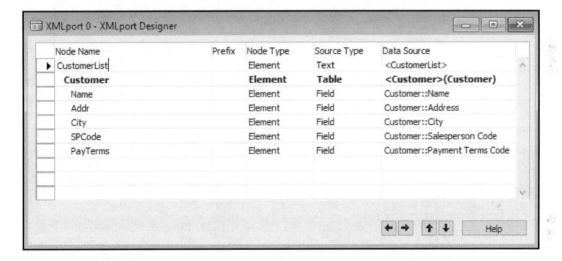

7. Save the XMLport by clicking on **File** | **Save** (or press *Ctrl + S*).
8. Give your XMLport an ID, 50001, and a name, Import Customer Data.
9. Click on the **OK** button.

The additional elements are indented using the icon and not by using the spacebar. There are many deep dive book on C/AL and AL languages, I would suggest *Programming Microsoft Dynamics NAV and Microsoft Dynamics 365 Business Central Development Quick Start Guide*, published by Packt.

The following are the elements of our XMLport:

- The **Node Name** column indicates the tag names that will be used in the XML document.
- The **Node Type** column is where we indicate which type of tag it will be, whether element or attribute.
- The **Source Type** column is from where we can select whether the mapping of the element or attribute is with a text, table, or field source.
- The **Data Source** column is where we indicate the text for the text sources, the Microsoft Dynamics NAV and Microsoft Dynamics 365 Business Central table for the table source types, and the Microsoft Dynamics NAV and Microsoft Dynamics 365 Business Central field for the field source types.

For both the table and field source types, we can click on the up arrow that appears in the column to select the appropriate Microsoft Dynamics NAV and Microsoft Dynamics 365 Business Central data structure. When a table source type is selected, a list of Microsoft Dynamics NAV and Microsoft Dynamics 365 Business Central tables is shown. When a field source type is selected, a lookup field appears for us to select a field in any of the tables selected as a table source type on the XMLport. When using a text source type, the information imported from the XML document is put in a text variable with the name specified in the **Data Source** column. This variable can be used as a global C/AL variable.

Child nodes have to be indented under their parent elements using one indentation per level. To indent the elements, use the left and right arrows that can be found in the lower-right corner of the **XMLport Designer** window. Nodes have to be entered in the exact same order in which they appear in the XML document.

If you check the XMLport properties by placing the cursor on the first empty line of the XMLport and clicking on **View** | **Properties** (or pressing the *Shift + F4* key combination), you'll see a property called **Format**, which is set to **xml**. The other options for this property are variable text and fixed text. By selecting either variable text or fixed text, you'll be able to import/export data in a plain text format rather than in an XML format. Let's leave this property alone for now.

It's also possible to create XMLports using extensions, using a `txmlport` snippet to create them. The development of XMLports with AL language will be illustrated in the next section.

Running the XMLport

We'll be importing a file called `Customer.xml`, which has the following structure and data:

```xml
<?xml version="1.0" encoding="UTF-16" standalone="no"?>
<CustomerList>
  <Customer>
    <Name>GDE Distribución S.A.</Name>
    <Address>Plaza del mercado 192</Address>
    <City>Barcelona</City>
    <SalespersonCode />

    <PaymentTermsCode>N30</PaymentTermsCode>
  </Customer>
  <Customer>
    <Name>Sellafrio S.L.</Name>
    <Address>Rambla de Teruel 153</Address>
    <City>Sabadell</City>
    <SalespersonCode />
    <PaymentTermsCode>COD</PaymentTermsCode>
  </Customer>
</CustomerList>
```

To import the file, follow these steps:

1. Open the Microsoft Dynamics NAV or Microsoft Dynamics 365 Business Central on-premise Development Environment.
2. Click on **Tools | Object Designer** (or press *Shift + F12*).
3. Select the **XMLport** option.
4. Click on the **Run** tab (or press *Alt + R*).
5. The Windows client will open, and the **Edit - Import Customer Data** page will also open.
6. Select the **Import** tag in the **Direction** field.
7. Click on the **OK** button.
8. Navigate to the XML file you want to import and click on the **Open** tab.
9. The file will be imported.

Check the customer list to see the records that have been created by the XMLport. You'll notice that the **OnInsert** and **OnValidate** triggers for each of the fields have been run (each customer has a number, so the **OnInsert** trigger has been run, and the field **Search Name** has been filled in, which means that at least the **OnValidate** trigger for the **Name** field has been run as well).

Writing code inside the XMLport

With an XMLport, you can write your own code to handle multiple situations. You can either write data on multiple Microsoft Dynamics NAV or Microsoft Dynamics 365 Business Central tables or create secondary records while importing the master data.

In our example, you can write code to create new `Payment Terms` if the `Payment Terms Code` filled for one customer does not exist on the database.

XMLports also offer the capability of importing data into different Microsoft Dynamics NAV or Microsoft Dynamics 365 Business Central tables that have a link relation between them, such as in a `Sales Order` table. In a `Sales Order` table, data has to be imported into the `SalesHeader` and `SalesLine` table, which have a header/line relation through the **Document Type** and **Document No.** fields.

The document structure

Imagine we have an XML document, such as the one shown in the following screenshot, that we want to import into Microsoft Dynamics NAV or in Microsoft Dynamics 365 Business Central:

```xml
<?xml version="1.0" encoding="UTF-16" standalone="no" ?>
- <SalesOrder>
  - <Header>
    - <SalesHeader Date="18/01/12">
        <CustomerName>Deerfield Graphics Company</CustomerName>
      - <Lines>
        - <SalesLine>
            <ItemNo>LS-10PC</ItemNo>
            <Quantity>12</Quantity>
            <UnitOfMeasureCode>BOX</UnitOfMeasureCode>
            <UnitPrice>57</UnitPrice>
            <LocationCode>WHITE</LocationCode>
          </SalesLine>
        - <SalesLine>
            <ItemNo>LS-150</ItemNo>
            <Quantity>8</Quantity>
            <UnitOfMeasureCode>PCS</UnitOfMeasureCode>
            <UnitPrice>120</UnitPrice>
            <LocationCode>WHITE</LocationCode>
          </SalesLine>
        </Lines>
      </SalesHeader>
    </Header>
  </SalesOrder>
```

We analyze the XML document tag structure and decide that we'll have to import the data into the `SalesHeader` and `SalesLine` tables, and we design an XMLport with the following structure:

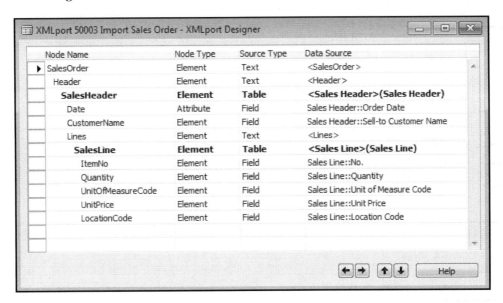

In this XMLport structure, we have used all of the XML tags detected on the XML document and mapped them to Microsoft Dynamics NAV or Microsoft Dynamics 365 Business Central tables (the `SalesHeader` element is mapped to the `SalesHeader` table, and the `SalesLine` element is mapped to the `SalesLine` table) and Microsoft Dynamics NAV or Microsoft Dynamics 365 Business Central fields in the corresponding tables.

Note that the `Date` tag, which has been mapped to the **Order Date** field of the `Sales Header` table, has a node type of attribute. We've designed it that way because, while analyzing the XML document, we can see the `Date` tag as an attribute of the preceding tag, `SalesHeader`:

```
<SalesHeader Date="18/01/12">
```

The following screenshot shows the properties page of `SalesLine`. In the properties of the `SalesLine` tag, which is mapped to the **Sales Line** table, we have indicated that this tag has a link relation with the `SalesHeader` table, we have specified which fields offer the link in the **LinkFields** property, and we have set the **LinkTableForceInsert** property to **Yes**. This means that we force the record on the link table (`SalesHeader`) to be inserted before we start writing anything in the linked table (`SalesLine`):

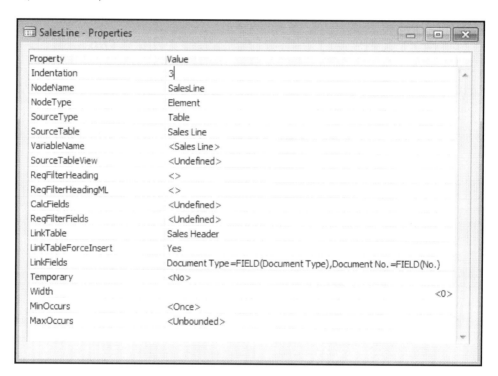

Filling data not included in the XML file

The data provided to you may not be enough. Different software have different fields that are considered mandatory, and Microsoft Dynamics NAV and Microsoft Dynamics 365 Business Central are no different. Therefore, we'll need to write some code to fill in the fields that don't appear in the XML document but are needed in Microsoft Dynamics NAV and in Microsoft Dynamics 365 Business Central to create a `Sales Order` table.

For example, we'll have to fill in the Document Type field in both the SalesHeader
and SalesLine tables. We'll also have to fill in the Type field in the SalesLine table.
In addition, we'll need to find the customer number as only the name of the customer
appears in the XML document, but in Microsoft Dynamics NAV and Microsoft
Dynamics 365 Business Central, we'll have to input the Sell-to Customer
No. field as well. Now, declare the global variables as shown in the following
screenshot:

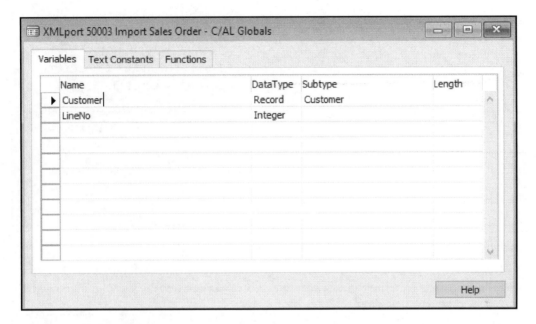

When initializing the Sales Header record, assign Order as the Document Type
field and assign an initial value of 10,000 to the LineNo global variable:

```
XMLport 50003 Import Sales Order - C/AL Editor
23  Sales Header - Import::OnAfterInitRecord()
24  //DEMOXMLPORT .snew
25  "Sales Header"."Document Type" := "Sales Header"."Document Type"::Order;
26  LineNo := 10000;
27  //DEMOXMLPORT .snew
28
```

Assign the `Document Date` field the same value as the `Order Date` field:

```
XMLport 50003 Import Sales Order - C/AL Editor
31  Sales Header - Import::OnAfterInsertRecord()
32
33  Sales Header - Import::OnBeforeModifyRecord()
34
35  Date - Import::OnAfterAssignField()
36    "Sales Header".VALIDATE("Document Date", "Sales Header"."Order Date");
37
```

Find the customer number by setting a filter on its `Name` field and assign it to the `Sell-to Customer No.` field, as shown in the following screenshot:

```
XMLport 50003 Import Sales Order - C/AL Editor
40
41  CustomerName - Import::OnAfterAssignField()
42    Customer.SETRANGE(Name, "Sales Header"."Sell-to Customer Name");
43    IF Customer.FINDFIRST THEN
44      "Sales Header".VALIDATE("Sell-to Customer No.", Customer."No.");
45
```

When initializing the `Sales Line` record, assign `Order` as the `Document Type` field, `Item` as the `Type` field, and the value of the `Line No.` global variable as the `LineNo` field. Then, the `LineNo` increment variable should be used in the next line:

```
XMLport 50003 Import Sales Order - C/AL Editor
60  Sales Line - Export::OnAfterGetRecord()
61
62  Sales Line - Import::OnAfterInitRecord()
63    "Sales Line"."Document Type" := "Sales Line"."Document Type"::Order;
64    "Sales Line".Type := "Sales Line".Type::Item;
65    "Sales Line"."Line No." := LineNo;
66    LineNo := LineNo+1000;
```

Save and compile the XMLport with the number `50003` and the name `Import Sales Order`.

 This is a very fast example of how to write code in the XMLport. As previously mentioned, to get a complete guide on programming for Microsoft Dynamics NAV, refer to *Programming Microsoft Dynamics NAV* published by Packt.

Validation order may change our data

Everything seems to be fine, except the dates, which were set to 01/18/12 in the XML document but have the value 2/16/2016 in the Sales Order table.

This is because, although the order and document dates were first set to 01/18/2012, when the OnInsert trigger for the Sales Header table was run, they get defaulted to Work Date, which was 02/26/2016. How do we know this? You can turn on the debugger (which will be covered in Chapter 11, *Debugging with Dynamics NAV and MSDYN365BC*, of this book) and follow through the code, or just ask a Microsoft Dynamics NAV or Microsoft Dynamics 365 Business Central developer.

Either way, we'll have to change something in our XMLport to prevent this behavior. What we'll do is save the Order Date field in a global variable and validate it against the table field after the OnInsert trigger is run.

Create a global variable named OrderDate as the Date field. Modify the code in the XMLport to insert the highlighted code lines in the Date - Import::OnAfterAssignField() trigger:

```
XMLport 50003 Import Sales Order - C/AL Editor
52 ⊟Date - Export::OnBeforePassField()
53
54 ⊟Date - Import::OnAfterAssignField()
55   "Sales Header".VALIDATE("Document Date", "Sales Header"."Order Date");
56   OrderDate := "Sales Header"."Order Date";
57
```

Also add the highlighted code line in the SalesLine - Import::OnAfterInitRecord() trigger.

When the Date tag is assigned to the Order Date field, we can also assign it to the variable named OrderDate.

When the sales line record is being initialized (it means the OnInsert trigger for the Sales Header table has already been run), we once again assign the saved date to the Order Date, Document Date, and Posting Date fields, and we modify the Sales Header record.

Back in Microsoft Dynamics NAV or in Microsoft Dynamics 365 Business Central, if we take a look at the Sales Order table that's been created, we'll see that, finally, all of the data is correct.

Creating XMLports in the Microsoft AL language

As already mentioned, to use an XMLport to import or export data, you first create an XMLport object, and after that, you can run the XMLport from a page or `codeunit` object.

To create a new XMLport in the AL language, you can use the `txmlport` snippet:

```
Typing the shortcut
txmlport
will create the basic layout for an XMLport object when using the AL
Language extension in Visual Studio Code
```

The XMLport `txmlport` snippet is shown as follows:

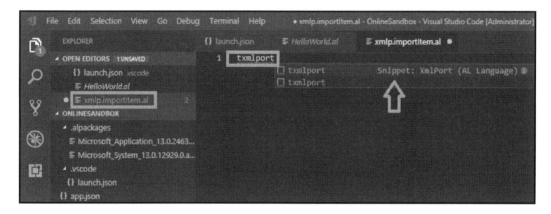

The XMLPort sample definition snippet is shown as follows:

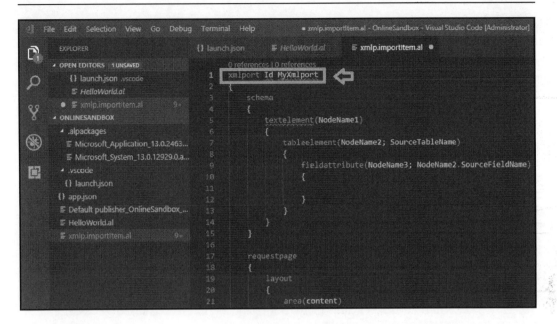

 Here is the link to the XMLport snippet page: `https://docs.`
`microsoft.com/en-us/dynamics365/business-central/dev-itpro/`
`developer/devenv-xmlport-object.`

Writing your own tools

The tools provided by Microsoft Dynamics NAV or Microsoft Dynamics 365 Business
Central to import data only allow you to do so in a very specific Microsoft Office
Excel format, in an XML format, or in plain text.

What if you have the data in a completely different format? In that case, you have two options:

- Manually manipulate the document you have to give it the format expected. This may be a good option for a one-time import process. Manual manipulation of data and formats may lead to errors, but if you just have to do it once, do it carefully, take your time, and check everything afterward. The time consumed in doing all of this work will probably not be as much as developing a tool to import the data, so yes, it is probably a good option.
- Write your own tool to import the data. Make your tool meet the exact format as it appears in the original document, so no manual manipulation of data is needed.

 You can use a **codeunit**, a report, or even a page to write your own code. You'll find several examples in the Microsoft Dynamics NAV or Microsoft Dynamics 365 Business Central code on how to read from files or how to use the `Excel Buffer` table to read from a Microsoft Excel file. Use variables of the `record` type for as many tables as you have to import data into.

We'll not be giving any examples on how to develop a tool to import data as it isn't within the scope of this book. We just wanted to point out that this is always an option although, if possible, it is better to use the tools provided by Microsoft Dynamics NAV or Microsoft Dynamics 365 Business Central as they will probably save you a lot of time.

APIs to import/export data

With Microsoft Dynamics 365 Business Central, APIs could be used to import/export data as well.

With Microsoft Dynamics 365 Business Central, you can create `Connect apps` that establish a point-to-point connection between Dynamics 365 Business Central and a third-party solution or service. Typically, this connection is created using a standard RESTful API to interchange data.

API Setup page

From API Setup page, you can configure the APIs, and there are some ready-to-use pre-configured demo APIs, for example, to import:

- Customers DOMESTIC
- Vendors DOMESTIC
- Item RETAIL

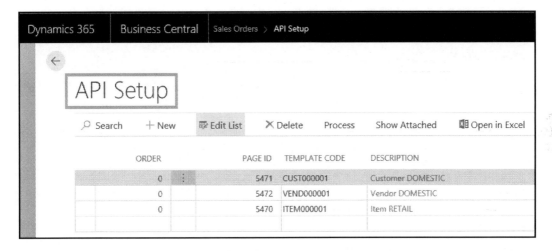

If you click on **Process | Integrate APIs**, the system asks whether you want to start importing the data:

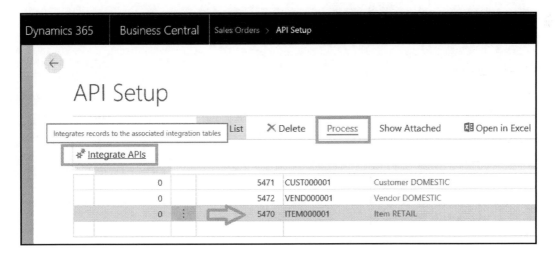

If you confirm to continue then select **Yes**, the system starts to import the data:

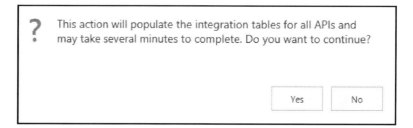

APIs entity pages

We can use a new page type (**API page**) called **entity**, created specifically for this purpose, there are several ready-to-use pages; in the following screenshot, you can see the **Item Entity** page:

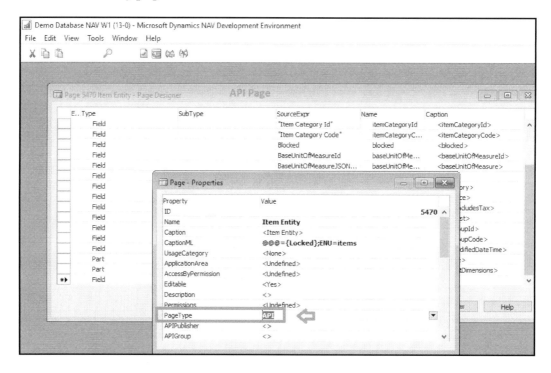

You can find more information about the APIs at `https://docs.`
`microsoft.com/en-us/dynamics-nav/fin-graph/` and `Developing`
`Connect Apps for Dynamics 365 Business Central.`

Converting data from the old system to Microsoft Dynamics NAV's or Microsoft Dynamics 365 Business Central's needs

The company's legacy system will probably have a very different data structure. However, in the meantime, a conversion process must be done. In this section, we'll give you a few tips for converting data to meet Microsoft Dynamics NAV's or Microsoft Dynamics 365 Business Central's needs.

In most of the Microsoft Dynamics NAV or Microsoft Dynamics 365 Business Central tables (including all master and document tables), the primary key uses a code field type. The code field type is alphanumeric and is stored in the database in uppercase characters. You can write either numbers or characters in a code field. If a code contains only numbers, people expect the data to be ordered by a number. But Microsoft Dynamics NAV does not act this way. A code is always sorted by a character, even if it only contains numbers. This may confuse the user, so using fixed-length number codes is recommended. Let's look at this with an example:

Number sort	Dynamics NAV/Business Central Sort	Fixed-length sort
1	1	01
2	10	02
3	2	03
10	3	10

As you can see, if you use fixed-length codes, the way these codes are sorted in Microsoft Dynamics NAV or in Microsoft Dynamics 365 Business Central is the same as the number sort. Therefore, we recommend that you identify those codes in the old system data and convert them before importing the data into Microsoft Dynamics NAV or Microsoft Dynamics 365 Business Central.

Fields particular to Microsoft Dynamics NAV and Microsoft Dynamics 365 Business Central

In Microsoft Dynamics NAV and Microsoft Dynamics 365 Business Central, posting groups are used in the master tables (customers, vendors, items, banks, fixed assets, and other such master tables) to identify which accounts must be used while posting entries related to them. This information may not be available in the old system or may need to be transformed. For instance, the company could be using a system that uses a single account for each customer. In Microsoft Dynamics NAV and Microsoft Dynamics 365 Business Central, just a few accounts are necessary, so you may have to figure out which posting group fits all of the master data best.

You also need to know which fields are mandatory for each master table in order to use its registers. For instance, a customer needs to have the **Customer Posting Group** field filled in to create a new order, and items need the **Base Unit of Measure** field. You may not find this information in the old system, but you need to define how to fill these fields during the migration process.

In general, find all Microsoft Dynamics NAV and Microsoft Dynamics 365 Business Central required fields and the fields required by the company's business logic, determine how they're going to be filled, and fill them during the migration process.

Master data

Master data can be defined as information key to the operation of a business that is often non-transactional but supports transactional processes and operations.

Customers are a good example of master data. Data about customers (their names, addresses, phone numbers, and so on) is not transactional data, but will support a transactional operation, for example, a sales order for a customer.

Microsoft Dynamics NAV and Microsoft Dynamics 365 Business Central have several master data tables, namely, Customer, Vendor, Item, Contact, Resource, and Fixed Asset. Each master data table is the primary table in an application area. The Customer table is the main table in the sales application area, while the Vendor table is the main table in the **Purchases** application area.

Secondary tables, such as Sales Prices, support transactions just as the master tables do. You'll also need to take the secondary tables into account when migrating the master data.

The master and secondary tables that will be used in Microsoft Dynamics NAV and Microsoft Dynamics 365 Business Central have to be identified and a migration plan has to be defined in order to get all of this information into the system.

The migration plan for the master data tables includes the following:

- The table name and number
- The list of fields that will be migrated and their possible values (if applicable)
- The format in which the data will be presented
- The possible requirement of data manipulation before importing it to Microsoft Dynamics NAV or Microsoft Dynamics 365 Business Central
- The tool that will be used to import the data
- The date on which a migration test will be done
- The go-live migration date
- The person responsible for providing the data
- The person responsible for importing the data into Microsoft Dynamics NAV or Microsoft Dynamics 365 Business Central
- The person responsible for testing and validating the migrated data

To import the master data into Microsoft Dynamics NAV or Microsoft Dynamics 365 Business Central, use the tool that best meets your requirements for importing into the database.

Open entries

Open entries are transactions that haven't reached their final status yet and aren't included in the *Open documents* section. You can only post open entries when the corresponding master data is already imported. In a common scenario, the open entries include the following:

- **Customer entries**: It means all of the money each customer owes on the day of the migration—basically, accounts receivable.
- **Vendor entries**: It means all of the money the company owes to each of their vendors on the day of the migration—basically, accounts payable.
- **Bank entries**: It means the money the company has in each bank account.
- **Item entries**: It means the stock the company has in each location on the day of the migration.

- **Accounting balances**: It means the balance that each account has on the day of the migration.
- **Fixed asset entries**: It means all of the company's assets with their initial cost and the amount depreciated, as on the day of the migration.

All of these entries must be posted through their corresponding journal and must use a specific posting date. The posting date must be at least one day prior to the migration date. For instance, if you choose to go live on January 1st, you should use December 31st as the posting date for all of the open entries. This way, we'll start off with a fresh year with the new data and it reflects when you actually start with a new system. The easiest way to migrate the open entries is to use the configuration worksheet described earlier in this chapter.

Customer entries

Customer entries refer to all of the money that each customer owes on the day of the migration. We need to create at least one customer entry to summarize all of the money that the customer owes. If the company wants to control the due dates from Microsoft Dynamics NAV or Microsoft Dynamics 365 Business Central for the open entries, we need to create at least one summarized entry for each due date, or we can create one entry for each pending invoice.

The minimum information needed is as follows:

- **Posting date**: Use one day before the migration day for all of the entries.
- **Account type**: Use the `Customer` option for all of the entries.
- **Account number**: Use the customer code given to the customer.
- **Document number**: You can use the invoice number extracted from the old system, or you can give it a document number, such as `OPENING`.
- **Description**: Give the entry a description. You can use the invoice description extracted from the old system, or you can give a description, such as `Opening Entries`, to all of the entries.
- **Currency**: Leave it blank if the amounts are in the local currency. Write the currency code otherwise. Keep in mind that if a currency code is filled, the amounts must be in that currency.
- **Amount**: The money the customer owes. Write a negative amount if it's the company that owes money to the customer, either because of credit memos or advance payments.

Other information that can be provided are as follows:

- **Document date**: In case you create one entry for each pending invoice, the document date corresponds to the date of the original invoice.
- **Due date**: In case you create one entry for each pending invoice, the due date corresponds to the date when the customer has to pay their debt.
- **Payment method**: In case you create one entry for each pending invoice, the payment method corresponds to how the debt will be paid.

Actually, you can provide information for any field included in the Gen. Journal Line table. However, for migration purposes, the previously listed fields are enough.

Let's use an example to show how to migrate the customer entries. We'll just take the minimum information needed. The following steps are involved when migrating a customer entry:

1. Provide a Microsoft Excel template; we'll use RapidStart Services. The data has
   to be imported into the General Journal to create the customer entries when posted.
2. Create an Excel template for table 81 and include the Account Type, Account No., Posting Date, Document No., Description, Currency Code, and Amount fields.
3. Ask someone in the company to fill in the template, extracting data from the old system using the extraction tools available. You are a Microsoft Dynamics NAV or Microsoft Dynamics 365 Business Central expert, and you may not know how the data is stored in the old system, so don't try to do it yourself.

Remember that your job is to import data into Microsoft Dynamics NAV or Microsoft Dynamics 365 Business Central the way Microsoft Dynamics NAV expects it. It is the company's responsibility to assure that the data is consistent and of good quality.
As a Microsoft Dynamics expert, you are responsible for filling in the fields corresponding to the primary key of the table. In this case, these are the Journal Template Name, Journal Batch Name, and Line No. fields.

4. Once the template is completely filled, it's time to import it into Microsoft Dynamics NAV or Microsoft Dynamics 365 Business Central and apply it.

5. Open the General Journal. The data is almost ready to be posted. Once posted, Microsoft Dynamics NAV or Microsoft Dynamics 365 Business Central won't allow you to delete or modify the created entries, so take your time before posting. Check, check, and check your work. Once you are done, check it again. Also, ask the user who provided you the information to check it. Use this checklist:

Question	Answer
Does the total balance shown in the journal correspond with the total accounts receivable?	
Does your accounts receivable match that of the general ledger A/R account?	
Does each customer owe the amount shown in its journal line?	

Don't check it with the template you just imported; you'll easily get a positive answer. Instead, ask someone in the company to check it with their old system. If you added extra fields to the template, add at least one question for each new field.

Once the lines are posted, new customer ledger entries will be created. G/L entries will also be created. When a new `Gen. Journal Line` table is created, Microsoft Dynamics NAV copies the posting group from the customer card to the `Gen. Journal Line` table. The receivables account found in each posting group is used to determine which account must be used to post the amount each customer owes. Now, add another question to your checklist:

Question	Answer
Group all of the lines by posting group. Get the receivables account for each posting group. Will each account receive the expected amount?	

Since G/L entries will be created, the accounting rules must be followed. One rule says that any transaction must be balanced. The sum of the debit amounts in each line must equal the sum of the credit amounts. The following screenshot shows the **GENERAL JOURNAL** page of the **INVOICES** journal batch:

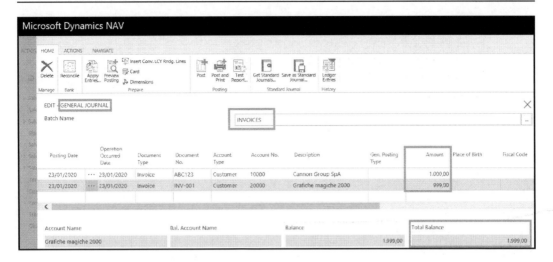

In Microsoft Dynamics NAV and Microsoft Dynamics 365 Business Central, the **Total Balance** entry shown at the bottom of the **GENERAL JOURNAL** field must be **0**.

6. In our example, the total available balance is **1,999.00**. We need to perform an extra step to make it **0** and balance the whole transaction. There are a few options we can use to accomplish this. Let's explain two of these options that we are aware of:

- Fill in the **Bal. Account Type** field with **G/L Account**.
- Fill in the **Bal. Account No.** field with the receivables account on the customer posting group assigned to each customer. In the example, both customers have the domestic customer posting group. In this case, the receivables account for them is **2340**.

Note that there are some accounts that you'll not be able to directly post into. This is because Microsoft Dynamics NAV and Microsoft Dynamics 365 Business Central have a mechanism to prevent accounts included in any posting group from receiving entries directly. You'll have to skip this control in order to post the customer open entries. Go to the account card and uncheck the **Direct Posting** field. Don't forget to check it again when the migration process is over!

Your journal lines will now look like the following screenshot, and the transaction will be balanced and ready to post:

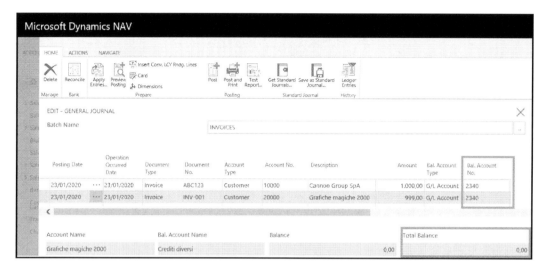

Of course, these two new fields can be added to the migration template to fill them at the outset.

Let's look at the **GENERAL LEDGER ENTRIES** that have been created after the posting process:

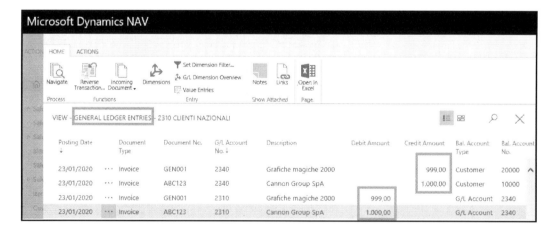

As you can see, the same account has been used. The balance of the account is **0.00**, even though it has four entries. If you run a balance report, you'll see that no amount is shown in the **Accounts Receivable** line. It feels weird, doesn't it? Don't worry, this will be solved once the balance open entries are imported. We are done with the accounts receivable! You can repeat this process as many times as you want.

Vendor entries

Vendor entries are pretty much the same as customer entries. Just follow the steps described in the *Customer entries* section. There are a few differences, explained as follows:

- When you fill in the data migration template, the account type must have the vendor value.
- You have to reverse the sign of the amounts.
- The balancing account will be found in the **Payables Account** field in the `Vendor Posting` group table.

Bank entries

Bank entries are pretty much the same as customer entries. Just follow the steps described in the *Customer entries* section. The few differences are explained as follows:

- When you fill in the data migration template, the account type must have the bank account value.
- The balancing account will be found in the **G/L Bank Account No.** field in the `Bank Account Posting Group` table.

Item entries

Item entries are a bit different from the entries described so far. First of all, another journal must be used—the item journal. Also, you can choose whether the posting of the item entries creates **GENERAL LEDGER ENTRIES**.

The data migration tool has limitations here, so follow the recommendations to work around them.

The minimum information needed is as follows:

- **Posting date**: Use one day before the migration day for all of the entries
- **Entry type**: Use **Positive Adjmt.** for all of the entries
- **Document number**: You can use a generic document number, such as OPENING
- **Item number**: Use the item code given to the item
- **Location code**: Leave it blank if the company is not using locations; otherwise, write the location code
- **Quantity**: Fill in the quantity in terms of the base unit of measurement of the item
- **Unit cost**: Fill in the unit cost in the base unit of measurement of the item

Note that the **Item Journal Line** table contains a field called **Unit of Measure Code**. So, you can use a different unit of measurement and therefore the quantity and unit cost will refer to the new unit. When you import data using RapidStart Services, the OnValidate trigger of each field is run. By default, the fields are validated in the same order that they are declared in the table. The **Unit Cost** field has a field number of **17**, whereas the **Unit of Measure Code** field has a field number of **5407**. The Unit Cost field will be validated before the **Unit of Measure Code** field. If you fill in the **Unit of Measure Code** field in the template, the code will be run. In this particular case, the unit cost will be recalculated and you'll not get the unit cost you input into the template. To avoid this situation, you have to change the default validation order, as explained in the *RapidStart Services* section.

Usually, the automatic cost posting is disabled, since in most scenarios it is not recommended that this functionality should be used.

To check whether the automatic cost posting is disabled, go to **Departments** | **Financial Management** | **Inventory** | **Setup** and open the **Inventory Setup** page. There's a field called **Automatic Cost Posting**. If this field isn't checked, the functionality is disabled.

Even if, in your case, the automatic cost posting must be used, disable the functionality while posting the initial item open entries. The cost will be posted in the corresponding account later on, when the accounting balances are imported.

Run the data migration tool to import the data into the item journal and post it. The item entries will be created.

Fixed-asset entries

Migrating fixed assets is a bit tricky. Here, we are not talking just about the assets that have pending depreciation but all of the active assets in the company. Two types of entries have to be posted—cost and depreciation. Plus, there's more than one account involved with a singular asset. You can post the fixed-asset entries from two different journals:

- The **GENERAL JOURNAL** will post the fixed-asset entries as well as the **GENERAL LEDGER ENTRIES**.
- The fixed-asset journal will only post the fixed-asset entries; the **GENERAL LEDGER ENTRIES** won't be posted.

We'll now explain how to post the fixed-asset entries using the fixed-asset journal. Accounting entries related to them will be posted when importing the accounting balances later on.

To use the fixed-asset journal, you must uncheck the G/L integration for the acquisition cost and the depreciation. Go to **Departments** | **Financial Management** | **Fixed Assets** | **Setup** | **Depreciation Book**. Open the **DEPRECIATION BOOK CARD** page and uncheck the fields, as shown in the following screenshot:

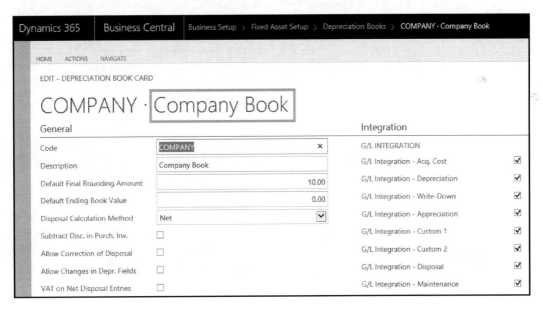

From the fixed-asset journal, the minimum information needed for the acquisition cost entries is as follows:

- **FA posting date**: Use one day before the migration day for all of the entries
- **Document number**: You can use a generic document number, such as `OPENING`
- **FA number**: Use the fixed asset code given to the asset
- **FA posting type**: Use the **Acquisition Cost** value
- **Amount**: Fill in this field with the amount of the original invoice

Import this information using the data migration tool and post it.

From the fixed-asset journal, the minimum information needed for the depreciation entries is as follows:

- **FA posting date**: Use one day before the migration day for all of the entries
- **Document number**: You can use a generic document number, such as `OPENING`
- **FA number**: Use the fixed asset code given to the asset
- **FA posting type**: Use the depreciation value
- **Amount**: Fill in this field with the total amount already depreciated for each asset
- **Number of depreciation days**: Count 30 days for each month depreciated

Import this information using the data migration tool and post it. Don't forget to check the G/L integration again in **DEPRECIATION BOOK CARD**. If you've been using a temporary account in the previous sections, we recommend that you post the **GENERAL LEDGER ENTRIES** for the fixed-assets entries that you just posted.

Summarize all of the asset-acquisition cost entries, grouped by posting groups. In the **GENERAL JOURNAL**, create one line for each posting group. Use the acquisition cost account found in the FA posting group. Use the `FA - Opening Cost entries` account to balance the whole transaction.

Do the same with the depreciation entries and use the `FA - Opening Depreciation entries` account to balance the transaction.

General Ledger balances

General Ledger balances are the backbone of all open entries. When the accounting balances are posted, everything else must match. It is like putting in the last piece of a puzzle. The sad part is that sometimes you find that your last piece does not fit. Don't worry about this right now; at the end of this section, we'll explain how to check whether everything is okay and how to solve problems.

While other open entries could be imported and posted in many iterations, the accounting balances must be posted all at once because the whole transaction must be self-balanced. Follow the steps described in the *Customer entries* section of this chapter, but keep in mind these few differences:

- When you fill in the data migration template, **Account Type** must have the G/L account value.
- If an account has a debit amount, the amount for that account must be positive.
- If an account has a credit amount, the amount for that account must be negative.

Make sure that the amount you are about to post is the same as the sum of all of the corresponding entries. You can run the following reconciliation reports:

- **Aged Accounts Receivable**: This report and the **Aged Accounts Payable** report can be found at **Departments | Financial Management | Receivables | Reports and Departments | Financial Management | Payables | Reports** respectively.
- **Inventory to G/L Reconcile**: This report can be found at **Departments | Financial Management | Inventory | Reports.**

No standard reconciliation report for the bank accounts or fixed assets exists, so you'll have to check it yourself.

Since accounting must always be balanced, if the reconcile reports show any difference, it will mean that some other account does not have the correct balance. Find this other account and you'll find the solution to your problem.

 The features seen here are available in Microsoft Dynamics NAV, Microsoft Dynamics 365 Business Central On-premise, and Microsoft Dynamics 365 SaaS.

Historical data

When moving from an ERP system to another ERP system, such as Microsoft Dynamics NAV or Microsoft Dynamics 365 Business Central, a lot of companies want to import their historical data into the new ERP. For example, companies may want to import all of the inventory entries made for the previous year for statistical purposes. If they start working with Microsoft Dynamics NAV or Microsoft Dynamics 365 Business Central in the middle of a fiscal year, they may want to import all of the G/L entries made in the old system for the current fiscal year.

In Microsoft Dynamics NAV and Microsoft Dynamics 365 Business Central, this kind of data is stored in ledger-entry tables. If you have to conduct a migration of such data, never import it directly into the ledger entry tables. Use journals instead and post the data. This way, Microsoft Dynamics NAV or Microsoft Dynamics 365 Business Central will create the ledger entries for you in a consistent way.

For the item ledger entries, for instance, not only is the item ledger entry created, but the value, item register, item application entries, and other entries are created as well. If a journal is used, all these entries will consistently be created for us and we won't have to worry about anything.

Several journals exist in Microsoft Dynamics NAV and Microsoft Dynamics 365 Business Central. Choose the right journal for the ledger entries that have to be imported. If item ledger entries have to be imported, use the item journal. If G/L entries have to be imported, use the General Journal. Some journals use the same underlying table but have specific values in some fields or use specific fields to differentiate what they're used for. General Journals and Recurring Journals use the same `Gen. Journal Line` table, and item journals and revaluation journals use the same `Item Journal Line` table.

If you have to import data into these tables, make sure the right fields are being filled in and that the right options are used.

A good idea would be to create some journal lines manually, through the interface provided by Microsoft Dynamics NAV, and compare these lines with the ones created through an import process. This way, we'll know whether we are missing something in our import process code and will be able to correct it.

Open documents

The day a company moves to Microsoft Dynamics NAV or to Microsoft Dynamics 365 Business Central, they can start creating all kinds of documents in the system for their daily work, such as sales orders, purchase orders, and production orders.

There may be cases where some documents on the old system have not yet been completed; for example, sales orders that have not yet been shipped, purchase orders that have not yet been received, or production orders that have yet not been finished.

What should be done with all of these documents?

The first recommendation is to have the fewest possible open documents on the old system on the day you start working with Microsoft Dynamics NAV or Microsoft Dynamics 365 Business Central. Make sure the customer calls their vendor, informs the production team, and notifies the shipping team that during this date all open orders should be closed in their legacy system.

For those documents that could not be finished before migrating to Microsoft Dynamics NAV or Microsoft Dynamics 365 Business Central, there are a few strategies you can follow:

- Finish them in the old system and recreate the movements in Microsoft Dynamics NAV or Microsoft Dynamics 365 Business Central. This will mean doing double the manual work and some manual checks, and asking the users to function somewhat differently from how they have been taught to in Microsoft Dynamics NAV or Microsoft Dynamics 365 Business Central. All of this added to the fact that the users may still not be 100 percent comfortable with the new system may lead to some errors. But it may be an option to take into account.

How should the users act if this is the chosen option? When an open sales order is shipped in the old system, you'll have to do a negative adjustment in Microsoft Dynamics NAV or in Microsoft Dynamics 365 Business Central to reflect the inventory decrease. No sales shipment will exist Microsoft Dynamics NAV or in Microsoft Dynamics 365 Business Central though; the person responsible for posting the sales invoices won't have the information Microsoft Dynamics NAV for what to invoice. They'll will have to check the old system and do a manual invoice in Microsoft Dynamics NAV or in Microsoft Dynamics 365 Business Central. This will be done using a G/L account and not the item number since we don't want the inventory decrease to be posted again while posting the invoice. You can think of similar strategies for all other kinds of documents that still exist on the old system and that will be finished at some point.

- Create them in Microsoft Dynamics NAV or Microsoft Dynamics 365 Business Central and finish them in the new system. This strategy may also involve some manual work, extra checks, and acting differently for these documents. You can create all of the open documents in Microsoft Dynamics NAV or Microsoft Dynamics 365 Business Central using any of the migration tools explained in this chapter, keeping in mind the folllowing:

    - If a sales order line, for instance, has already been partially shipped in the old system, only the pending quantity should be transferred to Microsoft Dynamics NAV or Microsoft Dynamics 365 Business Central.

    - In some cases, most of the lines of a document may have been finished, but the document could be open because of a still-pending single line. In this case, only this line should be transferred to Microsoft Dynamics NAV or Microsoft Dynamics 365 Business Central.

    - For tracing purposes, whenever it is possible, try to create the documents in Microsoft Dynamics NAV or Microsoft Dynamics 365 Business Central using the same document number they were given on the old system.

- If the documents are created in Microsoft Dynamics NAV or Microsoft Dynamics 365 Business Central, you'll be able to finish them without having to do any extra work or extra checks. You'll be able to proceed as normal in Microsoft Dynamics NAV or Microsoft Dynamics 365 Business Central.

- You'll probably have to do an extra check and extra work with all of the partially finished documents. Let's imagine you have a partially shipped sales order on the old system. Only the pending lines and quantities are transferred (and finished) in Microsoft Dynamics NAV or in Microsoft Dynamics 365 Business Central. Imagine the company does not post the invoice for the sales order until the sales order has been completely shipped. The sales order (and sales shipment) in Microsoft Dynamics NAV or in Microsoft Dynamics 365 Business Central will not have complete information about the original sales order. To be able to post the sales invoice in Microsoft Dynamics NAV or Microsoft Dynamics 365 Business Central, you'll have to use the sales shipment existing in Microsoft Dynamics NAV or Microsoft Dynamics 365 Business Central, but you'll also have to complete the sales invoice with information that's in the old system.

Open documents can be handled, but they imply extra work. This is actually why our recommendation was to try to finish as many documents as possible in the old system before migrating.

You can also think of some other strategies. For example, you could have created the open documents in Microsoft Dynamics NAV or in Microsoft Dynamics 365 Business Central in a way in which no extra work was needed in any of the processes to actually finish the document.

In the sales order case, you could have created the pending lines for the pending quantities and for the lines already shipped but not yet invoiced.

For those last lines, you could have used G/L accounts instead of items. After creating them in Microsoft Dynamics NAV or in Microsoft Dynamics 365 Business Central, they should be posted. This way, we have a scenario in which the following applies:

- The complete information of the sales order exists in Microsoft Dynamics NAV or Microsoft Dynamics 365 Business Central.
- Posting the already shipped but not yet invoiced lines as G/L entries doesn't lead to wrong inventory information for the items.
- Posting the already shipped but not invoiced lines creates a sales shipment that you'll be able to use while doing the sales invoice (although in Microsoft Dynamics NAV or Microsoft Dynamics 365 Business Central, the sales shipment may be given a different document number from what was given in the old system, which may lead to mistakes or misunderstandings).

Even more elaborate strategies can be used. Think of all of the possible strategies, analyze them, and determine how much work is needed in the migration process (define the data to be imported, the migration tool to be used, and so on), how much work is needed by the users to finish those documents, and so on. After analyzing all of them, choose the one that best meets your requirements.

Choosing a go-live date

If you ask any accountant which date to start working with Microsoft Dynamics NAV or Microsoft Dynamics 365 Business Central, they will always answer January 1st. The reason behind this answer is that, for most companies, January 1st is the beginning of their fiscal year. It has advantages, no doubt, but it also has drawbacks. The year has 364 additional days to work, but limiting yourself this much is not worth the hassle and stress.

In this section, we'll see the pros and cons of going live at the beginning of a fiscal year versus going live on any other date. With all of this information, you should be able to choose the best date in your case and know the consequences of your choice.

 There are no differences between on-premises and online releases in relation to the dates to go-live, they are just technical product differences.

Going live at the beginning of the fiscal year

All companies analyze information at least annually, because, among other reasons, the tax authorities require certain documentation be submitted annually as balance sheets. Starting to use Microsoft Dynamics NAV or Microsoft Dynamics 365 Business Central at the beginning of the year has another major advantage; there's no need to do anything special to get annual information. There's no need to seek information in two different systems and add it somewhere, and then repeat this process every time you need to analyze the information.

We are not just talking about accounting. Accounting information is the easiest to add. This is because accounting is an area where everything is regulated, and so there won't be many differences between the old system and Microsoft Dynamics NAV or Microsoft Dynamics 365 Business Central. No major problem here. But there are other areas where it may be impossible to obtain information from the old system. We'll never have complete information in the first year.

Let's see an example. Imagine a company that sells items. In their old system, the company had no way to classify the items by category, but in Microsoft Dynamics NAV or Microsoft Dynamics 365 Business Central, they do. Now they want to analyze the sales by item category. As you can imagine, there will be no way to have complete information on an annual basis, as the old system did not have this information. Therefore, the only way to get complete information from any area is migrating at the beginning of a fiscal year.

As you can see, the major (and the only) advantage here is having complete information on an annual basis for analytics and statistics purposes.

What are the cons?

A project, by definition, is a temporary endeavor with a defined beginning and end, undertaken to meet unique goals and objectives. Implementing Microsoft Dynamics NAV or Microsoft Dynamics 365 Business Central is a project. At the beginning of the project, you have some requirements, which give you the details of the amount of work needed to accomplish it. Along with the resources available, you can perfectly plan when each task must be completed in order to get the entire job done before January 1st. However, when it comes to software projects, changes in requirements are on the agenda all of the time.

Each project has three main constraints that must be balanced—time, cost, and scope. This is known as the **iron triangle**.

In order to keep the triangle balanced, any change in one of the sides modifies at least one of the other sides. Therefore, any change in the requirements (scope) produces a change in the cost, the time, or in both of them.

If you choose January 1 as the migration day, the time side will be pretty difficult to change. You'll have to wait a whole year for it to be January 1 again. Your other option is to increase the cost side. You can put in more resources to help finish the project on time. But this isn't an easy solution. Resources aren't always available, plus you'll have to teach them what the project is all about. Wouldn't it be easier if you could just go live two weeks later?

Another disadvantage is that the month prior to the go-live date is quite busy, both at the implementer's and the customer's ends. All of the training has to be done, all of the development has to be tested, and the new requirements usually come at the end! Plus, usually the customer is asked to leave as few things pending as possible and complete most of the tasks. This again means extra effort. Besides, December is not the best time of the year to ask people for extra effort. It's a vacation, kids are off school, and people want to spend time with their families.

Okay, there are not that many cons on the list. Just two, but they are important enough to consider another date.

Going live in the middle of a fiscal year

Here, the pros and cons are just the opposite of those in the case we discussed earlier.

The main advantage is that the starting date can be moved. Don't get us wrong; it does not mean that you can play with the date with no consequences. Your customer will always ask you to be committed with a date. But in case of some change within the iron triangle, you'll always have the chance to negotiate a change on the time side to balance the triangle.

It is better to go live a few days late with guarantees than to do it on time if a new feature hasn't been implemented or tested yet.

Choose a date, bearing in mind what your customer's busiest time of the year is and try to avoid it. As we mentioned earlier, the month before the go-live date is a pretty busy month. Actually, the month after it is also a very busy one.

The main con is that, in some cases, the company won't have complete information, on an annual basis, during the year they start to work with Microsoft Dynamics NAV or Microsoft Dynamics 365 Business Central. But don't worry, you also have the option of doing an extra job to mitigate it. You can post historical data, such as accountant entries or item entries, into Microsoft Dynamics NAV or Microsoft Dynamics 365 Business Central. Read the *Historical data* section for more information. If you choose to migrate the historical data, the main con of going live in the middle of a fiscal year is gone and only the pros stay.

So, there is no reason not to choose a date different from January 1.

Summary

Several kinds of data may be imported into Microsoft Dynamics NAV or Microsoft Dynamics 365 Business Central. There are different ways to import that data and a variety of ways to present that data.

Do you remember anything about statistics classes? Let's remember a few of the basics:

```
Several x Different x Many x A bunch = Too many options
```

This means that the migration processes should be carefully designed and planned. Everyone, both at the partner and at the customer end, should know what will be migrated, how it will be migrated, when it will be migrated, who is responsible for retrieving or filling in the data, how the data has to be presented, and what the result in Microsoft Dynamics NAV or Microsoft Dynamics 365 Business Central will be.

The tools that can be used, the ways you can use them, and the kind of data that is commonly migrated have been covered in this chapter. We hope all of this helps you to plan your migration process.

In the next chapter, we'll learn how to upgrade Microsoft Dynamics NAV from the previous versions to Microsoft Dynamics NAV 2018/Microsoft Dynamics 365 Business Central on-premise and how to move to Microsoft Dynamics 365 Business Central SaaS.

7
Upgrading to Dynamics NAV and MSDYN365BC

In the previous chapters, we covered the implementation process of Microsoft Dynamics NAV for new customers or companies that had not used Microsoft Dynamics NAV before.

What about companies already using Microsoft Dynamics NAV that want to upgrade to the latest version? Upgrading to a newer version of Microsoft Dynamics NAV, unfortunately, is not like upgrading Microsoft Office, where it can be done with clicks of buttons. It's a project that has to be planned and executed carefully.

In this chapter, we will explain the migration process that comes from almost all of the previous versions of the application. We will go through the steps that should be done and the tools that are out there to help us execute the upgrade process.

In this chapter, we will cover the following topics:

- An explanation of the upgrading philosophy in Microsoft Dynamics NAV
- A brief checklist of all the steps required to upgrade from the previous versions
- A detailed explanation of all the steps in the checklist
- The tools that must be used in the upgrade process
- The tools that can be used in the upgrade process to make the whole process easier

Why to upgrade?

The possibility to upgrade a customized Microsoft Dynamics NAV installation is very important—the customer always wants to be updated. An updated system is a competitive advantage, but if the system is very personalized, it may not be easy to upgrade to the latest version of the product.

For Microsoft Dynamics 365 Business Central SaaS, the subject is different—the continuous update is the basis of the philosophy of the product itself, born to be in the Cloud and automatically upgraded.

Having an updated version offers a number of advantages:

- Access to new features introduced by new releases of the product
- Possibility to upload fixes and updates
- Maintenance of the support for all updated to releases still under maintenance
- Being updated with the latest technologies available on the market
- If the company has updated and has modern software, it increases in value

For Microsoft Dynamics 365 Business Central, the model is different. If you have a lot of customizations in your old Dynamics NAV installation and if you have a Dynamics NAV release before Dynamics NAV 2016 or Dynamics NAV 2017, it's recommended (but not mandatory) to refactor the code in extensions (this process is not a simple conversion) and divide your customizations into a series of little packages. If you have old-style, monolithic customizations (for example, a horizontal layer that is deprecated for automatic upgrades), it's convenient in these cases to opt for a "new implementation project" by migrating the data.

Upgrading philosophy

Prior to the release of Microsoft Dynamics NAV 2015, an upgrade was a tremendous project that required hundreds (sometimes thousands) of hours to bring you to the latest version.

The upgrade required a lot of time because of modifications done in your database; essentially, the less you modify, the faster the upgrade. In fact, if you need to upgrade from versions prior to Microsoft Dynamics NAV 2013, you may see similar estimates during a new implementation.

Microsoft Dynamics NAV can be used with no customization at all, but that's almost unheard of. That's like buying a Ferrari and only driving it at 25 miles per hour. Once users discover the power of Microsoft Dynamics NAV and how flexible the software is, they will want to make changes so that they have a competitive edge in their industry. It's like the users suddenly discover the power of the force.

One of the greatest selling points for Microsoft Dynamics NAV is the ease of making changes to the software. You don't need other applications to edit the application code since Microsoft Dynamics NAV has its own code editor. There is no need for full compilations of code projects, and there's no need to deploy the new solution since modifications can be done on the fly and they get to the end users right away.

The customizations can be of the following types:

- **Minor customizations:** Adding an existing field to a page or creating a new field in an existing table
- **Mid-size customizations**: Modifying some minor standard behavior
- **Major customizations**: Developing a whole new functionality or changing the way the major standard functionalities behave

When you get a new version of Microsoft Dynamics NAV and a new application code file, a merge process has to be done to ensure that customizations done in a specific version of Microsoft Dynamics NAV are carried out into the new version of the application. The upgrade process can be done automatically with the PowerShell upgrade. This has been available since Microsoft Dynamics NAV 2015.

However, even with the automated PowerShell upgrade, some steps in the merge process and data-migration process will have to be done manually by a Microsoft Dynamics NAV developer because of conflicts in the automated process.

Upgrades prior to Microsoft Dynamics NAV 2013

An upgrade project from versions prior to Microsoft Dynamics NAV 2013 can be an easy task or a large project. It really depends on the amount of modifications that are done and the version of Microsoft Dynamics NAV you are upgrading from. The basic principle is that the older the version, the more involved it will be for you and your company.

To summarize, the steps to upgrade versions prior to Microsoft Dynamics NAV 2013 are as follows:

1. Back up your existing database (of course)
2. Compare and manually merge the codes that are modified to the latest version of Microsoft Dynamics NAV
3. Convert the database to the version you're upgrading to by opening it in the new version of the software
4. Import the merged objects (new version objects with customizations) to your current database
5. Run the processes to upgrade your data

 All of these steps are done manually and some steps are very time-consuming. There are horror stories of developers pulling all-nighters just so they can execute the next step in the upgrade process. It's not a very good use of time and money for both the partner and the customer.

Upgrades after Microsoft Dynamics NAV 2013

With the release of Microsoft Dynamics NAV 2015, Microsoft introduced the PowerShell upgrade, which automates code merging as well as data upgrades. In order to take advantage of the PowerShell upgrade process, you need to be at least on Microsoft Dynamics NAV 2013.

There are some limitations to the automated upgrade:

- If the names of your old variables are used in the newer version as a function or statement, you must change them before you upgrade
- If your old code calls functions do not exist anymore in the newer version, you must verify that the upgrade codeunits migrate data correctly
- If the code you're coming from causes some fields on the table to be dropped, you'll need to make sure that it doesn't
- If your company name uses special reserved characters in Microsoft Dynamics NAV (such as, ~, @, #, $, %, &, *, (), ., !, %, −, +, /, =, and ?), rename the company before proceeding
- Make sure that the system tables are in English

In the following section, we will do a checklist of the steps that have to be taken to upgrade to the latest version of Microsoft Dynamics NAV, from every version since Navision Attain 3.60. We will do that in reverse order; we will first explore the checklist of actions to upgrade from Microsoft Dynamics NAV 2013, which is the minimum version you must be on in order to initiate the automated PowerShell upgrade, and then work to cover the other versions prior to Microsoft Dynamics NAV 2013.

The upgrading-process checklist

As mentioned previously, using the PowerShell upgrade is only supported from Microsoft Dynamics NAV 2013 forward. There are ways to use the PowerShell upgrade if you're running earlier versions, but that is outside the scope of this book. So, the simple rule is to get to at least Microsoft Dynamics NAV 2013 to make upgrading easier in the future.

If you are on older versions, the official documentation tells you to follow the Microsoft Dynamics NAV upgrade guide for the respective versions for details. Essentially, if you are coming from versions previous to X, you will have to follow guide Y, and so on. If you follow all the steps detailed in all the guides, it will take a long time—hence the rule that the older the version you're on, the more time-consuming and more complex the upgrade.

But there is some good news: if you are planning to upgrade from the older versions, you can skip some steps since the ultimate goal is to get to the latest version.

 In the next section, we will look at the steps you need to follow to upgrade from Version 3.60 to Microsoft Dynamics NAV 2018. You can use this section as a checklist for your upgrade process.

How to upgrade to Microsoft Dynamics NAV 2018

The steps that you will have to follow to upgrade from any version to Microsoft Dynamics NAV 2018 can be spread out into three groups:

- Preparing to upgrade
- Upgrading the application code
- Upgrading the data

The first group will be the same for all versions. The second and third groups will be different depending on which version you intend to upgrade to regrading Microsoft Dynamics NAV 2018.

We will first enumerate the steps for the preparing-to-upgrade group, and then enumerate the steps in the other two groups, depending on the version.

Upgrading from Microsoft Dynamics NAV 2013, 2013 R2, 2015, 2016, or 2017

If you're currently using these versions, good for you! The PowerShell upgrade is ready for you to use. There are three steps you will need to follow to get Microsoft Dynamics NAV 2018:

1. Convert the database.
2. Upgrade the application code.
3. Upgrade the data.

Technical upgrades (converting the database)

Before anything can be done, you need to make sure that your database is converted. Simply put, this just means that the foundation of the database has to adhere to the standards of Microsoft Dynamics NAV 2018; to achieve a technical upgrade, it's necessary to perform the steps discussed in the following sections.

Building application objects and uploading the development license

Make sure that your existing Microsoft Dynamics NAV 2018 database works (or you can use the CRONUS Demonstration Database). This is done by using **Build Server Application Objects**, which can be found from the **Microsoft Dynamics NAV Development Environment**, as shown in the following screenshot:

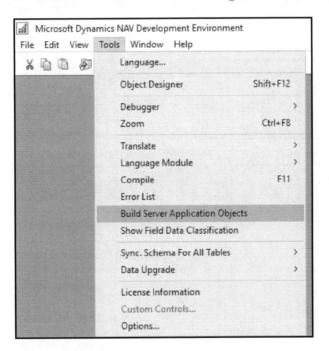

This step essentially converts the code you've written in C/AL into C# for Microsoft Dynamics NAV middle tier.

Upload your Microsoft Dynamics NAV 2018 license using the Microsoft Dynamics NAV Development Environment. The license can be obtained from your Microsoft Dynamics NAV partner or by logging in to **CustomerSource**, a portal for Microsoft Dynamics NAV customers. Once you have the license file (usually with a file extension of .flf), you can upload the license file onto your server by going to **Tools | License Information**:

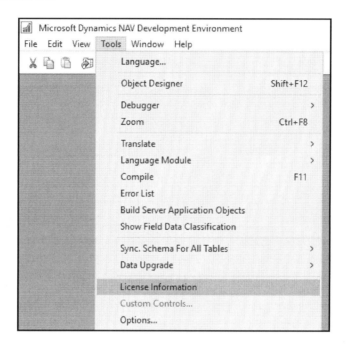

A new screen will pop up. Click on **Upload** and select the .flf file, and then your license will be updated to the latest version.

Converting the database

Start the Microsoft Dynamics NAV 2018 Development Environment and open your old database. A warning message will appear to confirm your actions to convert the database:

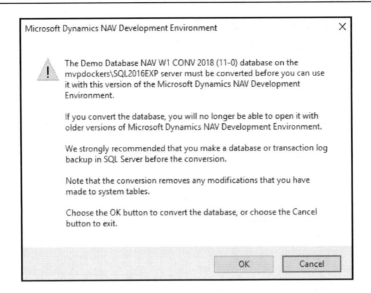

As the warning suggests, make sure that you really want to proceed. There's no turning back!

After the process completes in a few minutes, you will receive the **You must now run schema synchronization to finalize the conversion** message, basically telling you that you're ready to connect the new service tier to the database.

Now, you have your database with Microsoft Dynamics NAV 2013 functionalities, which have the Microsoft Dynamics NAV 2018 foundation (technical upgrade).

Connecting the Dynamics NAV Server

Once the database has been converted, we will need to set up the service tier to connect to the upgraded database.

Start the Microsoft Dynamics NAV 2018 Administration, select the **Microsoft Dynamics NAV Server** that was installed when you installed Microsoft Dynamics NAV, and edit the **Database Name** to the name of your database:

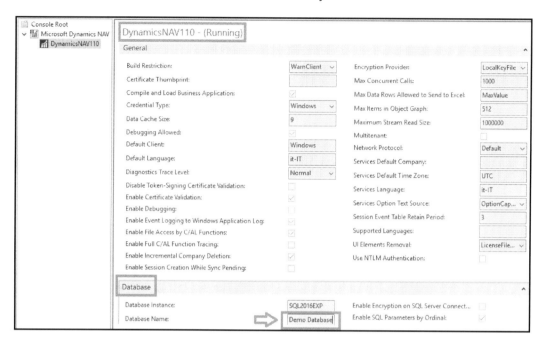

Once you've changed the database the service is pointing to, start the Microsoft Dynamics NAV service.

 If you want further information on how to configure the service tier for Microsoft Dynamics NAV, go to `https://docs.microsoft.com/en-us/dynamics-nav/configuring-microsoft-dynamics-nav-server`. Make sure that the user on the service has sufficient permission on Microsoft SQL Server, otherwise the service will not start.

Once the service is started, go back to the Microsoft Dynamics NAV 2018
Development Environment and navigate to **Tools | Sync. Schema For All Tables |
With Validation** so that the database matches the service tier:

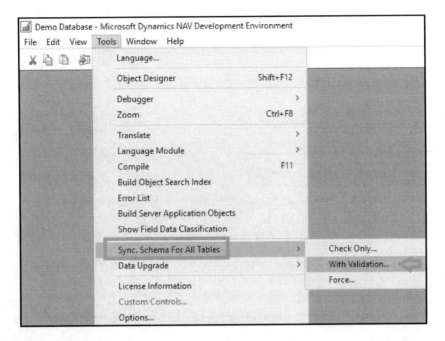

You will be prompted with a message and the ability to select the Microsoft
Dynamics NAV Service you want to synchronize the schema with.

It is also possible to achieve this from PowerShell through the
"**Sync-NAVTenant**" cmdlet with the **Check Only**, **With validation**,
and **Force** parameters (for more information, visit https://docs.
microsoft.com/en-us/dynamics-nav/synchronizing-table-
schemas).

Once the schema is synchronized, click on **Build Server Application Objects**. This will push what we've done to the service tier:

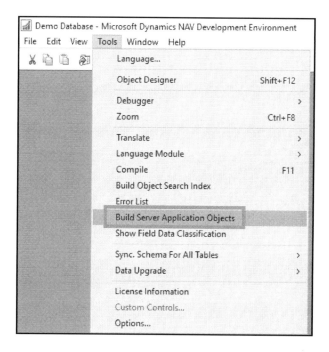

Not too much coding here—and we're done! You've now done what's called a technical upgrade. Basically this is upgrading the platform without upgrading the application code or the data.

Upgrading the application code

After the technical upgrade of the database to Microsoft Dynamics NAV 2018, you will need to upgrade the application code.

 Even after the technical upgrade, there could be a possibility that they have not been tested by the development team with the previous application version. It is highly recommended, if not mandatory, that you perform a complete upgrade—a so-called full upgrade—of both the platform and application files.

The application code is basically where the functionalities in Microsoft Dynamics NAV reside. Without upgrading the application code, you will not be able to utilize the new features with the new version.

To upgrade the application code using PowerShell upgrade, you will need the following:

- The original unmodified Microsoft Dynamics NAV 2013 objects in text format. Note that if you've applied any hotfix to the application code, you will need that version with the hotfix applied.
- Your current modified database objects in text format.
- The objects from the new version in text format.

Before you proceed to export the objects, let's create some folders, as shown in the following screenshot, on your computer to store the files:

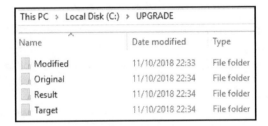

This will allow us to easily see what is being done where.

To get the objects for these databases, you will need the original unmodified Microsoft Dynamics NAV 2013 (with any hotfixes), your current Microsoft Dynamics NAV database, and a new Microsoft Dynamics NAV 2018 database.

If you're using versions of Microsoft Dynamics NAV 2013 R2 and prior, in order to get these objects in text format, you will need a developer's license. In the object designer, you can export the objects by clicking on **File | Export**, and then selecting the proper export format:

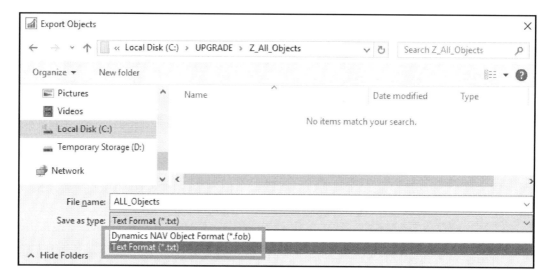

If you're using Microsoft Dynamics NAV 2015 or a newer version, you can use the Export PowerShell cmdlets to export objects and data:

- Export-NAVApplication: Used to break the application into multitenancy port application objects
- Export-NAVData: The surrogate of the old .fbk files (Financials Backup)
- Export-NAVApplicationObject: Used to export the objects from the specified database into the specified file

In this case, the cmdlet we want to use is Export-NAVApplicationObject. You will need the following when you run this command:

- The Microsoft Dynamics NAV service name
- The database name
- The directory where you want to export the object in text format to

Once you've obtained this information, type in the information into PowerShell:

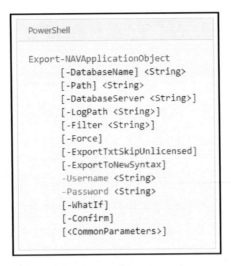

```
PowerShell

Export-NAVApplicationObject
    [-DatabaseName] <String>
    [-Path] <String>
    [-DatabaseServer <String>]
    [-LogPath <String>]
    [-Filter <String>]
    [-Force]
    [-ExportTxtSkipUnlicensed]
    [-ExportToNewSyntax]
    -Username <String>
    -Password <String>
    [-WhatIf]
    [-Confirm]
    [<CommonParameters>]
```

We are exporting the objects from the database that we did the technical upgrade on. You will need to repeat this process for the unmodified Microsoft Dynamics NAV 2013 database (after you do the technical upgrade) and the unmodified Microsoft Dynamics NAV 2018 database, and save it to the appropriate folders that we defined earlier.

You can read more about the Export-NAVApplicationObject cmdlet at https://docs.microsoft.com/en-us/powershell/ module/microsoft.dynamics.nav.ide/export-navapplicationobject?view=businesscentral-ps and some useful PowerShell cmdlets at https://robertostefanettinavblog.com/ 2016/07/11/some-links-about-powershell-cmdlets-for-nav/.

Merging the code

The next step is to merge the modifications that you've made to your existing database into the new Microsoft Dynamics NAV version.

The cmdlet we will use is Merge-NAVApplicationObject. In this example, the files are put into the appropriate folder in a subpath called upgrade.

The following screenshot shows the `Merge-navapplicationobject` cmdlet in action:

```
PS C:\Windows\system32> merge-navapplicationobject

cmdlet Merge-NAVApplicationObject at command pipeline position 1
Supply values for the following parameters:
OriginalPath[0]: c:\upgrade\original\original.txt
OriginalPath[1]:
ModifiedPath[0]: c:\upgrade\modified\modified.txt
ModifiedPath[1]:
TargetPath[0]: c:\upgrade\target\target.txt
TargetPath[1]:
ResultPath: c:\upgrade\result\result.txt

Summary:
  Merge operation processed 1129 application object(s) with a total of 1 indivi
  dual change(s). 100.0% of individual modifications were automatically merged.

Details:
  Processed 1129 application object(s):

    Merged        1 objects  - with changes in MODIFIED that were successfully m
                              erged with any changes from TARGET into RESULT.
    Conflict      0 objects  - with changes in both MODIFIED and TARGET that cou
                              ld only be merged partially.
                              Partially merged objects and corresponding .CONFL
                              ICT files are added to RESULT.
                              This also includes objects that are deleted in MO
                              DIFIED/TARGET and changed in TARGET/MODIFIED.
    Inserted      0 objects  - in MODIFIED that do not exist in TARGET and are i
                              nserted into RESULT.
    Deleted       0 objects  - that exist in ORIGINAL, but do not exist in MODIF
                              IED and are unchanged in TARGET.
    Unchanged  1128 objects  - in TARGET which are not changed in MODIFIED and a
                              re copied from TARGET to RESULT.
                              This also include objects deleted in both MODIFIE
                              D and TARGET and objects unchanged in MODIFIED an
                              d deleted in TARGET.
    Failed        0 objects  - that could not be imported, such as an object tha
                              t is not valid or that contains
                              unsupported features.

  Processed 1 individual changes:

    Conflict      0 changes
    Merged      100.0% of all changes

To see detailed explanation of these, type: "get-help Merge-NAVApplicationObjec
```

You can select multiple files to merge. If there is only one file, you can push *Enter* to go to the next file it's asking for.

After the merge is done, it will list out what was merged, has conflicts, inserted, and removed from the code. If there are any conflicts, they will be kept in the `Conflicts` folder in the `Result` folder. The conflicts will need to be resolved manually.

Importing the merged code

The merged file will be stored in the `Result` folder. You can now import the merged objects into your fresh Microsoft Dynamics NAV 2018 database. You can do this using the `Import-NAVApplicationObject` cmdlet. The files present in the Result folder are shown in the following screenshot:

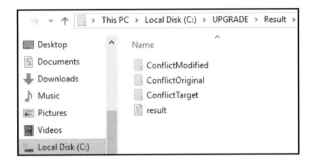

Once the merged code is imported successfully, you will need to start the Microsoft Dynamics NAV 2018 Development Environment, select all the objects, and click on **Tools | Compile**. Any errors that may come up will need to be resolved manually.

Congratulations! You've now upgraded the application code to the latest version of Microsoft Dynamics NAV (in this case, Microsoft Dynamics NAV 2018).

Upgrading the application data

So, we did a technical upgrade by converting the foundation to Microsoft Dynamics NAV 2018, and then we upgraded the application code so that the functionalities are now in Microsoft Dynamics NAV 2018. The last step of the process is to upgrade the data so that it utilizes the Microsoft Dynamics NAV 2018 functionalities.

First, we will need to import the `Upgrade ToolKit` that's included in the Microsoft Dynamics NAV installation files. These `.fob` or object files are located in the `Upgrade ToolKit` folder. Within the folder, you may see the `Data Conversion Tools` or `Local Objects` folder. If you see the `Local Objects` folder, you will want to use the contents in that folder since it's localized for your region.

Import the object into Microsoft Dynamics NAV by going to the Microsoft Dynamics NAV Development Environment and clicking on **File** | **Import**.

The file you choose will depend on the version you're coming from. In this case, the files are from US localization:

- `Upgrade7001100.US.fob`: If you're upgrading from Microsoft Dynamics NAV 2013
- `Upgrade7101100.US.fob`: If you're upgrading from Microsoft Dynamics NAV 2013 R2
- `Upgrade8001100.US.fob`: If you're upgrading from Microsoft Dynamics NAV 2015
- `Upgrade9001100.US.fob`: If you're upgrading from Microsoft Dynamics NAV 2016
- `Upgrade10001100.US.fob`: If you're upgrading from Microsoft Dynamics NAV 2017
- `Upgrade11001300.US.fob`: If you're upgrading from Microsoft Dynamics NAV 2018 to Microsoft Dynamics 365 Business Central on-premise (version 13.00)

The following screenshot shows the `import-navapplicationobject` command in action:

```
PS C:\Windows\system32> import-navapplicationobject

cmdlet Import-NAVApplicationObject at command pipeline position 1
Supply values for the following parameters:
Path[0]: c:\upgrade\result\result.txt
Path[1]:
DatabaseName: Demo Database

Confirm
Import application objects from C:\upgrade\result\result.txt into the Demo
Database database. If you continue, you may loose data in fields that are
removed or changed in the imported file.
[Y] Yes  [A] Yes to All  [N] No  [L] No to All  [S] Suspend  [?] Help
(default is "Y"):_
```

Once the objects are imported, we can run the upgrade by clicking on **Tools** | **DataUpgrade**, and then choosing **Show Progress**.

Once the process is complete, we're done. Welcome to Microsoft Dynamics NAV 2018!

Automating upgrading using PowerShell

As mentioned previously, there's a totally hands-off approach to upgrading to Microsoft Dynamics NAV 2018 using PowerShell scripts. Fortunately, Microsoft has provided sample scripts on automating that can be found in the installation files in the `WindowsPowerShellScriptsApplicationMergeUtilities` directory.

Configuring these scripts is outside the scope of this book. The scripts basically follow the same principle as the steps that are described in this section.

You can read more about these scripts at `https://docs.microsoft.com/en-us/dynamics-nav/automating-the-upgrade-process-using-sample-windows-powershell-scripts`.

Upgrading from Microsoft Dynamics NAV 2009, 2009 SP1, or 2009 R2

We will now see the steps necessary to upgrade from an old version of Microsoft Dynamics NAV to Microsoft Dynamics NAV 2018; the number of steps change according to how old our installation of Microsoft Dynamics NAV is.

You need to get to at least Microsoft Dynamics NAV 2013 in order to get to Microsoft Dynamics NAV 2018. Upgrading to Microsoft Dynamics NAV 2013 is only officially supported from those versions. In this section, we will enumerate the number of steps that have to be performed to upgrade from these versions.

Upgrading the Microsoft Dynamics NAV 2009 application code

The steps that have to be performed to upgrade the application code from Microsoft Dynamics NAV 2009 to Microsoft Dynamics NAV 2013 are listed as follows:

1. Get the objects' versions.
2. Convert the old objects' version files to the Microsoft Dynamics NAV 2013 format.
3. Compare your database objects to the standard objects of your current version to determine the objects that have been customized.
4. Carry out your customizations to the new standard code for the new version of Microsoft Dynamics NAV.

 You can use any generic text-comparing application to do this job. It will be easier, though, if you use an application that's specifically designed for Microsoft Dynamics NAV, such as **MergeTool**.

5. If you have a Microsoft Dynamics NAV 2009 classic client installation, transform your own forms to pages.
6. If you have a Microsoft Dynamics NAV 2009 classic client installation, carry out your customizations on the existing forms and put them into its corresponding page object.
7. Transform your reports to the new report definition of Microsoft Dynamics NAV 2013.
8. Revise and modify your customized code for better performance in Microsoft Dynamics NAV 2013.

Upgrading the Microsoft Dynamics NAV 2009 data

The data and field structure has changed between Microsoft Dynamics NAV 2009 and Microsoft Dynamics NAV 2013. That's why a data upgrade process has to be run. The data upgrade is done in two steps: one still in the old version and the other in the new version.

The data conversion process can be seen in the following diagram:

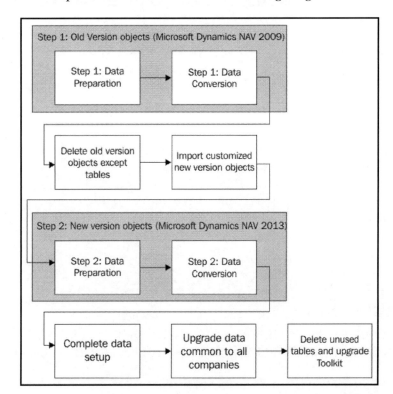

Perform these steps for the data-conversion process:

1. In your old customized database, import the `Upgrade Step 1 Objects` file
2. Run the data-conversion process for the objects of the old version
3. Create a new Microsoft Dynamics NAV 2013 database
4. Restore the database that was being upgraded
5. Import all the customized Microsoft Dynamics NAV 2013 objects
6. Import the `Upgrade Step 2 objects` file
7. Run the data-conversion process for the objects of the new version
8. Delete the `Upgrade ToolKit` objects

Upgrading from Microsoft Dynamics NAV 5.0 or 5.0 SP1

To upgrade to Microsoft Dynamics NAV 2013 from any Microsoft Dynamics NAV 5.0 version, you will have to upgrade to Microsoft Dynamics NAV 2009, and then follow the upgrade steps to upgrade from Microsoft Dynamics NAV 2009 to Microsoft Dynamics NAV 2013.

Even if you have to upgrade to Microsoft Dynamics NAV 2009 first, a full upgrade to the intermediate version will not be necessary. For example, you will not need to upgrade your application code to Microsoft Dynamics NAV 2009. The application code can be upgraded directly to Microsoft Dynamics NAV 2013. You don't need to perform the data-upgrade process while upgrading from Microsoft Dynamics NAV 5.0 to Microsoft Dynamics NAV 2009 since there is no table structure changes between these two versions.

Upgrading the Microsoft Dynamics NAV 5.0 application code

The steps that have to be performed to upgrade the application code from Microsoft Dynamics NAV 5.0 to Microsoft Dynamics NAV 2013 are listed as follows:

1. Import both your customized application code and the standard application code of your current version in a Microsoft Dynamics NAV 2009 database. Compile all the objects. Use those objects that are converted to the Microsoft Dynamics NAV 2009 format for comparison and merging purposes.
2. Get the objects' version (exporting them from the Microsoft Dynamics NAV 2009 database).
3. Compare your database objects to the standard objects of your current version to determine the objects that have been customized.
4. Carry out your customizations to the new standard code for the new version of Microsoft Dynamics NAV.

 You can use any generic text-comparing application to do this job. It will be easier, though, if you use an application specifically designed for Microsoft Dynamics NAV, such as **MergeTool**.

5. Transform your own forms to pages.

6. Carry out your customizations on the existing forms to their corresponding page objects.
7. Transform your reports to the new report definition of Microsoft Dynamics NAV 2013.
8. Revise and modify your customized code for better performance in Microsoft Dynamics NAV 2013.

Upgrading the Microsoft Dynamics NAV 5.0 data

The data and field structure has changed between Microsoft Dynamics NAV 5.0 and Microsoft Dynamics NAV 2013. That's why a data-upgrade process has to be run. However, the data and field structure did not change at all between Microsoft Dynamics NAV 5.0 and Microsoft Dynamics NAV 2009. Therefore, the data-upgrade tools available for Microsoft Dynamics NAV 2009 also apply to Microsoft Dynamics NAV 5.0. The only extra thing you will have to do is convert your database to Microsoft Dynamics NAV 2009. The data-conversion process can be seen in the following diagram:

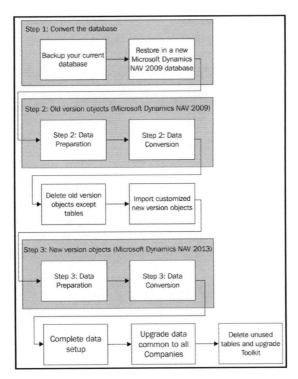

The steps required to upgrade the data are listed as follows:

1. Create a new Microsoft Dynamics NAV 2009 database.
2. Restore your Microsoft Dynamics NAV 5.0 database in the new Microsoft Dynamics NAV 2009 database.
3. Import the `Upgrade Step 1 Objects` file.
4. Run the data-conversion process for the objects of the old version.
5. Create a new Microsoft Dynamics NAV 2013 database.
6. Restore the database that was being upgraded.
7. Import all the customized Microsoft Dynamics NAV 2013 objects.
8. Import the `Upgrade Step 2 objects` file.
9. Run the data-conversion process for the objects of the new version.
10. Delete the `Upgrade ToolKit` objects.

Upgrading steps for Microsoft Dynamics NAV 2013

In the preceding sections, we saw all the steps that you have to follow to upgrade from the older versions of Microsoft Dynamics NAV to Microsoft Dynamics NAV 2013. In this section, we will explain those steps in more detail.

Preparing to upgrade

No matter what your current version of Microsoft Dynamics NAV is, before you can upgrade to Microsoft Dynamics NAV 2013, a migration to Microsoft SQL Server is needed if you are using a native database, as it is no longer available.

A test of the database is also needed before starting the upgrade process. In this section, we will explain how to perform these two processes.

Migrating to Microsoft SQL Server

Microsoft SQL Server (on its 64-bit version) is the only database supported in Microsoft Dynamics NAV 2013. The native database is gone. If you are using a native database in the older versions of Microsoft Dynamics NAV, you should upgrade to SQL before you start the upgrade process to Microsoft Dynamics NAV 2013.

The steps to upgrade to Microsoft SQL Server will not be explained in this book. You can use the official Microsoft Dynamics NAV documentation (`https://docs.microsoft.com/en-us/sql/database-engine/install-windows/upgrade-sql-server-using-the-installation-wizard-setup?view=sql-server-2017`) to do that.

Testing the database

This is a required step to upgrade to Microsoft Dynamics NAV 2013. The steps to test the database are as follows:

1. Open your current database in the classic client (testing the database can be done in any version of Microsoft Dynamics NAV; if you are upgrading to Microsoft Dynamics NAV 2013 from any version prior to Microsoft Dynamics NAV 2009, you can do the test of the database in your current version).
2. Go to **File | Database | Test**. The **Test Database** form will open.
3. Click on the **Options** tab.
4. Select the file's output and enter or browse to a path and filename.
5. Click on the **General** tab.
6. Choose **Normal** to test everything except the field relationships between the tables. If the test fails, follow the workflow for repairing damaged databases.
7. Open the **Test Database** form again (**File | Database | Test**).
8. Choose **Custom** and then check **Test field relationships between tables** to test the field relationships between the tables. This will determine whether there is any data inconsistency in your database. You should determine whether errors detected in this test will affect the upgrade process.
9. Compile all the objects in the database. Repair the objects that are not compiling correctly.

Upgrading the application code

Customers typically want all the customizations that were implemented in their old Microsoft Dynamics NAV databases to be implemented in their new Microsoft Dynamics NAV 2013 database.

To achieve this goal, a sequence of development actions, intended to fully transfer the functionality of a customer's solution to the latest version of Microsoft Dynamics NAV, have to be performed.

Getting object versions

When working with code upgrades, it is important to analyze and process the changes by comparing and evaluating three separate versions of the Microsoft Dynamics NAV database:

- **The old base version**: This is the standard version of the current version of the Dynamics NAV database
- **The old custom version**: This is the old base's database, plus the customer's changes and add-on solutions
- **The new base version**: This is the standard version of the Microsoft Dynamics NAV 2013 database

Follow these steps to obtain the three `.txt` files:

1. Open the standard Microsoft Dynamics NAV database of your current version.
2. Navigate to **Tools | Object Designer** (or press *Ctrl + F12*).
3. Click on **All** to see the list of all the application objects.
4. Select all the objects (click on the upper-left corner of the grid to select all the objects).
5. Go to **File | Export**.
6. Select the destination folder and name the file `OldBase.txt`.
7. Open your current customized Microsoft Dynamics NAV database.
8. Navigate to **Tools | Object Designer** (or press *Ctrl + F12*).
9. Click on **All** to see the list of all the application objects.
10. Select all the objects (click on the upper-left corner of the grid to select all the objects).
11. Click on **File | Export**.
12. Select the destination folder and name the file `OldCustom.txt`.
13. Open the standard Microsoft Dynamics NAV 2013 database.
14. Navigate to **Tools | Object Designer** (or press *Ctrl + F12*).

15. Click on **All** to see the list of all the application objects.
16. Select all the objects (click on the upper-left corner of the grid to select all the objects).
17. Go to **File** | **Export**.
18. Select the destination folder and name the file NewBase.txt. At this point, you should have three .txt files: OldBase.txt, OldCustom.txt, and NewBase.txt.

Converting objects into the Microsoft Dynamics NAV 2013 format

There is a tool called TextFormatUpgrade2013 that is explained later in this chapter, in the *Upgrading tools* section. Right after the OldBase.txt and OldCustom.txt files are obtained, they have to be converted into the format that's used in Microsoft Dynamics NAV 2013.

This will make comparisons to the new standard application code (the NewBase.txt file) much easier.

New custom objects that do not exist in the standard application but only in the customized application (custom objects in the range of 50000 to 99999, or in add-on ranges) cannot be directly imported in Microsoft Dynamics NAV 2013 in a .fob file (.fob is the extension of Microsoft Dynamics NAV object files). Doing so will cause the application to crash as soon as the objects are accessed. For these objects, you have to use the TextFormatUpgrade2013 tool to do the appropriate formatting change, import them in Microsoft Dynamics NAV 2013 in text format, and compile the objects in Microsoft Dynamics NAV 2013.

Refer to the *Upgrading tools* section to learn what exactly the tool does and how to use it.

Carrying out customizations on the new version

As explained in the *Upgrading philosophy* section, carrying out customizations to the new version is actually the main point of the whole upgrade process.

There are a couple of ways to achieve this:

- Rewriting your customizations from scratch in Microsoft Dynamics NAV 2013
- Using any merge tool to follow a compare-and-merge process to finally get the customized code into Microsoft Dynamics NAV 2013

As the implementer, feel free to use the approach that best suits your needs. You can probably go for the rewriting method when just a few customizations exist, and use the compare-and-merge one when the old database has been customized a lot.

Where do we draw the line between a few and a lot? We don't really know.

To rewrite your customizations, you will probably want to use a text-compare tool to compare your old base application code to your new base application code. That way, you will understand what the differences are and you will be able to write them again on a Microsoft Dynamics NAV 2013 database.

To do a compare-and-merge process, you need a tool that allows you to compare three text files at the same time (OldBase.txt, OldCustom.txt, and NewBase.txt) and automatically create the new application code (NewCustom.txt).

In the *Upgrading tools* section, we will talk about comparing the text tools and about MergeTool, which can be used for the purpose of the current section. Refer to them to get a detailed view of how to use them to carry out customizations on a new database.

Transforming forms to pages

The form object type is no longer available in Microsoft Dynamics NAV 2013. The process of transforming forms into pages had to be done when upgrading to Microsoft Dynamics NAV 2009 with an **RTC** (short for **RoleTailored Client**) installation.

If you intend to upgrade to Microsoft Dynamics NAV 2013 from Microsoft Dynamics NAV 2009 with an RTC installation, just skip this section. It's not for you.

For those using a classic installation in any previous version of Microsoft Dynamics NAV, this is a required step. Your own forms have to be transformed into pages. Also, the standard customized forms should be transformed into pages to carry out the customization that's done in the form to the standard page.

There isn't a form-transformation tool specifically for Microsoft Dynamics NAV 2013. The form-transformation tool that was released with Microsoft Dynamics NAV 2009 can be used.

 Refer to the *Upgrading tools* section to learn more about the form-transformation tool.

Transforming reports

The report definition had already changed in Microsoft Dynamics NAV 2009 compared to the previous versions of Microsoft Dynamics NAV. In Microsoft Dynamics NAV 2013, the report definition changes again. So, no matter which version you are upgrading to Microsoft Dynamics NAV 2013 from, you will have to go through a report-transformation process.

The report-definition changes in Microsoft Dynamics NAV 2013 include the following:

- The report sections and section triggers are no longer available
- The request form is no longer available
- The RDLC definition of reports has changed

With the release of Microsoft Dynamics NAV 2013, a tool for report transformation included in Microsoft Dynamics NAV 2013 Development Environment has been shipped. This is the tool to use. It can be used for reports in Microsoft Dynamics NAV 2009 that have both a classic definition and an RDLC definition, and for reports in Microsoft Dynamics NAV 2009, or any previous version, that only have a classic definition.

Refer to the *Upgrading tools* section to get detailed information on how to use this tool.

Upgrading the data

The steps to upgrade your data have been summarized to reflect the most important steps involved in this process. There are many other minor steps that are required to successfully upgrade your data to Microsoft Dynamics NAV 2013. A complete list of all the steps can be found in the official documentation provided by Microsoft, which can be downloaded from PartnerSource or from CustomerSource at `https://mbs.` `microsoft.com/customersource/northamerica/NAV/downloads/service-packs/` `MSDYN_NAV2013RTMDownload_CS`. From here navigate to the **Microsoft Dynamics NAV 2013 Documentation** section and download the **Upgrade Quick** guide.

> Actually, Microsoft Dynamics NAV 2013 is out of maintenance and out of support; only Microsoft Dynamics NAV releases after 2013 are in maintenance.

If you are upgrading from Microsoft Business Solutions-Navision 4.0 or from Navision Attain 3.xx, to do the first data upgrade to Microsoft Dynamics NAV 2009, you will not need a full application code upgrade to Microsoft Dynamics NAV 2009. You really only need to do an application code upgrade to Microsoft Dynamics NAV 2009 for your table objects, and even for those, you don't have to upgrade all your code—only your own customized fields.

Just compare your old database version object tables to the Microsoft Dynamics NAV 2009 standard object tables to determine which fields were created by customization, and create those same fields in a Microsoft Dynamics NAV 2009 database. There is no need to upgrade any other application code.

Upgrading tools

There are several tools that help us in the upgrading process. Some of them must be used at some point in the upgrade process (such as the text format upgrade tool). Others can be used to help us in the upgrade process, but are not mandatory (such as MergeTool). In this section, we will explain them all.

> **MergeTool** is a great product that was published several years ago but is still updated. Today, it's mainly recommended for merging with Microsoft Dynamics NAV. For more information, you can visit `http://www.mergetool.com`.

Upgrade ToolKit

Upgrade ToolKit is included in the Microsoft Dynamics NAV 2013 installation media.

For the Microsoft Dynamics NAV W1 version of Microsoft Dynamics NAV 2013, Upgrade ToolKit only includes two folders: Data Conversion Tools and Object Change Tools. For country versions, it also includes an extra folder: Local Objects.

In both the Data Conversion Tools and Local Objects folders, there are two .fob files that have to be used in the data upgrade process. If you are upgrading an old W1 version database, the objects found in Data Conversion Tools should be used. If you are upgrading any old localized version database, use the objects under the Local Objects folder instead.

 Microsoft Dynamics NAV is used throughout the world. Every country and region has a localized version of Microsoft Dynamics NAV, or a version that complies with the local government or tax regulations. Make sure you utilize the right version for your country.

In *Upgrading the data* section, regarding the different versions of Microsoft Dynamics NAV, we have explained at what point these objects have to be imported and used.

In the Object Change Tools folder, there is a .exe file that helps us transform our new customized objects that have a Microsoft Dynamics NAV 2009 object definition into objects with a Microsoft Dynamics NAV 2013 object definition.

The text format upgrade tool

As part of the Upgrade ToolKit, there is a folder called Object Change Tools, which contains a tool called TextFormatUpgrade2013. This tool has to be used during the application code upgrade process.

There are several object properties, parts, triggers, text in code, and so on, that are no longer available in Microsoft Dynamics NAV 2013. Some of them have been replaced by other properties, parts, or triggers. Some of them have just been removed.

As part of the code upgrade to Microsoft Dynamics NAV 2013, we have to get rid of all the old stuff and get a clean object for the new application version.

The text format upgrade tool does the following:

- Replaces the `LookupFormID` table and page property with `LookupPageID`
- Replaces the `DrillDownFormID` table property with `DrillDownPageID`
- Replaces the text form with the text page on the value of former table properties `LookupFormID` and `DrillDownFormID`
- Replaces `FORM.RUN(FORM::` and `FORM.RUNMODAL(FORM::` with `PAGE.RUN(PAGE::` and `PAGE.RUNMODAL(PAGE::`
- Replaces all form variables declared in the application code with a page variable, taking the same variable ID and name
- Deletes the whole definition of the request form in reports
- Replaces the `UseRequestForm` XMLport property with `UseRequestPage`
- Replaces the value form with the value page in the `MenuSuite` property, `RunObjectType`
- Replaces the `RunFormLink` page property with `RunPageLink`
- Replaces the `CardFormID` page property with `CardPageID`
- Replaces the `RunFormView` page property with `RunPageView`
- Replaces the `SubFormLink` page property with `SubPageLink`
- Replaces the `RunFormMode` page property with `RunPageMode`

We may have skipped some individual replacements, but we are pretty sure that you get the idea. Actually, to summarize, the tool does the following:

- Replaces all references to the former form object with the page object in the following:
    - Object properties
    - Application code
- Deletes the definition of request form in reports

Now, how do we use this tool? Well, it is a command-line tool that can just take one parameter, so it's pretty easy to use! Just follow these steps:

1. Open the Microsoft Dynamics NAV 2009 database.
2. Select all the objects except forms and data ports.
3. Export them in `.txt` format.
4. Open the command-line interface.

5. Execute the following command:

```
TextFormatUpgrade2013.exe <PathToTheTxtFileOrFolder>
```

This can, for instance, be as follows:

```
TextFormatUpgrade2013.exe
C:ImplementingDynamicsNAV2013OldCustom.txt
```

Alternatively, it can be as follows:

```
TextFormatUpgrade2013.exe C:ImplementingDynamicsNAV2013
```

In the second case, we just specified the folder containing the different `.txt` Microsoft Dynamics NAV files (`OldBase.txt` and `OldCustom.txt`). The tool will convert all the text files inside the folder during the same execution.

6. The tool will start its execution. Wait for the process to finish.
7. The result of the execution of the tool will be a text file with the same name as the original text file, but it will be stored in a directory, called `Converted`, inside the directory where the original file was.

You can now use these new text files for merging purposes by following the instructions explained in the previous sections. If you use the old text files instead, any comparison to the new standard application code of Microsoft Dynamics NAV 2013 will result in hundreds or thousands of modifications, purely because of object property changes, even if the object has not changed between the two versions. Using these new files instead will let us just compare real object modifications.

Form transformation

For those who upgrade to Microsoft Dynamics NAV 2013 from Microsoft Dynamics NAV 5.0 or previous versions, or from Microsoft Dynamics NAV 2009 in a classic environment, you have to know that your form objects have to be transformed into pages. Customizations done in the standard form objects have to be carried out to the corresponding standard page object, and new custom form objects have to be fully transformed to new custom page objects.

This process is not new for Microsoft Dynamics NAV 2013. It was already a requirement if you wanted to upgrade to Microsoft Dynamics NAV 2009 in an RTC environment.

There was a *form-transformation tool* available with Microsoft Dynamics NAV 2009. You will find the tool in the Microsoft Dynamics NAV 2009 installation media, in a folder called `TransformationTool`.

There is no form-transformation tool shipped with Microsoft Dynamics NAV 2013. So, if you have to transform forms into pages, you will have to use the tool shipped with the 2009 version.

 This tool permits transforming a Dynamics NAV form into a Microsoft Dynamics NAV page (it is a converter). We will not explain how to use this tool in this book. If you have never used the tool and want to learn how to use it, you can consult the online help that's available at

`http://msdn.microsoft.com/en-us/library/dd338789.aspx.`

Report transformation

With Microsoft Dynamics NAV 2009, a new way of reporting was introduced: **Reporting Definition Language Client-side (RDLC)**. The old way of reporting—the classic way—was kept for compatibility reasons so that we can use it with the classic client. That is, in Microsoft Dynamics NAV 5.0 and previous versions, only classic reporting was available; in Microsoft Dynamics NAV 2009, hybrid reporting was available (reporting in classic and RDLC at the same time); now, in Microsoft Dynamics NAV 2013, only RDLC reporting is available.

For RDLC in Microsoft Dynamics NAV 2009, classic sections were the base of constructing the layout of the report, and Report Viewer 2008 was used. In Microsoft Dynamics NAV 2013, the base of the RDLC layout is not the classic report structure anymore (because it has disappeared). The new report structure is the report dataset. Along with that, RDLC 2005 (the RDLC version used in Microsoft Dynamics NAV 2009) has been upgraded to RDLC 2008, and the report viewer that's used is the 2010 version.

All of this means that the old reports done in the previous versions of Microsoft Dynamics NAV 2013 will not run anymore in the new version. They have to be converted to the new report format and structure.

The method of upgrading reports to Microsoft Dynamics NAV 2013 differs for hybrid reports (those that have both a native Dynamics NAV and a RDLC definition) and classic reports (those that only have a native Microsoft Dynamics NAV definition).

Upgrading hybrid reports

The steps required to upgrade a hybrid report to Microsoft Dynamics NAV 2013 are as follows:

1. Export the hybrid report in `.txt` format from the Microsoft Dynamics NAV 2009 database.
2. Use the text-format-upgrade tool described earlier in this section to transform its definition into a Microsoft Dynamics NAV 2013 format.
3. Import them into the Microsoft Dynamics NAV 2013 database.
4. Compile the imported reports. The reports must be compiled in order to finish the report transformation. If there is any report that does not compile because it refers to tables, fields, or any structure that does not exist in Dynamics NAV 2013 anymore, make the report compile by redefining it.
5. In Microsoft Dynamics NAV 2013's Development Environment, go to **Tools | Upgrade Report**. When the **Upgrade Report** tool is run, the report data is upgraded to a valid Microsoft Dynamics NAV 2013 dataset definition and the layout is upgraded to RLDC 2008.
6. Save and compile the report.

Upgrading classic reports

The steps required to upgrade a classic report to Microsoft Dynamics NAV 2013 are as follows:

1. Export the classic report in `.txt` format from the Microsoft Dynamics NAV 2009 database.
2. Use the text-format-upgrade tool described earlier in this section to transform its definition into a Microsoft Dynamics NAV 2013 format.
3. Import them into the Microsoft Dynamics NAV 2013 database.
4. Compile the imported reports. The reports must be compiled in order to finish the report transformation. If there is any report that does not compile because it refers to tables, fields, or any structure that does not exist in Dynamics NAV 2013 anymore, make the report compile by redefining it.
5. In Microsoft Dynamics NAV 2013's Development Environment, go to **Tools | Upgrade Report**.

6. When the upgrade report tool is run, the report data is upgraded to a valid Microsoft Dynamics NAV 2013 dataset definition, the request form is deleted, and the RDLC 2008 layout is generated by using the layout suggestion tool.

7. Manually adjust the RDLC layout in Visual Studio.

8. Manually create a request page if needed, or use the form-transformation tool to transform the former request form into a request page.

9. Save and compile the report.

Comparing text tools

To upgrade your application code to a new version of Microsoft Dynamics NAV, you have to compare your customized application code with the old original standard application code to determine which customizations have been made and where they have been made.

A second comparison has to be done between the old original standard application code and the new original standard application code to determine what differences exist between these two versions so that we can decide whether the old customized objects can still be used (if the original object hasn't changed) or if the customization has to be manually carried out to the new version of Microsoft Dynamics NAV.

There are several generic compare-text tools that you can use for this purpose. A web search will present you with different tools that you can use. We will not explain any of these tools here. We just want to point out that you can use any of them for application code-upgrade purposes.

MergeTool

MergeTool is a third-party application that can be used for free by Microsoft partners. This application is developed inside Microsoft Dynamics NAV. Using this application to help you out in your application code upgrade will probably save you a lot of time in analyzing text, as it will let you concentrate on the real customizations.

When using any generic text-compare tool, you have to deal not only with customizations, but also with object structure changes that may exist between a Microsoft Dynamics NAV version and its preceding versions. Dealing with object structure changes is useless.

Downloading MergeTool

MergeTool can be downloaded from `http://www.mergetool.com/default.html`. In the download section of the web page, you will find a ZIP or RAR file containing all the objects of the application. Download it onto your hard disk and unzip the file.

The version of MergeTool at the time of writing was MGT1.50.24. This version contains four `.fob` files that can be imported into Microsoft Dynamics NAV 2013: two help files, one Microsoft Visio file, and one `README` file.

Installing MergeTool

The steps to install MergeTool are as follows:

1. Create a new Microsoft Dynamics NAV 2013 database.
2. Open the development environment for the new database.
3. Open the **Object Designer** page by navigating to **Tools | Object Designer** or by pressing *Shift + F12*.
4. Navigate to **File | Import**.
5. Select the `MGT1.30.37 NAV7 B33451.fob` file.
6. A message will be pop up saying that all the objects have been examined and no conflicts were found. Choose **Yes** to import all the objects.

The steps to install the help files for MergeTool are as follows:

1. Copy the `addin_e.hh` file into the `C:Program FilesMicrosoft Dynamics NAV70ServiceENU` folder in the server where the Microsoft Dynamics NAV 2013 services are installed.
2. Copy the `addin_e.chm` file to the `C:Program FilesMicrosoft Dynamics NAV70RoleTailored Clienten-US` folder in all the PCs where the Microsoft Dynamics NAV 2013 client is installed.
3. Restart the Microsoft Dynamics NAV 2013 service.
4. Restart the Microsoft Dynamics NAV 2013 client.

Using MergeTool

MergeTool allows us to compare our customized application code with the old standard application code and merge the customizations with the new standard application code thus creating new, customized application code.

Follow the steps explained in the *Upgrade steps in detail* section and then perform these steps:

1. Get the object's version to get the `OldBase.txt`, `OldCustom.txt`, and `NewBase.txt` files
2. Open your Microsoft Dynamics NAV MergeTool database
3. Open the MergeTool menu by navigating to **Departments | MergeTool**

In this menu, you will find everything that can be done with MergeTool. We will start by importing the old base version of our current Microsoft Dynamics NAV database (that is, the `OldBase.txt` file).

Importing the old base version

To import the old base version, follow these steps:

1. Click on **Version**.
2. Click on the **Import Object Text File** process option that appears on the ribbon bar.
3. Select the `OldBase.txt` file, give this version a name in the **Version** field, and put a check mark on **Navision Version**.
4. Click on **OK**. The text file will be imported.
5. In the example we are using, the old version is a Microsoft Dynamics NAV 2009 R2 database. This version has, **4232** different objects (excluding forms and data ports), which get reflected in the version list of MergeTool once the file is completely imported.

Importing the old custom version

We will now import our old customized database, that is, the `OldCustom.txt` file. The steps are as follows:

1. Click on the **Import Object Text File** process option that appears on the ribbon bar.
2. Select the `OldCustom.txt` file, give this version a name in the **Version** field, select **OLDBASE** in the **Based on Navision Version Code** field and also in the **Compare Old Version** field, and select **Delete Equal Objects**.
3. Click on **OK**. The text file will be imported.

When importing the old custom version, we have selected a version in the **Based on Navision Version Code** and **Compare Old Version** fields and have also selected **Delete Equal Objects** because this will allow us to concentrate only on the customizations done on the base code.

By selecting **Based on Navision Version Code**, the import process will skip those objects in our custom version that do not exist in the base version. The objects that exist in a custom version but do not exist in its base version are objects that have been created for the customization. You don't need to compare them to anything; you will just import those in the new custom database. That's why we skip them.

By selecting **Compare Old Version** and **Delete Equal Objects**, the import process will first compare the custom objects against those in the base version and, if they have not changed at all, will skip them. As we saw in the first import process, a Microsoft Dynamics NAV database has thousands of objects. In a customization, probably not all of them have been customized. Probably only a few dozen, or even a few hundred, objects have been modified, but not all 7,000 objects are customized. We want to skip objects that have not been modified because we want to concentrate only on those that have actually been modified.

Once the old custom version has been imported, compared against the old base version, and equal objects have been deleted, our old custom version has only 927 objects. Only 927! We don't need to go through all 4,232 objects for the application code upgrade. We only need to concentrate on those 927 that have actually been modified. That's great! That will save us a lot of time!

But we can further reduce these 927 objects. How can we do that? Well, sometimes it happens that you open an object in design mode through the **Object Designer** page because you want to check something. You finally leave the object without modifying anything at all, but the editor asks you whether you want to save the changes made to the object. If you say yes, the object properties, such as Date and Time, will be modified. Since there is something that has changed, even if it's just those object properties, MergeTool determines that you will have to compare and merge those objects. Wouldn't it be great to be able to delete those objects from the comparison so that only real modifications have to be compared and merged?

This is possible with MergeTool. That's cool, right?

Let's look at how we can delete objects that have only object property changes (date, time, and version list):

1. Navigate to **Departments | MergeTool | Versions**
2. Click on the **Navigate** tab that can be found on the ribbon bar
3. Click on **Find Object Properties Changes**
4. The **Find Object Properties Changes** process will open
5. Select the **OLDCUSTOM** version in the **Version** field
6. Select **Delete Objects**

If we go back to the **Versions** list, only **914** objects are on the **OLDCUSTOM** version now. This means that 13 objects only had object property changes and have been removed. Great! As we go on, we will be saving more and more time. Now, we will only have to concentrate on 914 objects!

Importing the new base version

Now, it is time to import the new base version, that is, the `NewBase.txt` file:

1. Click on the **Import Object Text File** process option that appears on the ribbon bar.
2. Select the `NewBase.txt` file, give this version a name in the **Version** field, place a checkmark on **Navision Version**, and select **OLDCUSTOM** in the **Must Exist** in **Version** field.
3. Click on **OK**. The text file will be imported.
4. When importing the new base version, we have selected a version in the **Must Exist in Version** field because this will allow us to concentrate only on the customizations done on the base code. In the previous steps, we saw that only 914 objects were really modified or new in the custom application code used in that example. For the new version, we only want to import these 914 objects. Microsoft Dynamics NAV 2013 has 4,053 objects, but we only want to focus on the 914 that were modified or are new in our custom version. For the rest of the objects, we will use the standard objects of Microsoft Dynamics NAV 2013. By selecting the **OLDCUSTOM** version in the **Must Exist in Version** field, we are telling MergeTool that we only want to import the new objects of the new version if it was an object modified in our custom version.

5. Only 182 objects are shown in the new base version. This means that 732 objects that were modified in the old custom version do not exist anymore in Microsoft Dynamics NAV 2013, or they were new customized objects.

6. We have just a few objects to concentrate on. Our customizations on those objects will have to be carried out to the new application code version. To do so, the first thing we need to know is whether the standard code for these 182 objects has been modified at all. If there are no modifications in the standard code, carrying out our customizations will be easy. If there are modifications in the standard code, we will have to take a closer look to see how to carry out our customizations to the new objects.

Comparing the old base and new base versions

Let's first compare the old base and new base versions:

1. On the ribbon bar, click on **Compare Objects**
2. Select **OLDBASE** in the **Old Version** field
3. Select **NEWBASE** in the **New Version** field
4. Click on **OK**. The compare process will start
5. A message saying that the versions have been compared will appear once the compare process has finished
6. Click on **OK**

Take a new look at the **Version** list. Contrast fields have been updated. A contrast is a group of code lines that have some differences (change in code, added code, or deleted code) between the two versions. MergeTool does not treat modifications on a line-by-line basis. It actually treats modifications as groups of line codes.

Imagine that the modification in an object consists of creating a new function with hundreds of code lines and a call to that function from within the same object. There aren't hundreds of modifications for the hundreds of code lines being added. There are only two modifications: added code for the definition of the function, and added code for the call to that function. It's easier to deal with two modifications than with hundreds of modifications. And that's what MergeTool does.

MergeTool groups contrasts in **Contrast Headers**. There is one contrast header per object in the new base version. Each contrast header may have several contrasts inside.

NEWBASE gets compared against **OLDBASE**, and it tells us that there are **182** contrasts:

- **Equal Contrast Headers - 9**: These contrasts correspond to **9** whole objects out of the 182 new base version's contrasts that have not changed at all.
- **Changed Contrast Headers - 168**: These contrasts correspond to 168 objects that have changed.
- **New or Added Contrast Headers - 5**: These contrasts correspond to **5** objects that are new in **NEWBASE** (they did not exist in **OLDBASE**). Even if they did not exist in **OLDBASE**, they did actually exist in **OLDCUSTOM**, otherwise they would not be on **NEWBASE** because of the import options we have selected. Standard objects that were not in **OLDBASE** but were in **OLDCUSTOM** now remain the same in **NEWBASE**. This may seem weird, but it's not. They probably correspond to hotfixes or new functionalities released by Microsoft that we have applied to our customized version of Microsoft Dynamics NAV, and that were not part of the original standard code for our old version of the application.

We can navigate to the contrast to analyze the differences. To do so, click on the type of contrast you want to analyze (for all, click on the **ContrastHeaders** field; for equal contrasts, click on the **Equal Contrast Headers** field; for changed contrasts, click on the **Changed Contrast Headers** field; for new contrasts, click on the **New Contrast Headers** field) and the list of contrasts will be shown. Select the specific contrast you want to analyze and click on **Lines** (log), which can be found on the ribbon bar.

The code lines in green remain the same in both the versions (**Line Status** is **Equal**). The code lines in red tell us what the code was in the old version (**Line Status** is **Before**). The code lines in orange tell us what the code is in the new version (**Line Status** is **After**).

In the example, a line of code has been replaced by three lines of code. The three lines of code are involved in the change, but there is only one change: a local variable has been defined for an action in **Page 143 Posted Sales Invoices**.

In the **Contrast Headers** list, we can see how many groups of changes exist between the two versions. In the example, we have 182 contrast headers (objects) with a total of 4,018 groups of changes: 330 changes in properties groups, 2,368 changed groups, 893 inserted groups, and 427 deleted groups.

We definitely do not want to deal with all 4,018 groups of changes by manually looking at all the differences in code. We want MergeTool to deal with them automatically and just let us decide on those that cannot be merged automatically by the application. That's what we are going to do in the last part of this section.

The following screenshot shows MergeTool in action (**Manual Merge Form**):

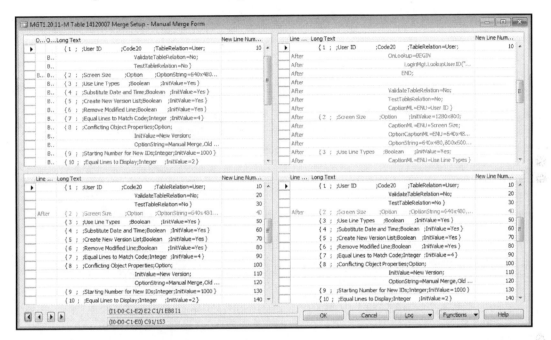

Merging all versions

We will go back to the version list page of MergeTool and we will follow these steps:

1. Click on the **Merge Version** action that can be found on the ribbon bar.
2. Select **OLDBASE** in the **Old Base** field.
3. Select **NEWBASE** in the **New Base** field.
4. Select **OLDCUSTOM** in the **Custom Version** field.
5. Write **NEWCUSTOM** in the **New Custom Version** field.
6. Give this new version a description in the **New Custom Version Description** field.

7. Put a check mark in the **Skip if Manual Merge** field. We select this option because on the first merge, we want MergeTool to automatically merge everything that can be merged without our intervention. In the second run, we will uncheck this option to deal with those changes that MergeTool cannot automatically deal with.

8. Leave the rest of the options as their default values.

9. Click on **OK**. The merge process will start.

10. When the merge process has completed, a message will appear saying that the **NEWCUSTOM** version has been created, and the number of objects that require manual merging.

11. Click on **OK**.

If we go back to the MergeTool version list, we will see that a new version, **NEWCUSTOM**, has been created with a few objects – the ones that were completely merged automatically.

We will now do a second run of the merge process, unselecting the **Skip if Manual Merge** field. Once the merge process starts again, the process will prompt a page with all the versions (the old base code, the old custom code, the new base code, and the new merged custom code) when a manual merge is required. After MergeTool merges the changes to the new merged custom code, we have to decide whether we accept the merge or we want to do any extra modification. Let's see an example of this.

The first subpage corresponds to the old base code. Earlier, we had the assignment of a value to a field, then a record was inserted into the database, and finally the call to a function to store document dimensions.

The second subpage corresponds to the new base code. In the new application code, there is an extra code line between the assignment of a value to a field and the insertion into the database, and the call to a function to store document dimensions has disappeared.

The third subpage corresponds to the old custom base code. To see the whole customization, we will have to scroll through the subpage. The customization consists of a group of 11 code lines, which has been added between the assignment of a value to a field and the insertion of the record into the database.

The fourth subpage corresponds to the new custom code. There is a conflict. The custom code inserts the code lines in a specific place, and the new code inserts different code lines in the same place. MergeTool cannot automatically merge this because the tool cannot decide whether only the custom-added code lines have to be inserted, only the new code lines have to be inserted, or both the added code lines have to be inserted in the new custom version—and, in this case, in which order.

Let's take a better look at the fourth subpage (The **Merge Subform New Custom** section), at the proposal made by MergeTool:

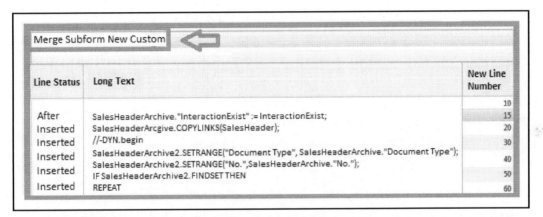

As you can see, the merge proposal consists of using only the customized code. Even the old call to the `StoreDocDim()` function has been used in the custom-merged code. MergeTool has made this proposal because of the **Default Manual Merge Lines** option used in the merge options, which we left to its default value, **Custom**. That is, we have actually told MergeTool to use the custom version for the first proposal when merging lines manually.

In this particular example, we actually want both the groups of added lines (the ones coming from the old customization version and the ones coming from the new base version) to be added to the new customized version, and we want the call to the function to be deleted from the new customized version, as this function is no longer available in Microsoft Dynamics NAV 2013 because of the dimension functionality redesign.

The way to move the code lines from any version to the new customized version in MergeTool is through the **New Line Number** field, which can be found in any of the subpages. If there is a number in the **New Line Number** field in any line code of the three first subpages, which correspond to the three code versions used for the merge process, that line will show up on the fourth subpage, in the new customized code. The number used in this field will determine the order in which the code lines will be shown in the fourth subpage.

In this particular example, we want to do the following:

1. Delete the **New Line Number** field values on the third subpage (custom version) for lines 140 to 170. That is, we do not want the call to the StoreDocDim() function to be in our new customized version.

2. Leave the proposed **New Line Number** field values as is, on the third subpage for lines 20 to 120. That is, we want our 11 customized code lines to be in our new customized version.

3. Give a value of **15** to the **New Line Number** field on the second subpage (new version) to the second line:

   ```
   SalesHeaderArchive.COPYLINKS(SalesHeader);
   ```

4. To do so, we will use the functions found on the **Actions** tab of the ribbon bar.

5. In the **New Lines** action, there are several functions to assign a value to the **New Line Number** field to code lines in the second subpage, the one corresponding to the new base version.

6. In the **Custom Lines** action, we will find the same functions, but they apply to the code lines in the third subpage, the one corresponding to the old custom version.

7. The final result is the one that can be seen in the preceding screenshot (**Merge Subform New Custom**).

8. In the new custom version, we have our customized code and we have the code line added in the new version, and the call to the StoreDocDim() function is not there anymore.

9. Once we are done, we will click **OK**, and MergeTool will move on to the next merge conflict.

Exporting the new custom version

Once we are done with the whole merge process and we have a good, new custom version, we can go back to the MergeTool versions list and export this version as a .txt file. To do so, there is an action in the **Actions** tab of the ribbon bar, called **Export Object Text File**. Select **NEWCUSTOM** as the version to export and select a destination folder and file name.

Importing the new custom version to a Microsoft Dynamics NAV 2013 database

The last part of the merge process is to get a new database, with all the new objects, and import into that database the .txt file we have just exported with the customizations merged into the new code version. After importing the .txt file, we will have to compile all the objects and solve any additional issues that may exist.

And that's it! We have brand new, full application code with standard objects for all those objects that we have not modified in the old version and with the customizations carried out to this new version.

We still have to import the new objects that we created in our customization into this new database. To do so, we will first have to do the following:

- Transform form objects to pages
- Transform reports to the new RDLC definition

Upgrading from Microsoft Dynamics NAV to Microsoft Dynamics 365 Business Central on-premise

Now, let's discuss how to migrate from Microsoft Dynamics NAV to Microsoft Dynamics 365 Business Central on-premise.

On-premises versus online environments – differences

In upgrades with an on-premise architecture, you have complete control over your infrastructure's upgrades (hardware and software), and you can decide on what type of upgrade to apply and when to apply it. In an online architecture, you could have some aspects of the infrastructure where upgrades are not completely under your control, but they can be deployed globally from the solution provider (in this case, Microsoft) and the upgrades are managed automatically (a continuous upgrade detected).

 Here's a comparison between the different types of Microsoft Dynamics NAV/Microsoft Dynamics 365 Business Central on-premise installations (pros and cons). We will talk about these differences in `Chapter 13`, *Microsoft Dynamics 365 Business Central*.

In the next few paragraphs, we will talk about the upgrade to Microsoft Dynamics 365 Business Central on-premise, starting from an older release of Microsoft Dynamics NAV.

Upgrading to Microsoft Dynamics 365 Business Central on-premise

In this scenario, we want to check the steps required to upgrade from Microsoft Dynamics NAV to Microsoft Dynamics 365 Business Central on-premise. In this case, we want to upgrade starting from Microsoft Dynamics NAV 2018. From older versions of Microsoft Dynamics NAV, obviously the steps seen in the previous paragraphs are valid, up to Microsoft Dynamics NAV 2018.

 We want to start from Microsoft Dynamics NAV 2018 because Microsoft Dynamics 365 Business Central is the evolution of NAV; I think it's an upgrade scenario that many will use soon.

To migrate from an old version of Microsoft Dynamics NAV to Microsoft Dynamics 365 Business Central on-premise, you need a series of steps based on the starting release of the product; the upgrade steps are related to data-migration and object merge activities.

Here is a table showing a schema of the necessary steps, starting from Navision Attain 3.70:

From release	To release	Steps
Case 1 – Dynamics NAV 2015/2016/2017/2018	Dyn365BC on-premise	1
Case 2 – Dynamics NAV 2013	Dyn365BC on-premise	2
Case 3 – Dynamics NAV 2009/NAV 5	Dyn365BC on-premise	3
Case 4 – Navision Attain 3.70/MBS Navision 4.0	Dyn365BC on-premise	4

Upgrade ToolKit

The main tool for upgrades is the `Upgrade ToolKit` (we have also talked about it in the previous sections), a tool available on the Microsoft Dynamics 365 Business Central on-premise DVD and in previous versions of Microsoft Dynamics NAV.

On the Microsoft Dynamics 365 Business Central on-premise DVD, we have two `Upgrade ToolKit` available:

- `Data Conversion Tools`
- `Local Objects`

The `Data Conversion Tools` (W1-Worldwide DVD) folder content is shown here:

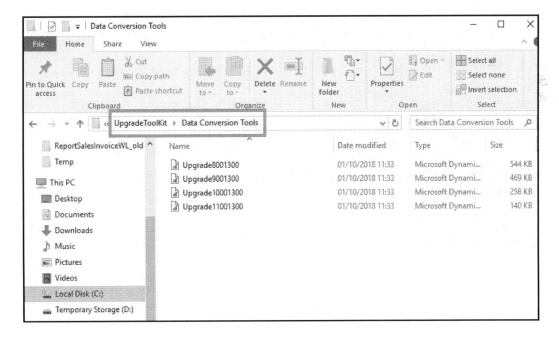

Here is the `Local Objects` (for localized releases—for example, DVD for ITA localization) folder content:

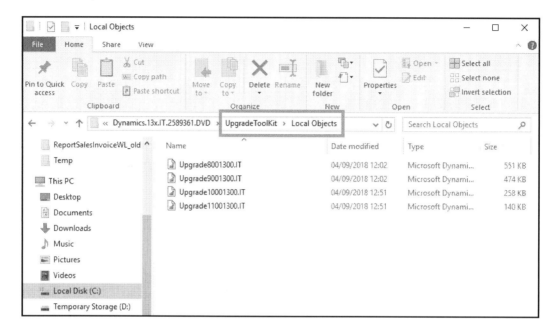

Case 1 – starting from Microsoft Dynamics NAV 2015/NAV 2016/NAV 2017/NAV 2018

Starting from Microsoft Dynamics NAV 2015, 2016, 2017, and NAV 2018, Microsoft has released one-step upgrade codeunits to upgrade to Microsoft Dynamics 365 Business Central on-premise.

Case 2 – starting from Microsoft Dynamics NAV 5.0/NAV 2009

Starting from Microsoft Dynamics NAV 5.0, a no data `Upgrade ToolKit` to upgrade to Microsoft Dynamics NAV 2009 version is the only required object merge.

Starting from Microsoft Dynamics NAV 2009, you need to upgrade to Microsoft Dynamics NAV 2013 to maintain dimensions; after that, you can upgrade with a one-step upgrade to Microsoft Dynamics NAV 2015.

Starting from Microsoft Dynamics NAV 2013, Microsoft have a one-step upgrade to upgrade to Microsoft Dynamics NAV 2015.

Starting from Microsoft Dynamics NAV 2015, it's a one-step upgrade to Microsoft Dynamics 365 Business Central on-premise.

Case 3 – starting from Microsoft Dynamics NAV 2013

Starting from Microsoft Dynamics NAV 2013, Microsoft have a one-step upgrade to Microsoft Dynamics NAV 2015, and a one-step upgrade to Microsoft Dynamics 365 Business Central on-premise.

Case 4 – starting from Navision Attain 3.70/MBS Navision 4.0

Starting from Navision Attain 3.70 and MBS Navision 4, Microsoft have a one-step upgrade to Microsoft Dynamics NAV 2009.

Starting from Microsoft Dynamics NAV 2009, you need to upgrade to Microsoft Dynamics NAV 2013 to maintain dimensions.

Starting from Microsoft Dynamics NAV 2013, Microsoft have a one-step upgrade to Microsoft Dynamics NAV 2015, and a one-step upgarde to Microsoft Dynamics 365 Business Central on-premise.

How to upgrade to Microsoft Dynamics 365 Business Central on-premise

We can have an *upgrade* to Microsoft Dynamics 365 Business Central on-premise from one of the following versions of Microsoft Dynamics NAV:

- Microsoft Dynamics NAV 2015
- Microsoft Dynamics NAV 2016
- Microsoft Dynamics NAV 2017
- Microsoft Dynamics NAV 2018

To perform a full upgrade, you need to perform three steps:

1. Upgrade the application code
2. Upgrade the data
3. Run the data-upgrade process

We will discuss these steps in detail in the following sections.

Upgrading the application code

A lot of customers want all the customizations that have been implemented in their existing Microsoft Dynamics NAV installations to be migrated to their new Microsoft Dynamics 365 Business Central on-premise installation. The amount of code changes between the two versions can vary (if you have a lot of customizations, this process can be more expensive). To upgrade the application code, you must merge code from different versions of the application; this merge process is known as a code upgrade or application upgrade.

During an upgrade, you have to first identify which changes you have to make, and then you'll have to upgrade the application objects and the application code, and finally, you might have to upgrade data so that it fits the new database schema.

You can use any tool or set of tools to help you compare and merge code. Microsoft Dynamics NAV and Microsoft Dynamics 365 Business Central include Windows PowerShell cmdlets and sample scripts that can help you upgrade your application. The cmdlets are available through the Microsoft Dynamics NAV Development Shell and Microsoft Dynamic NAV Development Shell, or by importing the `Microsoft.Dynamics.NAV.Model.Tools.psd1` module into the Windows PowerShell **Integrated Scripting Environment** (**ISE**). You can find the sample scripts on the product installation media in the `WindowsPowerShellScripts\ApplicationMergeUtilities` folder. We recommend that you use these cmdlets and sample scripts because they can make it faster to merge most changes.

 You must upgrade the application before you upgrade the data. Upgrade the application code, as shown here `https://docs.microsoft.com/en-us/dynamics365/business-central/dev-itpro/upgrade/upgrading-the-application-code`.

Upgrading the data

You must use data-conversion tools that have been provided with Microsoft Dynamics 365 Business Central to convert the old data with the old version's table and field structure so that it functions together with the new version's table and field structure. Mainly, only table objects and table data are modified during the data-upgrade process. Other objects, such as pages, reports, codeunits, and XMLports are upgraded as part of the application code upgrade process.

 The data-upgrade process leads you through the database conversion (technical upgrade) and then the upgrade of the actual data, which is achieved by using `Upgrade ToolKit`/upgrade codeunits.

Running the data-upgrade process

A data upgrade runs the Upgrade ToolKit objects (as seen in the preceding paragraph) to migrate business data from the old table structure to the new table structure. You can start the data upgrade from the Microsoft Dynamics NAV Development Environment or from Microsoft Dynamics 365 Business Central Administration Shell.

When you upgrade to Microsoft Dynamics NAV 2018, you must first upgrade the application code, and then you can upgrade the data. By using Windows PowerShell, you can automate both parts of the upgrade process. Also, you can use the same scripts to test each step in your upgrade process before you upgrade production databases; you can reduce the time that you spend upgrading each database by using Windows PowerShell scripts.

Upgrade considerations for releases after Microsoft Dynamics NAV 2015

Now, we will look at some features related to upgrades for higher versions of Microsoft Dynamics NAV 2015, starting from Microsoft Dynamics NAV 2016 forward.

Data Upgrade from Microsoft Dynamics NAV Development Environment and PowerShell

Since Microsoft Dynamics NAV 2016, it is possible to launch the **Data Upgrade** procedure directly from the Microsoft Dynamics NAV Development Environment or PowerShell script (as already mentioned). The Microsoft Dynamics NAV Development Environment already contains the necessary information to proceed with the data upgrade without having to read the developer toolkit files. You can launch it from a command, as shown in the following screenshot:

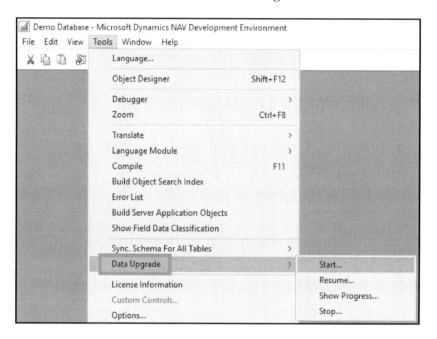

Once you click on **Start**, you will see a confirmation box:

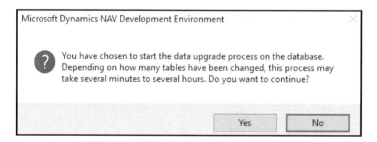

You can also launch the **Data Upgrade** procedure from the Microsoft Dynamics NAV Administration Shell. Open the Microsoft Dynamics NAV Administration Shell as an administrator, and then run the **Start-NavDataUpgrade** cmdlet:

```
Start-NavDataUpgrade -ServerInstance <ServerInstanceName> -Force
```

Wait for completion as it happens in Microsoft Dynamics NAV Development Environment.

Generating symbols

Make sure that **Enable loading application symbol references** at server startup is set on the Dynamics NAV server instance. To generate the application symbol references for running C/SIDE and AL side-by-side, open a Command Prompt, change to the directory where the `Finsql.exe` file has been installed as part of Microsoft Dynamics NAV 2018, and then run the following command:

```
finsql.exe Command=generatesymbolreference, Database=<MyDatabaseName>,
ServerName=<DatabaseServerName>\<DatabaseInstance>
```

As this is only the first step, to complete the operation, it is necessary to follow other steps indicated in the following info box.

> You can also refer to this post by Duilio Tacconi for complete syntax and all of the steps to generate symbols: https://blogs.msdn. microsoft.com/nav/2018/01/16/generate-symbols-in-a-modern-development-environment-with-microsoft-dynamics-nav-2018/.

Upgrading installed extensions

The installed extensions must also be updated; you need to upgrade the V1 extensions by reinstalling them.

Extension V1 must be rewritten to Extension V2 using Microsoft AL, so you need to perform the following steps:

1. Unpublish the V1 extension (`Uninstall-NAVApp`).
2. Install the V2 extension (`Publish-NAVApp`).

3. Synch the V2 with the database schema (`Sync-NAVApp`).
4. Execute the upgrade code to V2 (`Start-NAVAppDataUpgrade`). The upgrade logic must be written in an Upgrade codeunit in your V2 extension.

To get a list of the published extensions on the server instance, run the following `Get-NAVAppInfo` command, as follows:

```
Get-NAVAppInfo -ServerInstance <ServerInstanceName>
```

For each V1 Extension that you want to upgrade to a V2 Extension, you can run the `Unpublish-NAVApp`, `Sync-NAVApp`, and `Start-NAVAppDataUpgrade` commands:

```
>Unpublish-NAVApp -ServerInstance <ServerInstanceName> -Name <Name> -
Version <N.N.N.N>
>Sync-NAVApp -ServerInstance <ServerInstanceName> -Name <Name> -
Version <N.N.N.N>
>Start-NAVAppDataUpgrade -ServerInstance <ServerInstanceName> -Name
<Name> -Version <N.N.N.N>
```

For each V1 Extension that you want to reinstall or upgrade, run the following `Install-NAVApp` command, as follows:

```
Install-NAVApp -ServerInstance <ServerInstanceName> -Name <Name> -
Version <N.N.N.N> -Tenant <Tenant>
```

Upgrades permission sets

It is possible to import upgraded permission sets and permissions by using the **Roles and Permissions XMLports**. For this, you can use the NAV Development Environment.

The steps to upgrade the permission sets are as follows:

1. Delete all permission sets in the database except the **SUPER** permission set
2. In **Object Designer**, run `Page 9802 Permission Sets`, and then delete the permission sets
3. Run `XMLport 9171` and `XMLport 9172` to import the permission sets and permission XML files

Now, you can use the updated permissions sets in the upgraded release of Microsoft Dynamics NAV.

General considerations about Data Upgrade

We have mentioned general concepts related to the upgrade of multiple versions of Microsoft Dynamics NAV. In addition to the official Microsoft links (that I have already added in the following tip box), I want to share another post (in the following tip box) because it is really complete and well done, by Suraj Patel.

 Data Upgrade from Microsoft Dynamics NAV 2013 to Microsoft Dynamics NAV 2018 (https://suraj-nav.blogspot.com/2018/07/data-upgrade-from-nav-2013-to-nav-2018.html) and *Confessions of a Dynamics NAV 2018 Upgrade* (https://dynamicsuser.net/nav/b/peik/posts/confessions-of-a-dynamics-nav-2018-upgrade).

Automating the upgrade process using sample Windows PowerShell scripts

You can use automation to upgrade a single Microsoft Dynamics NAV database as well as multiple Microsoft Dynamics NAV databases that use the same application. Microsoft Dynamics 365 Business Central provides sample scripts that you can adapt for your deployment architecture.

You can learn more about automating upgrades using PowerShell scripts at https://docs.microsoft.com/en-us/dynamics-nav/automating-the-upgrade-process-using-sample-windows-powershell-scripts.

The sample scripts for upgrading code

Microsoft Dynamics NAV includes sample scripts that illustrate how you can use Windows PowerShell cmdlets to upgrade your application to the latest version of Microsoft Dynamics NAV. The sample scripts are located in the `ApplicationMergeUtilities` folder under the `WindowsPowerShellScripts` folder on the Microsoft Dynamics NAV product media. The sample scripts illustrate how you can create scripts that you run in the Microsoft Dynamics NAV Development Shell or the Windows PowerShell ISE.

 Merging application objects using the example scripts: https://docs.microsoft.com/en-us/dynamics-nav/merging-application-objects-using-the-example-scripts.

The sample scripts for upgrading data

Microsoft Dynamics NAV includes sample scripts that illustrate how you can automate the upgrade of data to the latest version of Microsoft Dynamics NAV. The sample scripts are located in the `Upgrade` folder under the `WindowsPowerShellScripts` folder on the Microsoft Dynamics NAV product media. The sample scripts include a `HowTo` script that illustrates how you can use the Microsoft Dynamics NAV cmdlets and sample scripts.

The `HowTo-UpgradeNAVDatabase.ps1` script illustrates how you can create a script that upgrades a database from an earlier version of Microsoft Dynamics NAV to a new version through a set of upgrade tasks. You can run the sample script using a partner license or a customer license.

 Upgrade to Microsoft Dynamics 365 Business Central: `https://docs.microsoft.com/en-us/dynamics365/business-central/dev-itpro/upgrade/upgrading-to-business-central`.

Upgrading to Microsoft Dynamics 365 Business Central SaaS

For this upgrade, we have two problems to manage: Data Migration and Porting of Customizations.

First, let's talk about data migration. Actually, you should use the configuration packages (RapidStart Services), exporting data from Microsoft Dynamics NAV and importing data into Microsoft Dynamics 365 Business Central via Excel files. In some scenarios, where data to load has a very high volume, it is recommended to use different methods such as loading data using web services or APIs.

Other ways could be through XMLport extensions, or you could even use Azure functions to import files and then process them afterwards.

 For more information, you can refer to *Working with Configuration Packages* at `https://docs.microsoft.com/en-us/dynamics365/business-central/across-import-data-configuration-packages`.

You can also use Intelligence Cloud for moving data from Microsoft Dynamics 365 on-premise to a SaaS tenant; obviously, all must be rewritten using extensions (we will talk about Intelligent Cloud and Intelligent Edge in `Chapter 13`, *Microsoft Dynamics 365 Business Central*).

 Intelligence Cloud or Intelligence Edge could be the tool to move the whole on-premise database into the cloud. You can learn more about it at: `https://docs.microsoft.com/en-us/dynamics365/business-central/about-intelligent-cloud` and `https://docs.microsoft.com/en-us/dynamics365/business-central/dev-itpro/administration/about-intelligent-edge`, respectively.

Now, about porting customizations: all existing customizations must be refactored into Extensions for Microsoft AL—you can only upload extensions in Microsoft Dynamics 365 Business Central SaaS.

Limitations for migrating to Microsoft Dynamics 365 Business Central SaaS

As already mentioned in the first chapters of this book there are some limitations in Microsoft Dynamics 365 Business Central SaaS, also in relation to data migration, data export/import, and data backup. They are listed as follows:

- No backup/restore database feature is available (Microsoft create backups with its policies—you can only request a restore if necessary)
- We have no access to the database
- PowerShell is not available (no PowerShell cmdlets and PowerShell database functions: we don't have import and export data functions such as `NAVDATA`, `EXPORTDATA`, `IMPORTDATA`)
- No Export\Import data from pages (these pages are not available)

Given these limitations, for now, a new implementation is recommended by migrating only the data with the tools we've described.

 For more information, have a look at *Data Migration from Microsoft Dynamics NAV to Microsoft Dynamics 365 Business Central* SaaS (`https://github.com/Microsoft/AL/issues/2476`) and *Importing Business Data from Other Finance Systems* (`https://docs.microsoft.com/en-us/dynamics365/business-central/across-import-data-configuration-packages`).

Summary

Upgrading used to take a considerable amount of time and effort. With the release of the PowerShell upgrade, it doesn't have to. Companies that already use Microsoft Dynamics NAV will want to get to, at least, Microsoft Dynamics NAV 2013, so upgrading in the future will be easier. To do so, they have to go through an upgrade process to get their current implementation to the latest version. In this chapter, we covered upgrading to Microsoft Dynamics NAV 2016 by using PowerShell to upgrade from NAV 2013. Even upgrading to Microsoft Dynamics NAV 2013 is only supported from Microsoft Dynamics NAV 2009. We also explained how to upgrade from the previous versions of the application.

Upgrading to Microsoft Dynamics 365 Business Central on-premise is similar to upgrading to Microsoft Dynamics NAV 2018. The main difference is that it is necessary to convert the existing developments to extensions in order to prevent system updates from touching the source code. Sometimes, it is necessary to choose a new implementation instead of the upgrade, through a data migration.

In the next chapter, we will be talking about developing in Microsoft Dynamics NAV 2018 and in Microsoft Dynamics 365 Business Central.

Development Considerations

8

Almost every Microsoft Dynamics NAV implementation will have some development. The customized code must fit inside the standard code within Microsoft Dynamics NAV, and it should look like it was a part of the standard Microsoft Dynamics NAV. This makes it easier for the users to understand how the customized modules work and for the partners to support it. A good initial development also makes any future changes easier and more efficient, for both the customer and the partner.

Now let's talk about development in Microsoft Dynamics 365 Business Central on-premise and SaaS. Microsoft Dynamics 365 Business Central will have some development, but the development model is different. For the on-premise release, it is still possible to develop applications defined "internal" (not based on extensions), but they will be deprecate in the near future-year 2020; for the SaaS release, it's not possible to modify the standard code, and only extensions can be used to develop and install customizations.

In this chapter, we will go through the main development considerations you should take into account while developing for Microsoft Dynamics NAV and Microsoft Dynamics 365 Business Central.

In this chapter, we will cover the following topics:

- For Microsoft Dynamics NAV, we look at the following:
    - Setup versus customization
    - The data model principles
    - How posting processes are developed
    - Where to write customized code
    - How to write customized code
    - The old development model (CSIDE)

- For Microsoft Dynamics 365 Business Central on-premise and SaaS, we look at the following:
  - The new development model (powered by extension)
  - Differences between the old and the new model
  - Dynamics 365 Business Central on-premise versus SaaS
  - Developing for the cloud environment and SaaS world
  - Development FAQ

Development in Microsoft Dynamics NAV and Business Central general concepts – setup versus customization

Microsoft Dynamics NAV and Microsoft Dynamics 365 Business Central offer many configuration options within all of the modules. These options make ERPs work differently in different companies, depending on the option selected; for example, you could define that your locations will use warehouse documents for shipping or process shipping directly from the sales order.

When you set up a new company, you will find more than 200 tables that can be considered setup tables. You will find the setup table of each module, its journals, and its sections. In addition, there are global setups, such as the accounting periods, the payment terms, and dimensions.

You will find there are hundreds of setup options in the base Microsoft Dynamics NAV and Microsoft Dynamics 365 Business Central product. It is really difficult for a person who does not work with ERPs full time to be aware of all the options and the impact that a single option can have on the system. Even some consultants or developers may not know the consequence of certain settings in Microsoft Dynamics NAV or Microsoft Dynamics 365 Business Central without research.

A good consultant or developer will not be tempted to start developing right away. Before starting, it is important to invest time to understand exactly what the client company needs and why, as well as investigating all the setup options that are related to the client's core business. For example, if the client is a manufacturing company, the partners better make sure they thoroughly understand the basic manufacturing principles and the manufacturing functionality in Microsoft Dynamics NAV and in Microsoft Dynamics 365 Business Central and how they can be applied to the client's business, based on their requirements.

How can we discover how all the features work? Basically, there are three options: read, research, and ask for help. Let's look at these in more detail:

- **Read**: Microsoft now publishes all the documentation with regards to Microsoft Dynamics NAV and Microsoft Dynamics 365 Business Central in MSDN. You do not need a subscription to MSDN in order to view it. In fact, when you search anything on the functionality of Microsoft Dynamics NAV or Microsoft Dynamics 365 Business Central, one of the results may point to the MSDN article. For example, for the current release, Microsoft Dynamics 365 Business Central, the full documentation can be found at `https://docs.microsoft.com/en-us/dynamics365/business-central/`. Not only does the MSDN article go through all the technical aspects of the product, it also shows you step-by-step instructions on the functional aspects of the program, that is, how to create a new sales order.

- **Research**: This is one of the best ways to discover all the features that Microsoft Dynamics NAV and Microsoft Dynamics 365 Business Central can offer, in a step-by-step manner. Every time a customer raises a query or has a particular requirement, do investigate. Do not simply start to develop a new feature; before that, you must try to answer the query or meet the requirement using the standard options. For example, if the your customer's query is related to items, start by looking at each single field in the item table. If you don't know what a certain field is used for, use tools to help you see where the field is used and why.

- **Ask for help**: Microsoft Dynamics NAV and Microsoft Dynamics 365 Business Central have a large online community that can help you with a specific problem. Microsoft has an official community called Microsoft Dynamics Community (`https://community.dynamics.com`) and a lot of MVPs are always available for questions.

> There are also paid online communication groups such as the Microsoft Dynamics NAV user group or the Microsoft Dynamics 365 Business Central user group named **NAVUG** (`http://www.navug.com` for both systems) and free online communities, such as **MIBUSO** (`http://www.mibuso.com`) and **DynamicsUser** (`http://Dynamicsuser.net`).

Our recommendation is to ask the community just after you have tried to solve the problem yourself. You can state the problem by explaining what you have tried so far. Generally, the community will be more receptive if you have tried first, rather than you throwing out the question without investigating beforehand. You must understand that the community is there to help you, not to work for you.

Lastly, if you still can't get the help you need, pay for the help by contacting your partner. Or if you're a partner, contract a Microsoft Dynamics NAV or Business Central person with better knowledge than your company has. Investing in training is better than paying for mistakes down the road.

As we have seen, it is important to invest time in finding ways to use the standard features before starting to develop. This implementation project will be easier, and you will also increase your knowledge of the product, which will be very useful in your future projects.

For the customer, the benefit is also clear. Apart from saving the cost of unnecessary developments, you will also save the grief of creating unnecessary business processes because the solution was not fully thought through.

Data model principles

After analyzing the standard functionality, if there are needs to do custom development, it is important to develop the solution with the same structure that Microsoft Dynamics NAV and Microsoft Dynamics 365 Business Central on-premise use in their modules (it's necessary to follow the standard of product).

 For Microsoft Dynamics 365 Business Central, SaaS is different because it is not possible to access the source code and it is possible to develop customizations only through extensions; this will be discussed in the following paragraphs.

The users that are going to use the functionalities are users that are also going to use the standard parts of the application. To avoid confusing them, it is essential to use the same philosophy and the same structure everywhere. This way, once a user knows one part of the application, they can intuitively use the other modules.

This is something that will also help us; we do not have to reinvent the wheel every time. There is no need for us to consider how to structure our data for each development. Take the existing structure as your basis, and just grow its functionality to meet your needs. With this, we are making not only the developer's life easier, but also the life of others who will participate in the project, such as the consultant, the implementer, the trainer, and the person who will support the customer once they start to run with Microsoft Dynamics NAV or Microsoft Dynamics 365 Business Central. To develop our own application, using the principles and structure of what already exists, it is important to know what already exists. This is what we will cover in the next section.

Basic objects

With Microsoft Dynamics NAV 2018 and in Microsoft Dynamics 365 Business Central on-premise in CSIDE Development Environment, you can find seven basic object types. They are as follows:

Object	Description
Table	This object is used to store data in the database. Most of the time, it is within this object that data is validated or calculated so that it follows the business rules described in each application area. Understanding tables is the key to using all the other objects.
Page	This object is used to display data to users. Pages allow the users to add records to a table and to view and modify the records. Pages can also be exposed as web services so that the other applications can also read, insert, modify, or delete data, just like the users do.
Report	These objects are mostly used to summarize and print detailed information by using filters and sorting, selected by the users. On some occasions, reports are also used to batch process data.
XMLport	This object is used to export and import table data in XML format.
Codeunit	This object is used to group code of a particular functional area.
MenuSuite	This object contains the menus that are displayed in the Department page. It is the user's door to access the functionalities of a certain area. Note: Department is not available in Microsoft Dynamics 365 Business Central SaaS.
Query	This object is used to specify a set of data coming from more tables.

Even if we talk about objects, it is important to note that Microsoft Dynamics NAV and Microsoft Dynamics 365 Business Central are not object-oriented, but object-based. You have seven object types that you can use, but you cannot create new object types. This may seem limiting, but it also makes development work much easier.

Tables – how tables are structured

Tables are the most fundamental objects among any databases. They store records that are collected through pages; for example, customers, sales, and inventories. These records are then presented to the users through pages and reports.

The table's structure is the base of the structure of the whole application. We have already covered the table structure in `Chapter 3`, *General Considerations*, but we will go a bit deeper in this section. In the standard application, we find different kinds of tables that are used for different purposes:

- **Master tables**: We will find master tables in each area of the application; they are the ones that are used to store the more important information of each module. In the sales area, the most important table is the `Customer` table; in the purchase area, it is the `Vendor` table; and in the warehouse management module, the `Item` table is the most important table. Therefore, they are called master tables.

- **Secondary or subsidiary tables**: These are the tables that store secondary data, usually related to the master table, or that can be selected from a master table. An example of a secondary or subsidiary table is the `Customer Price Group` table. This table contains the distinct price groups that are set up in the `Company` table. A value from this table can be selected and assigned to a customer from the `Customer` table.

- **Setup tables**: All the modules have their own setup table; different options can be selected to specify how the module is going to work.

- **Document tables**: We always find the document tables in pairs, because a document always has a `Header` table and a `Lines` table. Orders, shipments, or invoices are all examples of documents. The documents can also be divided between live documents and posted documents. The posted documents are stored in different tables that cannot be edited, but can be deleted.

- **Entry tables**: Entry tables are used to keep track of all the transactions related to a master table. On the `Customer ledger Entry` table, for instance, we can find an entry for each invoice, credit memo, or payments for a single customer.

- **Register tables**: Register tables are used to keep track of entries created on the same posting process. For instance, the posting of a single sales invoice creates different G/L entries (an entry in the customer account, another in the sales account, another in the VAT account, and so on). All these entries are grouped in the `G/L Register` table as they all belong to the same posting process, the posting of a specific sales invoice.

- **Journal tables**: These are the tables that the posting process uses to create entries. It is the system that introduces data as a previous step on the journal tables while posting a document. The user can also manually introduce data on a journal table if he wants to post a transaction without a document. We can find many processes that create data on journal tables but don't post them. The user is responsible for checking that data and finally posting it. That's what the calculate depreciation process does. For each fixed asset, it calculates the corresponding depreciation, and creates a line that reflects those calculations. The user has to go to the journal, review the lines, and post them.

Object elements

Each object has its own attributes; the structure of a table has four sections:

- The first block contains metadata for the overall table—the table type
- The fields section describes the data elements that make up the table—their name and the type of data they can store
- The keys section contains the definitions of the keys that the table needs to support
- The final section details the triggers and code that can run on the table

A table then contains **Table properties**, **Fields**, **Keys**, and **Triggers**, as we can see in the following diagram:

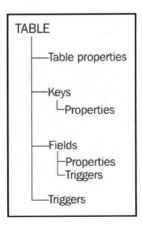

Understanding table structures

The best way to understand a concept is to see it in practice. This is why we are going to analyze the structure of the tables in a particular area, the warehouse management area.

Master tables

The master table of the warehouse management area is the `Item` table. It holds the main data in this area, and everything else relates to it. Usually, the primary key of a master table is a field named `No.`. Typically, a series number is used to assign a new `No.value` each time a new item is created. The field `No.` gets replicated on different tables to refer to a specific item.

Secondary tables

In the item card page, you will find fields that can be filled by selecting data from a secondary table, such as the `Base Unit of Measure` field, which can be filled by selecting data from the `Item Unit of Measure` table. For each item, you can indicate its sales price on the `Sales Price` table, which is also a secondary table:

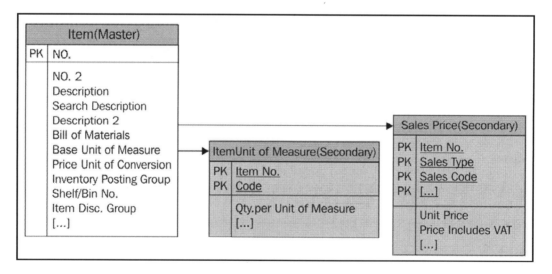

Any table (it doesn't matter whether it's a master table, a secondary table, a setup table, or any other kind of table) can be used in the other application areas. The `Sales Price` table, which we've seen, is also a secondary table of the sales area.

In the preceding example, we only saw a couple of secondary tables related to the `Item master` table. We'll find many other secondary tables, such as the `Item Category` table, the `Product Group` table, the `Tariff Number` table, the `Item Tracking Code` table, and the `Item Variant` table, just to give a few examples.

Setup tables

The setup table of the warehouse management area is called the `Inventory Setup` table. The number series used to code the items can be set up on this table. In addition, other information such as whether we want the item cost to be automatically posted to the general ledger or not is controlled through here. Other setup tables also affect how the warehouse management area works. For instance, in the `General Ledger Setup` table, you can indicate the rounding precision of the unit prices of the items in the `Unit-Amount Rounding Precision` field:

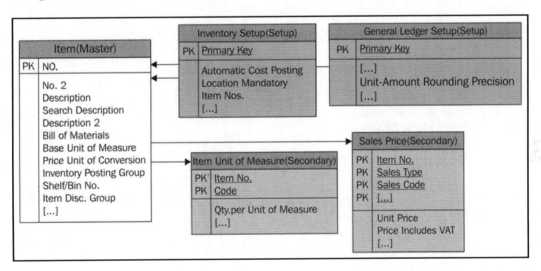

Document tables

It's time to start using the item on documents, to purchase or sell them. The item can now be used on the lines of a document. In the following example, we will use a sales order to put in an item line in the sales order. There are other sales documents where an item can be used, such as the sales quote, the sales invoice, the sales return order, or the sales credit memo. In fact, all these sales documents are stored on a single document structure composed of the `Sales Header` table and the `Sales Line` table. Each one is identified by the `Document Type` field that is part of the primary key of the tables:

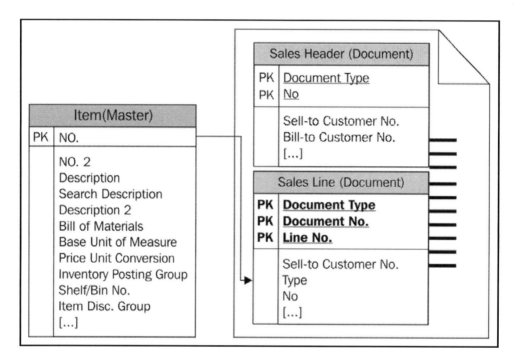

When an item is used in a document, not only the item number is stored in the `Sales Line` table, but many other fields from the `Item` table are also copied. Fields such as the `Inventory Posting Group` field, the `Description` and `Description 2` fields, the `Gen. Prod. Posting Group` field, or the `VAT Prod. Posting Group` field—just to name a few—are copied from the `Item` table to the `Sales Line` table.

It may seem redundant, but why are all these fields copied if the information is already stored in the item card? Well, this information is copied for two reasons. Firstly, the information is considered default data; secondly, it gets copied to allow the users to change a field value on a specific order. As an example, you can change the item description, the sales unit of measure, or the item description on a specific order. Other fields, such as `Inventory Posting Group`, are also replicated in the `Sales Line` table, but the users cannot modify their values. It may take some time between creating the order and finally posting it. In the meantime, the item configuration may have changed. However, it is not acceptable for a specific order to post something different to when it was created, which is probably when the user checked it.

The same is true for the item price. When we create a sales order for the item, the system calculates and proposes a price for the item. This is the price we configure, either on the item card or in the `Sales Price` table. We tell our customer the selling price so that he can approve the order before we ship the item. Imagine that, in the meantime, the item price changes. We all agree that the new price is for the new orders. It will be unacceptable for the system to change the existing price without warning.

Copying data from the master table to a document table is part of Microsoft Dynamics NAV philosophy. It is something that we can find in all the application areas and in all the documents. It has a clear pro: it makes the system flexible. It also gives us a lot of traceability. It also has a con: any change on a master table is not reflected immediately. The existing document lines keep the old configuration. The user has to refresh the line if the new configuration is needed. From our experience, some users have difficulty understanding this. They don't know when to refresh a line. During training, we will have to invest time to tell them and make sure they understand when to refresh a line. When the order is ready and the item has been shipped to the customer, the order can be posted. The posting routines, which are explained later on, are in charge of verifying that all data is correct and creating all the required entries to reflect the transaction.

Concerning documents, a shipment is created by inserting records on the `Sales Shipment Header` and `Sales Shipment Lines` tables. In the next step, the invoice will be created by inserting the records on the `Sales Invoice Header` and `Sales Invoice Lines` tables.

Records representing the shipment and the invoice are almost the exact copies of the original order. Take a look at the fields found on the `Sales Line` table, which is shown in the following screenshot:

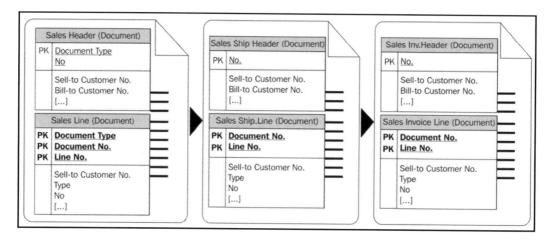

Now take a look at the fields found on the `Sales Shipment Line` table, which is shown in the following screenshot:

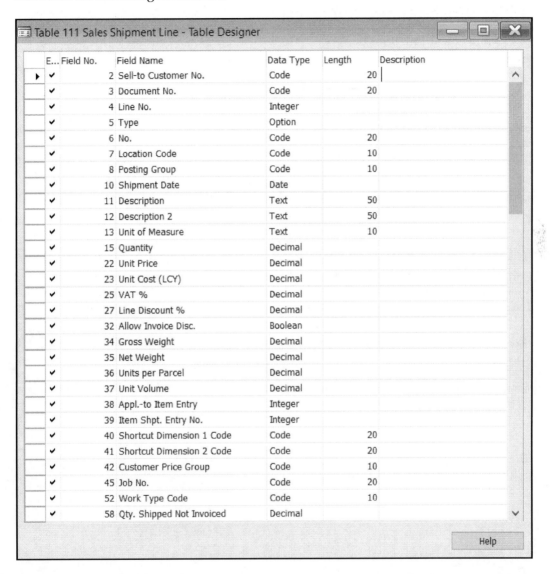

Table 111 Sales Shipment Line - Table Designer

E...	Field No.	Field Name	Data Type	Length	Description
✔	2	Sell-to Customer No.	Code	20	
✔	3	Document No.	Code	20	
✔	4	Line No.	Integer		
✔	5	Type	Option		
✔	6	No.	Code	20	
✔	7	Location Code	Code	10	
✔	8	Posting Group	Code	10	
✔	10	Shipment Date	Date		
✔	11	Description	Text	50	
✔	12	Description 2	Text	50	
✔	13	Unit of Measure	Text	10	
✔	15	Quantity	Decimal		
✔	22	Unit Price	Decimal		
✔	23	Unit Cost (LCY)	Decimal		
✔	25	VAT %	Decimal		
✔	27	Line Discount %	Decimal		
✔	32	Allow Invoice Disc.	Boolean		
✔	34	Gross Weight	Decimal		
✔	35	Net Weight	Decimal		
✔	36	Units per Parcel	Decimal		
✔	37	Unit Volume	Decimal		
✔	38	Appl.-to Item Entry	Integer		
✔	39	Item Shpt. Entry No.	Integer		
✔	40	Shortcut Dimension 1 Code	Code	20	
✔	41	Shortcut Dimension 2 Code	Code	20	
✔	42	Customer Price Group	Code	10	
✔	45	Job No.	Code	20	
✔	52	Work Type Code	Code	10	
✔	58	Qty. Shipped Not Invoiced	Decimal		

Help

As you can see, we can find almost the same fields, with the same name and the same type. The most important part is that the fields have the same value in the `Field No.` property. This is important because to copy values from one table to another, the `TRANSFERFIELDS` instruction is used. This instruction copies the fields based on the `Field No.` property. For each field in the `Record` (the destination) table, the contents of the field with the same `Field No.` property in the `FromRecord` (the source) table will be copied, if such a field exists. Note that in order for the function to work, the fields that are being transferred need to have the same data type. You cannot transfer a text value into a date field. You will receive an error if the field type is different when this function is called.

So, if you create a new field on the `Sales Line` table and you need to copy the value of the field along the different documents, you just have to create the same field with the same `Field No.` property on the tables where the documents are stored. There is no need for extra coding.

There are other document tables related to the warehouse management area. For instance, the `Transfer Header` and `Transfer Line` tables, with the corresponding `Transfer Shipment Header`, `Transfer Shipment Line`, `Transfer Receipt Header`, and `Transfer Receipt Line` historical documents. Historical documents are part of the Microsoft Dynamics NAV protected tables. Data on the protected tables cannot be changed, nor can you directly insert new records on these tables; the posting routines are the ones in charge of inserting data in these tables.

To refresh our memory, so far we have covered the types of tables that are shown in the following diagram:

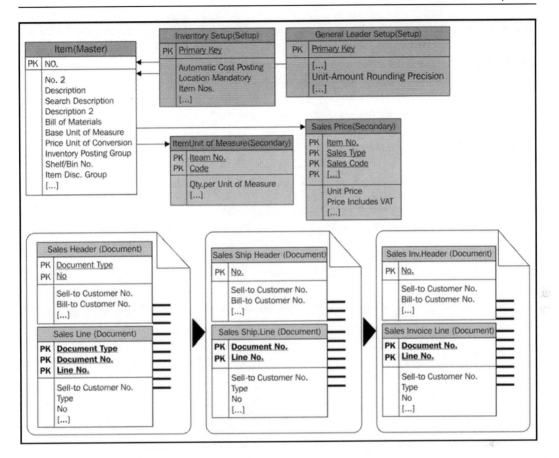

Only the `Entry` and `Journal` tables are left, and we will cover them in the following section.

Entry tables

As we have mentioned, the purpose of entry tables is to keep track of all the transactions done with a master table. Each time we purchase an item, we have to record the stock increase. Every time we sell an item, we have to record the stock decrease. It gives us valuable information about the item, such as the inventory quantity we have at any time.

We might think that we don't need an entry table to determinate the stock. When we purchase or sell, we create the appropriate purchase and sales document. Theoretically, we can just add all the purchases and sales document lines and get the same data. Again, we seem to be duplicating information. It is true that for one transaction the same information has to be copied to a lot of tables. However, in each case we want to see the information in a different way. Also, the tables that are used for sales and purchase documents are different; to get the stock, we will have to search between multiple tables. This will make the whole system slower.

Another element to consider is that on some occasions we need to register an item transaction but have no documents. What if we break an item? Or if an item "magically" disappears? We need to decrease the item stock, but there is no document to reflect this. In this case, we want to create a new record in the table entry without creating a purchase or sales document.

Some master tables need more than one entry table. This is the case of the warehouse management area, where we find the `Item Ledger Entry` and `Value Entry` tables. The `Value Entry` table is used to store the costing details related to each item ledger entry:

Item Ledger Entry (Entry)		Value Entry (Entry)	
PK	**Entry No.**	PK	**Entry No.**
	Item No.		Item No.
	Posting Date		Posting Date
	Entry Type		Item Leader Entry Type
	[...]		[...]

The primary key for all the entry tables is a field called `Entry No.`, which is an auto-incremental integer. All the entry tables also have a field named `Posting Date`.

Additionally, when new records are inserted on the entry tables, the system also creates new records on tables called `Register`. In the warehouse management area, we find the `Item Register` table. The `Item Register` table is used to keep track of when entries are created (regardless of the posting date), which user created them, and also how many entries have been created for each transaction. The `Item Register` table can be considered a secondary table:

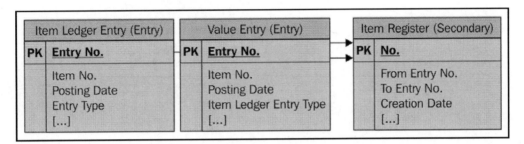

Journal tables

Last but not the least, we find the journal tables. Journal tables are very important since they contain most of the business logic of the application. All the posting processes found on the application are based on journal tables. In the warehouse management area, we find the `Item Journal Line` table.

If the posting is made from a document, the posting process converts the document lines to journal lines by creating temporary registers on the `Item Journal Line` table. The user can also manually create lines on the `Item Journal Line` table and then post them, without using a document at all:

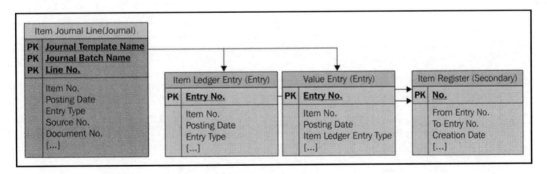

The final picture

And at last, we can see the final picture of how the tables are structured in Microsoft Dynamics NAV and in Microsoft Dynamics 365 Business Central, as shown in the following diagram:

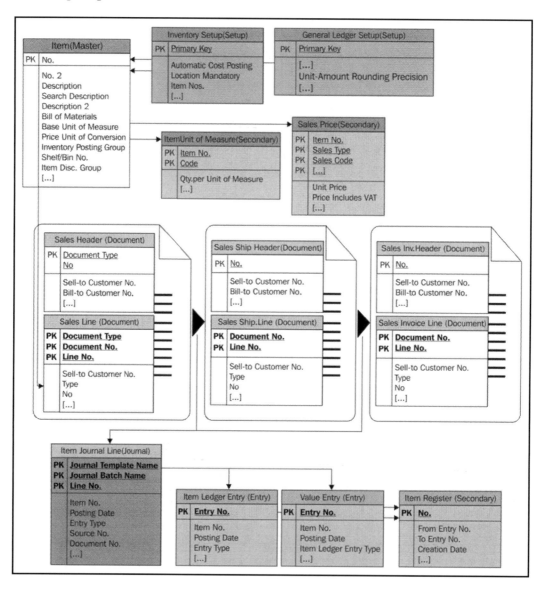

You will find many other secondary tables, setup tables, document tables, and entry tables that are not shown in the diagram, but the structure remains the same.

Remember that all the existing areas in the applications follow this structure; therefore, users are used to it. Keep this structure in mind while building your own applications.

The structure of pages

In the previous section, we saw the tables' structure and how important it is to keep the same structure in all the areas to help the users understand how the area works. Pages are also important; they are the objects through which the users interact with Microsoft Dynamics NAV and with Microsoft Dynamics 365 Business Central. The users do not see tables, but pages. Thus, maintaining consistency in the page structure is vital for the user to perceive the consistent application structure. In the standard application, we find different kinds of pages that are used for different purposes, such as the following:

- **Role center pages**: This is the first page that the users see when accessing Microsoft Dynamics NAV and Microsoft Dynamics 365 Business Central. Depending on each user's role, the page shows a quick view of the work that the user is responsible for. This page is displayed differently in web client compared to Windows client for on-premise releases.

- **Card pages**: Card pages show data from a single table and also from a single record. All the master tables have a card page associated with them, which is also the only way to insert, edit, or delete records. Some secondary tables with sufficient entities (many fields) also use card pages.

- **List pages**: List pages show multiple records from a single table. For each card page, you will find a list page that shows data from the same table. In fact, the users access the card page from the list page. These pages are not editable and are only used to show data, not to modify or delete it. Most secondary tables don't have a card page, but all of them have a list page. When no card page can be found for a table, the list page is editable. We are allowed to insert, modify, or delete records from the list page.

- **Document pages**: These pages are used to show the two tables related to a document: the header and the lines. Document pages are used to show data related to the header, and they include a link to a ListPart page where the lines are shown.

- **ListPart pages**: ListPart pages are pages with the same characteristics as those of a list page, but the difference is that they are always used inside other pages.

- **Worksheet pages**: These pages are based on a template, batch, or name structure, and have a control for selecting a template, batch, or name. Journals are a good example of worksheet pages.

- **ConfirmationDialog pages**: These are pages that pose a question to the user, have no input fields, and require that the user select **Yes** or **No**.

- **NavigatePage pages**: These pages are used for wizards, which consist of a number of user input screens or steps linked together, enabling the user to carry out infrequently performed tasks.

- **API pages:** Pages of this type are used to generate web service endpoints and cannot be shown in the user interface.

- **Headline pages:** The headlines can provide users with up-to-date information and insight into the business and daily work. Typical categories of headlines might include: getting started information, productivity tips, and other information. Headline pages are working only with Web client and are not available in Windows client).

Understanding page structures

As in the previous section, we will analyze the *structure of pages* in a particular area, the warehouse management area.

Role Center pages

The following screenshot shows the default **Role Center** page for a user who has the **Sales Order Processor** profiles assigned. The **Role Center** page page looks different between the Windows client and the Web client:

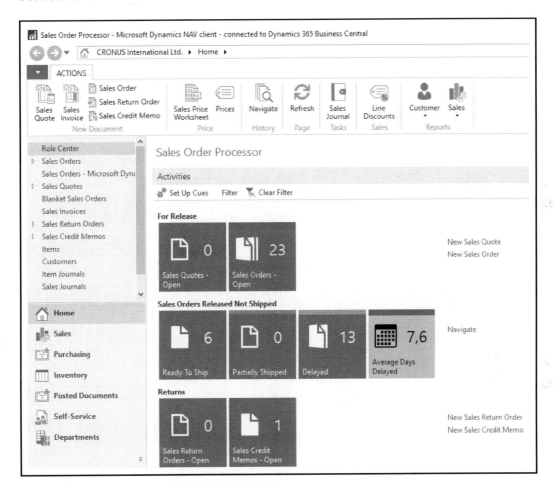

The **Role Center** page has a central area called **Activities**. This area contains a few cues that provide a visual indicator of the work that a user has to do each day. Cues are different for each role. The **Activities** area also contains actions so that the user can start new transactions right from the role center. The following is the role center page in the Microsoft Dynamics 365 Business Central web client (SaaS):

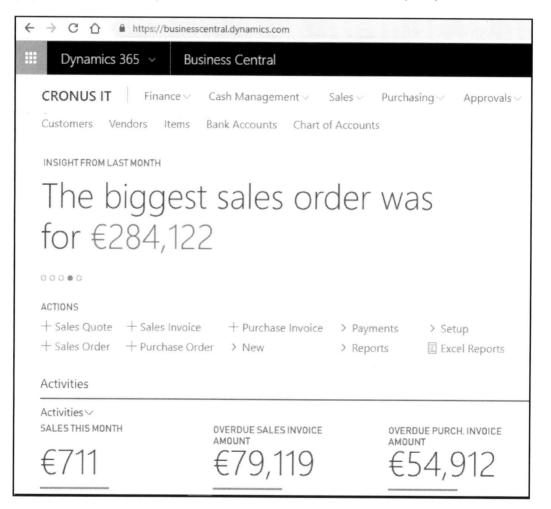

 The next screenshots will be related to the Microsoft Dynamics 365 Business Central Web client; soon only the Web client will be available.

Card pages

Card pages show data from a single table and also from a single record. In the following screenshot, you can see the **ITEM CARD** page. It contains all the fields that can be stored in the `Item` table, except for a few fields that are used for internal purposes:

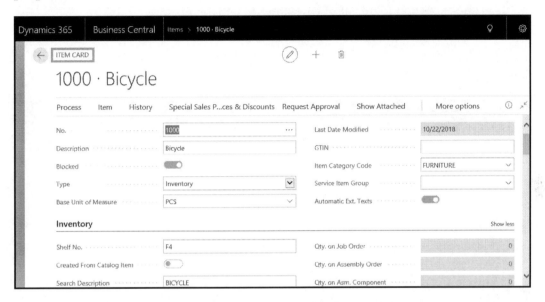

Data is shown in different tabs, grouping fields that are used for similar purposes. In the **ITEM CARD** page, we can find all these tabs—**Inventory, Cost & Posting, Price & Sales, Replenishment, Planning, Item Tracking,** and **Warehouse:**

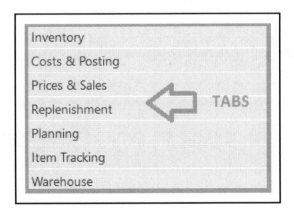

If you need to create your own card page, keep a similar structure. The card pages are always editable, which means that the user can insert, modify, or delete data on this page. Only a few fields are not editable, such as the **Last Date Modified** field. But you don't have to define this as an editable page because it is a property of the field in the table where you define whether a field is editable or not.

There is one exception to this. If one field has to be editable only in certain circumstances, you cannot define it on the table. You will need to do that on the page.

Find the **Planning** tab from the item card. Note that fields such as **Safety Stock Quantity** can only be editable with certain values from the **Reordering Policy** field:

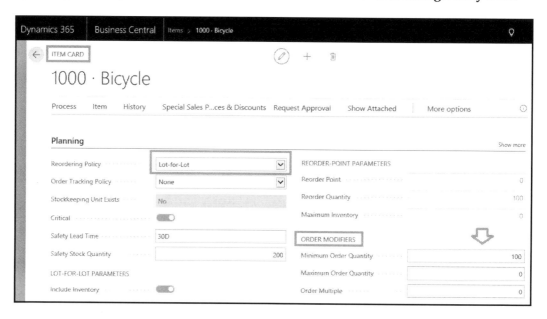

When the **Reordering Policy** field has no value entered into it, the **Safety Stock Quantity** field is not editable. This is recognizable because the field has a grey background. When you change the value to **Lot-for-Lot**, the **Safety Stock Quantity** field becomes editable. You can identify it because the fields have a white background.

As we mentioned earlier, this behavior has to be coded from the card page. Follow these steps to see how it is achieved in the item card page:

1. Open **Microsoft Dynamics NAV Development Environment**.
2. Navigate to **Tools | Object Designer.**
3. Find **Page 30 Item Card** and click on the **Design** button.
4. Navigate to **View | C/AL Code**. The following screenshot shows what you will see:

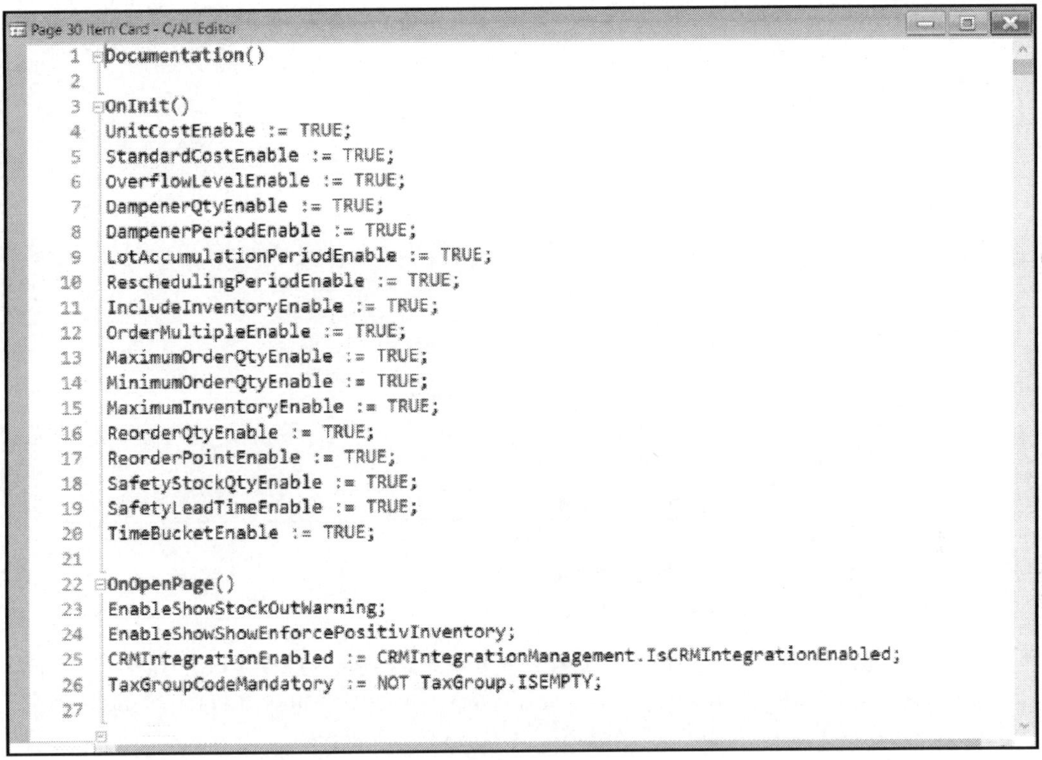

```
Page 30 Item Card - C/AL Editor
  1  Documentation()
  2
  3  OnInit()
  4  UnitCostEnable := TRUE;
  5  StandardCostEnable := TRUE;
  6  OverflowLevelEnable := TRUE;
  7  DampenerQtyEnable := TRUE;
  8  DampenerPeriodEnable := TRUE;
  9  LotAccumulationPeriodEnable := TRUE;
 10  ReschedulingPeriodEnable := TRUE;
 11  IncludeInventoryEnable := TRUE;
 12  OrderMultipleEnable := TRUE;
 13  MaximumOrderQtyEnable := TRUE;
 14  MinimumOrderQtyEnable := TRUE;
 15  MaximumInventoryEnable := TRUE;
 16  ReorderQtyEnable := TRUE;
 17  ReorderPointEnable := TRUE;
 18  SafetyStockQtyEnable := TRUE;
 19  SafetyLeadTimeEnable := TRUE;
 20  TimeBucketEnable := TRUE;
 21
 22  OnOpenPage()
 23  EnableShowStockOutWarning;
 24  EnableShowShowEnforcePositivInventory;
 25  CRMIntegrationEnabled := CRMIntegrationManagement.IsCRMIntegrationEnabled;
 26  TaxGroupCodeMandatory := NOT TaxGroup.ISEMPTY;
 27
```

Only a few lines of code are present for the non-editable fields, but there is no code for inserting or deleting a record or validating a field.

List pages

List pages show multiple records from a single table. For each card page, you will find a list page that shows data from the same table. In fact, the users access the card page from the list page. These pages are not editable and are only used to show data, not to modify or delete it.

The following screenshot shows the **Items** list page:

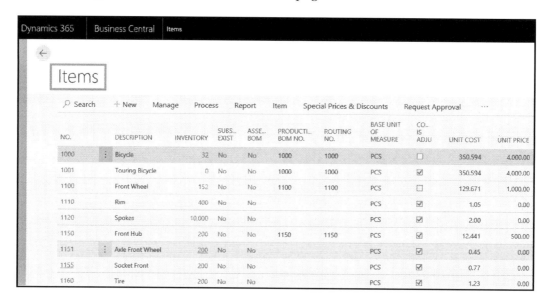

The list pages show fewer fields than the card pages. Only the most important fields of each master table are shown in the list.

All options that can be found on the **Actions** pane can also be found on the item card page. Therefore, while creating a new option, remember to make it accessible from the list page and also from its corresponding card page.

Most secondary tables don't have a card page, but all of them have a list page. When no card page can be found for a table, the list page is editable. We are allowed to insert, modify, or delete records from the list page.

This is the case of the **Item Units of Measure** page, which can be accessed from the **Actions** pane, the **Navigate** tab, the **Item entry**, and the units-of-measure icon. You will find the option both from the item card and the items list:

The list pages need to show all the fields (except internal use fields) to the user, so that he/she can fill them with the required data. By default, the **Item Units of Measure** page shows only two fields, but many others are also available to the user.

Document pages

These kinds of pages are used to show the two tables related to a **document**: the header and the lines. The document pages are used to show data related to the header, and they include a link to a ListPart page where the lines are shown.

An example of this is on the **SALES ORDER** page (with the **Lines** sections):

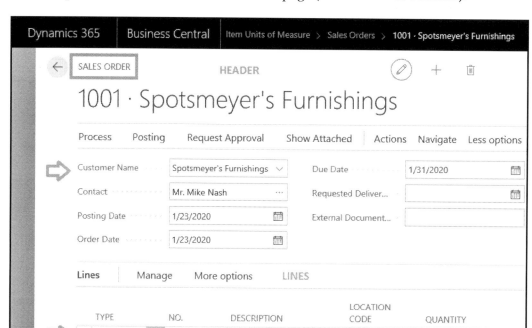

As with the card pages, the users access the document pages from a list page. The actions *and* related information found on the document page and its corresponding list page must remain the same while adding new options.

The document pages are organized in tabs, like the card page. The only difference is that the **Lines** tab shows another page—a ListPart page that is embedded into the document part.

On the right-hand side of the preceding screenshot, you can find a few tabs showing data related to the document, the customer, or the item on the order. These tabs are a particular type of page, called **CardParts**. These pages are associated to the FactBox pane of the document page.

ListPart pages

ListPart pages are pages with the same characteristics as of a list page, but the difference is that ListPart pages are always used inside other pages. Actions can also be defined for ListPart pages.

In the example of the **SALES ORDER** page listed previously, the line areas where you enter the items are created using the ListPart pages.

Worksheet pages

Worksheet pages are based on a template, batch, or name structure, and have a control for selecting a template, batch, or name. Journals are a good example of worksheet pages, but there are other worksheet examples, such as the account schedule or the requisition worksheet functionality.

The following screenshot shows the **ITEM JOURNALS** page:

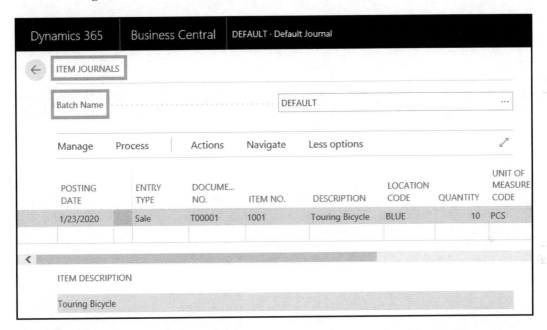

The **ITEM JOURNALS** page is based on a batch and has a control for selecting the batch name. Only the lines associated with the selected batch are shown in the page. It's similar to the header-lines structure. In this case, the header is the batch and has only one field, its name.

The users can create as many batches as needed on each journal.

Different batches on a journal can be set up as a distinction between the journal adjustments for different people. In the **Item Journal Batches** page, the **No. Series** field, the **Posting No. Series** field, or the **Reason Code** field can be filled for each batch. You will find other options on other journals.

Another reason for creating different batches on the same journal is that different people can input data on the same journal but in different batches. Doing so, the users will not disrupt each other's work.

ConfirmationDialog pages

ConfirmationDialog pages are pages that pose a question to the user, have no input fields, and require that the user selects the **Yes** or the **No** button.

The **SALES ORDER** un-posted check page shown in the following screenshot is a good example of a ConfirmationDialog page:

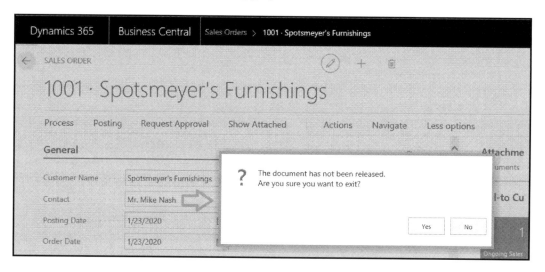

This page will pop up when a user exits from a sales order page where the sales order has not yet been processed.

NavigatePage pages

NavigatePage pages are used for wizards, which consist of a number of user input screens or steps linked together, enabling the users to carry out infrequently performed tasks.

Microsoft Dynamics NAV has a functionality called **NAVIGATE**, and the page that shows this functionality is a NavigatePage type of page:

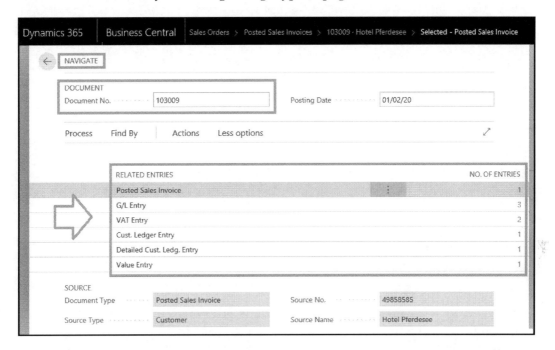

The **NAVIGATE** functionality shows all the documents and entries posted using the same document number on the same posting date. This is a very useful way to see all the entries of a particular transaction that have been posted. If you create your own entry or posted document tables, don't forget to add them to the **NAVIGATE** functionality.

Personalization feature versus "In-client" Designer feature in Web client

What are the differences between using the personalization feature and in-client designer feature with Web client? In Microsoft Dynamics 365 Business Central SaaS, with sandboxes you have both at hands, while in production you only have personalization. In shorts, there is also personalization feature that could be used if you want to add fields hidden on a page.

"In-client" Designer—you can use the "In-client" Designer feature to personalize your page:

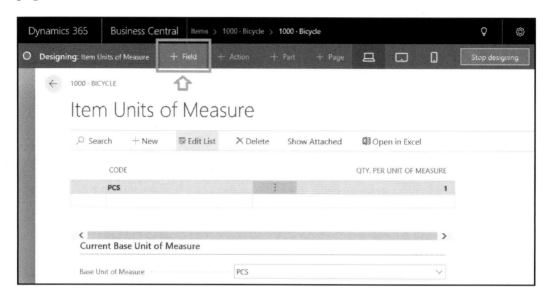

Put the cursor on **Customize Fields** and select the **Add Field to Page** option. After a drag and drop operation on a selected field (in this case, the **Height** field), the field will be added to the **Items** list page, as shown in the following screenshot:

When you have completed the customization, click on **Done** to save it:

The customized **Item Units of Measure** page now has the new fields added, as you can see in the following screenshot:

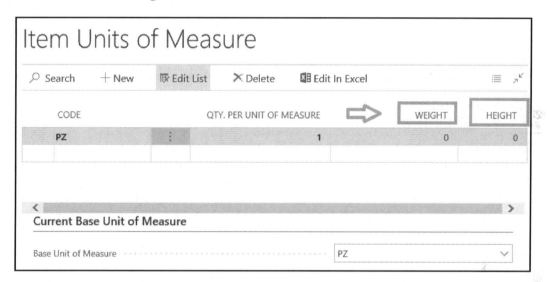

So, remember that if you want a field from a secondary table to be filled by the users, you have to make the field available from the list page (if the field is not directly accessible, you would need an extensions to make it available in the add fields selection list).

 With the master tables, you will have to make the field available from the card page and then decide whether the new field is important enough to make it available on the list page.

Development methods – the CSIDE Development Environment and the New Modern Development Environment

It's possible to develop both with the CSIDE Development Environment and with the New Modern Development Environment in Microsoft Dynamics NAV 2018 and in Microsoft Dynamics 365 Business Central on-premise; for Microsoft Dynamics 365 Business Central SaaS, it is possible to use only the New Modern Development Environment.

Working with the CSIDE Development Environment

Though it is still possible (at the time of writing this book) to develop with the CSIDE Development Environment. To open the Development Environment, you have to install **Microsoft Dynamics NAV Development Environment** (or **Microsoft Dynamics 365 Business Central Development Environment**, the appearance and the name are similar). Open it and navigate to **Tools** | **Object Designer** (or press *Shift + F12*). The following window will open:

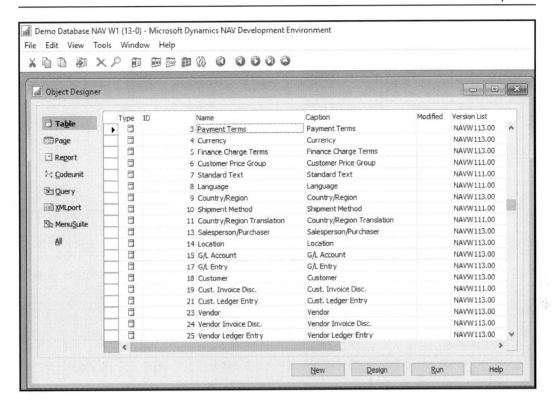

On the left-hand side, you will find a number of icons representing the different objects available. On the right-hand side, you will see a list of all the existing objects of the object type selected. In the previous screenshot, we can see a list of objects of the Table type.

All application objects are identified by an ID number. There are, however, restrictions about which numbers can be used while creating application objects. As a general rule, when you are developing for a customer, you use ID numbers between 50000 and 99999 when creating new objects, although you will have to check the exact IDs that can be used for a specific customer license. You will be allowed to modify the standard objects, but you cannot create them.

To modify an existing object, you must select it and then click on the **Design** button. This will open the object in its corresponding designer. In the following screenshot, we can see the **Table 18 Customer - Table Designer** window:

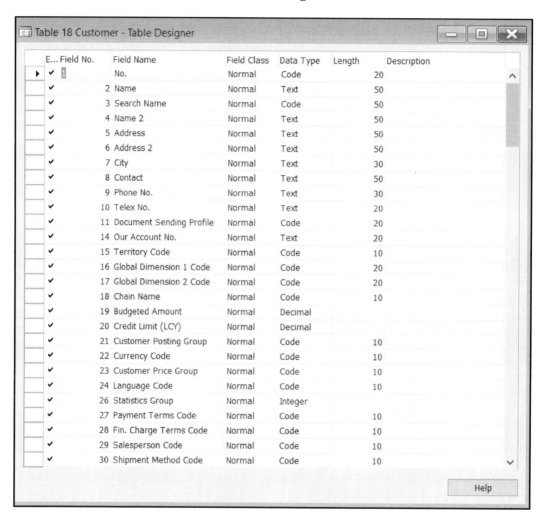

Working with CSIDE Development Environment – table properties

In **Microsoft Dynamics NAV Development Environment**, to access the table properties, scroll down from the **Table Designer** and put the cursor on an empty line at the bottom of the **Table Designer**. Then navigate to **View | Properties**, or click on the properties icon on the toolbar, or press *Shift + F4*. The **Table - Properties** window opens and shows the properties of the table. In the following screenshot, the developers can view and modify the properties for the Customer table:

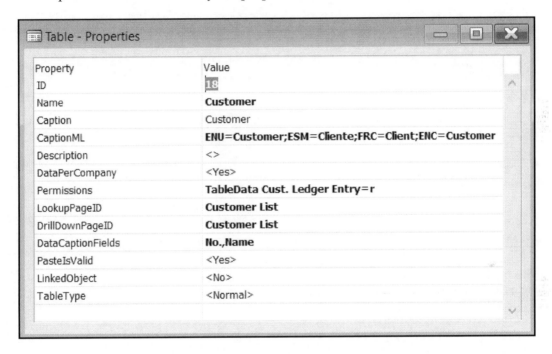

To access the triggers from the **Table Designer**, go to **View** | **C/AL Code** (or press *F9*). The following window will open, showing all the triggers of the table, including the field triggers:

```
Table 18 Customer - C/AL Editor
   1  Documentation()
   2
   3  OnInsert()
   4  IF "No." = '' THEN BEGIN
   5    SalesSetup.GET;
   6    SalesSetup.TESTFIELD("Customer Nos.");
   7    NoSeriesMgt.InitSeries(SalesSetup."Customer Nos.",xRec."No. Series",0D,"No.","No. Series");
   8  END;
   9  IF "Invoice Disc. Code" = '' THEN
  10    "Invoice Disc. Code" := "No.";
  11
  12  IF NOT InsertFromContact THEN
  13    UpdateContFromCust.OnInsert(Rec);
  14
  15  DimMgt.UpdateDefaultDim(
  16    DATABASE::Customer,"No.",
  17    "Global Dimension 1 Code","Global Dimension 2 Code");
  18
  19  OnModify()
  20  "Last Date Modified" := TODAY;
  21
  22  IF (Name <> xRec.Name) OR
  23    ("Search Name" <> xRec."Search Name") OR
  24    ("Name 2" <> xRec."Name 2") OR
  25    (Address <> xRec.Address) OR
  26    ("Address 2" <> xRec."Address 2") OR
  27    (City <> xRec.City) OR
  28    ("Phone No." <> xRec."Phone No.") OR
100 %
```

Field properties can be accessed from the **Table Designer**. Put the cursor on the field you want to check and then navigate to **View** | **Properties**, or click on the properties icon on the toolbar, or press *Shift + F4*.

The **No. - Properties** window for the selected field opens, as shown in the following screenshot:

The properties that are changed from the default settings will be highlighted in bold. Keys can be accessed from the **Table Designer** by navigating to **View** | **Keys**, as shown in the following structure:

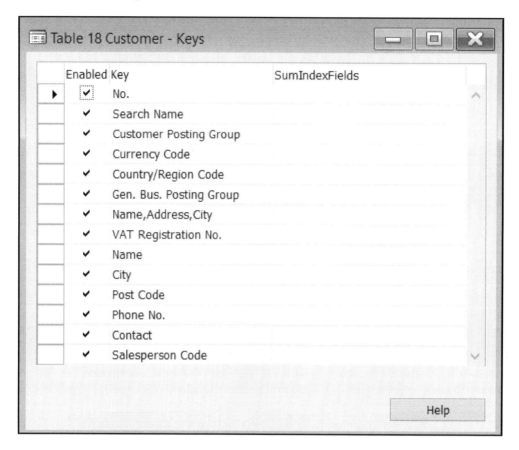

The properties of the keys can be accessed the same way you accessed the table properties or the field properties. Select the key you want to check, and navigate to **View** | **Properties**. Not all the objects have the same elements as the ones shown for the tables, but they have similar elements that can be accessed in a similar way.

Working with the New Modern Development Environment

To use the New Modern Development Environment, you need to install **Visual Studio Code** and **Microsoft AL Language extension**. In this environment, it is only possible to develop extensions to create new objects or extend existing ones; you can use some ready-to-use shortcuts named **snippets** to create the predefined structures of the objects. The following screenshot shows the Microsoft Visual Studio Code and Microsoft AL language extension environment:

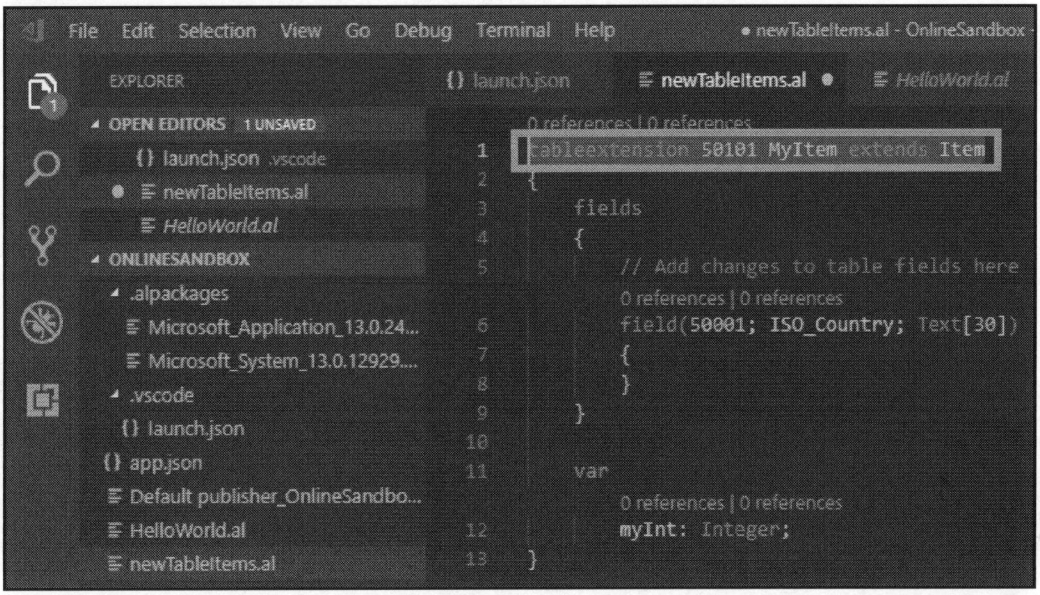

Working with the New Modern Development Environment – table properties

If you are using the New Modern Development Environment, you can set the properties for a table directly from the AL code while you are creating the object. For example, you can add the caption for the table or define properties for each field:

```
table 50104 Address
{
    caption = 'Sample table';        ⇐  Property
    DataPerCompany = true;

    fields
    {
        field(1; Address; Text[50])      ⇐  Property
        {
            Description = 'Address retrieved by Service';
        }
        field(2; Locality; Text[30])
        {
            Description = 'Locality retrieved by Service';
        }
        field(3; "Town/City"; Text[30])
        {
            Description = 'Town/City retrieved by Service';
```

You can find how to develop tables in AL language at `https://docs.microsoft.com/en-us/dynamics365/business-central/dev-itpro/developer/devenv-tables-overview`, and you will find all the information related to table properties at `https://docs.microsoft.com/en-us/dynamics365/business-central/dev-itpro/developer/properties/devenv-table-properties`.

Snippet table

Typing the shortcut table will create the basic layout for a table object when using the AL language extension.

The following is an example of a table that stores address information and has two fields: Address and Locality:

```
table 50104 Address
{
    caption = 'Sample table';
    DataPerCompany = true;

    fields
    {
        field(1; Address; Text[50])
        {
            Description = 'Address retrieved by Service';
        }
        field(2; Locality; Text[30])
        {
            Description = 'Locality retrieved by Service';
        }
    }
    keys
    {
        key(PrimaryKey; Address)
        {
            Clustered = TRUE;
        }
    }
    trigger OnInsert();
    begin
    end;

    procedure MyMethod();
    begin
        Message(Msg);
    end;
}
```

Table extension object

The **table extension object** allows you to add additional fields or to change some properties on a table provided by Microsoft Dynamics 365 Business Central. In this way, you can add data to the same table and treat it as a single table.

When developing a solution for Microsoft Dynamics 365 Business Central, you follow the code layout for a table extension, as shown in the following sections.

Snippet ttableextension

Typing the shortcut `ttableextension` will create the basic layout for a table extension object when using the AL language extension.

The following is an example of a table extension object that extends the `Customer` table object by adding a `ShoeSize` field:

```
tableextension 50115 RetailWinterSportsStore extends Customer
{
    fields
    {
        field(50116;ShoeSize;Integer)
        {
            trigger OnValidate();
            begin
                if (rec.ShoeSize < 0) then
                begin
                    message('Shoe size not valid: %1', rec.ShoeSize);
                end;
            end;
        }
    }

    procedure HasShoeSize() : Boolean;
    begin
        exit(ShoeSize <> 0);
    end;

    trigger OnBeforeInsert();
    begin
        if not HasShoeSize then
            ShoeSize := Random(42);
    end;
}
```

 Extension objects can have a name with a maximum length of 30 characters.

The posting process

The posting process is the most important process in Microsoft Dynamics NAV. It commits the data entered by the users into the financial ledgers. There are a few different posting processes; however, they all follow the same structure. The posting process runs through a lot of code from a lot of functions. In fact, many functions are executed many times. This section does not cover the posting process in depth; instead, it shows the overview of the codeunits and how they are structured.

There are several posting routines, one for each journal table and one for each group of documents. All posting routines use more than one codeunit. In Microsoft Dynamics NAV, you can find more than 80 codeunits with the word *post* in their description. That's quite a few!

Let's see a couple of examples of the posting codeunits' structure. The first example is the posting codeunits for sales documents. In the second example, we will see posting codeunits for **General Journal** lines.

The codeunit structure for sales posting

The sales posting routine starts with four codeunits. The following diagram shows the schema that shows how each codeunit relates to the others:

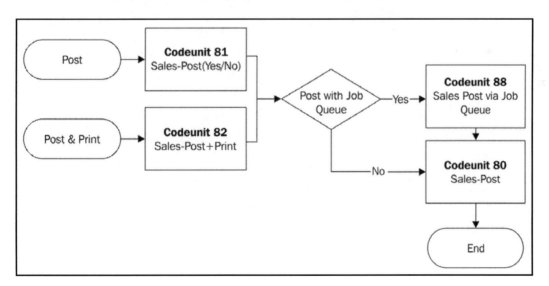

A user can start the posting process by selecting the **Post** or the **Post & Print** action, which will run **Codeunit 81 Sales-Post (Yes/No)** or **Codeunit 82 Sales-Post + Print** respectively. Both codeunits perform the same action; the only difference is that the **Codeunit 82 Sales-Post + Print** prints the posted sales document at the end.

Both codeunits ask a confirmation from the user and check whether the post with the job queue is activated. If the post with the job queue is activated, they call the **Codeunit 88 Sales Post via Job Queue**, which is an automatic process to post documents when the system is not busy.

When the record in the queue is processed, **Codeunit 80 Sales-Post** is called in order to end the posting routine. If the post with the job queue is not activated, **Codeunit 80 Sales-Post** is called from **Codeunit 81 or Codeunit 82**.

Codeunit 80 Sales-Post is the most important one. It checks the data, inserts records into the historical document tables, and creates all the required journal lines. It also calls the posting routines for the journal lines. You will find similar structures in the other document-posting routines.

The codeunit structure for general journal posting

The general journal routine consists of seven codeunits. The following screenshot shows us the schema of how each codeunit relates to each other:

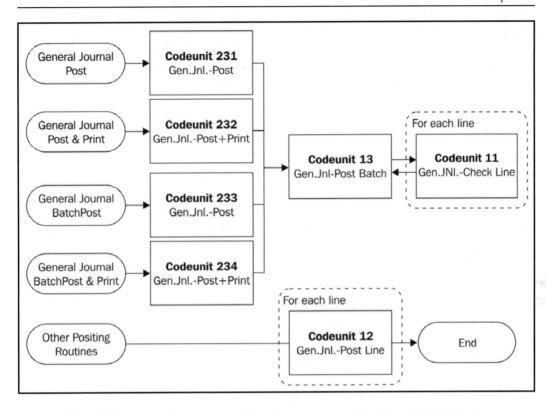

The general journal posting routine can start from several places. Either from a general journal page or a general journal batch page. When the user clicks on **Post** or **Post & Print**, this will run one of the following codeunits: **Codeunit 231 Gen. Jnl.-Post, Codeunit 232 Gen. Jnl.-Post + Print, Codeunit 233 Gen. Jnl.-B.Post**, or **Codeunit 234 Gen. Jnl.-B.Post + Print**.

All these codeunits ask for confirmation from the user, and **Codeunit 232** and **Codeunit 234** also print the posted entries at the end. After that, they all call **Codeunit 13 Gen. Jnl.-Post Batch**. This codeunit checks the consistency of all the lines individually, by calling **Codeunit 11 Gen. Jnl.-Check Line**. **Codeunit 13** also checks that all the lines in the transactions are balanced, and, if so, it inserts some secondary data into the records.

Finally, **Codeunit 13** calls **Codeunit 12 Gen. Jnl.-Post Line** for each line. **Codeunit 12** is the one in charge of creating the corresponding ledger entries. If some other posting routines need to post General Journal Lines, they do so by calling **Codeunit 12** directly.

Validating fields

When a field is filled, a special trigger runs the OnValidate trigger of the field. For a given field, you will find an OnValidate trigger on the page where the user enters the data and also on the table itself. Whenever possible, write your code on the OnValidate trigger of the table.

A field can be shown on multiple pages. If you choose to validate the field on the page, you will have to replicate your code in all the pages where the field is shown. This will make your code difficult to maintain.

Batch jobs through reports objects

Batch jobs are written using report objects. Typically, batch jobs are not to be done for all the records on a table, but for a set of them. In most cases, it is the user who selects which set of data has to be processed. The report objects are the ones that best suit these requirements, since they have an interface that allows the users to select options or filter the data:

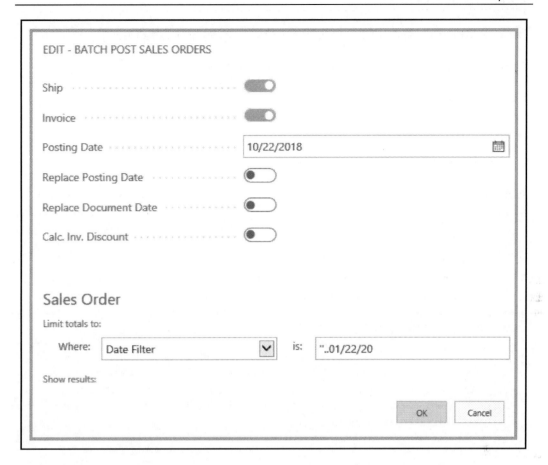

The previous screenshot is an example of a **BATCH POST SALES ORDER** report. It is used to post multiple sales orders at once. As we can see in the screenshot, there is a **Sales Order** tab that allows the users to filter the data.

In this section, we saw where to write customized code. Besides following the guidelines given in this book, there are other options that will help you choose where to write your code.

When you need to write a new functionality, you can search for a similar functionality on the standard application and try to mimic the structure (this tip is valid for Microsoft Dynamics NAV, Microsoft Dynamics 365 Business Central on-premise and SaaS, AL Extension code for Microsoft standard is open. You can download or even submit your changes for improvements).

Where to write customized code

While writing your own customized code for Microsoft Dynamics NAV, it is important to choose where to write that code. Code can be written in different places, and the application will still work as you had intended. Unfortunately, not all places are good choices. Depending on where you write your code, it may be easier or more difficult to expand or change functionality.

As already mentioned, developing Microsoft Dynamics 365 Business Central on-premise and Microsoft Dynamics NAV can be done in the same way. However, developing Microsoft Dynamics 365 Business Central SaaS is different because of the following reasons:

- It's not possible to modify the standard
- It's possible to develop only through extensions
- Microsoft extension code is open. It is possible to see the source code of published extensions (It depends if showmycode is set to true or false).

Therefore, the model of development changes radically.

 In this section, we will give you some guidelines for choosing where to write your code in Microsoft Dynamics NAV. At the end of the chapter, we will see the differences between Microsoft Dynamics NAV and Microsoft Dynamics 365 Business Central SaaS and the different development methods.

Formatting customized code

Your customized code should look like the standard code. Keep in mind that any code you write today will probably be maintained by others in the future. If you follow your own programming conventions, we are pretty sure you'll find it easier to write and read. Unfortunately, others may not be used to your conventions, so you'll be making their lives a lot harder.

All Microsoft Dynamics NAV and Microsoft Dynamics 365 Business Central on-premise developers are used to reading code from the standard application. If everyone writes customized code like the standard application does, everybody will only be able to read their own code. To make it easy to maintain an application, it is important to follow a few strict guidelines while writing C/AL or AL code, the standards can be found in the C/AL programming guide and AL programming guide.

The C/AL guide can be found published on MSDN at `https://docs.microsoft.com/en-us/dynamics-nav/programming-in-c-al`. The AL guide can be found published on MSDN at `https://docs.microsoft.com/en-us/dynamics365/business-central/dev-itpro/developer/devenv-programming-in-al`.

Development in Microsoft Dynamics 365 Business Central SaaS

In this section, some differences related to the development for native applications for the cloud compared to the development of applications for on-premises will be listed; what works correctly on on-premise deployments may not work on the cloud as some restrictions existing on the cloud are not present in on-premise.

General considerations

Developing for the cloud is different than developing for on-premise because the architecture is very different: You can't have access to hardware, operating systems, installations, and components.

In the case of development for the Dynamics 365 Business Central SaaS platform, the developer must be aware of some of the following constraints:

- The database cannot be accessed (data, managing, queries, and so on)
- We do not have a local backup of the data (we can only ask for a recovery)
- It is not possible to access server services (only for some functions and telemetry)
- The standard product cannot be changed
- The system updates automatically (and you can set the time slot when the tenant can be updated)
- We should always test the apps in a sandbox before installing them (this is a best practice but not a constraint)
- We can/must open a support request to Microsoft for maintenance and requests

The following is a list of some of the benefits:

- It offers modern, innovative, and professional development environment (this is not a limitation and not a constraint, is a feature
- There is no risk of breaching the standard and the apps are safe (check the installation)
- The system is more scalable, high-performing, secure, and highly reliable (and it is all managed and monitored by Microsoft hosted in a public cloud through several Windows Azure services)
- Infrastructure costs are lower (everything is in the cloud)
- The upgrade is automatic (the system always updated)
- The user only logs once with a nominal user and uses it everywhere
- With Docker, local development environments can be used if needed

 See behind the scenes of Microsoft Dynamics 365 Business Central on Public Azure at `https://pssiusa.blog/2018/08/21/behind-the-scenes-of-dynamics-365-business-central-and-the-public-cloud-azure-version/`, and reasons to buy or move to Business Central in 2018 at `https://msdynamicsworld.com/story/reasons-buy-or-move-business-central-2018`.

Microsoft Dynamics 365 Business Central Roadmap for development

The Roadmap for Microsoft Dynamics 365 Business Central, presented at the Directions EMEA 2018 conference, shows how the development environment will change in the next few years:

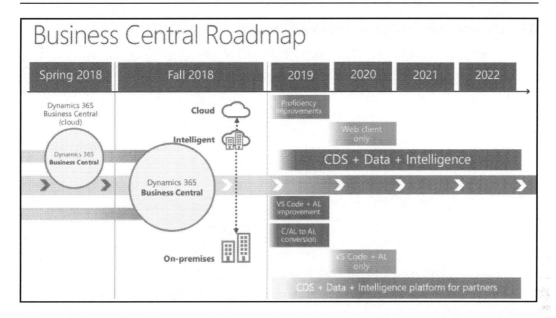

The Microsoft Dynamics 365 Business Central Roadmap (2018-2022) makes these predictions for the following years:

In 2019:

- Proficiency improvements
- Conversion from C/L to AL time
- Hybrid system (intelligence cloud to move data to SaaS)

In 2020:

- Web client only
- VS Code and AL only

After 2020:

- Welcome to SaaS with web and apps

How to become a 2.0 Microsoft ERP solution developer

A Microsoft 2.0 ERP solution developer should know about the following:

- AL development
- Docker
- Source control
- Azure cloud ecosystem
- Integration aspects (web services and APIs)
- SaaS versus on-premise differences
- Common data services and Dynamics 365 family overview

2020 is not so far! You need to be ready and compliant

Best lessons learned for developers

Every developer should take into consideration that Microsoft has these things in mind:

- Cloud and Mobile first is the motto.
- Move solutions to AL, use repeatable IP when possible, and create lean and smart apps.
- Forget Windows client. Demo only with Web client.
- Integrate artificial intelligence and machine learning when possible.
- VS Code and the Microsoft AL language extension are modern solutions with continuous improvements.
- Intelligent cloud is the solution to move your customers to (transition from on-premise to SaaS).
- Collaboration and suggestions are the keys. Use Microsoft Ideas for suggestions, the Microsoft AL Issue page on GitHub for bug/improvements, and the Collaborate portal to test insider releases ; all these portals are useful for creating a valuable product that reflects the real needs of the customers and partners.
- MVPs are a great opportunity for collecting ideas and sharing knowledge (or people's opinions).
- Get ready for SaaS development.

If you are interested in the news presented to the Directions EMEA 2018, you can consult my blog where you will find a diary of the event. Use the following link: `https://robertostefanettinavblog.com/2018/10/29/directions-emea-2018-wip-diary/`.

The new extension model (2.0)

The **new extension model** is the new way to develop applications for Microsoft Dynamics NAV or Microsoft Dynamics 365 Business Central for on-premise and cloud, based on extensions. For Microsoft Dynamics 365 Business Central SaaS, it is the only one development method possible.

According to Microsoft, an extension is an installable feature for Microsoft Dynamics NAV and Dynamics 365 Business Central built in a way that doesn't directly alter source resources and is distributed as a preconfigured package.

The package is developed by the New Modern Development Environment (VS Code plus AL language extension), which extends standard objects and uses events for creating custom business logic or existing standard objects:

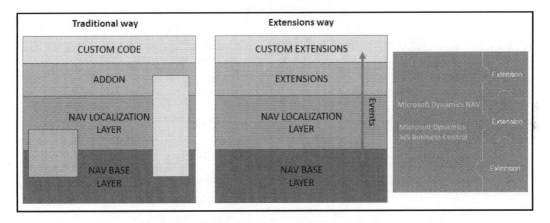

Diagram taken from Dynamics 365 Business Central Development Quick Start Guide by Stefano Demiliani

So, are extensions customizations? Yes! If you're familiar with the Dynamics NAV customization model, then you're probably used to making changes directly on objects. The extension model asks you to design your changes differently—namely, make those changes by extending the core objects and linking to code using events.

New era for developer skills

Extensions are the right way to build for SaaS, as they allow you to sell your product in Microsoft AppSource, and you can take advantage of the upgrade investments.

Extensions also offer additional protection for your IP compared to the very open source nature of classic Dynamics NAV, as well as platform stability and a reduced time to deployment.

We are in a new era for developer skills. The following table compares the skills of today with those of tomorrow:

Today	Tomorrow
Business process	Business process
C/SIDE	Visual Studio Code
C/AL	AL
Windows and web client	Web client
Integrations (WS and API)	Integrations (WS and API)
Data tier management	No access to data tier, platform restrictions, no database access (on cloud)
Database full control	Events and extensions
Customize: do what you want	Source control (Git, GitHub)
	Docker, sandbox
	Different debug

Microsoft suggestions for developers

Microsoft has just released some useful information for developers, which make us understand in which direction they are going.

The most important are these:

- Microsoft is converting all base apps to AL (moving completely from C/AL to AL)
- Some releases of Business Central will be shared for preview after conversion
- Txt2AL is upgrading and evolving to support best automatic code conversion
- You need to familiarize with AL, VS Code, and Git
- Use a ready-to-go platform to be ready and compliant

Extensions 2.0 – .fob package versus .app package

Some specifications about the .fob and .app packages are as follows:

- They were developed on the New Modern Development Environment (VS Code plus AL extension language)
- All functionalities are coded as objects, the objects are stored in AL code in .al files
- A single .al file can contain multiple objects
- Table and page extensions, are used for defining additive or overriding changes to a standard object in the customization layer
- They are compiled as .app package files; the package can be deployed to server/tenant
- .NET variables support is possible only for the on-premises releases

The following table compares the .fob and .app packages:

.fob objects (old model)	.app objects (new model)
Package—final object, standard old package	Package: Extension-based—AL files, app.json, launch.json
Source code visible in C/SIDE	No
Include standard objects plus new objects, standard code can be changed	Extension of standard objects plus additional business logic plus new objects; Event-based
Imported in NAV server via C/SIDE	Deploy via PowerShell, VS Code, manual upload

> For more details about differences between old and new development models, take a look here: https://msdn.microsoft.com/en-us/dynamics-nav/developer/devenv-differences.

The New Modern Development Environment (VS Code plus Microsoft AL extension language)

The following diagram depicts the old and new development environments. The New Modern Development Environment comprises two elements:

- **VS Code** is the new open source development environment.
- **AL language extension** is the file-based AL extension language for VS Code:

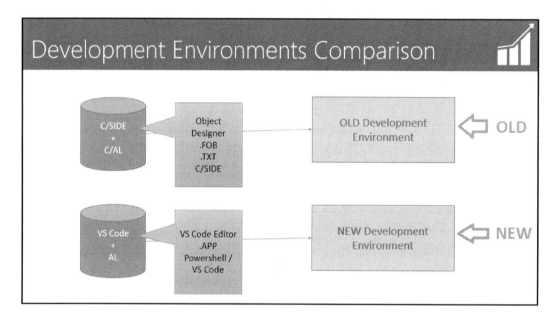

Visual Studio Code (VS Code)

VS Code is a modern tool for development in the modern era. According to Microsoft, it is an open source, cross-platform, multi-language development environment that puts writing code at its center.

Some core specifics are as follows:

- Free, open source (MIT license)
- Code-centric (AL language extensibility)
- Folder-based environment (not project-based)
- Native version control (Git)

- Cross-platform (Windows, macOS X, Linux-not supported with AL language)
- Symbols (`AL:DownloadSymbols`)
- Debugger
- Code optimized
- Extensions
- Community supported
- Always updated—monthly/nightly build

The following screenshot shows the `launch.json` file in the VS Code editor:

> You can view the VS Code main page here: `https://code.visualstudio.com/`.

Microsoft AL language extension

Microsoft AL is the extension programming language that is used for manipulating data (such as retrieving, inserting, and modifying records) in Dynamics 365 Business Central, and controlling the execution of the various application objects, such as pages, reports, or codeunits.

With AL, you can create *business rules* to ensure that the data that is stored in the database is meaningful and consistent with the way customers do business.

Through AL programming , you can do the following for example:

- Add new data or transfer data from one table to another, for example, from a journal table to a ledger table
- Combine data from multiple tables into one report or display it on one form or page

Where to write AL code? You can only extend the code by subscribing to published events.

 For more details, see the Microsoft AL language extension link given here: `https://msdn.microsoft.com/en-us/dynamics-nav/developer/devenv-programming-in-al`.

Events instead of triggers

In all Microsoft Dynamics NAV objects, we can have triggers; triggers are predefined functions that are fired when certain actions are executed. Since Microsoft Dynamics NAV 2016 *events* have been introduced; events are integration points inside a Microsoft Dynamics NAV application. The new development model for developing extensions is based on events.

We can have three different elements for events:

- **Event**: Declaration of the action in application
- **Publisher**: Contains the event declaration to expose
- **Subscriber**: Object that listens for published events

An event can have multiple subscribers. In this case the execution order is random; this situation must be kept in mind during development to avoid mistakes.

We can have five types of events:

- **Database events**: Raised automatically by the system for insert, delete, modify, and rename
- **Page events**: Raised automatically by the system
- **Business events**: Custom events raised by the system, not changed in future releases

- **Integration events**: Custom events raised by the system, may be changed in future releases
- **System events**: Predefined system events raised by system

For more info about events, see my blog article: *Publish, Raise, and Subscribe* (`https://robertostefanettinavblog.com/2015/10/27/publish-raise-and-subscribe/`).

Txt2AL – conversion tool from C/AL to AL

The Txt2AL free conversion tool (a `.exe` file) can be used to convert from C/AL to AL language.

If you need or convert the code from C/AL to AL language using the Txt2AL tool, it converts the code from the C/AL format to AL format.

Currently, the tool is still working and is being constantly updated and improved to help developers to convert existing solutions to extensions; Microsoft is converting localizations by bringing them into extension mode as well.

The Txt2AL tool specifics can be seen here: `https://docs.microsoft.com/en-us/dynamics365/business-central/dev-itpro/developer/devenv-txt2al-tool`.

What's new for Microsoft Dynamics 365 Business Central for development?

The major new features in Microsoft Dynamics 365 Business Central that have become available since October 2018 release and they are as follows:

- Per-tenant customizations
- The new Business Central CSP administration portal (from the CSP portal—a complete set of management tools ready to use)
- Creation of sandboxes with production data and isolation (also from the CSP portal)
- Telemetry for all customers/tenants (from the CSP portal)—you can monitor everything (events fired, GDPR activities, and so on) for each customer/tenant

You can find a lot of info about extension development in my blog, (`https://robertostefanettinavblog.com/?s=extension`) or in my SlideShare page `https://www.slideshare.net/RobertoStefanetti/presentations`.

Naming guidelines for development

It's necessary to use and follow some coding rules in order to make clear what the extensions we are preparing to develop will do. Let's look at the following rules:

- **Full object rules**: `<Type><Id>.<ObjectName>.al` (for example, `Tab.50100.MyTable.al`)
- **Extension rules**: `<Type>.<BaseID>-Ext<ObjectId>.<ObjectName>.al` (for example, `page 50100 "MyPage" extends "Customer Card"`: `Pag21-Ext50100.MyPage.al`)
- **Prefix/suffix tag**: It's required to use a prefix or suffix for the name property of the fields in your extension; the tag must be three characters, and the object/field name must start or end with the tag (for example, `MYPREFIXSalesPersonCode`)

 To read an interesting page about best practices for AL code, see `https://docs.microsoft.com/en-us/dynamics365/business-central/dev-itpro/compliance/apptest-bestpracticesforalcode`.

Extension translations (XLIFF file extension)

Microsoft Dynamics 365 Business Central is multilanguage enabled, which means that you can display the **user interface** (**UI**) in different languages. To add a new language to the extension, you have built you must first enable the generation of XLIFF files.

The XLIFF file extension is `.xlf`; the generated XLIFF file contains the strings that are specified in properties, such as `Caption` and `Tooltip`.

Generating the XLIFF file

To enable generation of the translation file, you must add a setting in the manifest. In the `app.json` file of your extension, add the following line:

```
"features": [ "TranslationFile" ]
```

Now, when you run the `build` command (*Ctrl + Shift + B*) in VS Code, a `\Translation` folder will be generated and populated with the `.xlf` file that contains all the labels, label properties, and report labels that you are using in the extension. The generated `.xlf` file can now be translated.

> Make sure to rename the translated file to avoid the file being overwritten next time the extension is built.

Source Control Management (SCM)

SCM is necessary to keep projects under control, especially on multi-projects spanning different environments.

A good SCM system should manage the following:

- Versioning and chronological changes
- Comparing and merging
- Restoring to checkpoint

Git and GitHub

If you need to use Microsoft Dynamics NAV or Microsoft Dynamics 365 Business Central with SCM integration, Git is the best solution (free, open source and natively integrated with VS Code).

What is Git? Git is a version control system for tracking changes (SCM) in computer files and coordinating work on those files among multiple people. Git is an open source distributed version control engine. VS Code supports Git natively.

Some Git commands are as follows:

- cmd: `git remote add origin master <repo url>`
- cmd: `git push -u origin master`
- cmd: `git push -u add master`

The Git local repository commits to GitHub, pushes the content of the local repository into the branch called `master`.

The following screenshot shows Git commands through the command palette:

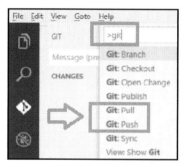

What is GitHub? GitHub is a web-based hosting service for version control using Git.

Install Git from `https://git-scm.com/`. You can learn more about Git specifics at `https://www.git-scm.com/about/free-and-open-source`.

Publishing your apps on AppSource

Let's now learn how to publish an app on Microsoft Store. Publishing an app is simple: you can do it either as a Microsoft partner or as an individual. Partners can already use the partner account to do this. For individual people, a registration is required as a personal publisher, and a one-time cost for publication is required. The app, after being proposed and evaluated, must be verified for publication, and will be assigned an ID with a dedicated number; once published it will be available for download/installation.

The **Microsoft | Store** home page looks as shown:

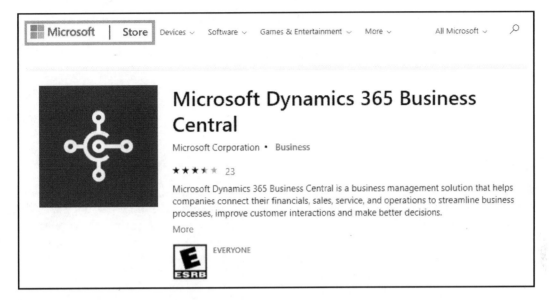

Steps to publishing an app

Two steps are necessary to publish an app on Microsoft Store:

1. Create an account
2. Send your idea of an app

To create an account, you can choose an account type: partner or developer

- **Partner account:** You need an MPN partner ID
- **Developer account:** A private account granted to a developer

To be a developer—if you aren't a partner, you can register as a developer here:
`https://developer.microsoft.com/it-it/store/register`.

The following are some resources for proposing and publishing an app:

- **Propose and upload your app**: `https://appsource.microsoft.com/it-it/ partners/list-an-app`
- **Checklist before submitting**: `https://docs.microsoft.com/it-it/ dynamics-nav/developer/devenv-checklist-submission`
- **Signing an extension**: `https://docs.microsoft.com/it-it/dynamics- nav/developer/devenv-sign-extension`

Summary

In this chapter, we saw that Microsoft Dynamics NAV and Microsoft Dynamics 365 Business Central offer many configuration options and workarounds that we should use before starting to write our own code. If you need to write customized code, it is important to do it following the same structure as the standard application, to avoid confusing the users. The structures of the tables and the pages are the most important ones, and we've seen them in depth.

The posting processes, or posting routines, are the ones in charge of creating historical documents and entries. If you need to modify them, you have to be careful and know what you are doing. That's why we have explained the main idea of posting routines. Last but not least, we saw where and how to write customized code on the Microsoft Dynamics NAV objects.

Almost every Microsoft Dynamics NAV or Microsoft Dynamics 365 Business Central implementation will need some kind of changes.

In the old development model, the customized code could also be inserted inside the application standard code, and it looked as if it was part of the standard. This made it easier for users to understand how customized modules worked and easier for partners to support it. A good initial development also makes any future change easier and cheaper for both the customer and the partner.

In the new development model (based on extensions), the customized code exists only in extensions, and it is not possible to modify the standard in any way, which is the right choice to develop in the SaaS world.

In the following chapter, we will see how to implement functional changes on existing and running Microsoft Dynamics NAV implementations and in Microsoft Dynamics 365 Business Central.

9
Implementing Functional Changes

The world changes constantly; therefore, the demands for every company that's interested in keeping doing business will need to change with it.

A company may require functional changes on their Microsoft Dynamics NAV or Microsoft Dynamics 365 Business Central implementation as more and more demands from external parties they do business with emerge. The new project may not be an implementation project, but some of the steps that have to be taken on an implementation project also apply. There are some other things to take into account and this chapter will explain how to handle a project like this one, by analyzing the actions to be performed using four examples of a functional change in an installed and operative system:

- The Requisition Worksheet
- Fixed Assets
- Item Tracking
- Extending a customized functionality

General guidelines

Depending on the requirements, the functional changes will be different. Some will just require a few actions to complete the change; others may require many actions, which are not just related to the functionality being changed. There are a few things to take into account when implementing a functional change. In this section, we will provide some general guidelines. Later on, we will follow the guidelines for all the examples in the chapter.

The following diagram shows the general steps that should be performed to implement a functional change:

The steps in detail are as follows:

1. The first step is to clearly define the functional change.
2. Think about how this change will affect existing Microsoft Dynamics NAV or Microsoft Dynamics 365 Business Central functionalities and whether those functionalities will need to be changed as well.
3. Define a list of all the actions that will have to be completed to be able to implement the functional change.
4. Choose the right time to implement the change.
5. Actually implement the change into the system.

What is a functional change?

A functional change in a Microsoft Dynamics NAV or Microsoft Dynamics 365 Business Central implementation involves using an application functionality not used before, or to change the way certain application functionalities were used in the past.

From the introduction of Microsoft Dynamics NAV 2016 to Microsoft Dynamics 365 Business Central, the development model has changed. As already said, it is not recommended to change the standard of the product as done previously with the old versions of Microsoft Dynamics NAV (in Microsoft Dynamics 365 Business Central SaaS it is not possible to change the standard code). It is mandatory to use the extension model supported by the events for development; in this way, it is possible to preserve the standard product's code and easily remove the customizations installed in the system.

Here are some examples of some new functionalities that a company might want to explore after these ERP systems are implemented.

Scenario – the Requisition Worksheet

Imagine a distribution company that purchases items from its vendors and sells those same items to its customers. This company does not have any kind of automation in its purchase order creation process. It manually determines when purchase orders have to be created, for which items, and in what quantities.

The aim of automating this process to reduce the time invested in purchase order creation is that the company wants to start using the **Requisition Worksheet** based on the replenishment parameters established in every item. This function will calculate the replenishment needs of the company and allow the user to automatically create the corresponding replenishment purchase orders:

Fixed Assets

You could also think of a company that has never used the **Fixed Assets** functional area and has been keeping its fixed assets by posting manual accounting transactions using the **Fixed Asset G/L Journal**. The company may want to start using the **Fixed Assets** functionality to better manage its fixed assets and automate some of its depreciation entries:

Item Tracking

A company may have been working with items for a long time, but now it has developed new products and the company wants to start keeping track of their lot and serial numbers. Implementing the **Item Tracking** feature allows the company to have detailed control (traceability) of all the movements that need to be traced. From the page in the following screenshot (named **Item Tracing**), it is possible to search existing tracking entries for items, filtering for both the lot and serial numbers:

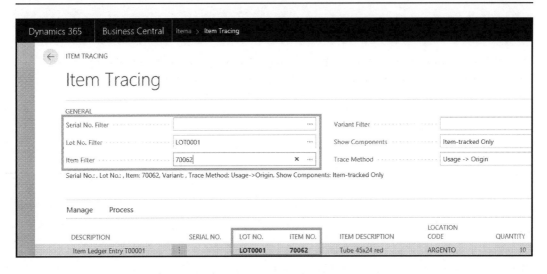

Extending a customized functionality

Sometimes, the existing functionality may not meet what your business needs. In this case, customization will be required. The custom requirements will be as follows:

- Volume discounts were calculated for each sales invoice line, according to a set of predefined rules, and they were stored as **volume discount ledger entries**.
- When thousands of volume discount ledger entries existed in the system, the company wanted to be able to apply those ledger entries to other ledger entries, so that they could know which entries are still open, partially open, or closed. This is similar to how an application of customer ledger entries or vendor ledger entries works in standard Microsoft Dynamics NAV or in Microsoft Dynamics 365 Business Central.

Interactions with other functionalities

If you have to make a functional change in a Microsoft Dynamics NAV or Microsoft Dynamics 365 Business Central implementation that has been working for a while, the questions that should be answered are as follows:

- Does the functionality being changed (or that will begin to be used) have interactions with other functionalities?
- What are those interactions?
- How will the other functionalities have to change?
- How many of these features could have an invasive impact on the standard product with a view to installing updates?

The Requisition Worksheet

The Requisition Worksheet has interactions with the **Purchase** functionality of Microsoft Dynamics NAV or Microsoft Dynamics 365 Business Central, since purchase orders can be created as the result of running the Requisition Worksheet.

However, it also has interactions with items (as they hold the replenishment parameters that the Requisition Worksheet will use, and since the Requisition Worksheet will check this functionality to establish the demand for items), and with other functionalities that represent the demand of items (item transfers between locations, production components, service orders, and so on), and again with the **Purchase** functionality (since the Requisition Worksheet will check this functionality to get the supply of items) and other functionalities that represent the supply of items (item transfers between locations, inventory, production, and so on).

The answer to the question of how those functionalities will have to change, in the case of using the Requisition Worksheet, is that they do not have to change at all. Not in a standard product at least.

What will definitely have to change is the way users create purchase orders. The old procedure will not be used anymore, as it will be replaced by a new procedure.

Fixed Assets

The **Fixed Assets** functionality interacts with the **Financial Management** functionality:

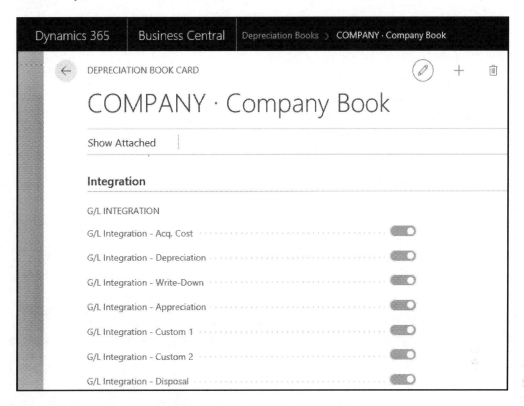

The acquisition costs and depreciation of the company's fixed assets have probably already been posted to the general ledger by posting manual transactions using the general journal. But, this will have to change in the future. Those transactions will not be posted by creating manual transactions anymore, but by using the standard functionality offered by the Microsoft Dynamics NAV or Microsoft Dynamics 365 Business Central Fixed Assets module. The accounting procedure will have to be changed.

Fixed Assets also interact with Microsoft Dynamics **Sales** and **Purchase** functionalities, as fixed assets can either be sold or purchased using those functionalities. The user's procedures to post those transactions will change when the new functionality starts being used.

Item Tracking

The **Item Tracking** functionality interacts with all the Microsoft Dynamics NAV or Microsoft Dynamics 365 Business Central areas that use items to post item transactions, such as these:

- Sales and marketing
- Purchase
- Warehouse
- Manufacturing
- Jobs

Every single item posting a transaction will have to change since **Item Tracking** will have to be informed prior to posting. Examine all the places where you use items. Very often, items have some kind of customization in Microsoft Dynamics NAV. When determining interactions with other functionalities, take into account those customizations. They may not have been developed to support **Item Tracking**.

Item Tracking also interacts with **Item Ledger Entry**. Even if the actual inventory of an item is 0, the **Item Tracking** feature, that involves either **SN Specific Tracking** or **Lot Specific Tracking** if the item has had any kind of movement in the past, is not permitted.

This is a big problem for most companies, as the only way (without customizing Microsoft Dynamics NAV or Microsoft Dynamics 365 Business Central) to start using **Item Tracking** for already used items is to use the official workaround, which involves the following steps:

1. For the item in question, reduce the quantity in hand to 0 by making a negative adjustment.
2. Rename the item in question.
3. Create a new item and give it the name of the original item.
4. Set up an **Item Tracking Code** for the new item.
5. For the new item, increase the quantity in hand to the original amount by making a positive adjustment.

Companies don't like this workaround. It involves a lot of work and a lot of problems:

- This workaround involves doubling your list of items (if **Item Tracking** has to be used in all items).
- It involves "losing" your item's history (entries, orders, and so on), as this will be under the renamed item and not under the new item.
- When renaming, not only the history of the item will be renamed, but also all kinds of related data (units of measure, sales and purchase prices, sales and purchase discounts, item variants, extended texts, cross references, stockkeeping units, bills of materials, and so on) and other documents. However, not only historical documents (posted documents) will point to the renamed item, but pending documents as well. So, you will have to go to all pending documents, one by one, and change the **Item No.** field so that the new item is shipped, received, or manufactured, instead of the old one. You will also have to check bills of materials where that item was used, because you probably also want to point it to the new item.
- Creating a new item involves not only creating the item itself, but also its related data (units of measure, sales and purchase prices, sales and purchase discounts, item variants, extended texts, cross references, stockkeeping units, bill of materials, and so on).

If you have to do this for thousands of items and you have a lot of data related to your items and a bunch of pending documents, then completing all those steps can take many hours (even days).

You could also think about customization. Do not check whether **Item Ledger Entry** exists for the item and allow the **Item Tracking** functionality to be turned on. If you do so, we recommend a lot of testing work. If Microsoft doesn't allow this change to be made, it is probably because the application has not been designed to do it under those circumstances. If you plan on turning on **Item Tracking** on your existing items without using the official workaround and allowing it through customization, test the application so that no data inconsistency is introduced due to the change.

By testing, you may find odd behaviors that you will have to take into account in the future.

For instance, an undo action on a **Sales Shipment** posted prior to the change (so posted without any **Item Tracking** information) may not work as expected. There is no tracking information for the undo action to use, but the item now requires this information. The standard functionality of Microsoft Dynamics NAV and Microsoft Dynamics 365 Business Central hasn't been designed to allow the user to introduce **Item Tracking** information when undoing a **Sales Shipment**. The posting action will require **Item Tracking** but there will be no way to introduce that information, so there will be no way to undo a **Sales Shipment** posted prior to the change.

Let's actually take a look at that situation in a step-by-step example. We will create a new item (with no **Item Tracking**) and post a purchase order for it. We will also post a sales order for that same item. Having **Item Ledger Entry** for the item, we will enable the **Item Tracking** functionality for it and will try to undo the **Sales Shipment** to see what happens.

Creating a new item

Follow these steps to create a new item:

1. Navigate to the item list.
2. On the **Home** tab, click on **New** to create a new item.
3. Place the cursor on the **No.** field on the **General** tab.
4. Press *Enter*. A new item number is given. The item number in this example is 70062.
5. Enter the following information for the item:

Tab name	Field name	Field value
Item	Description	Item Tracking Test
Item	Base Unit of Measure	PCS
Invoicing	Gen. Prod. Posting Group	MISC
Invoicing	VAT Prod. Posting Group	TAX25
Invoicing	Inventory Posting Group	RESALE
Invoicing	Tax Group Code	MATERIALS

The following screenshot shows the input fields related to Item Master Table:

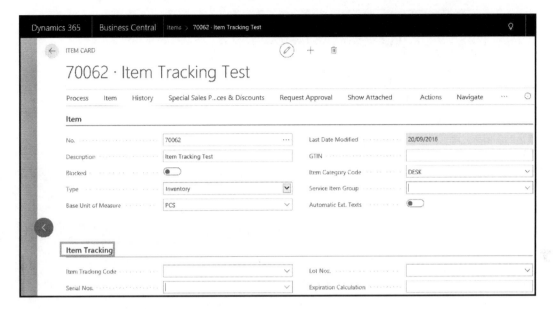

Creating and posting a purchase order for the new item

Follow these steps to create and post a purchase order for the new item:

1. Navigate to the **Purchase Orders** list.
2. On the **Home** tab, click on **New** to create a new purchase order.
3. Place the cursor on the **No.** field on the **General** tab.
4. Press *Enter*. Microsoft Dynamics NAV will give you a new purchase order number.

5. Enter the following information for the purchase order:

Tab name	Field name	Field value
General	**Buy-from Vendor No.**	106024
Lines	**TYPE**	**Item**
Lines	**NO.**	70062
Lines	**LOCATION CODE**	BLUE
Lines	**QUANTITY**	10
Lines	**DIRECT UNIT COST EXCL. VAT**	1

The **Purchase Orders** page for vendor **106024** is shown in the following screenshot:

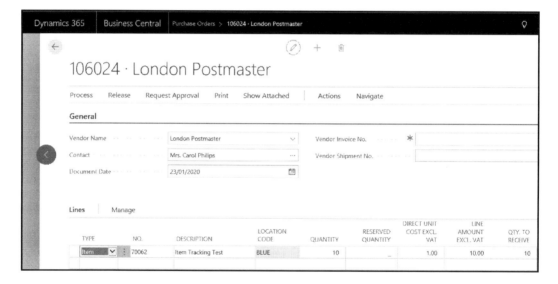

6. Make sure the **QUANTITY** field in the line has a value of 10.
7. On the **Home** tab, click on **Post** to post the purchase order.
8. A dialog will open with the options **Receive**, **Invoice**, and **Receive and Invoice**. Select **Receive** and click on **OK**.
9. The purchase order has been posted (received).

Creating and posting a sales order for the new item

Follow these steps to create and post a sales order for the new item:

1. Navigate to the **Sales Order** list.
2. On the **Home** tab, click on **New** to create a new **Sales Order**.
3. Place the cursor on the **No.** field on the **General** tab.
4. Press *Enter*. Microsoft Dynamics NAV will give you a new **Sales Order** number.
5. Enter the following information for the sales order:

Tab name	Field name	Field value
General	Sell-to Customer No.:	20000
Lines	TYPE	Item
Lines	NO.	70062
Lines	LOCATION CODE	BLUE
Lines	QUANTITY	2
Lines	UNIT PRICE EXCL. VAT	1.5

6. Make sure the QUANTITY field in the line has a value of 2.
7. On the **Home** tab, click on **Post** to post the sales order.
8. A dialog will open with the options **Ship**, **Invoice**, and **Ship and Invoice**. Select **Ship** and click on **OK**.

9. The sales order has been posted (shipped). The sales order page is shown in the following screenshot:

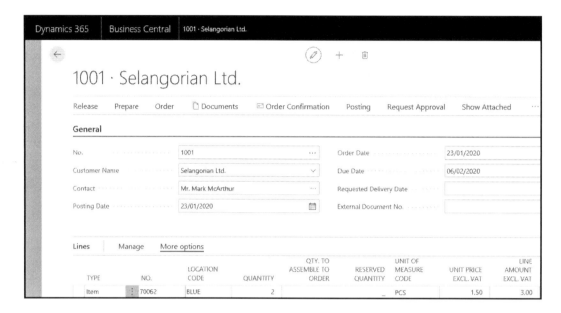

Turning on Item Tracking for the new item

Follow these steps to turn on **Item Tracking** for the new item:

1. Navigate to the items list.
2. Select item **70062**.
3. On the **Home** tab, click on **Edit**.
4. The **ITEM CARD** for item **70062** opens.

5. On the **Item Tracking** tab, enter the `LOTALL` value in the **Item Tracking Code** field:

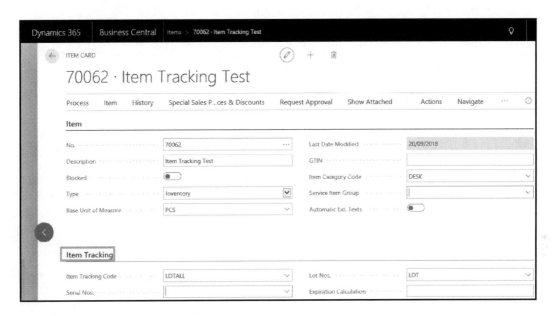

An error message will be displayed:

> `"You cannot change Item Tracking Code because there are one or more`
> `ledger entries for this item."`

This step-by-step example was meant to show you a problem you may encounter if you turn on **Item Tracking** on an item that had one or more Item Ledger Entries.

If you test around, you will probably find many other problems. If you do customizations, you will need to know all the problems you may encounter in the future.

Extending a customized functionality

In this example, we will talk about a customized functionality in which volume discounts were calculated for each sales invoice line, according to a set of predefined rules, and stored as volume discount ledger entries.

The functionality had to be extended to allow users to apply those ledger entries to other volume discount ledger entries, so that they could know whether volume discount ledger entries were completely open, partially open, or closed.

In this case, there are no interactions with other Microsoft Dynamics NAV functionalities. The interaction is actually with the customized Volume Discount functionality itself.

Since the functionality was developed to follow the same philosophy behind customer ledger entries and vendor ledger entries, the extension of the functionality had to follow the same philosophy as well.

This means creating a Detailed Volume Discount Ledger Entry table (similar to the `Detailed Cust. Ledg. Entry` and `Detailed Vendor Ledg. Entry` tables) and then creating extra fields, the most important ones being **Remaining Amount**, **Open**, and **Amount To Apply**, in the already existing volume discount ledger entry table.

For all of this to work, the development of the functionality extension had to do the following:

- Insert a detailed volume discount ledger entry of type **Initial Entry** when inserting a volume discount ledger entry.
- Develop the functionality to be able to select which volume discount ledger entries have to be applied to.
- Develop the posting process of volume discount ledger entry applications, which should include the following:
  - Inserting detailed volume discount ledger entries of type **Application**
  - Updating the **Open** field for the corresponding volume discount ledger entries

That is great and the extended functionality will work for new volume discount ledger entries. But, what happens with existing volume discount ledger entries? They do not have a **Detailed Ledger Entry** of the **Initial Entry** type. Furthermore, their **Open** field will indicate **No** (the default value for fields of type **Boolean**), but some of the existing volume discount ledger entries, especially the newest ones at the moment of implementing the new functionality, are probably open, so their **Open** field should actually indicate **Yes**.

When implementing the new functionality, some actions will have to be performed to create detailed volume discount ledger entries for all existing volume discount ledger entries. In addition, a process will have to be run so that only existing volume discount ledger entries that are indicated will be open.

Writing documentation to implement changes

Several actions will have to be performed to implement a functional change. All of them will have to be written down so that everyone is aware of what has to be done for the new functionality to work properly. Documentation on developments is fundamental; it is not possible to develop and modify without tracing what has been done, and it is always advisable to have the test reports of the new implementation signed, so that no one can contest what has been done.

All Microsoft Dynamics NAV and Microsoft Dynamics 365 Business Central developers should always write documentation about changes.

The Requisition Worksheet

Let's examine the Requisition Worksheet implementation. The actions that have to be performed are as follows:

1. Study the different reordering policies Microsoft Dynamics NAV and Microsoft Dynamics 365 Business Central offer.
2. Determine which replenishment parameters apply to each reordering policy. Notice that some replenishment parameters are not editable when you select a specific reordering policy. This means that those parameters do not apply to the selected reordering policy.
3. The **Maximum Inventory** field is non-editable when the **Fixed Reorder Qty.** reordering policy is selected.
4. Establish which reordering policies will be used in every group of items. Different kinds of items will probably be the best fit in different reordering policies.
5. Calculate the appropriate replenishment parameters for every item using statistical information on sales or any other information.
6. Set the **Vendor No.** for every item.
7. Set the **Lead Time Calculation** for every item.
8. If the company manages different locations, and replenishment parameters are different for every location, create stockkeeping units and inform the replenishment parameters in the stockkeeping unit card rather than on the item card.

9. If the company uses item variants, and replenishment parameters are different for every variant, create stockkeeping units and inform the replenishment parameters in the stockkeeping unit card, rather than on the item card.

10. If the company uses both different locations and item variants, create stockkeeping units per variant and per location.

That's a lot of clicks and some of them may require a lot of time and effort to complete. As you go on, you may find several other actions that have to be done. Write them all down so that nothing is forgotten. Consider using flow charts for a clearer picture of what has to be done and in which order, if the order matters.

If you have a reasonable number of items, this project will not be difficult or time consuming.

If you have thousands of items, you may want a Microsoft Dynamics NAV or Microsoft Dynamics 365 Business Central developer to help you out with some of the steps, especially in the calculation of the replenishment parameters. You could think of an algorithm to calculate and inform replenishment parameters in your items or stockkeeping units and ask a developer to develop it for you:

Fixed Assets

Imagine a company that has been using Microsoft Dynamics NAV or Microsoft Dynamics 365 Business Central for a while. This company has never used the **Fixed Assets** functionality. Now, they want to start managing their fixed assets with the ERP.

How many actions do you think will be needed to complete the project? Let's go through them:

1. Get a list of the fixed assets. This may require that you perform a **Fixed Asset Physical Inventory** in your company.
2. Check the existing FA posting groups. Modify the existing FA posting groups if they do not meet your accounting requirements, or create new ones if you need to. To do so, navigate to **Departments | Financial Management | Administration** and click on **FA Posting Groups**.
3. Study the different depreciation methods Microsoft Dynamics NAV and Microsoft Dynamics 365 Business Central offer. The **Depreciation Method** field can be found on a fixed asset card; the options for this field are shown in the following screenshot:

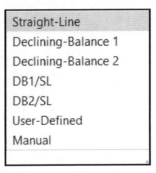

4. Choose the appropriate **FA Posting Group** for each fixed asset in your list.
5. Choose the appropriate **Depreciation Method** for each fixed asset in your list.
6. Determine **Depreciation Starting Date** and **Depreciation Ending Date** for each fixed asset in your list.
7. Determine **Acquisition Cost** for each fixed asset in your list.

8. Manually create all the fixed assets in Microsoft Dynamics NAV or in Microsoft Dynamics 365 Business Central, or choose a data migration tool and format to create fixed assets from an archive.

 You will find more information about data migration tools in `Chapter 6`, *Migrating Data*.

9. Uncheck all G/L integrations of all depreciation books your company will be using. Fixed asset movements have to be posted with the acquisition cost and depreciation that your fixed assets have had prior to using the Microsoft Dynamics NAV or Microsoft Dynamics 365 Business Central **Fixed Asset** functionality. We do not want all of those movements to be posted to the general ledger because they have probably already been posted to the general ledger by posting manual transactions. That is why we want to uncheck all kinds of integrations between fixed assets and the general ledger.

10. Use the **FA Journals** to post an **Acquisition Cost** movement for each fixed asset. You can either create the lines in the FA Journal manually or use a data migration tool to create them from an archive.

11. Use the FA Journal to post depreciation movements for each fixed asset. You can either create the lines in the FA Journal manually or use a data migration tool to create them from an archive.

12. Make sure both acquisition costs and depreciation movements match with transactions previously posted to the general ledger.

13. Check the G/L integrations again of all the depreciation books your company will be using.

In this example, 13 actions had to be completed to implement this functional change. All the steps can be done by an end user using standard Microsoft Dynamics NAV or Microsoft Dynamics 365 Business Central functionality.

If you have a reasonable number of fixed assets, this project will not be difficult or time consuming.

If you have thousands of fixed assets, you may want a developer to help you out with some of the steps, especially in the creation of thousands of FA Journal lines to post acquisition costs and depreciations:

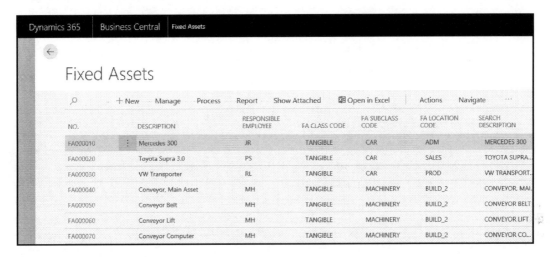

Item Tracking

In this example, we are talking about turning on **Item Tracking** for existing items that have at least one **Item Ledger Entry**. This is casuistry in which Microsoft Dynamics NAV or in Microsoft Dynamics 365 Business Central will not allow us to turn **Item Tracking** on.

In the previous section, we already talked about some of the steps that will have to be performed for this to be possible. We will follow the official workaround to implement this functional change, as we have seen that some other solutions can lead to data inconsistency, unpredictable behavior, or some other functionalities not working as expected.

Let's write down the list of actions we need to perform in order to turn on **Item Tracking** for existing items that have at least one **Item Ledger Entry**:

1. Reduce the quantity in hand to zero by making negative adjustments of all items for which **Item Tracking** will be turned on.
2. Rename all those items.
3. Create new items and give them the name of the original items.

4. Create and configure related data for the new items, which includes the following:
   - Units of measure
   - Sales prices
   - Sales discounts
   - Purchase prices
   - Purchase discounts
   - Vendors
   - Item variants
   - Extended texts
   - Translations
   - Cross references
   - Stockkeeping units
   - Bills of materials
   - Substitutions
   - Dimensions
   - Customized related data

5. Set up the **Item Tracking Code** for the new items.

6. Do a physical inventory of those items, specifying quantities and their tracking (serial number, lot number, and expiration date).

7. Increase the quantity in hand of the new items by making positive adjustments in which quantities and tracking will have to be specified.

8. Review open documents and change the item number to point to the new item instead of the renamed one, so that the item that will be shipped, received, or manufactured is actually the new one and not the renamed one. You need to change the item number in the following documents:
   - Sales documents
   - Purchase documents
   - Service documents
   - Transfer orders
   - Manufacturing documents
   - Job planning lines
   - Item journals
   - Warehouse journals
   - Requisition Worksheets

The following screenshot shows the **ITEM CARD** for **Bicycle**:

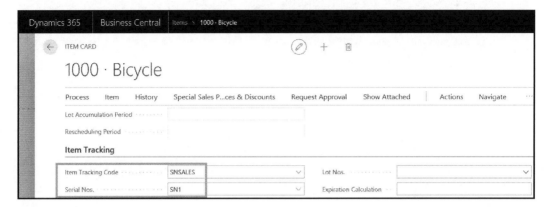

Extending a customized functionality

In this example, we are talking about a customized functionality in which volume discounts were calculated for each sales invoice line, according to a set of predefined rules, and stored as volume discount ledger entries.

The functionality had to be extended to allow users to apply those ledger entries to other volume discount ledger entries, so that they could know whether volume discount ledger entries were completely open, partially open, or closed.

In the *Interactions with other functionalities* section, we said that this extension actually had only interactions with the functionality itself, and we have already pointed out some of the actions that will have to be performed. These include creating detailed volume discount ledger entries of the **Initial Entry** type for all existing volume discount ledger entries, and doing a big initial application of volume discount ledger entries so that only real open volume discount ledger entries indicate so in their **Open** field.

The actions to be performed in this example are as follows:

1. Develop the extended functionality as per requirements.
2. Develop a process that will create detailed volume discount ledger entries of the **Initial Entry** type for all existing volume discount ledger entries.
3. Develop a process that will set the recently created **Open** field to **Yes** in the **Volume Discount Ledger Entry** table.

4. Determine which existing volume discount ledger entries are actually open and what remaining amount they should have.

5. Implement the development change.

6. Execute the process that will create detailed volume discount ledger entries of the type **Initial Entry** for all existing volume discount ledger entries.

7. Execute the process that will set the recently created **Open** field to **Yes** in the **Volume Discount Ledger Entry** table.

8. Use the new **Volume Discount Application** functionality to do a big initial application posting so that at the end of this process, only real open volume discount ledger entries are marked as open and they have the correct remaining amount.

Choosing the "right time" to release and implement the changes, and analyzing the risks

It is important to choose the right time to make a functional change on an existing Microsoft Dynamics NAV or in Microsoft Dynamics 365 Business Central implementation. Some functional changes can be deployed at any time, others not. Some of them may require a lot of time and no users to be working and changing data; you may want to choose a weekend for that. Some others could be implemented at any time, but to keep a better track of the time at which it began to work differently, you might want to choose the start of a fiscal year or the start of a month.

The important thing is to think about it, analyze it, and choose the right time for every functional change implementation, as a wrong choice could cost you dearly. It is always useful, in cases with complex procedures, to draw up a risk analysis in order to have a way out in case of problems that could arise.

The Requisition Worksheet

Using the Requisition Worksheet to automatically calculate and plan the replenishment of items is something that could be done at any time. It could even be done progressively, starting with a few items to get familiar with the requisition functionality, and adding new items to this process by progressively configuring their replenishment parameters.

In this case, the right time is anytime, whenever you are ready for it.

Fixed Assets

In the previous section, when talking about the actions required to start using the Microsoft Dynamics NAV or Microsoft Dynamics 365 Business Central Fixed Assets functionalities, we said that fixed assets' movements will have to be posted with the acquisition cost and depreciation–the fixed assets without G/L integration–before starting to utilize them, and the fixed assets' functionality, to calculate your depreciations.

Item Tracking

If you turn **Item Tracking** on for your items, it is because you want or need to be able to have traceability of your products.

Choose an appropriate time to do so because you will have to know when your traceability begins and that before that date there is no traceability at all.

You may have a legal requirement that says that after a specific date, traceability will be mandatory for the kinds of items you sell or manufacture. If this is the case, that date will probably be the right time.

If this is not the case, or you have a period of time to implement it, you will have to choose a specific date. The beginning of a fiscal year or the beginning of a specific month are dates that are easy to remember for anyone. They could be good candidates.

But you also have to take into account that turning **Item Tracking** on, especially if it has to be done for a large number of items, or if you have a lot of data related to your items or a lot of pending documents, is something that will be time consuming. You will have to rename old items, create new items, create their related data, and go through all pending documents. You will also have to reduce the quantity in hand of the old items and do a physical inventory of the new items to write down their tracking, and be able to increase the inventory of the new items and assign them the right tracking.

Even if you develop a process to rename items, create new items and all their related data, and go through all pending documents, you have to know that this will be a time consuming process if that has to be done for a lot of items, because the renaming instruction in Microsoft Dynamics NAV or in Microsoft Dynamics 365 Business Central takes an extremely long time to execute.

There is something else to take into account. When doing all of this, you do not want any users to be posting any item entries as they will either be locked up as the process is running, or they may transact on an item that may not have all of the settings completed yet.

Keeping all of this in mind, you will probably have to choose a time to implement the change on items outside regular working time. This could be a long weekend or a holiday period.

You could also choose to implement **Item Tracking** progressively, a few items at a time. That will take a shorter time per partial implementation, so it will be easier to find the time to do it, but the global process will take longer and there will not be a single date on which **Item Tracking** functionality was turned on.

Extending a customized functionality

In this example, in which a functionality of volume discounts—which has volume discount ledger entries—needs to be extended by adding application functionality similar to how applications work both in customer ledger entries and vendor ledger entries, any time is good to implement the change. Whenever it is developed and ready to go live will be considered a good time to implement this change.

The only thing to take into account is that the list of open ledger entries has to be prepared for the initial application to be done. Some manual work will have to be done to post this initial application, but there is no need for the users to stop working with the system.

Planning the change

Good planning (and actually sticking to it) is something you always need. As we have seen, some implementations may require a lot of actions to be carried out some of them before the new functionality is implemented, some during the implementation process, and some others right after the implementation process is completed. Some implementations can even be done progressively, so they could last weeks or even some months.

Everything has to be planned and scheduled so that all the work needed for the implementation of the functionality is ready on the chosen date to go live.

Take the to-do list written in the previous section and determine the following for each action:

- Determine when the action has to be performed:
  - Before the implementation date
  - During the implementation process
  - After the implementation process is completed
- Estimate the time that will be needed to complete the action.
- Establish relations between actions (some actions have to be completed so that other actions can start; some actions have no relations with other actions, so two or more actions can be performed simultaneously).
- Determine the date on which the actions should be completed.
- Determine the person or persons responsible for performing the action.

The Requisition Worksheet

Let's take a look at the actions required for this implementation and determine relations between them, estimation of time, and when they should be performed. In the example, we will not be determining the due date and the people responsible for the action.

The estimation of time will depend upon the number of items the company implementing this functionality may have:

1. Study the different reordering policies that Microsoft Dynamics NAV or Microsoft Dynamics 365 Business Central offer:
   - **When**: Before the implementation
   - **Estimation of time**: A day
   - **Previous action**: None

2. Determine which replenishment parameters apply to each reordering policy:
   - **When**: Before the implementation
   - **Estimation of time**: Half a day
   - **Previous action**: Action 1

3. Establish which reordering policies will be used in every group of items:
   - **When**: Before the implementation
   - **Estimation of time**: A day
   - **Previous action**: Action 2

4. Calculate the appropriate replenishment parameters for every item using statistical information on sales or any other information:
   - **When**: Before the implementation
   - **Estimation of time**: Three days
   - **Previous action**: Action 3

5. Set **Vendor No.** for every item:
   - **When**: Before the implementation
   - **Estimation of time**: A day
   - **Previous action**: None

6. Set **Lead Time Calculation** for every item:
   - **When**: Before the implementation
   - **Estimation of time**: A day
   - **Previous action**: None

7. If the company manages different locations, and replenishment parameters are different for every location, create stockkeeping units and inform the replenishment parameters in the stockkeeping unit card rather than on the item card:
    - **When**: Before the implementation
    - **Estimation of time**: Half a day
    - **Previous action**: None

8. If the company uses item variants, and replenishment parameters are different for every variant, create stockkeeping units and inform the replenishment parameters in the stockkeeping unit card rather than on the item card:
    - **When**: Before the implementation
    - **Estimation of time**: Half a day
    - **Previous action**: None

9. If the company uses both different locations and item variants, create stockkeeping units per variant and per location:
    - **When**: Before the implementation
    - **Estimation of time**: Half a day
    - **Previous action**: None

Fixed Assets

Let's take the actions required for this implementation and determine relations between them, estimation of time, and when they should be performed. In the example, we will not be determining the due date and the people responsible for the action.

The estimation of time will depend upon the number of fixed assets the company implementing this functionality may have:

1. Get a list of fixed assets:
    - **When**: Before the implementation
    - **Estimation of time**: Two days
    - **Previous action**: None

2. Check the existing **FA Posting Groups**. Modify the existing **FA Posting Groups** if they do not meet your accounting requirements, or create new ones if you need to:
   - **When**: Before the implementation
   - **Estimation of time**: Half a day
   - **Previous action**: None

3. Study the different depreciation methods that Microsoft Dynamics NAV offers:
   - **When**: Before the implementation
   - **Estimation of time**: Half a day
   - **Previous action**: None

4. Choose the appropriate **FA Posting Group** for each fixed asset in your list:
   - **When**: Before the implementation
   - **Estimation of time**: Half a day
   - **Previous action**: Actions 1 and 2

5. Choose the appropriate depreciation method for each fixed asset in your list:
   - **When**: Before the implementation
   - **Estimation of time**: Half a day
   - **Previous action**: Actions 1 and 3

6. Determine depreciation starting date and depreciation ending date for each fixed asset in your list:
   - **When**: Before the implementation
   - **Estimation of time**: A day
   - **Previous action**: Action 1

7. Determine the acquisition cost for each fixed asset in your list:
   - **When**: Before the implementation
   - **Estimation of time**: A day
   - **Previous action**: Action 1

8. Create all the fixed assets in Microsoft Dynamics NAV:
   - **When**: Before or during the implementation
   - **Estimation of time**: Half a day
   - **Previous action**: Actions 1 to 7

9. Uncheck all G/L integrations of all depreciation books your company will be using:
   - **When**: During the implementation
   - **Estimation of time**: Half an hour
   - **Previous action**: None

10. Use the FA Journals to post an acquisition cost movement for each fixed asset:
    - **When**: During the implementation
    - **Estimation of time**: Half a day
    - **Previous action**: Actions 8 and 9

11. Use the FA Journal to post depreciation movements for each fixed asset:
    - **When**: During the implementation
    - **Estimation of time**: Half a day
    - **Previous action**: Action 11

12. Make sure both acquisition costs and depreciation movements match with transactions previously posted to the general ledger:
    - **When**: During the implementation
    - **Estimation of time**: Half a day
    - **Previous action**: Action 11

13. Check GL integrations again for all the depreciation books your company will be using:
    - **When**: After the implementation
    - **Estimation of time**: Half an hour
    - **Previous action**: Action 12

Item Tracking

Let's take the actions required for this implementation and determine the relations between them, the estimation of time, and when they should be performed. In the example, we will not be determining the due date and the people responsible for the action.

The estimation of time will depend upon the number of items the company implementing this functionality may have:

1. Reduce the quantity in hand to zero by making negative adjustments to all items for which **Item Tracking** will be turned on:
   - **When**: During the implementation
   - **Estimation of time**: Half a day
   - **Previous action**: None

2. Rename all those items:
   - **When**: During the implementation
   - **Estimation of time**: 1-2 days
   - **Previous action**: Action 1

3. Create new items and give them the names of the original items:
   - **When**: During the implementation
   - **Estimation of time**: Half a day
   - **Previous action**: Action 2

4. Create and configure related data for the new items:
   - **When**: During the implementation
   - **Estimation of time**: Half a day
   - **Previous action**: Action 3

5. Set up the **Item Tracking Code** for the new items:
   - **When**: During the implementation
   - **Estimation of time**: Half a day
   - **Previous action**: Action 3

6. Do a physical inventory of those items, specifying quantities and their tracking (serial number, lot number, and expiration date):
   - **When**: During the implementation
   - **Estimation of time**: A day
   - **Previous action**: None

7. Add the quantity on hand of the new items by making positive adjustments in which quantities and tracking will have to be specified:
    - **When**: During the implementation
    - **Estimation of time**: Half a day
    - **Previous action**: Action 6

8. Review open documents and change the **Item No.** field to point to the new item instead of to the renamed one, so that the item that will be shipped, received, or manufactured is actually the new one and not the renamed one:
    - **When**: After the implementation
    - **Estimation of time**: Half a day
    - **Previous action**: Action 2

Extending a customized functionality

Let's take the actions required for this implementation and determine relations between them, the estimation of time, and when they should be performed. In the example, we will not be determining the due date and the people responsible for the action.

The estimation of time will depend upon the number of volume discount ledger entries the company implementing this functionality has:

1. Do the required development of the extended functionality:
    - **When**: Before the implementation
    - **Estimation of time**: four days
    - **Previous action**: None

2. Develop a process that will create detailed volume discount ledger entries of the Initial Entry type for all existing volume discount ledger entries:
    - **When**: Before the implementation
    - **Estimation of time**: Half a day
    - **Previous action**: Action 1

3. Develop a process that will set the recently created **Open** field to **Yes** in the table volume discount ledger entries:
    - **When**: Before the implementation
    - **Estimation of time**: Half a day
    - **Previous action**: Action 1

4. Determine which existing volume discount ledger entries are actually open and what remaining amount they should have:
    - **When**: Before the implementation
    - **Estimation of time**: A day
    - **Previous action**: None

5. Implement the development change:
    - **When**: During the implementation
    - **Estimation of time**: Half an hour
    - **Previous action**: Action 1

6. Execute the process that will create detailed volume discount ledger entries of type Initial Entry for all existing volume discount ledger entries:
    - **When**: During the implementation
    - **Estimation of time**: Half an hour
    - **Previous action**: Action 5

7. Execute the process that will set the recently created Open field to Yes in the table volume discount ledger entries:
    - **When**: During the implementation
    - **Estimation of time**: Half an hour
    - **Previous action**: Action 5

8. Use the new Volume Discount Application functionality to do a big initial application posting so that, at the end of this process, only real open volume discount ledger entries are marked as open and they have the correct remaining amount:
    - **When**: After the implementation
    - **Estimation of time**: Half a day
    - **Previous action**: Action 4

Changes in Microsoft Dynamics 365 Business Central

I would like to mention that the Microsoft Dynamics 365 Business Central on-premises and SaaS environments are different. For the Microsoft Dynamics 365 Business Central SaaS environment, we must remember some restrictions:

- The SaaS environment is always on.
- Only the web client exists.
- The standard cannot be changed.
- It's possible to develop only with Visual Studio Code.
- The extensions must always be used to load the customizations.
- In multitenant environments, it may be more costly and time consuming to implement the changes.
- If a problem emerges, we do not have a physical server in front of us.
- We do not have access to the SQL Azure database.
- The times of implementation, release, and application of the changes are quite different (more expensive).
- If something is not successful, it could be a problem.

For the rest, the concepts seen earlier (as general concepts) are valid and applicable for both Microsoft Dynamics NAV and Microsoft Dynamics 365 Business Central.

Before implementing, always take a look at the Microsoft Dynamics 365 Business Central pages. Sometimes, Microsoft itself provides advice on how to approach a problem, providing *best practices* on related topics. The site is always continuously updated. For example, this topic is very interesting: *Setup Best Practices: Supply Planning* (`https://docs.microsoft.com/en-us/dynamics365/business-central/setup-best-practices-supply-planning`).

Summary

In this chapter, we have seen that Microsoft Dynamics NAV and Microsoft Dynamics 365 Business Central implementations are not only for companies that have never used these ERPs before and will start doing so. An implementation can also be done for companies already using Microsoft Dynamics NAV or Microsoft Dynamics 365 Business Central. They will not be complete implementations, of course, probably just the implementation of a new module or functionality. There are some things to take into account in these kinds of implementations. We have talked about them using different examples.

In the next chapter, we will be talking about reporting in Microsoft Dynamics NAV and in Microsoft Dynamics 365 Business Central, and how to analyze the data stored in the database.

Data Analysis and Reporting

10

Data analysis and reporting are an important part in the management of a company. Having a system where you can do accounting, invoicing, warehouse management, and all kinds of things a company does is great. Microsoft Dynamics NAV and Microsoft Dynamics 365 Business Central are very good data entry systems and offer ways to provide a flow to the information and make it available when it is needed in order to complete the company's processes. Sales processors enter the sales orders, which are then available to the warehouse employees so that they know what has to be shipped. Once the warehouse employees are done with the shipping, the invoicing people have the information required to compile the invoice.

But companies also need to analyze all this information. Do we ship our orders on time? Which item category is the most profitable? Are our departments generating value for the company? We have to be able to answer these kinds of questions. That is what analysis and reporting can do.

In this chapter, we will explore the tools available to analyze Microsoft Dynamics NAV and Microsoft Dynamics 365 Business Central data, both inside and outside the application.

We will cover the following topics:

- Analyzing data using Filters and FlowFilters
- Statistics
- Charts
- Reports
- Analysis views
- Account schedules

- Extracting Microsoft Dynamics NAV and Microsoft Dynamics 365 Business Central data
- Query objects and Power BI connectors (Power BI will be discussed in a later chapter)
- Report development

Using Filters and FlowFilters

A good and powerful way to view and analyze data is to use Filters and FlowFilters inside the application.

We have explained the use of filters in the *Navigating through your data* section in Chapter 3, *General Considerations*. Refer to that chapter to get some examples on how to use filters to analyze your data.

In that same chapter, we explained what the SIFT is and how to define fields on tables to use that technology. What we did not explain in that chapter is that FlowFilters can be applied over the defined to use SIFT to narrow down the calculated results. That is actually what we will be explaining now.

We will be looking at the **Chart of Accounts** page to explain how to apply FlowFilters and the results they produce. The procedure is as follows:

1. Enter Chart of Accounts in the search box of the Microsoft Dynamics NAV Windows client.
2. Select **Chart of Accounts**.
3. The **Chart of Accounts** page will be shown. The following screenshot shows part of the **Chart of Accounts** page (Web client):

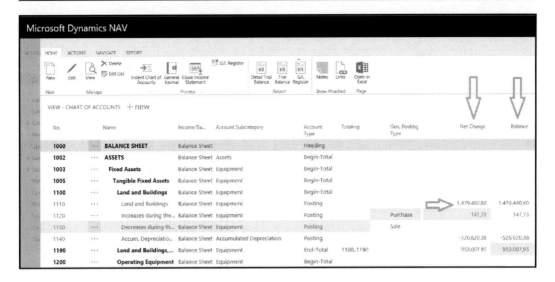

The fields that are shown are **No.**, **Name**, **Net Change**, and **Balance**, because these are the relevant fields for this example. **Net Change** and **Balance** are FlowFields that use the SIFT technology. They both show the sum of G/L entry amounts for the different accounts. On the Windows client, now that we are on a page that uses FlowFields, let's apply FlowFilters and look at the result.

 The **Limit totals** function is currently available in the Windows client and in the Microsoft Dynamics 365 Business Central Web client, both on-premise and online

4. Click on **Chart of Accounts** and select **Limit totals**, the following screenshot shows the **Limit totals** option for the Windows client:

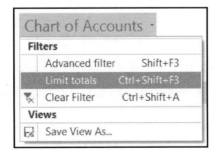

The following screenshot shows the **Limit totals** option for the Web client:

5. Select **Date Filter** and set 01/01/18..12/31/18 as the filter.
6. The **Net Change** field will be updated as shown:

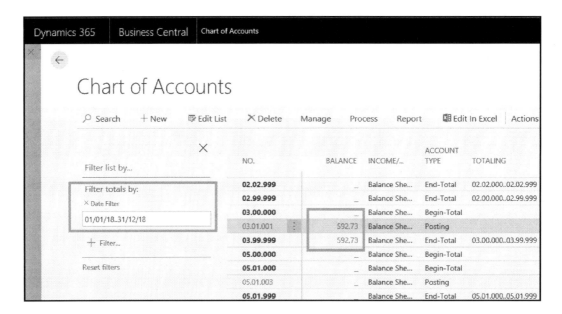

Not all FlowFilters apply to all FlowFields; however, FlowFilters only apply to FlowFields. In the preceding example, we saw that after applying a date FlowFilter, the **NET CHANGE** field got updated and now shows only the sum of G/L entry amounts in the specified period, while the **BALANCE** field has remained the same. This is because of the definition of the fields. The definition of the **NET CHANGE** field states that the calculation of this field will take into account a date filter, while the **BALANCE** field does not.

Limit total is the place where a user can apply FlowFilters. It can be found in all the application pages where a FlowFilter is available, and also in the **Filter** section of reports, which will be seen later in this chapter.

 Filters and FlowFilters in Business Central Fall Release: In the October release of Microsoft Dynamics 365 Business Central, Filters have been enhanced for the Web client as well. Their utilization is explained in `Chapter 13`, *Microsoft Dynamics 365 Business Central*.

Creating views

So we have seen how to apply filters and FlowFilters to the application. But once we leave the page and come back to the same page, the filter is gone. We have to apply the same filter or FlowFilter over and over again if we want to see the same results. Wouldn't it be great if we could save applied filters so that we could apply them as many times as we wished without having to select the fields we want to filter and writing the filter expression again? This is possible with Microsoft Dynamics NAV Views (we have already talked about this in a previous chapter). This feature might also be introduced in relation to Microsoft Dynamics 365 Business Central and Microsoft Dynamics NAV Web client; at present, it is not available.

To create a view, perform the following steps:

1. Perform the steps from the previous section to apply a FlowFilter to the **Chart of Accounts** page.

2. Click on **Chart of Accounts** and select **Save View As**, as demonstrated in the following screenshot:

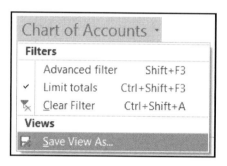

3. The **Save View As** dialog will open.

4. Enter `Chart of Accounts - 2018` in the **Name** field and select **Home** in the **Activity Group** field:

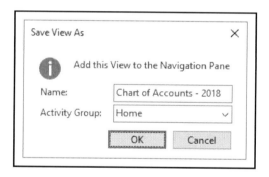

5. Click on **OK**.

6. The view will be saved.

Every time you want to see your saved view, perform the following steps:

- Click on **Home**.
- Click on your saved view, as demonstrated in the following screenshot:

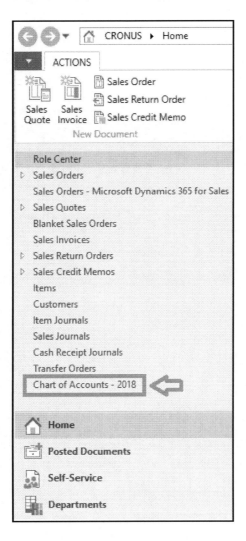

Statistics

All master data has one or more associated statistical pages, where the most important statistical information pertaining to the record is shown.

The statistics function of Microsoft Dynamics NAV collects a lot of information related to the document retrieved. For example, if we retrieve a customer card, we can see the following in detail: Sales Amount, Cost Amount, Profit, and Outstanding Orders. Sometimes, there are relative columns pertaining to the current and also to previous periods.

Statistics are a useful tool for consulting data quickly without going through reports and can be found under the **NAVIGATE** tab of the ribbon.

Perform the steps outlined as follows to view Customer Statistics:

1. Type `Customers` in the search box of the Microsoft Dynamics NAV Client.
2. Select **Customers**. The customer list will be shown, as demonstrated in the following screenshot:

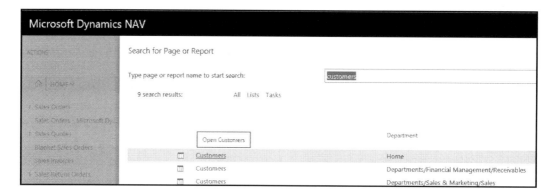

3. Click on the **NAVIGATE** tab in the ribbon:

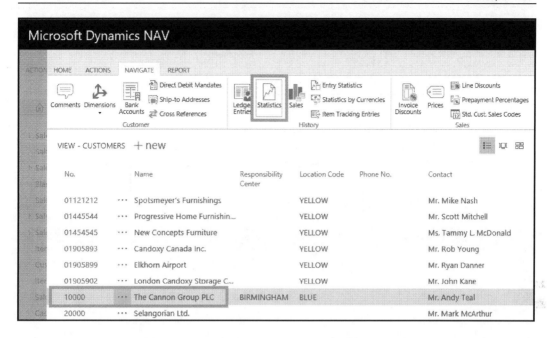

4. Select **Statistics**. The **CUSTOMER STATISTICS** page for the customer currently selected will be shown. This page shows the most important economic information pertaining to the customer:

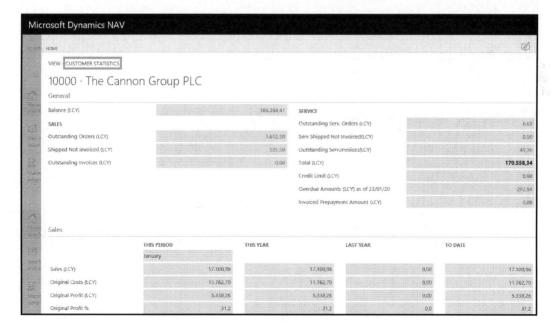

Other statistics pages offer dynamic information; for example, the **CUSTOMER SALES** statistics show, the sales for that customer for a specific period. To open the **CUSTOMER SALES** statistics page, perform the following steps:

1. Type `Customers` in the search box of the Microsoft Dynamics NAV Client.
2. Select **Customers**. The customer list will be shown.
3. Click on the **Navigate** tab in the ribbon.
4. Select **Sales**. The **CUSTOMER SALES** page for the currently selected customer will be shown. This page shows customer sales over time (for example, in the following screenshot, filters are applied to **View by | Month** and **View as | Net Change**):

Charts – representing data in graph form

Graphical information is always useful when analyzing data. Microsoft Dynamics NAV and Microsoft Dynamics 365 Business Central offer various ways of viewing data in graph form, and we can also use a number of ready-made graphs, or easily create new ones.

The Show as Chart option (the Windows client only)

Whenever the information displayed on screen can be viewed as a chart, the **Home** tab of the ribbon will contain a section called **View** where users can switch the view of the information from **List** to **Chart**, and vice versa. This feature is currently only available on the Windows client:

On Windows client, let's see an example of how to build a chart based on the customer list:

1. Type `Customers` in the search box of the Microsoft Dynamics NAV client.
2. Select **Customers**. The customer list will be shown.
3. Click on **Show as Chart**. An empty chart will be shown. We will have to select a measure and the dimensions we want to use to build our chart:

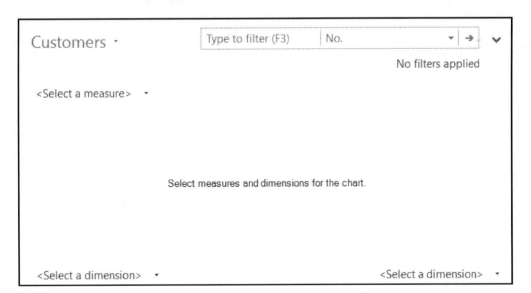

4. Select **Sales ($)** as the measure.
5. Select **Country/Region Code** as the dimension for the right-hand side of the chart. The chart will be drawn as shown in the following screenshot:

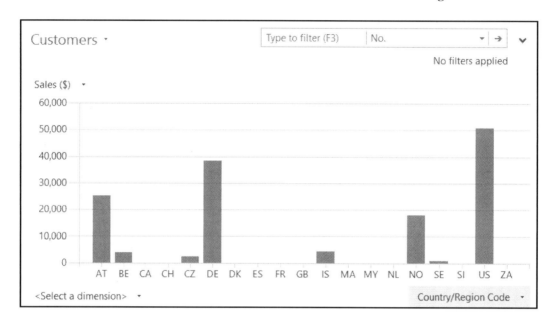

We can quickly see that the **US** is the country where our sales are concentrated.

Adding charts to the Role Center page – on the Windows client

Microsoft Dynamics NAV has a set of predefined generic charts that can be added to the **Role Center** page. You can add **Charts Part** using the **Customize the Role Center** feature.

To add a chart to the home page, perform the following steps:

1. Click on **Home**.
2. Click on the **Application** icon, choose **Customize**, and then **Customize This Page**. The **Customize the Role Center** window will open, as demonstrated in the following screenshot:

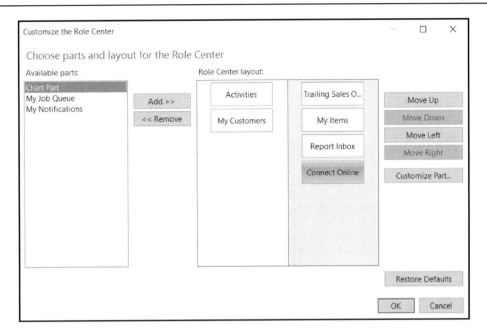

3. Select **Chart Part** from the **Available parts** field and click on the **Add** button. A blank chart will appear in the **Role Center layout** field.

4. Select the blank chart and click on the **Customize Part** button. A list of available charts will appear as shown:

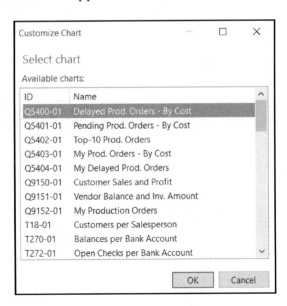

5. Select the **Customer Sales and Profit** chart. Click on **OK**.

6. Click on **OK** to close the **Customize the Role Center** window. The selected chart will be displayed on the **Role Center** page as follows:

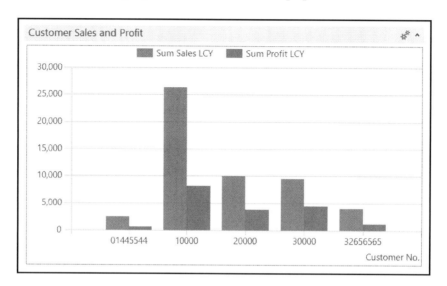

The data in this chart is displayed after the customers on the **My Customer** list. If you have no customers on the **My Customer** list, this chart will be devoid of data.

Creating and configuring charts

If the predefined generic charts are not enough for you, you can define other generic charts and make them available to all users so that they can add your chart to their **Role Center** page.

To create and define a generic chart, perform the following steps:

1. Type `Generic Charts` in the search box of the Microsoft Dynamics NAV Client (you can use both the Windows client or the Web client in this case).

2. Select **Generic Charts**. The **Generic Charts** list will be shown.

3. Click on **New** to create a new generic chart.

4. Give the new generic chart an **ID** (MY CUSTOMER CHART) and **Name** (MY CUSTOMER CHART).

5. Select **Table** as the **Source Type**.

6. Select **18** as the **Source ID**:

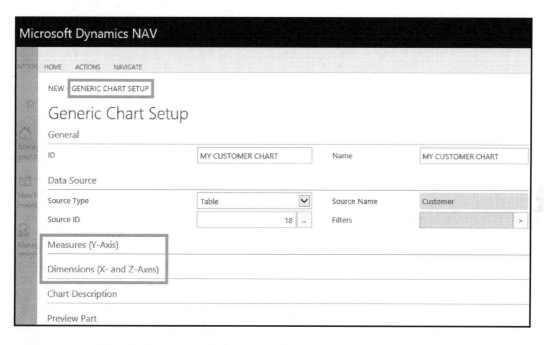

7. In the **Required Measure** row, select **Sales (LCY)** in the **Data Column** field, **Sum** as **Aggregation**, and **Column** as **Graph Type**.

8. In the **Optional Measure** row, select **Profit (LCY)** in the **Data Column** field, **Sum** as **Aggregation**, and **StepLine** as **Graph Type**.

9. Select **Country/Region Code** in the **X-Axis field**. The entire configuration of the generic chart is shown in the following screenshot:

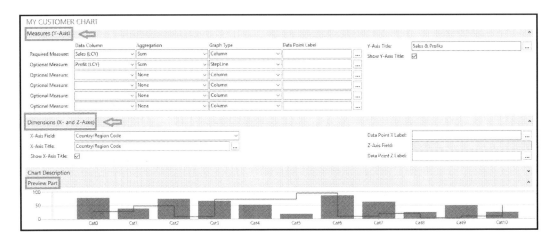

10. Click on **OK**.

A new chart is now created and configured. Perform the steps in the previous section to add this new chart to your Role Center page. The following screenshot shows the defined chart:

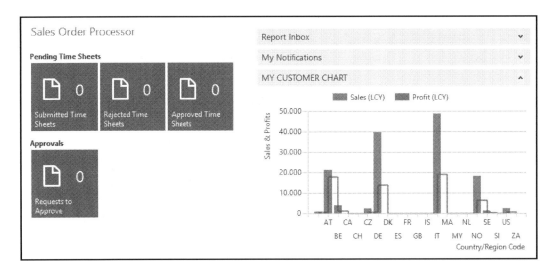

Personalizations on the Web client

It is possible to use the Web client in a different way from how this is achieved using the Windows client. It is possible to use the modality, which allows personalizations to be executed on-the-fly. Obviously, there are a number of limitations but, for example, you can alter the appearance and filters in a chart in a simple manner, as demonstrated in the following screenshot:

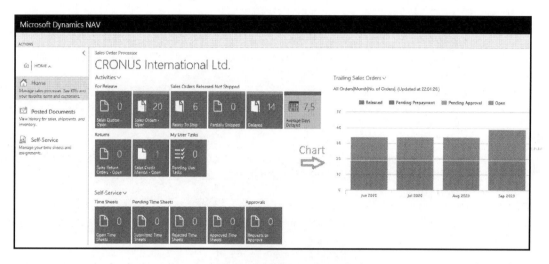

The Home view in Dynamics NAV

We can change **Chart Format** and **Filters** in a simple way. For example, it's possible to change the chart format from **All Orders** to **Only Open Delayed Orders**. The system immediately applies the filters and shows the filtered data:

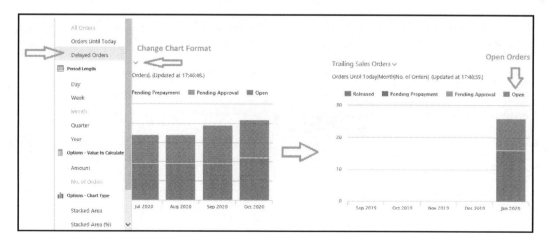

Personalize and design the Web client via the In-client Designer feature

It is possible to customize the Web client in a similar way to the Windows client, although the Web client obviously has limitations via-à-vis the Windows client.

The In-client Designer feature is not enabled by default, but you can activate it. Here, there is a difference between personalize and design.

- **Personalize:** Any changes I make are applicable just to me; this highly valuable feature in production environments enables me to optimize my workspace specifically to how I work.
- **Design:** Applies to all users in that environment. It is intended for developers or power users to create lightweight extensions that will ultimately be used by everyone within the organization. The extension produced by In-client Designer could be imported into a customer's production environment to customize Microsoft Dynamics NAV and Microsoft Dynamics 365 Business Central, as demonstrated in the following screenshot:

To personalize the Web client of Microsoft Dynamics NAV (in this case the **Sales Order** Role Center), perform the following steps:

1. Click on the Open the designer icon on the **Role Center** page:

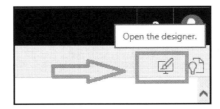

2. The In-client Designer will be open (in this case from the Microsoft Dynamics NAV Web client). Configure it as you see fit:

In this case, we will try to remove the **Trailing Sales Order** chart page using the following steps:

1. Click on **Stop designing** to terminate any saved personalization.
2. The **Trailing Sales Order** chart page is hidden by the saved personalization:

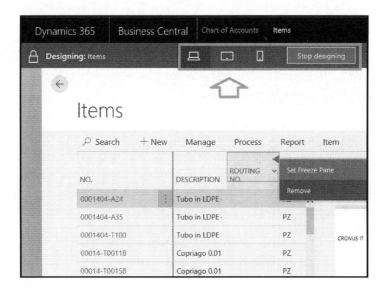

Designer gives you a few more features, such as being able to preview your creation as it would appear on a tablet or phone.

> We have already talked about this topic in detail in `Chapter 2,` *Microsoft Dynamics NAV 2018 – An Overview.*

Using reports

Microsoft Dynamics NAV and Microsoft Dynamics 365 Business Central have a bunch of reports that can be used out-of-the-box. Some other reports may have been added by a partner and can also be used. The first thing you need to know to be able to execute application reports is where to find them.

Finding reports in the Windows client and Web client

From the Windows client: To find application reports from the Windows client, perform the following steps:

1. Click on **Departments** and then select any functional area, **Sales & Marketing**, for instance.
2. The main menu for the selected functional area will appear on the screen. Every item you can find inside a menu for an application area has a category associated with it. In the menu, there is a way to view items according to their category. The following screenshot illustrates the existing categories in Microsoft Dynamics NAV:

Select **Reports and Analysis**.

3. All items under the **Reports and Analysis** category for the functional area selected will be shown, as follows:

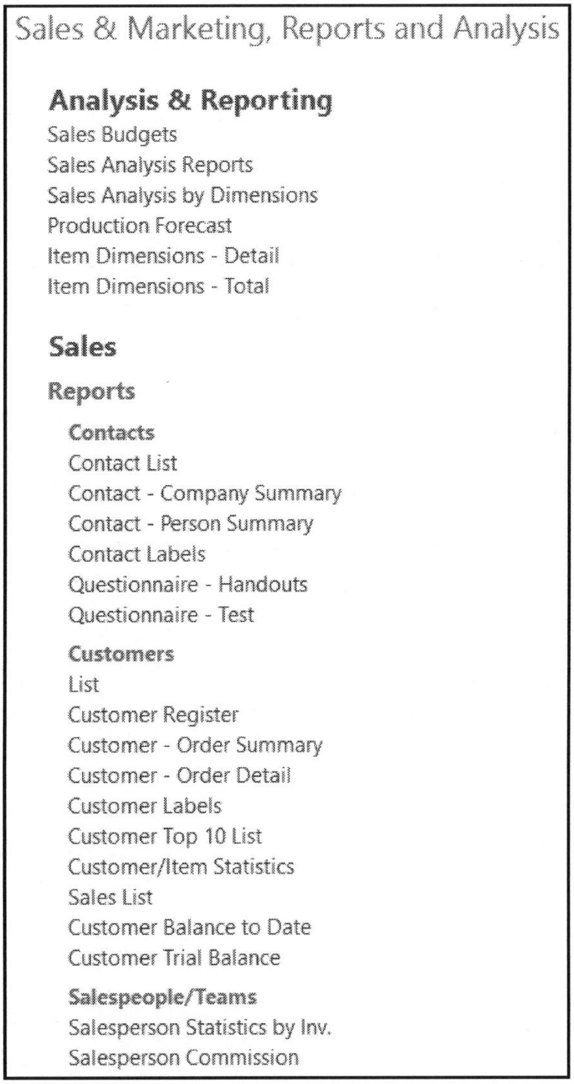

Sales & Marketing, Reports and Analysis

Analysis & Reporting
Sales Budgets
Sales Analysis Reports
Sales Analysis by Dimensions
Production Forecast
Item Dimensions - Detail
Item Dimensions - Total

Sales

Reports

Contacts
Contact List
Contact - Company Summary
Contact - Person Summary
Contact Labels
Questionnaire - Handouts
Questionnaire - Test

Customers
List
Customer Register
Customer - Order Summary
Customer - Order Detail
Customer Labels
Customer Top 10 List
Customer/Item Statistics
Sales List
Customer Balance to Date
Customer Trial Balance

Salespeople/Teams
Salesperson Statistics by Inv.
Salesperson Commission

From the Web client : To find application reports from the Web client, you can use the **Search** menu (**Tell me what you want to do** in Microsoft Dynamics 365 Business Central October's release):

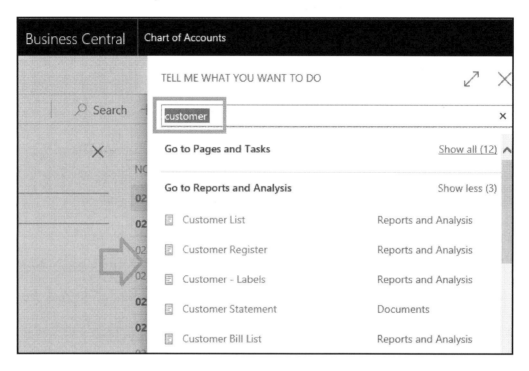

However, reports are not only found on the main menu or in the Search menu; they can also be found in many application pages where only reports that are valuable for the data shown on the page will be found.

Perform the following steps in order to see an example:

1. Click on **Customers** to open the customer list. In the **HOME** tab of the ribbon, a section called **Report** contains the most relevant reports pertaining to customers. The following screenshot is taken from the Microsoft Dynamics NAV Web client:

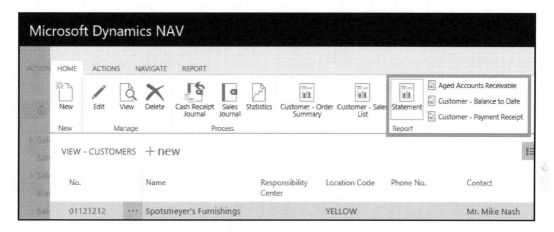

2. On the **REPORT** tab of the ribbon, the reports for customers will be shown and grouped according to the application area to which they belong, as demonstrated in the following screenshot:

Running reports

Now that we have found all the available reports, it is time to execute them and see what kind of information they show. To execute a report, perform the following steps:

1. Click on the report that you want to execute. For instance, click on **Customer - Top 10 List**.
2. The **Request** page for the report will be shown. The following screenshot shows the **Request** page for the **Customer - Top 10 List** report:

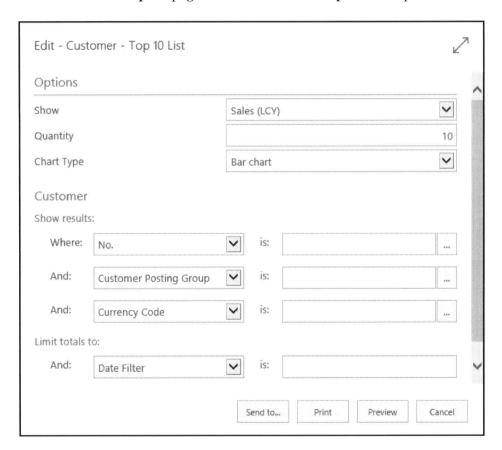

3. Request pages for reports have three different sections:
    - **The Options section**: Here, users can choose from among different options to define the behavior of the report. This section is always called **Options** and is shown as the first section of a report request page. The **Options** section may not be shown in some reports if the report actually has no options for the user to select.

        In the **Customer - Top 10 List** report, the **Option**s section is shown and users have three different fields (**Show**, **Quantity**, and **Chart Type**) to define what they want to see (using the **Show** field), how many customers they want to list (using the **Quantity** field).

    - **The filter section**: Here, users can apply filters over their data so that the report only shows the data the users are interested in. The Filter sections may take different names depending on which data the filters can be applied to. In the **Customer - Top 10 List** report, the filter section is called **Customer** because the filters will be applied over the **Customer** table.

        The filter sections are always shown after the **Options** section. A report may have no filter sections if there are no filters that users can apply to the data shown in the report, or it may have several filter sections if the report combines data from multiple tables and filters can be applied to the data of the different tables.

        The **Customer - Top 10 List** report has a single filter section, **Customer**, but the **Customer - Order detail report**, which can be found under the **Reports and Analysis** category of the **Sales & Marketing** functional area, has two filter sections—**Customer** and **Sales Order Line**.

    - **The buttons section**: Here, users can choose to either print the report in different formats (print it using one of the available printers in the system by using the **Print** option, print the report to a PDF archive by using the PDF option, print the report to a Microsoft Word archive by using the **Microsoft Word** option, or print the report to a Microsoft Excel archive by using the **Microsoft Excel** option), schedule the report to be printed at a later time, preview the report on screen, or cancel the execution of the report.

4. The **Print** and **Send to** options in the Windows client and the Web client are shown in the following screenshot:

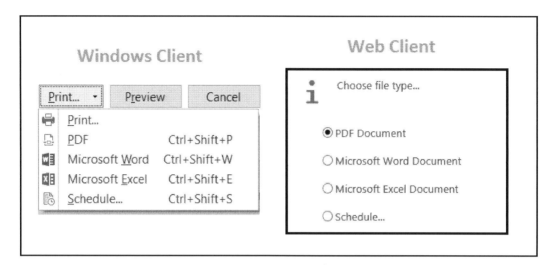

Using the Web client does not allow for a direct interaction between browser and printers. You always have to generate a file first.

5. Click on **Preview** to see the results of the report on screen, as demonstrated in the following screenshot:

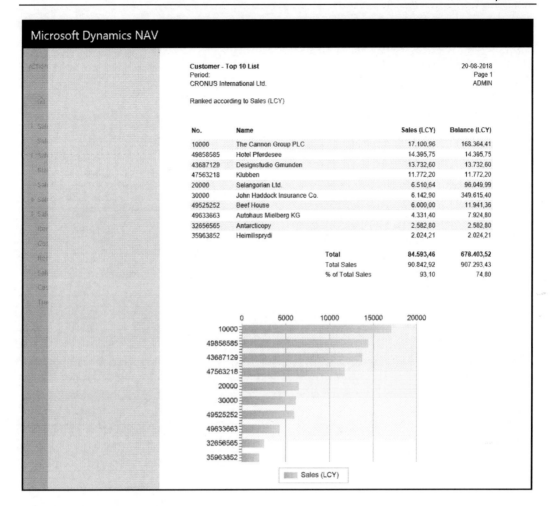

Types of report

Reports in Microsoft Dynamics NAV and in Microsoft Dynamics 365 Business Central have several purposes:

- Printing information from the database in a structured way
- Printing documents, such as the **Sales Invoice**
- Testing data posting before execution
- Automating recurring tasks, such as updating all the prices in an item list (since Microsoft Dynamics NAV 2015, it is possible to schedule report execution on demand)

There are different types of report available in Microsoft Dynamics NAV and Microsoft Dynamics 365 Business Central. We will discuss these in the forthcoming sections.

List reports

A list report is intended to print a list of records from a table, usually a table containing master data or secondary master data. Each column contains a field from the table. Most of the data is printed from that table and sometimes brought in or calculated from the other tables. The name of the list report is usually the name of the table followed by the `List` term.

The following are examples of list reports:

- Customer list
- Inventory list

Test reports

A test report is printed from unposted transactions, such as entries in a journal or sales/purchase documents. The purpose of this kind of report is to test each line of the journal according to the posting rules so that all errors can be found and fixed before posting. If you try to post, and the posting routine encounters an error, the posting routine will stop and will show the first error encountered. If several errors exist, they will be shown and, thus, corrected one at a time. A test report will show all the existing errors. The name of the test report is usually the name of the corresponding journal, followed by the `Test` term.

The following are examples of test reports:

- General journal—test
- Resource journal—test

Posting preview reports

A posting preview report is a report designed to test (simulate) effective data posting. These reports allow you to intercept any errors or missing setups (for example, an unassigned dimension, an incomplete accounting setup, and missing posting groups).

Posting reports

A posting report prints from a register table. It lists all the transactions (ledger entries) that are posted to the register. This kind of report can be very useful for auditing. The name of the posting report is usually the name of either the register table or the master table of the corresponding ledger entries.

The following are examples of posting reports:

- G/L register
- Job register

Transaction reports

A transaction report has the following characteristics:

- It lists all the ledger entries for each record in the ledger table.
- It contains a subtotal for each master table record, and a grand total for all the tables printed.
- It is used to view all the transactions for a particular master record.
- It has no standard naming convention. A transaction report usually has one or more data items, including the master and the corresponding ledger table.

The following are examples of transaction reports:

- Detail trial balance
- Customer—detail trial balance

Document reports

A document report prints a document, such as a **Sales Invoice** or a **Purchase Order**. Document reports have a different layout from all the other reports. The header information of the document is printed as if filling out the document at the top of the page and is repeated on every page. The information on the lines of the document resembles other kinds of report because it is printed in rows and columns. These types of report are typically modified for every implementation because each company will want documents sent out to vendors and customers to have their own unique design.

The following are examples of document reports:

- Sales invoice
- Order

Report selection

A user can select which document report will be printed with each document type. To view and select the document reports that will be printed with each document type, perform the following steps:

1. Type `Report Selection` in the search box of the Microsoft Dynamics NAV Client.
2. Select **Report Selection | Sales**. The **EDIT – REPORT SELECTION – SALES** window will open. The following screenshot shows that report number **1304** will be used to print the sales quotes:

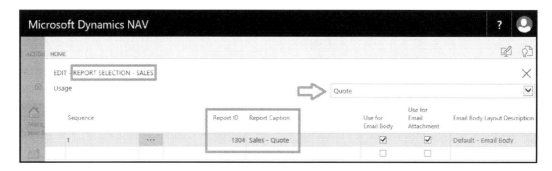

3. By selecting other usages (**Order, Invoice, Credit Memo, Shipment, Order Archive**, and so on), you will be able to choose which report(s) to print for each type of sales document. The selection types available (for Sales in this case) are shown in the following screenshot:

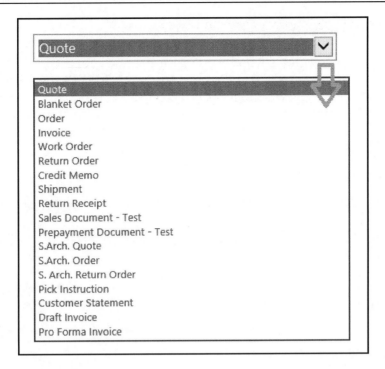

By default, there is usually only one report selected for each type of document, but you can add more reports to the list so that more than one record is printed for each document type.

Other reports

Most reports consist of a tabular listing with records listed horizontally and each field displaying in its own column. Frequently, there is a group heading or total to split the lines among various categories and to subtotal the lines by categories.

The following are examples of other reports:

- Customer/item sales
- Vendor/item purchases

Scheduling a report

As has already been mentioned, it is possible to schedule a report (on-demand). This is very useful when you need to print reports that take a long time to calculate (for example, an inventory evaluation, printing the general ledger journal). Once the report has been processed, it will be saved in the required format (for example, PDF format) and a notification sent to the user with a link to the report ready to allow immediate opening.

Benefits of report scheduling include the following:

- The execution of the report takes place on the Microsoft Dynamics NAV server (server-side execution)
- The client immediately frees resources for other operations (increased productivity)

For example, the following screenshot shows the scheduling of the **Customer – Top 10 List** report:

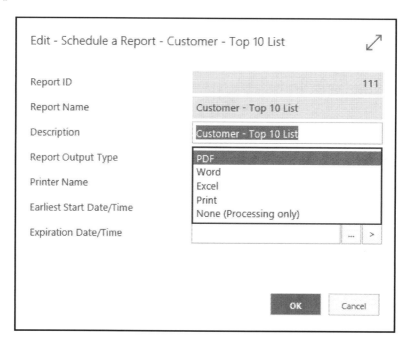

Account schedules

The account schedules functionality is part of the **Analysis and Reporting** section of the **Financial Management** area. It is meant to create customized financial reports based on general ledger information, budget information, or on the analysis views information. Account schedules can group data from various accounts and perform calculations that are not possible directly on the **Chart of Accounts**.

When defining account schedules, the information that will be displayed on both rows and columns can be defined.

To see how it works, we will create a simple account schedule that will compare budgeted amounts with real amounts. To do this, we will perform the following steps:

1. Navigate to **Departments** | **Financial Management** | **Reports and Analysis** and choose **Account Schedules**.
2. Click on **New** to create a new account schedule, as demonstrated in the following screenshot:

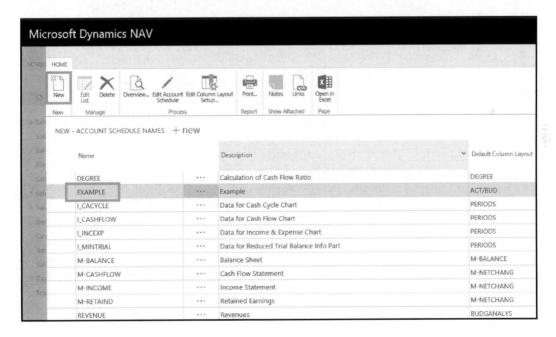

3. For the new account schedule, select **EXAMPLE** as **Name**, comparing budget versus actual as **Description**, and **ACT/BUD** as **Default Column Layout**.

4. Click on **Edit Account Schedule**. An empty page will open. We will define our account schedule on that page.

5. Define the account schedule, as shown in the following screenshot:

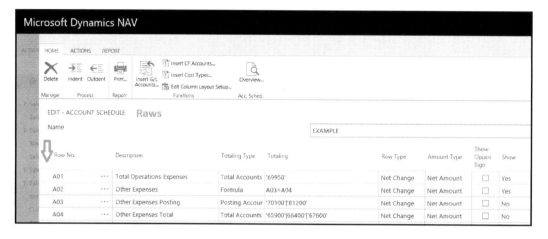

Let's discuss a few terms shown in the preceding screenshot:

- The first row gets the net amount of account **'69950'**; this is a totaling account that summarizes all the operating expenses.

- The second row uses a formula to sum up the results of rows **A03** and **A04**. This is because the other expenses couldn't be summarized together in a single account schedule row, since some of them are summarized in **Chart of Accounts** on totaling accounts, but there are a couple of other expenses that have to be taken directly from the posting accounts.

- The third row gets the net amount of other expenses from the posting accounts. The posting accounts used are **'70100'** and **'81200'**. As this row is only used for calculation purposes, and is not intended to be shown in the report, the **Show** field has been set to **No**.

- The fourth row gets the net amount of other expenses from totaling accounts. The totaling accounts used are **'65900'**, **'66400'**, and **'67600'**. As this row is only used for calculation purposes, and is not intended to be shown in the report, the **Show** field has been set to **No**.

The account schedule is fully defined now. The account schedule defines the rows that will be shown in the report.

Columns are defined under **COLUMN LAYOUT**. In the preceding example, we used an existing column layout called **ACT/BUD**. Let's see what this column layout will show.

6. On the **EDIT – ACCOUNT SCHEDULE** page, where we were defining our account schedule, click on the **ACTIONS** tab and then click on **Edit Column Layout Setup**. The **EDIT – COLUMN LAYOUT** page will open.

7. Select **ACT/BUD** for the **Name** field.

8. The **ACT/BUD** column layout definition will be shown as follows:

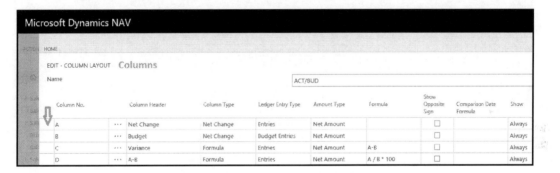

Let's discuss a few terms shown in the preceding screenshot:

- The column layout defines that the report will have four columns called **Net Change**, **Budget**, **Variance**, and **A-B.**
- The **Net Change** column will show the net amount for the G/L entries.
- The **Budget** column will show the net amount for the budget entries.
- The **Variance** column will show the difference between the first and second columns.

- The **A-B** column will calculate the percentage that the first column represents versus the second column.
- Now that we have both the account schedule and the column layout defined, it's time to see the results of our account schedule.

9. Navigate to **Departments | Financial Management | Reports and Analysis** and select **Account Schedules**.
10. Select the account schedule that we have created in this section.
11. Click on **Overview**. The report will be shown on screen, as demonstrated in the following screenshot:

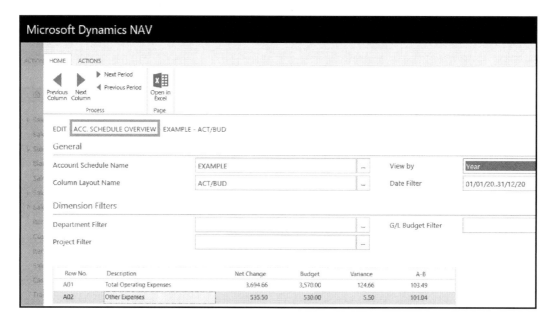

The results can be seen for different time periods and filters applied to the calculation to get a more refined dataset that you may be looking for. The results can be exported to Excel and can also be printed.

Analysis views

Analysis views are used to analyze information about dimensions from general ledger entries, budgets, and cash flow forecast entries. It is a very powerful tool that can create even very complex analysis scenarios, and the configuration matrix is very detailed, with many applicable filters.

Let's first have a look at what dimensions are, and then we will be able to see how to analyze the information that dimensions provide using analysis views.

Understanding dimensions

A dimension can be seen as information linked to an entry, something like a tag or a characteristic. The purpose of dimensions is to group entries with similar characteristics so that you can report on the data in a way that is meaningful to the company. Each company can define its own dimensions according to how they need to analyze their data.

Posted entries and posted documents can contain analyzable dimension information as well as budgets. The term **dimension** is used to describe how analysis occurs. A two-dimensional analysis, for example, would be sales per area. You can also apply more than two dimensions when posting a document or a journal. This will allow you to carry out a more complex analysis, for example, sales per sales campaign, sales per customer, or group per area.

Each dimension can have unlimited dimension values that are subunits of the dimension. For example, a dimension called `Department` can have subunits called `Sales`, `Administration`, and so on. These departments are dimension values.

Microsoft Dynamics NAV and Microsoft Dynamics 365 Business Central support unlimited dimensions. This means that you can create as many dimensions as needed according to how you are currently categorizing areas of the business. However, even if you can create unlimited dimensions, there are some restrictions on how they are stored and how easy it is to access their information.

In both Microsoft Dynamics NAV and Microsoft Dynamics 365 Business Central, all dimensions are stored in special dimension tables. Some dimensions are also stored in fields inside the table they refer to. We can group dimensions in three categories according to their access level (how easy it is to access them):

- **Global dimensions**: Their value is stored on special dimension tables and also on fields inside the table they refer to. We can use up to two global dimensions.
- **Shortcut dimensions**: Their value is stored on special dimension tables. Although the value is not stored inside the table they refer to, occasionally they are shown on pages as if they were stored on the table. We can use up to eight shortcut dimensions. Two of them correspond to global dimensions.
- **The rest of the dimensions**: Their value is only stored on special dimension tables.

Setting up new dimensions

Imagine that, in our company, we have two different divisions: one responsible for selling items, and another responsible for renting items. We decide to use dimensions to analyze the results of each division. So, we are going to create a dimension called DIVISION.

To create new dimensions, access **Departments | Financial Management | Setup | Dimensions** and follow the steps described in this section:

1. Click on the **New** icon found on the ribbon bar.
2. Create a new dimension by assigning some values, as shown in the following screenshot:

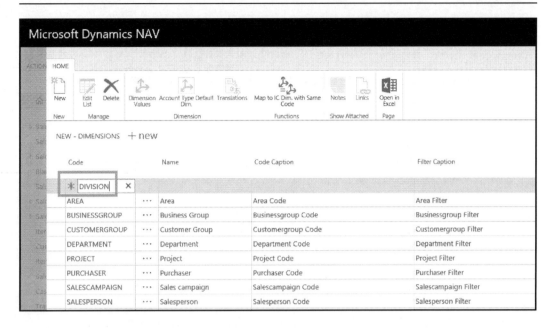

3. Click on the **Dimension Values** icon found on the ribbon bar. A new page will open.

4. Create two different dimension values by giving them the values shown in the following screenshot:

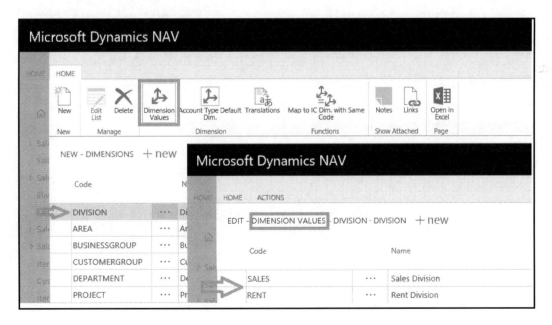

Categorizing dimensions

We have already created a new dimension along with its dimension values. Now, we must determine whether it is going to be a global dimension, a shortcut dimension, or dimension.

To do so, open General Ledger Setup by navigating to **Departments** | **Financial Management** | **Setup** | **General Ledger Setup**. Select the **Dimensions** tab:

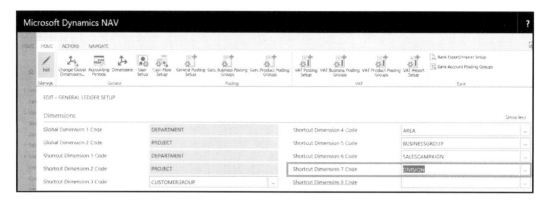

In the CRONUS International company, global dimensions are already defined. The company has already defined up to six shortcut dimensions.

Select DIVISION in the Shortcut Dimension 7 Code field in order to define our new dimension as a shortcut dimension.

Accessing dimensions

As we said earlier in this chapter, the difference between global, shortcut, and the remaining dimensions lies in how easy it is to access them.

We are going to see how to access the **DEPARTMENT** global dimension, the **DIVISION** shortcut dimension, and the **SALESPERSON** dimension, which is one of the remaining dimensions.

To see how dimensions can be accessed so we can fill them when creating documents, perform the following steps:

On the Windows client:

> 1. Open the **Sales Invoices** page that you will find by navigating to **Departments** | **Sales & Marketing** | **Order Processing** | **Sales Invoices**.

2. Click on the **New** icon found on the ribbon bar to create a new sales invoice.

3. In the **Sell-to Customer No.** field, select customer **62000**.

4. Create a line for item 1000 to sell 23 PCs.

5. On the **Lines** tab, click on the setup icon and select **Choose Columns**, as demonstrated in the following screenshot:

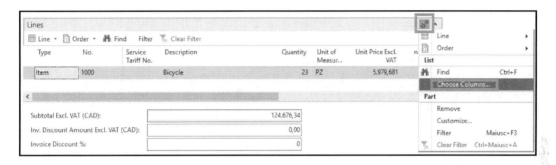

6. Add **Department Code** and **Division Code** in the column entitled **Show columns in this order**. Then click on **OK**. A **Salesperson Code** cannot be selected because it is not a global dimension or a shortcut dimension:

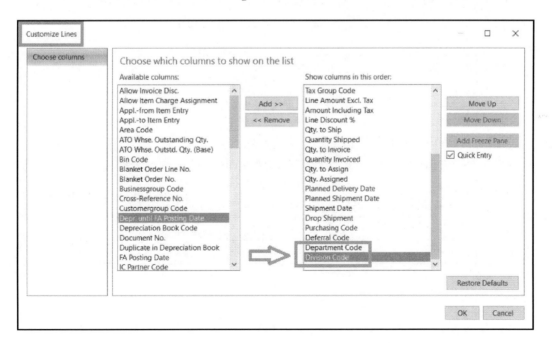

7. Returning to the sales line, fill in the value for the **Sales** for the **Department Code** field. Also fill in the value for **Sell** for the **Division Code** field.

8. To fill in a value in the **Salesperson Code** field, click on **Line** and then **Dimensions** to open the **Edit Dimension Set Entries** page, as demonstrated in the following screenshot:

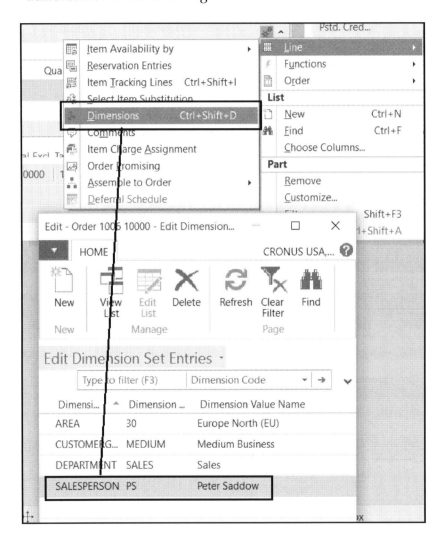

9. Post the **Sales Invoice**.

10. Open the **Posted Sales Invoices** page. You will find it by navigating to **Departments | Sales & Marketing | History | Posted Sales Invoices**. Locate the invoice we have just posted and open it by double-clicking on it.

11. Open the **Customize Lines** page, as we did in step 6.

12. Add **Department Code** to the column entitled **Show columns in this order**. Note that you will not find a **Division Code** available in the column entitled **Available columns**. This is because **Division** is a shortcut dimension. As we said earlier, shortcut dimensions are, in some instances, shown on pages as if they were stored on the table. Usually, they are shown in pages meant to intended for data entry, but not on pages meant to show posted information.

13. Access all the dimensions by clicking on **Line** and then **Dimensions**, as we did in step 8.

Dimensions on the Web client:

On the Web client, the dimension assignment process is also similar to that for the Windows client. The following screenshots are from the Microsoft Dynamics 365 Business Central Web client, the first one showing the **Dimensions** selection in the **Sales invoice** line:

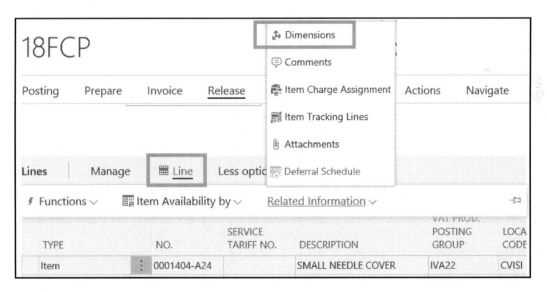

The following screenshot shows dimension codes and value assignments in the sales invoice **Line**:

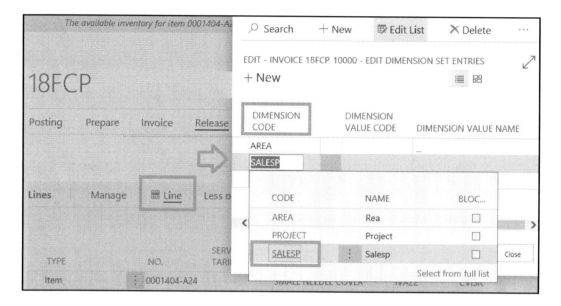

Creating an analysis view

As we have seen, there are several dimensions that are not easily accessed by users, especially when the document or the entry has been posted. This is when we need to analyze the data.

Analysis views are specifically meant to access all dimensions in the same easy way, in groups of a maximum of four dimensions at the same time. The four dimension groups may seem like a limitation, but they are not, since we can create as many analysis views as needed, combining all the dimensions we require.

With an analysis view, we can view data from the general ledger. Entries are grouped by criteria, such as:

- G/L accounts
- Period
- Business units
- Up to four dimensions

In other words, if a G/L entry has been posted to a particular account with one of the four dimensions selected, the G/L entry information will be included in the analysis view as an analysis view entry. You can also include G/L budget entries in an analysis view to compare the reality with the budget.

Perform the following steps to set up an analysis view:

1. Open the **ANALYSIS VIEW LIST** page by navigating to **Departments** | **Administration** | **Application Setup** | **Financial Management** | **Dimensions** | **Analysis View List**. The **ANALYSIS VIEW LIST** page will open, showing the existing analysis views:

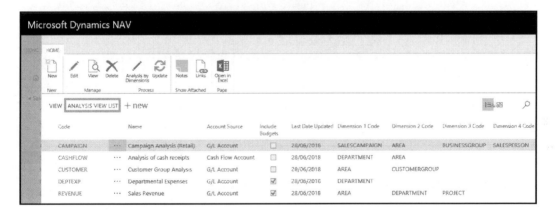

2. Click on the **New** icon found on the ribbon bar. The **ANALYSIS VIEW CARD** page will open.

3. Fill up the **ANALYSIS VIEW CARD** page with the data shown in the following screenshot:

4. Click on the **Update** option found on the ribbon bar to create analysis view entries based on the criteria that you set up on the card. The system will create one summarized analysis view entry for each G/L account, period, and dimension combination. In the preceding example, we will get one entry for each G/L account from account numbers **6210** to **6910**, for each month, and also for each combination of dimension values of the **Division**, **Salesperson**, and **Department** dimensions.

5. Open the **Analysis View Entries** page to see the entries created by the system. You can find it by navigating to **Departments** | **Financial Management** | **General Ledger** | **History** | **Analysis View Entries**, as demonstrated in the following screenshot:

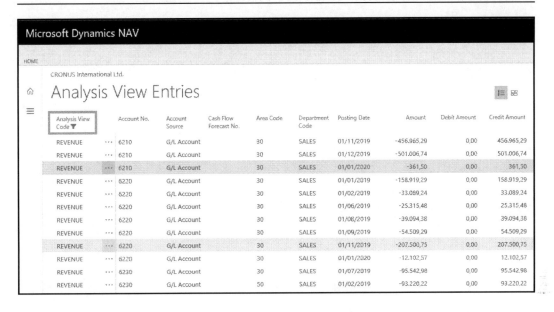

Updating analysis views

An analysis view is a fixed photo of posted G/L entries grouped with specific criteria.

If you change any of the fields found on the **Analysis View Card** page, for instance, if you change the **Starting Date** field, you will get the following message:

If you select **Yes**, all entries will be deleted and you will have to click on the **Update** option again to create analysis view entries according to the new criteria.

You will also have to use the **Update** action to include new general ledger entries posted after you last updated the analysis view. You can also let the system update it automatically when new G/L entries are posted by checking the **Update on Posting** field found on the **Analysis View Card** page.

 It's not recommended you use the **Update on Posting** option because it could penalize performance when posting, obviously depending on the size of the data managed in each company.

Using analysis views

Analysis views can be used in different scenarios:

- In the **Analysis by Dimensions** functionality
- As a source for account schedules

In this section, we are going to see an example of using analysis views on each of the scenarios detailed.

Analysis by Dimensions

The **Analysis by Dimensions** functionality is used to display and analyze the amount derived from the existing analysis views.

Perform the steps to see an example of how **Analysis by Dimensions** works:

1. Open the Analysis View List page by navigating to **Departments | Financial Management | General Ledger | Analysis & Reporting | Analysis by Dimensions**.
2. Locate the **REVENUE** analysis view that we created earlier in this chapter. Then click on the **Edit Analysis View** option found on the ribbon bar.
3. A new page opens. In the **Division Filter** field, select **RENT**.
4. Click on the **Show Matrix** icon found on the ribbon bar. The **Analysis by Dimensions Matrix** page now shows the amounts posted on the general ledger under the **RENT** value of the **Division** dimension, as demonstrated in the following screenshot:

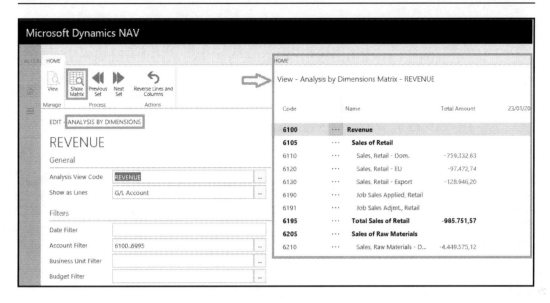

5. Close the current page and go back to the **Analysis by Dimensions** page.
6. Select different values for the following fields, and click on **Show Matrix** to see the results. The main fields you can change to analyze data are **Show as Lines**, **Show as Columns**, **Dimension Filters**, **Show**, **Show Amount Field**, **View by**, and **View as**.

Analysis views as a source for account schedules

If analysis views are selected as a source for account schedules, the amounts in the account schedules are calculated based on the analysis views entries. Since analysis views entries are based on general ledger entries, the result should be the same.

The difference is that, when analyzing account schedules, you can only filter amounts based on global dimensions. If you use analysis views as a source for account schedules, then you can filter on any of the four dimensions selected on the **Analysis View Card** page. These dimensions can be global dimensions, shortcut dimensions, or any other dimensions.

To use analysis views as a source for account schedules, perform the following steps:

1. Open **ACCOUNT SCHEDULE NAME** by navigating to **Departments** | **Financial Managemen**t | **General Ledger** | **Analysis & Reporting** | **Account Schedules**.

2. Locate the **REVENUE** account schedule. Note that an analysis view is selected in the **Analysis View Name** field. This is what makes it possible to use the analysis view as a source for the account schedule:

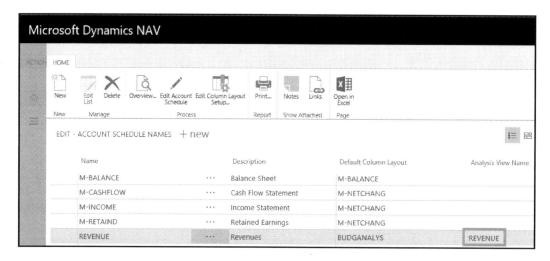

3. Click on the **Overview** option found on the ribbon bar.

4. The **ACC. SCHEDULE OVERVIEW - REVENUE** page opens. Note that you can now filter on any of the three dimensions that were set up on the analysis view. Select different values on these fields to see the results, as demonstrated in the following screenshot:

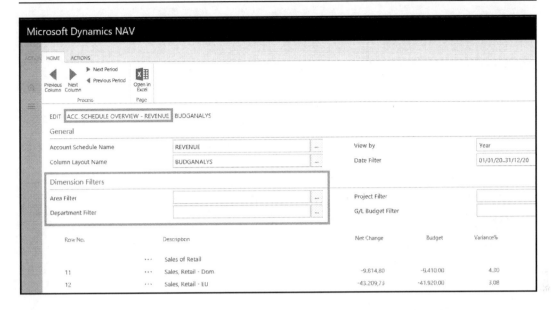

Extracting data

Microsoft Dynamics NAV and Microsoft Dynamics 365 Business Central offer several ways to analyze and report data inside the application. If that is not enough, you can also extract data from the application and use external tools to report and analyze your data.

In this section, we will see the different ways in which you can extract your data from Microsoft Dynamics NAV and Microsoft Dynamics 365 Business Central. Once it is outside the application, you can use the most convenient tool for you.

Data in Microsoft Dynamics NAV and Dynamics 365 Business Central can be extracted in multiple ways:

Feature	Dynamics NAV	Dynamics 365 Business Central on-premise	Dynamics 365 Business Central SaaS
Copying and pasting	Yes	Yes	Yes
Extracting data through Microsoft SQL Server	Yes	Yes	No
Any external data/reporting tools that can connect to Microsoft SQL Server	Yes	Yes	No
Web services (OData) published	Yes	Yes	Yes

Electronic Data Interchange (EDI)	Yes	Yes	Yes
Microsoft PowerShell Scripts	Yes	Yes	No
Microsoft Power BI connector	Yes	Yes	Yes
Export with Microsoft Dynamics Data Tools for Audit (available only in certain localizations)	Yes	Yes	Yes
APIs	Yes	Yes	Yes
RapidStart Packages	Yes	Yes	Yes

The list goes on and on...

 Not all options are currently available in the Web client; some are only available in the Windows client. Take a look at the following link for Web client limitations: `https://docs.microsoft.com/en-us/dynamics-nav/feature-limitations-of-the-microsoft-dynamics-nav-web-clientm`.

In this section, we'll focus solely on two ways of exporting data:

- Sending data to Microsoft Office applications
- Using web services

Sending data from pages to Microsoft Office applications

Let's first discuss the Windows client. Microsoft Dynamics NAV and Microsoft Dynamics 365 Business Central On-premise data can be sent to either Microsoft Word or Microsoft Excel by users; this can only be effected from the Windows client.

Whenever that is possible, which is on all the pages in Microsoft Dynamics NAV except on the **Role Center** page and on menu pages in the **Department** area, the export option will be available on the application menu, as demonstrated in the following screenshot:

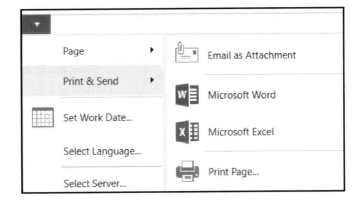

The data exported will be data that the user is seeing at the moment, including filters and columns shown/hidden on a list. Imagine you are looking at the customer list. In that list, you have only chosen the columns **No.**, **Name**, and **Contact**, and you have applied a filter so you only see blocked customers. When you export these to either Microsoft Word or Microsoft Excel, you will export only those three fields, and only the customers within the filter.

Now we will talk about the Web client. There are a number of limitations. It is not possible to export data directly from pages as for the Windows client. You can use the **Edit in Excel** function and then save the generated file, or use the **Copy** and **Paste** feature, as demonstrated in the following screenshot:

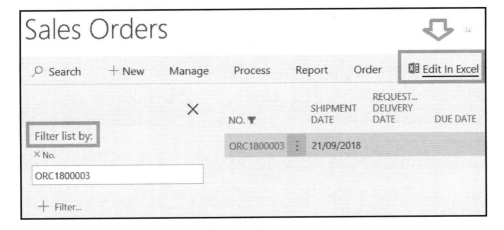

Sending data to Microsoft Word

The following screenshot shows how data exported to Microsoft Word appears:

Customers

No.	Name	Responsibility Center	Location Code	Phone No.	Contact	Balance (LCY)	Balance Due (LCY)	Sales (LCY)
01121212	Spotsmeyer's Furnishings		YELLOW		Mr. Mike Nash	0,00	0,00	0,00
01445544	Progressive Home Furnishings		BLUE		Mr. Scott Mitchell	2.322,63	2.322,63	2.322,63
01454545	New Concepts Furniture		YELLOW		Ms. Tammy L. McDonald	344.207,60	344.207,60	0,00
01905893	Candoxy Canada Inc.		YELLOW		Mr. Rob Young	0,00	0,00	0,00
01905899	Elkhorn Airport		YELLOW		Mr. Ryan Danner	0,00	0,00	0,00
01905902	London Candoxy Storage Campus		BLUE		Mr. John Kane	0,00	0,00	0,00

When data changes in Microsoft Dynamics NAV, it has to be sent to Microsoft Word again if you want your data in Microsoft Word to be updated with the most recent changes.

Sending data to Microsoft Excel

The following screenshot shows how data exported to Microsoft Excel appears:

	A	B	C	D	E	F	G
1	Customer List						
2	No.	Name	Phone No.	Contact	Balance (LCY)	Balance Due (LCY)	Sales (LCY)
3	01121212	Spotsmeyer's Furnishings		Mr. Mike Nash	0,00	0,00	0,00
4	01445544	Progressive Home Furnishings		Mr. Scott Mitchell	2.322,63	2.322,63	2.322,63
5	01454545	New Concepts Furniture		Ms. Tammy L. McDonald	344.207,60	344.207,60	0,00
6	01905893	Candoxy Canada Inc.		Mr. Rob Young	0,00	0,00	0,00
7	01905899	Elkhorn Airport		Mr. Ryan Danner	0,00	0,00	0,00
8	01905902	London Candoxy Storage Campus		Mr. John Kane	0,00	0,00	0,00
9	10000	Cannon Group SpA		Sig. Franco Verdi	260.354,79	260.354,79	26.762,09
10	20000	Grafiche magiche 2000		Sig. Ivan Gagliardi	148.667,31	148.667,31	10.009,43
11	20309920	Metatorad Malaysia Sdn Bhd		Mrs. Azleen Samat	0,00	0,00	0,00
12	20312912	Highlights Electronics Sdn Bhd		Mr. Mark Darrell Boland	0,00	0,00	0,00
13	20339921	TraxTonic Sdn Bhd		Mrs. Rubina Usman	0,00	0,00	0,00
14	21233572	Somadis		M. Syed ABBAS	0,00	0,00	0,00
15	21245278	Maronegoce		Mme. Fadoua AIT MOUSSA	0,00	0,00	0,00

Note the **Microsoft Dynamics NAV** tab on the Microsoft Excel ribbon and the **Refresh** button in that tab. When data changes in Microsoft Dynamics NAV, there is no need to send it to Microsoft Excel again. You can click on the **Refresh** button and the data in Microsoft Excel will be updated with the most recent data from Microsoft Dynamics NAV.

The Microsoft Dynamics NAV add-in for Microsoft Excel gets installed when you install the Microsoft Dynamics NAV Windows client.

Extracting data through web services

Any Microsoft Dynamics NAV codeunit, page, or query can be published as a web service. Codeunits are published as SOAP web services. Pages are published as both SOAP web services and OData web services. Queries are published as OData web services.

Any application that can consume SOAP web services or OData web services will be able to extract Microsoft Dynamics NAV data.

In Chapter 12, *Popular Reporting Options*, we include an example of consuming a query OData web service using Microsoft Excel.

Extracting data through APIs

APIs are the real future of REST services. They are available for both Microsoft Dynamics NAV and Microsoft Dynamics 365 Business Central. With APIs, it is possible to integrate these ERP systems with other services.

API Services are bounded on OData services. It's possible to configure APIs services from a setup named API Setup (it's illustrated in the Chapter 13, *Microsoft Dynamics 365 Business Central*).

Export data using the Microsoft Dynamics NAV Export to a Data File feature (and importing it)

Let's first discuss the **Export to a Data File** feature.

It's also possible to export (and import) data from Microsoft Dynamics NAV through a dedicated export function called **Export to a Data File**, which you can find in the **Search** menu, as demonstrated in the following screenshot:

How does it work?

In practice, the system allows you to export files and objects (similar to the old Microsoft Dynamics NAV backup) in a file. in this way, it is possible to make backup copies of data or to create new companies (using the Import tool); the system creates a file of the **NAV Data File** type with the extension `.navdata`:

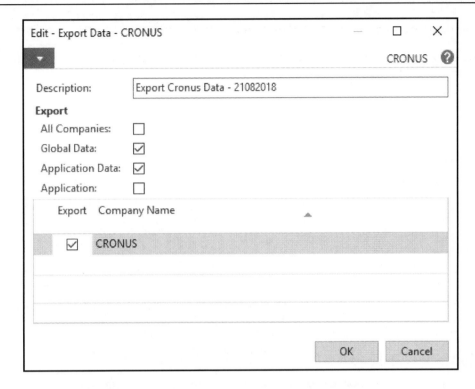

Export to **NAV Data File** as shown in the following screenshot:

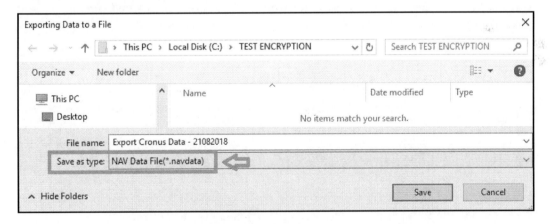

Now, let's move on to importing from a data file.

In the same way as exporting, it is possible to import data into Microsoft Dynamics NAV using the **Import from a Data File** function. The system reads the data contained in the `.navdata` file and loads it into the system, as demonstrated in the following screenshot:

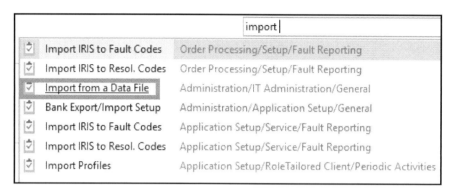

Exporting data from PowerShell

It is also possible to export data from PowerShell using just a single command—`Export-NAVData`—that runs server-side (take a look at the Microsoft website for more details). In practice, it is the same function illustrated previously and can also be executed by PowerShell.

Other ways to extract data

Just with on-premise releases, the data is actually stored in a Microsoft SQL database, and thus all available tools that let Microsoft SQL Server extract data can be used; it's also possible to use PowerShell scripts (from Microsoft Dynamics NAV, Microsoft Dynamics 365 Business Central on-premise, and Microsoft SQL Server) to export data.

Understanding report development

Report development is completely different from what it used to be. The report development experience changed in Microsoft Dynamics NAV 2009 with the introduction of the **Report Definition Language Client-side** (RDLC) report, but it changed again with the actual release of the application.

With Microsoft Dynamics NAV 2009, RDLC-based reports were introduced, but reports were still compatible with the classic definition of reports in Microsoft Dynamics NAV. RDLC reports were actually based on the classic definition of the report.

From Microsoft Dynamics NAV 2013, the classic definition of reports has disappeared and only RLDC-based reports are available. This is why the report development experience has changed again. It now resembles the development experience for pages, queries, or XML ports.

With the advent of Microsoft Dynamics NAV 2015, a new way of managing reports was introduced: Word Report Layout. A Word report layout is based on a Word document (.docx file type) that acts as a template for viewing and printing reports from Microsoft Dynamics NAV clients. Word report layouts are built on custom XML parts in Word.

Report anatomy

Creating reports includes designing both the business logic that covers the kind of information the report will contain, and the layout that deals with how the report will look when it is printed. In this section, we will look at these different types of report (RDLC reports and Word layout reports)

RDLC reports

In Microsoft Dynamics NAV 2018, to design a client report definition (RDLC), you design the data model with Report Dataset Designer and the layout with Visual Studio Report Designer. To do this, you must use Microsoft Visual Studio 2017 with an appropriate extension installed; you can use also Report Builder (embedded on SQL Server) if you do not have Visual Studio.

 For editing RDLC report layouts, use Report Builder for SQL Server 2016 or Visual Studio 2017 with Microsoft RDLC Report Designer for Visual Studio installed. For editing Word layouts, use Microsoft Word 2013 or later.

Visual Studio Report Designer offers several new options and features. Furthermore, due to its deep integration with Microsoft SQL Server, it is possible to take advantage of the reporting capabilities of Microsoft Report Viewer, including the following:

- Richer formatting
- Interactive sorting
- Graphics and charts
- Export possibilities (PDF, Microsoft Office Excel, and Microsoft Office Word)

A report object is composed of a report dataset and a visual layout. You design a report by first defining the dataset and then designing the visual layout. The Report objects also contain properties, triggers, code, and an optional request page.

The following diagram shows components of a report and how they are related in Microsoft Dynamics NAV:

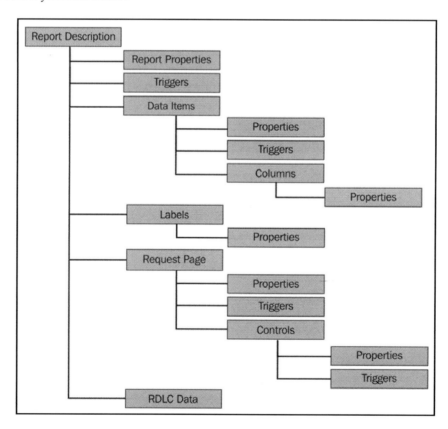

Reports in Microsoft Dynamics NAV 2018 are executed in two steps, reflecting the two steps in the report design. The first is dataset design in C/SIDE, followed by report layout design in Visual Studio.

The C/AL runtime retrieves the data from the involved source tables, performs the necessary calculations, and combines the data in a single flattened dataset. This is performed by the Microsoft Dynamics NAV server. The dataset produced is transferred to the report viewer's runtime hosted on the Microsoft Dynamics NAV client, which, in turn, renders the dataset data according to the report layout definition.

Word layout reports

A Word layout report is based on a Word document (`.docx` file type) that acts as a template for viewing and printing reports from Dynamic's NAV clients. Word layout reports enable you to design report layouts using Microsoft Word 2013. Word layouts report are built on custom XML parts in Word. A custom XML part is structured XML that represents the dataset of a Dynamics NAV report; the custom XML part is used to map the data into a report at runtime.

Defining the dataset

The dataset is defined on Report Dataset Designer in the Microsoft Dynamics NAV Development Environment. The report dataset is built from data items and columns. A data item is a table. A column can be one of the following:

- A field in a table
- A variable
- An expression
- A text constant

Typically, the data items correspond to the fields in a table. When the report is run, each data item is iterated for all records in the underlying table with an appropriate filter defined.

When a report is based on more than one table, you must set relations between the data items so you can retrieve and organize the data. In Report Dataset Designer, you indent data items to establish a hierarchy of data items and control how the information is gathered.

For example, to create a report that displays a list of customers and lists sales orders that were placed by each customer, you must define the following data items:

- A data item that corresponds to the `Customer` table
- A data item that corresponds to the `Sales Line` table

You indent the second data item, which is the `Sales Line` table. As the report works through the records in the `Customer` table, it finds each customer's sales orders by examining the records in the `Sales Line` table that's related to the customer number.

The following screenshot shows the dataset definition of **Report 108 Customer – Order Detail**:

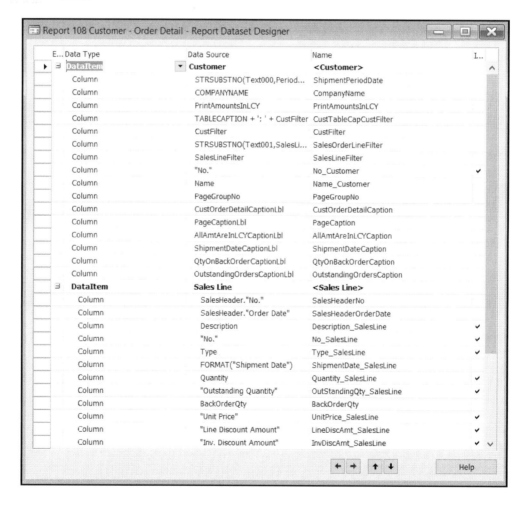

If you can't open the Visual Studio Editor, check the flag shown in the **Options** section:

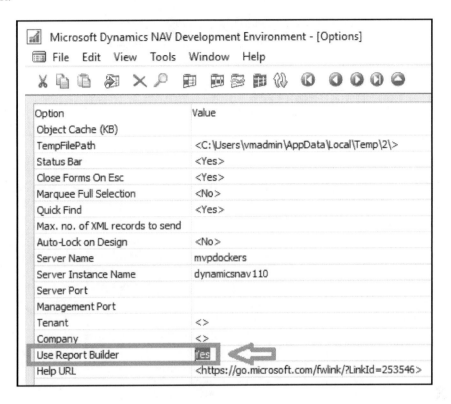

And the following is how the dataset looks on Visual Studio (Report Builder in this case):

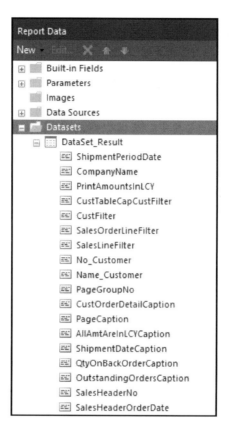

Designing the visual layout

You build the visual layout of a report by arranging data items. A report that is displayed or printed must have a client report definition (RDLC) layout. You use Visual Studio Report Designer to design the RDLC layout. You generally display most data in the body of a report, and you use the header to display information before any data item record is displayed. For example, you can display a report title, company, and user information in the header of a report.

With Visual Studio Report Designer, you can add useful features to your report layouts, such as the following:

- Providing links from a field on a report to either a page or another report
- The inclusion of images and graphs
- The ability to toggle columns so you can hide or display data
- The ability for users to interactively change the column on which the data in the report is sorted
- The ability to display HTML text

A report in Visual Studio always has exactly one body, and it is not possible to add more than one. Optionally, it can have a header and footer on a single page. Extra headers or footers cannot be added. However, you can dynamically change the visibility property of objects on the report layout to control how the report will look.

When the report runs, it first runs the page header, then the page body, and then the page footer. It will not run the page body for each record. Looping through records is done by using a data region in the body section.

Reports use a variety of report items to organize data on a report page. The design surface is not based on the *What You See Is What You Get* Approach. Report items have an initial layout position that can change when the report is processed. The following list describes typical uses for different report items:

- **Textbox**: This is used on titles, date stamps, and report names.
- **Table**, **Matrix**: This is used to display tabular data from a report dataset. Table and matrix are templates of a Tablix data region and provide a starting grid layout for data from a report dataset.
- **Chart**: This is used to graphically display data from a report dataset.
- **Gauge**: This is used to present a visual image for a single value within a range of values.
- **List**: This is used to create a free-form layout, such as forms on a web page.
- **Image**: This is used to add existing images to a report.
- **Line**: This uses lines as graphical elements.
- **Rectangle**: This can be used as a container for other report items. Rectangles are often used to help control how report items appear on a report page when the report is rendered.

The following screenshot shows the layout definition of the **108, Customer – Order Detail** report:

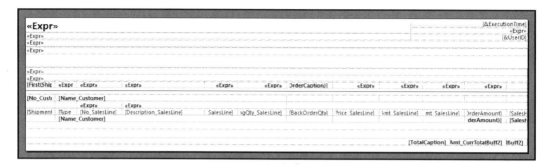

The layout definition view

 Detailed report writing using Visual Studio is beyond the scope of this book. For more in-depth detail on writing your own reports in Microsoft Dynamics NAV, check out Microsoft Dynamics NAV 2015 Professional Reporting, also published by Packt Publishing.

Using Word layout reports

The development of reports varies according to whether you use the CSIDE Development Environment or the New Modern Development Environment. Remember that, for Microsoft Dynamics 365 Business Central SaaS, it is not possible to change the standard code and you can develop reports only with VS Code plus the AL language extension. The chapter on Microsoft Dynamics 365 Business Central explains how to create a report from VS Code.

From the Dynamics NAV Development Environment

From Microsoft Dynamics NAV Development Environment, you can create and modify built-in Word layouts report on reports. The layouts that you create on reports in the development environment become part of the report objects in the database.

From the Microsoft Dynamics NAV clients, Microsoft Dynamics NAV users can manage Microsoft Word report layouts that are used on reports. This includes adding a built-in Word report layout, creating custom Word layouts report on a report, and changing which report layout is currently active on a report, as demonstrated in the following screenshot:

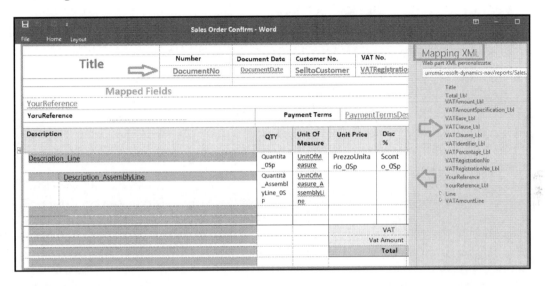

From the New Modern Development Environment

In Microsoft Dynamics 365 Business Central SaaS, you cannot modify standard reports and, as yet, it is not possible to create report extensions; it is only possible to create new reports.

You can create them manually or convert them from C/SIDE objects reports through a specific application named: `txt2AL`; once converted, it is possible to manage them in VS Code.

From VS Code, you can do the following:

- Recreate/change the report, adding the RDLC layout
- Create the dataset in AL
- Generate the RDLC layout from VS Code
- Customize it with Report Builder
- Import the new layout as a Custom Layout for new reports

 Take a look at my blog post: *How to develop a Word Layout report in Visual Studio Code*, available at `https:// robertostefanettinavblog.com/2018/09/30/how-to-develop-a- word-layout-report-in-visual-studio-code/`.

Summary

In this chapter, we learned that there are several ways of analyzing and reporting data inside Microsoft Dynamics NAV and in Microsoft Dynamics 365 Business Central. We can use filters and FlowFilters, create views, take a look at the statistics pages of Microsoft Dynamics NAV and Microsoft Dynamics 365 Business Central, define charts and use them in multiple pages, use all the available reports, use analysis views to analyze our data based on dimensions, and use account schedules to analyze our accounting information.

If that is not enough, we also learned that there are several ways to extract data from Microsoft Dynamics NAV and from Microsoft Dynamics 365 Business Central and do the analysis and reporting outside the application by using external tools. We have seen the options for using both RDLC reports and Word layout reports in Microsoft Dynamics NAV.

In the next chapter, we will learn how to debug error messages while users work through the system.

11
Debugging with Dynamics NAV and MSDYN365BC

Microsoft introduced a new debugger from the Microsoft Dynamics NAV 2013 release. The purpose of the revamped debugger is to allow IT people to easily pinpoint the problem any specific user is facing while using the software, for example, with conditional breakpoints, debugging other user sessions, and debugging C/AL code in the Windows client, instead of in incomprehensible C# code. All these new features make the debugging experience a happy one.

The following topics are covered in this chapter:

- The art of debugging
- Starting the debugger
- Placing breakpoints
- Line-by-line execution
- How to debug in the new AL Development Environment

 On 1st October 2018, Microsoft coined this new name for the New Modern Development Environment, that is, AL Development Environment, in relation to the launch of Microsoft Dynamics 365 Business Central on-premise.

The art of debugging

By definition, **debugging** is a methodical process of finding and reducing the number of bugs in an application. Normally, the first step in debugging is to attempt to reproduce the problem. On some occasions, the input of the program may need to be simplified to make it easier to debug. Then, the debugger tool is used to examine the program stats (values of variables, call stacks, and so on) to track down the origin of the problem and finally fix it.

Debugging, however, can do so much more than just solving issues. It is a fantastic way to understand how an application works. You could just open the object involved, read the written code, and follow it up. However, this will be hard.

First of all, Microsoft Dynamics NAV code is run after an event occurs. If you take a look at an object, you will see code in the events, but it will be hard to know when an event occurs or which event is the one that first causes the code to be executed.

It will also be hard to just read the code because you don't know which values a variable is taking. If you turn the debugger on, you read the code with a specific example that makes variables take specific values. This is really helpful!

Of course, this means that, depending on specific variable values, some lines of the code won't be executed and you won't be able to follow them. Therefore, you will have to create significant and varied examples in order to cover all (or almost all) the code in a given object.

Debugging in Microsoft Dynamics NAV 2018 and in Microsoft Dynamics 365 Business Central on-premise

The debugger starts from the **Microsoft Dynamics NAV Development Environment** both for Microsoft Dynamics NAV 2018 and from Microsoft Dynamics 365 Business Central on-premise. This is true for C/AL code. For AL code, you can debug from Visual Studio Code directly. The user with which you are logged in must be assigned as a user in Microsoft SQL Server.

Go to **Tools** | **Debugger** | **Debug Session;** the **Session List** page will open, as shown in the following screenshot (the screenshot is taken from the Microsoft Dynamics 365 Business Central on-premise October release):

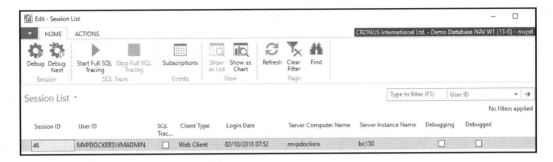

 Note that the page shows all sessions on the current database from all companies.

The session you select can be any of the following:

- A **Windows Client** session
- A **Web Client** session
- A **Mobile (Universal App Client)** session
- An **OData Web Services** session
- An **SOAP Web Services** session
- An **NAS (Navision Application Server) Services** session

Place the cursor on the line corresponding to the session you want to debug and then click on the **Debug** button from the ribbon bar. You can select your own session or any other session from any other user. You can also click on the **Debug Next** option to debug a session that is not on the session list. The next session can be a session of any client mentioned previously.

The user won't be able to work with his/her session while you are debugging; therefore, whenever possible, open your own session and debug your session. If you cannot reproduce the bug because of user setup conditions, debug the session of the user that is encountering the problem, but remember to warn him/her.

The **Debugger** page will now open, as shown in the following screenshot:

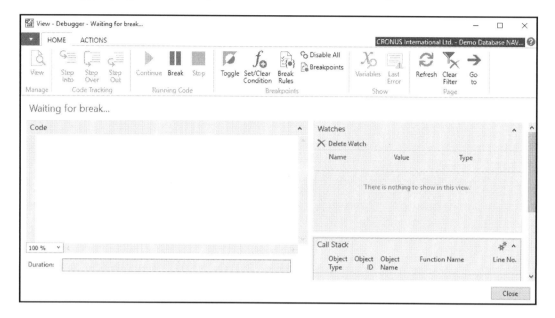

Note that the **Code** area is blank. You can still work with the session you have selected, but no code appears in the debugger. There are three options to start to debug code:

- Place a breakpoint on an object and wait until the session reaches the breakpoint. The *Placing breakpoints* section of this chapter explains how to do this.
- Click on the **Break** icon on the ribbon bar. The debugger will stop on the next line of code that the session executes.
- When the user you're targeting the debugger on runs into an error message using Microsoft Dynamics NAV or Microsoft Dynamics 365 Business Central.

You will notice that, on the **Debugger** page, you can only see the **Code** area, but you are missing two important parts that you will need to debug. The **Call Stack** FactBox is a list that shows the functions and triggers that are currently active. The **Watches** FactBox will allow you to select variables to see their current value.

Break Rules

This can be considered as the debugger setup. From the **Debugger** page, click on the **Break Rules** icon found on the ribbon bar. The **Debugger Break Rules** page opens, as shown in the following screenshot:

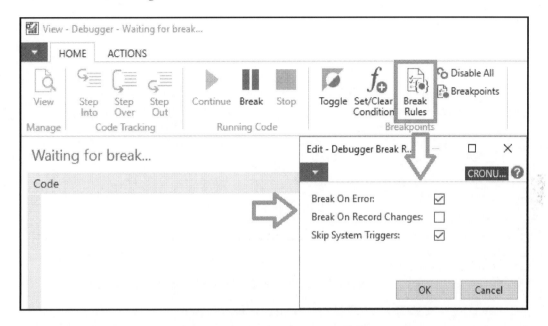

In Microsoft Dynamics NAV 2018 and in Microsoft Dynamics 365 Business Central, you can find three basic options for the debugger feature:

- **Break On Error**: If the debugger is set to **Break On Error**, it breaks execution both on errors that are handled in code and on unhandled errors. By default, the debugger is set to **Break On Error**.
- **Break On Record Changes**: If the debugger is set to **Break On Record Changes**, it breaks before creating, modifying, or deleting a record. Therefore, the debugger stops on any of the following statements: INSERT, MODIFY, MODIFYALL, DELETE, and DELETEALL. By default, the debugger is not set to **Break On Record Changes**.

- **Skip Codeunit 1** or **Skip System Trigger**: Many of the triggers in codeunit 1 Application Management or in System triggers are not important for debugging a business scenario. In the Dynamics 365 Business Central fall update, codeunit 1 is missing. This is due to the fact that it is seldom important for debugging and because the codeunit 1 triggers are called frequently in the application. So, you can specify that the debugger skips all code in codeunit 1. If you skip codeunit 1, the debugger does not break on code when you break on the next statement in codeunit 1. It continues until the first line of code after codeunit 1. In addition, when you step through the lines of code, the debugger does not step into code in codeunit 1. If you skip codeunit 1, you also implicitly skip all code that is called from codeunit 1.

Codeunit 1 has been replaced with System triggers in Microsoft Dynamics 365 Business Central.

If you explicitly set a breakpoint in codeunit 1 or in code that is called from codeunit 1, the debugger breaks execution when it hits the specific breakpoint, regardless of whether you have selected the setting to **Skip Codeunit 1** or **Skip System Trigger.**

By default, the debugger is set to **Skip Codeunit 1** or **Skip System Trigger.**

If the debugger is set up to **Break On Error**, the best way to determine the cause of a runtime error is to disable all breakpoints and click on **Continue**. The debugger will automatically stop the execution of the code when it encounters an error.

Placing breakpoints

A **breakpoint** is an intentional stop or pause placed in an object. It is a mark that you can set on a statement. When the program flow reaches the statement, the debugger intervenes and suspends execution until you instruct it to continue. During the interruption, you can inspect the environment, or start line-by-line code execution.

There are several methods for placing and removing breakpoints. This section will show you all the different ways, so that you can choose the one that best suits your debugging needs.

From the Object Designer

From the Microsoft Dynamics NAV Development Environment (both for Microsoft Dynamics NAV and Microsoft Dynamics 365 Business Central), select **Table 270 Bank Account** and click on the **Design** button to open the **Table Designer** window. Then, press *F9* or click on **View | C/AL Code** to open the C/AL Editor.

Place the cursor on one statement, a line of code, and press *F9*. A red bullet will appear on the left-hand side of the statement, as seen in the following screenshot. Press *F9* again; the bullet is now a white bullet. Press *F9* again and the bullet disappears; you have removed the breakpoint:

The red bullet indicates that a breakpoint is enabled for that statement. The debugger will stop when the program flow reaches that statement.

The white bullet indicates that a breakpoint was placed before, but it is now disabled. This means that the debugger will not stop on that statement.

In the current statement of the debugger

With the debugger in action, insert a new record in the **270 Bank Account** table; when the `OnInsert` trigger on table **270** is fired, the **Debugger** window will open:

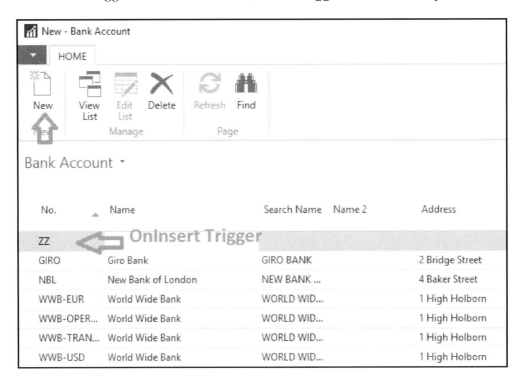

Place the cursor on a line of code and press *F9*. A red bullet will appear on the left-hand side of the statement. Press *F9* again; the bullet is now a white bullet. Press *F9* again and the bullet disappears. You have now removed the breakpoint.

Instead of pressing *F9*, you can also use the **Toggle** icon found on the ribbon bar, as shown in the following screenshot:

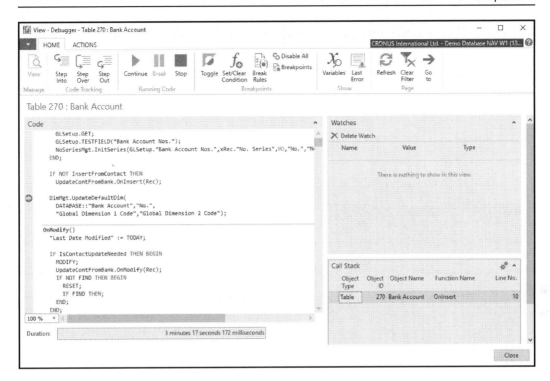

Red and white bullets indicate the same breakpoints as explained in the last section. This means that you can place breakpoints from the **Object Designer** window or from the debugger with the same effect.

The only difference is that breakpoints placed from the **Object Designer** window are seen from the debugger, but breakpoints placed from the debugger cannot be seen from the **Object Designer** window.

The end of each function contains a blank statement where you can also place a breakpoint. If you do so, the execution flow will stop right after all the code in the function has been executed and right before returning to the calling function. This is something we could not do in previous versions of Microsoft Dynamics NAV and Microsoft Dynamics 365 Business Central on-premise.

Conditional breakpoint

You can place a conditional breakpoint in Microsoft Dynamics NAV or in Microsoft Dynamics 365 Business Central on-premise. The debugger will only stop the execution if the program flow reaches the breakpoint and the condition is true. Otherwise, the execution continues.

The condition can include any variables or fields that are currently in the scope of the following types: BigInteger, Boolean, Code, Decimal, Integer, Option, Text, and WideText.

Place the cursor on the statement where you want to place the conditional breakpoint and then click on the **Set/Clear Condition** icon found on the ribbon bar. The following page will now open:

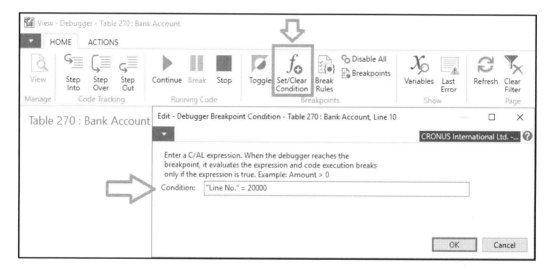

Write your condition using any of the supported operators: =, <>, <, >, <=, and >=. Then, click on **OK** to go back to the debugger.

On the left-hand side of the statement, a red bullet with a white cross inside will appear. This indicates that the statement has a conditional breakpoint.

Debugger Breakpoint List

From the debugger breakpoint, you can view, set, enable, disable, or delete breakpoints. You can also set, modify, or delete conditions for the breakpoints.

From the **Debugger** page, click on the **Breakpoints** icon found on the ribbon bar to open the **Debugger Breakpoint List** window, as shown in the following screenshot:

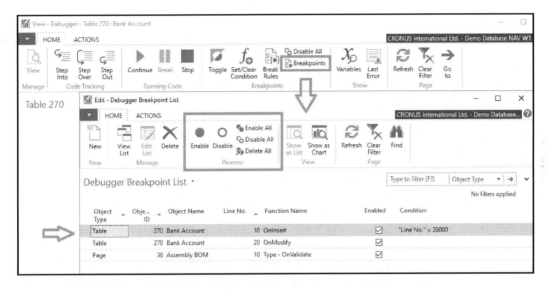

On the ribbon pane of the page, you will find options to create new breakpoints and to enable or disable the existing ones. You can also modify the **Condition** column of any existing breakpoint.

Line-by-line execution

When the debugger stops the execution of the program flow, you have four options to continue the execution. You can find those options on the ribbon pane of the **Debugger** page, as shown in the following screenshot:

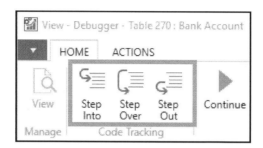

The following is a description of each of the options available to continue execution:

- **Step Into**: Click on the **Step Into** icon or press *F11* to execute the current statement. If the statement contains a function call, execute the function and break at the first statement inside the function.
- **Step Over**: Click on the **Step Over** icon or press *F10* to execute the current statement. If the statement contains a function call, execute the function and break at the first statement outside the function.
- **Step Out**: Click on the **Step Out** icon or press *Shift + F11* to execute the remaining statements in the current function, and break at the next statement in the calling function.
- **Continue**: Click on the **Continue** icon or press *F5* to continue until the next break.

Let's see an example of each execution mode: the insertion of a new record into the Bank Account table. We will use the same example for all the four options.

The Step Into option

The **Step Into** execution starts with the first statement of the OnInsert trigger of the Bank Account table. The arrow (shown in the following screenshot) shows the line that is currently going to be executed:

```
Table 270 Bank Account - C/AL Editor
   1  Documentation()
   2
   3  OnInsert()
   4  IF "No." = '' THEN BEGIN
   5    GLSetup.GET;
   6    GLSetup.TESTFIELD("Bank Account Nos.");
   7    NoSeriesMgt.InitSeries(GLSetup."Bank Account Nos.",xRec
   8  END;
   9
  10  IF NOT InsertFromContact THEN
  11    UpdateContFromBank.OnInsert(Rec);
  12
  13  DimMgt.UpdateDefaultDim(
  14    DATABASE::"Bank Account","No.",
  15    "Global Dimension 1 Code","Global Dimension 2 Code");
  16
```

```
Codeunit 396 NoSeriesManagement - C/AL Editor
  20      ERROR(PostErr,DocumentNo);
  21  END;
  22
  23  [External] InitSeries DefaultNoSeriesCode : Code[20];
  24  IF NewNo = '' THEN BEGIN
  25    NoSeries.GET(DefaultNoSeriesCode);
  26    IF NOT NoSeries."Default Nos." THEN
  27      ERROR(
  28        Text003,
  29        NoSeries.FIELDCAPTION("Default Nos."),NoSeries.
  30    IF OldNoSeriesCode <> '' THEN BEGIN
  31      NoSeriesCode := DefaultNoSeriesCode;
  32      FilterSeries;
  33      NoSeries.Code := OldNoSeriesCode;
  34      IF NOT NoSeries.FIND THEN
  35        NoSeries.GET(DefaultNoSeriesCode);
  36    END;
  37    NewNo := GetNextNo NoSeries.Code,NewDate,TRUE);
  38    NewNoSeriesCode := NoSeries.Code;
  39  END ELSE
```

```
Codeunit 396 NoSeriesManagement - C/AL Editor
  88    NoSeries.MARKEDONLY := TRUE;
  89
  90  [External] GetNextNo NoSeriesCode : Code[20];SeriesDate :
  91  EXIT(GetNextNo3(NoSeriesCode,SeriesDate,ModifySeries,FALSE
```

If you press *F11* (**Step Into**) repeatedly, you will see how each statement is executed. Four statements later, we find a function call. The debugger then stops on the first statement of the `InitSeries` function. A few statements later, we find a new function call, and the debugger goes to the first statement of the `GetNextNo` function.

Using these options, the debugger stops on each and every single statement. If you keep on debugging this example, you will see that after pressing *F11* a few hundred times and visiting numerous functions and triggers, the new bank account will get inserted.

For a person who wishes to learn the ins and outs of how to develop in Microsoft Dynamics NAV or in Microsoft Dynamics 365 Business Central, going through this process will give you a good sense of what code is run at what time. Many developers learned how the application worked when they started out in Microsoft Dynamics NAV development.

Try to avoid this option unless you don't know what you are looking for and you have no other option than executing all the statements one by one, especially for long transactions.

The Step Over option

In the last section, we used the **Step Into** option until we reached the first statement of the `GetNextNo` function. We will continue debugging from that point, but using the **Step Over** option, as shown in the following screenshot:

```
Codeunit 396 NoSeriesManagement - C/AL Editor

    [External] GetNextNo(NoSeriesCode : Code[20];SeriesDate : Date;ModifySeries : Boolean)
    EXIT(GetNextNo3(NoSeriesCode,SeriesDate,ModifySeries,FALSE));

    [External] GetNextNo3(NoSeriesCode : Code[20];SeriesDate : Date;ModifySeries : Boolean
    IF SeriesDate = 0D THEN
      SeriesDate := WORKDATE;

    IF ModifySeries OR (LastNoSeriesLine."Series Code" = '') THEN BEGIN
      IF ModifySeries THEN
        NoSeriesLine.LOCKTABLE;
      NoSeries.GET(NoSeriesCode);
      SetNoSeriesLineFilter NoSeriesLine,NoSeriesCode,SeriesDate);
      IF NOT NoSeriesLine.FINDFIRST THEN BEGIN
        IF NoErrorsOrWarnings THEN
          EXIT('');
        NoSeriesLine.SETRANGE("Starting Date");
        IF NOT NoSeriesLine.ISEMPTY THEN
          ERROR(
            Text004,
            NoSeriesCode,SeriesDate);
        ERROR(
          Text005,
          NoSeriesCode);
      END;
```

If you press *F10* a few times, you will see that the debugger stops on each statement, just as the **Step Into** option does.

The seventh statement of the function is a call to the `SetNoSeriesLineFilter` function. If you use the **Step Over** option on that statement, the debugger will execute all the code inside the function without stopping and will stop on the first statement after the function call, that is, the next statement in the current function.

Use this option when you already know the code that executes inside the function and you know that the function that is going to be called does not contain the bug you are looking for.

The Step Out option

In the last section, we used the **Step Over** option until we reached the first statement after the SetNoSeriesLineFilter function call, which is the GetNextNo function. We will continue debugging from that point, but using the **Step Out** option. Please refer to the following screenshot before proceeding:

```
 89
 90 ⊟[External] GetNextNo(NoSeriesCode : Code[20];SeriesDate : Date
 91   EXIT(GetNextNo3(NoSeriesCode,SeriesDate,ModifySeries,FALSE));
 92
 93 ⊟[External] GetNextNo3(NoSeriesCode : Code[20];SeriesDate : Dat
 94   IF SeriesDate = 0D THEN
 95     SeriesDate := WORKDATE;
 96
 97   IF ModifySeries OR (LastNoSeriesLine."Series Code" = '') THEN
 98     IF ModifySeries THEN
 99       NoSeriesLine.LOCKTABLE;
100     NoSeries.GET(NoSeriesCode);
101     SetNoSeriesLineFilter(NoSeriesLine,NoSeriesCode,SeriesDate);
102
103     IF NOT NoSeriesLine.FINDFIRST THEN BEGIN
104       IF NoErrorsOrWarnings THEN
105         EXIT('');
106       NoSeriesLine.SETRANGE("Starting Date");
107       IF NOT NoSeriesLine.ISEMPTY THEN
108         ERROR(
109           Text004,
110           NoSeriesCode,SeriesDate);
111       ERROR(
112         Text005,
113         NoSeriesCode);
114     END;
115   END ELSE
```

The **Step Out** option executes all the statements in the current function, and stops on the first statement of the calling function.

We are now on the GetNextNo function that was called from the InitSeries function, as we have seen in the *The Step Into option* section. If you click on the **Step Out** option, the debugger will execute all the remaining statements in the GetNextNo function, including the statements inside the new function call. After that, the debugger will stop on the next statement of the calling function, the InitSeries function.

Use this option if you have stepped inside a function to see its code and variables but, once inside the function, you have realized that the bug you are looking for is not there.

The Continue option

In the last section, we used the **Step Out** option until we reached the next statement after calling the GetNextNo function. We will continue debugging the code from that point, but using the **Continue** option.

With the **Continue** option, the execution of the code continues until the following:

- A breakpoint is reached
- We click on the **Break** option again
- An error occurs

Now, click on the **Continue** option in our example and see what happens:

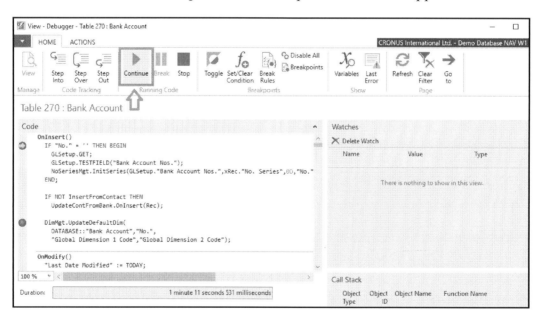

In the **Code** part of the debugger, we keep seeing the code we had before the **Continue** option was clicked. But the yellow arrow that showed us the current line is not there anymore. At the top of the preceding screenshot, we can read that the debugger is now waiting for a break.

The execution of the code has continued, a new bank account has been created, the user gets back control of the execution, and the debugger is waiting for a new breakpoint.

You can use this option if you don't need to follow the code line by line and want to wait for a breakpoint instead. You also can use this option if an error occurs in a process and you want to know where the error has occurred. In this case, you can turn on the debugger, reproduce the process that is causing the problem, and use the **Continue** option to let the debugger find the line causing the error. Of course, you will need the **Break On Error** option enabled. You can read the *Break Rules* section for more information about this option.

The Call Stack FactBox

The **Call Stack** FactBox shows the active functions of the current execution. The **Call Stack** FactBox gives us information about the function that is currently being executed, and also from where this function has been called:

Call Stack				
Object Type	Object ID	Object Name	Function Name	Line No.
Codeunit	396	NoSeriesManagement	InitSeries	21
Codeunit	5058	BankCont-Update	InsertNewContact	54
Codeunit	5058	BankCont-Update	OnInsert	5
Table	270	Bank Account	OnInsert	8

In the preceding screenshot, we can see the call stack corresponding to the code execution we were analyzing in the **Step Into** option.

We started debugging on the OnInsert trigger of the Bank Account table. We used the **Step Into** option until we reached a call to the InitSeries function. With this, we kept using the **Step Into** option until we reached the GetNextNo function. The *The Step Into option* section stopped there.

This is exactly what we see in the **Call Stack** FactBox.

The top line shows us the current function, while the bottom line shows the first function from where we started debugging. It also gives us valuable information, such as the object that contains the functions that are executed.

You can select any of the lines of the **Call Stack** FactBox. We have selected the bottom line. Now, in the following screenshot, you can see that the **Code** area of the debugger changes, showing the code of the line selected in the **Call Stack** FactBox:

```
Code
    OnInsert()
      IF "No." = '' THEN BEGIN
        GLSetup.GET;
        GLSetup.TESTFIELD("Bank Account Nos.");
        NoSeriesMgt.InitSeries(GLSetup."Bank Account Nos.",xRec."No. Series",0D,"No.","No. Series");
      END;

      IF NOT InsertFromContact THEN
        UpdateContFromBank.OnInsert(Rec);

      DimMgt.UpdateDefaultDim(
        DATABASE::"Bank Account","No.",
        "Global Dimension 1 Code","Global Dimension 2 Code");

    OnModify()
      "Last Date Modified" := TODAY;

      IF (Name <> xRec.Name) OR
        ("Search Name" <> xRec."Search Name") OR
        ("Name 2" <> xRec."Name 2") OR
        (Address <> xRec.Address) OR
        ("Address 2" <> xRec."Address 2") OR
        (City <> xRec.City) OR
        ("Phone No." <> xRec."Phone No.") OR
```

The arrow points to where the code is reading.

Note that an arrow shows us the last statement executed before the execution flow jumped to a new function.

We can now place a new breakpoint on the function, as can be seen a couple of statements after the green arrow.

The Watches FactBox

The **Watches** FactBox is used to view the values of variables. You can select some variables from the **Debugger Variables List** window and add them to the **Watches** FactBox. Those variables will be shown until you delete them, even if they run out of scope. If this happens, the **<Out of Scope>** text will be displayed in the **Value** column of the **Watches** FactBox. All the variables added to the **Watches** FactBox persist between debugging sessions.

There are two ways to add a variable to the **Watches** FactBox:

- From the **Debugger Variable List** window
- From the **Code** viewer

Adding variables from the Debugger Variables List window

To add variables from the **Debugger Variables List** window, follow these steps:

1. On the **Debugger** page, click on the **Variables** option found on the **ACTIONS** pane. The **Debugger Variable List** page will open, as shown in the following screenshot:

2. Select a variable from the list and click on the **Add Watch** icon. Then, click on the **Close** button.

3. Back on the **Debugger** page, you will see the selected variable on the **Watches** FactBox. You can view the **Name** of the variable, its **Value**, and its **Type**, as shown in the following screenshot:

Watches			
✕ Delete Watch			
Name	Value	Type	
"<Globals>".InsertFromContact	False	Boolean	

Adding variables from the code viewer

To add variables from the code viewer, follow these steps:

1. In the code viewer, hover the mouse pointer over the variable that you want to watch or select it, as shown in the following screenshot:

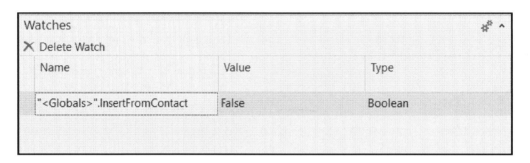

```
Codeunit 396 : NoSeriesManagement
```

```
Code
      IF NOT NoSeries."Default Nos." THEN
        ERROR(
          Text002 +
          Text003,
          NoSeries.FIELDCAPTION("Default Nos."),NoSeries.TABLECAPTION,NoSeries.Code);
      IF OldNoSeriesCode <> '' THEN BEGIN
        NoSeriesCode := DefaultNoSeriesCode;
        FilterSeries;
        NoSeries.Code := OldNoSeriesCode;
        IF NOT No   Globals
          NoSerie        NoSeries.Fields.Code (Code[10]) = 'BANK'
        END;
      NewNo := GetNextNo(NoSeries.Code,NewDate,TRUE);
      NewNoSeriesCode := NoSeries.Code;
      END ELSE
        TestManual(DefaultNoSeriesCode);
```

2. A data tip appears, as you can see in the preceding screenshot. Click on the **Add Watch** icon found on the left-hand side of the data tip (the glasses with a green plus symbol).

3. The variable will now be shown in the **Watches** FactBox, as shown in the following screenshot:

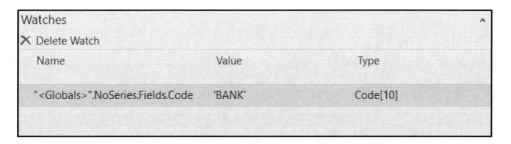

Debugging in the AL Development Environment

As already mentioned, debugging can also be done with the Modern Development Environment composed of Visual Studio Code and Microsoft AL Language Extension. Working with `.al` files and with the Visual Studio Code environment, debugging can be done differently than in a Microsoft Dynamics NAV development environment.

Debugging in Visual Studio Code

With Visual Studio Code and the AL Language extension, you get an **integrated debugger** to help you inspect your code to verify that your application can run as expected. You start a debugging session by pressing *F5*. (`https://docs.microsoft.com/it-it/dynamics-nav/developer/devenv-debugging`)

To bring up the debug view, click on the debug icon in the activity bar on the side of Visual Studio Code. You can also use the keyboard shortcut *Ctrl + Shift + D*.

The debug view displays all information related to debugging and has a top bar with debugging commands and configuration settings.

The Microsoft Al Language debugger can be enabled in different ways:

- From a shortcut (*F5*)
- From a palette command (*Ctrl* + *Shift* + *P*)
- From the menu bar Start Debugging

The following screenshot shows how to start debugging by pressing the green button:

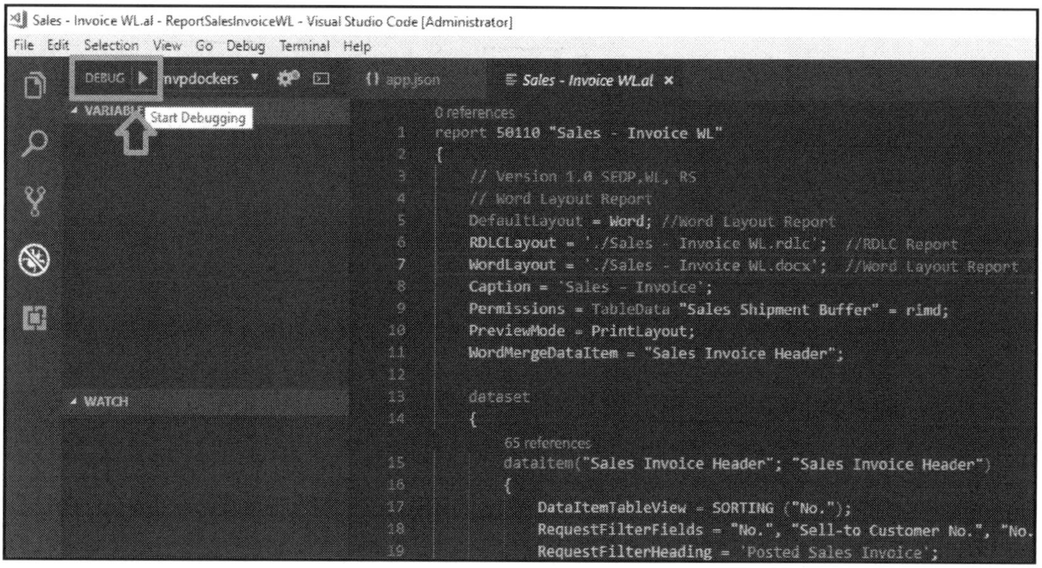

The following screenshot shows how to start debugging from the command menu or with the *F5* key:

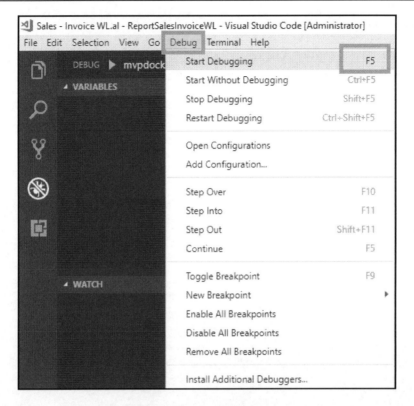

The following screenshot shows the **DEBUG CONSOLE**:

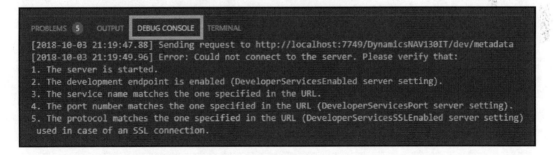

To enable debugging, the NetFx40_LegacySecurityPolicy
setting in the Microsoft.Dynamics.Nav.Server.exe.config
file must be set to false. This requires a server restart. External
code can only be debugged if the code has the showMyCode flag set
(For more information refer to: https://code.visualstudio.com/
docs/editor/debugging).

The debugger view

The debugger view includes four different sections: debug activity pane with several tiled sub panes, debug console, code pane, and debug activity buttons. The **VARIABLES** tile displays the global and local variables for the specific call stack. You might want to expand or collapse global elements from the current example to check their values. Clicking on the other tiles (such as **WATCH** and **CALL STACK**) will collapse them to give you a better overview of the content of **VARIABLES**.

Then, in the debugger view, we have four sections:

- Debug activity pane
- Debug console
- Code pane
- Debug activity buttons

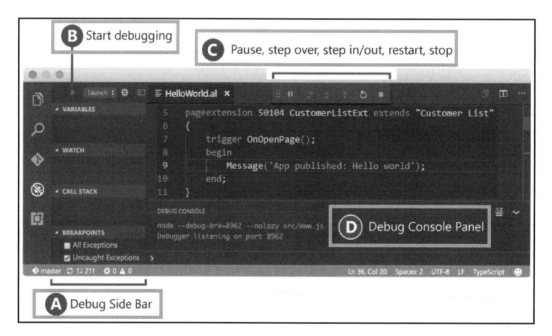

The **VARIABLES** pane displays the global and local variables for the specific call stack; when the debugger is activated, you can choose different debug actions manually, or using the following buttons related to **Step Over**, **Step Into**, **Step Out**, as already seen for debugging with Microsoft Dynamics NAV Development Environment:

The following screenshot shows the list of **VARIABLES, WATCH, CALL STACK,** and **BREAKPOINTS**:

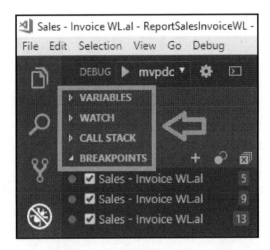

Debugging shortcuts in Visual Studio Code

The following table provides an **overview of shortcut keys for debugging** that you can use when you are working with Microsoft Dynamics 365 Business Central in Visual Studio Code; they may be useful:

Keyboard shortcut	Action
F5	Start debugging session
Shift + F5	Stop debugging
F10	**Step Over**
F11	**Step Into**
Shift + F11	**Step Out**

You can find a complete list of keyboard shortcuts here: `https://docs.microsoft.com/en-us/dynamics365/business-central/dev-itpro/developer/devenv-debugging#debugging-shortcuts`.

Example of debugging in Visual Studio Code

These are the usual steps followed in debugging:

1. Place a breakpoint
2. Execute a section of code
3. Move step by step to check the variable values in Visual Studio Code
4. Watch the values of variables

Step-by-step debugging sample

Let's take a scenario to debug the OnAfterGetRecord trigger in the item table.

1. Start running Visual Studio Code with AL language for Dynamics 365 Business Central:

You can use a local or online sandbox to test debugging; take a look at the Chapter 14, *Working and Developing with Docker and Sandboxes,* example with Microsoft Cloud Sandbox (https://businesscentral.dynamics.com/sandbox).

```
{} launch.json ●      ☰ HelloWorld.al
 1   {
 2        "version": "0.2.0",
 3        "configurations": [
 4
 5            {
 6                "type": "al",
 7                "request": "launch",
 8                "server": "Microsoft Cloud Sandbox",
 9                "startupObjectId": 31,
10                "startupObjectType": "Page",
11                "breakOnError": true
12            }
13        ]
14   }
```

2. Create a new HelloWorld sample.
3. Change launch.json to start with page 31 (item list).

4. Change the `app.json` file to look like the following by adding two extra parameters, showMyCode and `target`:

```json
{} app.json    ×
1    {
2        "id": "04e59cbf-a380-4d2f-9a14-a184acd5d7f1",
3        "name": "OnlineSandbox",
4        "publisher": "Roberto Stefanetti",
5        "brief": "",
6        "description": "",
7        "version": "1.0.0.1",
8        "privacyStatement": "",
9        "EULA": "",
10       "help": "",
11       "url": "",
12       "logo": "",
13       "capabilities": [],
14       "dependencies": [],
15       "screenshots": [],
16       "platform": "13.0.0.0",
17       "application": "13.0.0.0",
18       "target": "Extension",
19       "showMyCode": true,
20       "idRange": {
21           "from": 50100,
22           "to": 50149
23       },
24       "runtime": "2.0"
25   }
```

5. Download the symbols.

6. Rename `HelloWorld.al` to `PAGEEXT.50100.Item.al`.

7. Change the code internally as follows:

```
Trigger OnAfterGetRecord();
Begin
    Message('You are on record # ' + rec."No.");
End
```

8. Add a Breakpoint to line **6** by pressing *F9*:

```
≡ PAGEEXT.50100.Item.al  ×
    1
       0 references | 0 references
    2  pageextension 50100 PageExtension50100 extends "Item List"
    3  {
    4      trigger OnAfterGetRecord();
    5      begin
 ● 6          Message('You are on record #' + rec."No.");
    7      end;
    8  }
```

9. Build the extension (*Ctrl + Shift + B*).
10. Run with debugging (*F5*).

 The **DEBUG CONSOLE** is activated.

When the item list page pops up in your browser and you try move between records, the `OnAfterGetRecord` trigger is fired, the AL debugger is activated, and Visual Studio Code is presented to you:

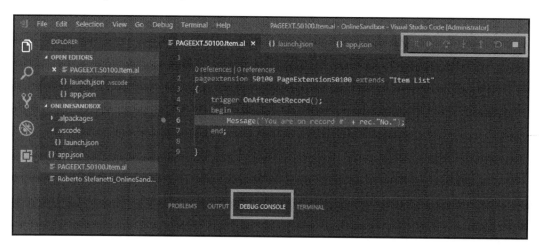

When the AL debugger is activated, you could choose to take different debug actions by using the buttons or manually:

Practice with all the buttons; inspect how **Step Over**, **Step Into**, and **Step Out** influence the debugger Activity Pane (**VARIABLE** and **CALL STACK**), and press Stop when finished.

 Note about extension code protection: Debugging into an extension to view the code is not allowed; if you want to allow debugging into a extension to view the source code, you can add the ShowMyCode property in the app.json file and set the property value to TRUE.

Summary

In this chapter, you saw that debugging is kind of an art that is used to examine program stats, find bugs, and enable them to be fixed. In addition, you saw that debugging can also be used to understand how an application works.

You also learned how to use the Microsoft Dynamics NAV debugger: how to start it, select a session to debug, place breakpoints, and do line-by-line execution. We also explained the **Call Stack** FactBox and the **Watches** FactBox.

We have also seen how to debug in Microsoft Dynamics 365 Business Central using Visual Studio Code and Microsoft AL Language Extension.

In the next chapter, we will talk about the query object, an object type included in Microsoft Dynamics NAV and in Microsoft Dynamics 365 Business Central, which will quickly summarize data for charts and reporting.

Popular Reporting Options

12

Without messing with the standard out-of-the-box reports, which require a very seasoned developer to create and customize, you can utilize external reporting and spreadsheet tools with live data from Microsoft Dynamics NAV or Microsoft Dynamics 365 Business Central.

It's no secret that Microsoft is trying to make printing reports obsolete in favor of real-time analyses that can be consumed with any of your electronic devices. Printed reports, in essence, are obsolete the moment you print them out. Imagine that you can look at the important metrics of your company with real-time data at any given moment and make impactful decisions right away. Think about how much of an impact that will have on your business. This is the future we're looking at.

With every release of Microsoft Dynamics NAV, there are more and more companies that are designing their applications around it. In addition, with Microsoft's introduction of Microsoft Office 365, there is now a native integration to Microsoft Power BI.

You can also utilize web services to publish queries data so that it can be consumed by any external applications, such as Excel. Third-party reporting developers, such as Jet Reports Express and Jet Basics NAV offer a free version of their Excel-based reporting that integrates with Microsoft Dynamics NAV.

This chapter will explain some of these popular reporting options and how they can be used with your existing Dynamics implementation. In this chapter, we will cover the following topics:

- Defining queries and charts
- Defining web services for external applications
- Configuring and using Microsoft PowerPivot in Excel
- Configuring and using Microsoft Power BI with Office 365
- Downloading and installing Jet Reports Express

What is a query?

Query is the name of a Microsoft Dynamics NAV or Microsoft Dynamics 365 Business Central application object that was first introduced in Microsoft Dynamics NAV 2013. This application object is only meant to retrieve data from the database. It is a read-only object. It cannot modify, delete, or insert new data into the database.

There are many things about queries in Microsoft Dynamics NAV and in Microsoft Dynamics 365 Business Central that point to the future of our reporting world:

- They allow us to retrieve data from multiple tables at the same time
- They allow us to retrieve only specific fields in a table
- They allow us to group the retrieved data according to certain fields without the need of any explicit key for them
- They allow us to total the retrieved data using different totaling methods (sum, count, average, minimum, and maximum)

If you are a Microsoft Dynamics NAV or Microsoft Dynamics 365 Business Central developer, and you have worked with the previous versions of Microsoft Dynamics NAV, you will see the advantages and the possibilities of this new object right away. The Query object makes summarizing data much easier, without complicated coding in reports. It makes data retrieval a lot faster, the queries can also be used in code.

In this chapter, we will show you how to define a query using the query editor and where and how to use queries on your developments. Once we know how to write and execute queries, we will compare them both in time/effort of development and in speed, against the old ways of retrieving the exact same data out of the application.

Query Designer

Queries, just as any other objects in Microsoft Dynamics NAV or in Microsoft Dynamics 365 Business Central on-premise, have their own designer or editor with CSIDE.

These steps are identical both for Microsoft Dynamics NAV and Microsoft Dynamics 365 Business Central On-premise. The screenshots are taken from Microsoft Dynamics 365 Business Central on-premises October 2018 release.

To open **Query Designer**, perform the following steps:

1. Open the Microsoft Dynamics NAV Development Environment. The **Object Designer** window will open.
2. On the left pane of the **Object Designer** window, click on **Query** to see the list of existing queries:

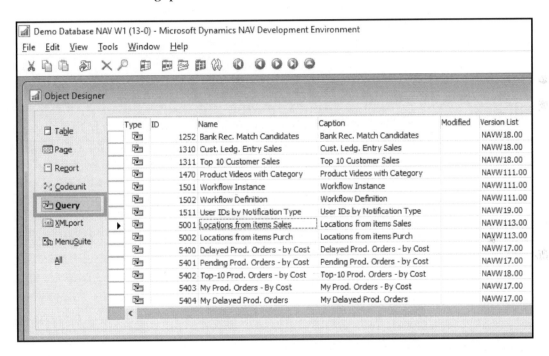

3. Select the query **9150 My Customers** (or any other existing query) and click on **Design**. The **Query Designer** window will open:

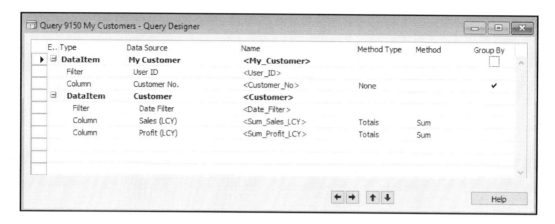

The **Query Designer** window looks a lot like **Page Designer** or the new **Report Dataset Designer**. This will make it easier to get used to developing queries.

In the **Query Designer** window, we can select one or more **DataItem** values to define the database table from which we want to retrieve data for the query. Through properties, we can define the relationship between different **DataItem** values. We can also select the columns or fields that will be included in the query and specify the totaling methods and groupings for the fields. Finally, using properties, we will be able to define filters and modify the behavior of certain columns, such as reversing their sign.

We will see the fields and properties of the **Query Designer** window by creating our first query.

Defining our first query

In our first query, we will try to retrieve the items that our customers buy per month. To do so, we will use the `Item Ledger Entry` table as our main data source, but we will also use the `Customer` and the `Item` tables to get additional information from customers and items, such as their name or description.

First, let's define the main data source and the fields that will be retrieved:

1. Open the **Object Designer** window in the Microsoft Dynamics NAV Development Environment and select the **Query** object type on the left pane of the **Object Designer** window.
2. Click on **New** to create a new query. An empty **Query Designer** window will open.
3. On the first line, in the **Type** column, choose **DataItem** from the drop-down list:

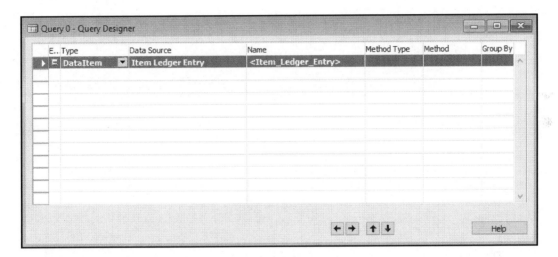

The first line in the **Query Designer** window must be a **DataItem** field and not a **Column** field.

4. Select **Item Ledger Entry** in the **Data Source** column.

You can choose the up arrow that will appear on the right-hand side of the **Data Source** column to view a table list and select the desired table. You can also type in the name or the number ID of the table (if you know it) you want to use on your query.

5. The **Name** column will be automatically populated once a **Data Source** value has been selected. Default names are usually fine, but you can change them if you want to.

6. Display the **Properties** window for the data item. To do so, select the **DataItem** row and click on **View** | **Properties** (or press *Shift + F4*).

Names in queries must be **Common Language Specification (CLS)** compliant. The first character must be a letter. Subsequent characters can be any combination of letters, integers, and underscores.

7. Select the `DataItemTableFilter` property and click on the **Assist Edit** button. The **Table Filter** window will open. Set **Field** to **Entry Type**, **Type** to **CONST**, and **Value** to **Sale**. Click on **OK**.

8. Back at the **Properties** window, the value for the `DataItemTableFilter` property should be what is shown in the following screenshot:

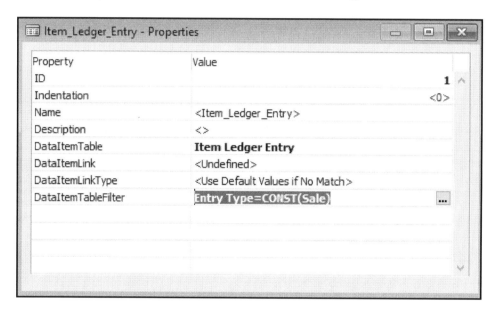

Using the `DataItemTableFilter` property, we have applied a filter so that only entries of the **Sale** type are retrieved on this query. We are analyzing sales; we do not want other types of entries to be shown in our query.

9. Close the **Properties** window.

10. For the **Item Ledger Entry** data item, select the **Item No.**, **Posting Date**, **Quantity**, and **Source No.** fields as **Column** in the rows below **DataItem**.

11. Once you have selected all of those fields, the **Query Designer** window should look like what's shown in the following screenshot:

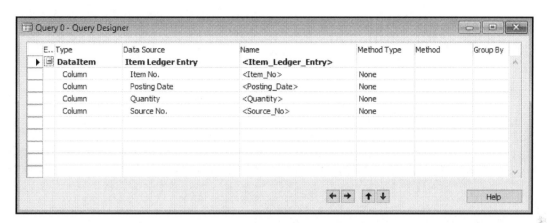

12. For the **Posting Date** row, select **Date** as **Method Type** and **Month** as **Method**.

13. For the **Quantity** row, select **Totals** as **Method Type** and **Sum** as **Method**.

Notice that, in the following screenshot, right after a **Totals** method type is selected, the **Group By** field is automatically selected for all the other columns in the query that are not of the **Totals** type. This defines how the results of the query will be grouped:

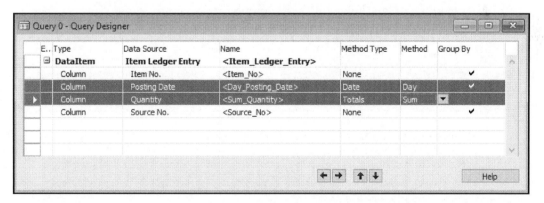

Group By is a read-only field that is automatically calculated. The value of this column cannot be modified.

14. In the **Properties** window of the **Quantity** field, select **Yes** for the **ReverseSign** property:

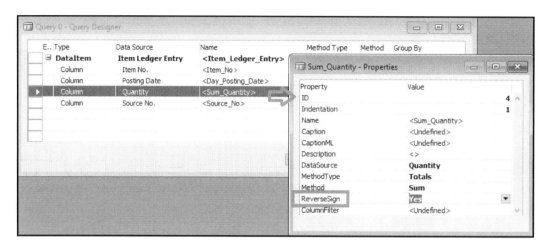

We are analyzing sales. Sales represent a decrease in the item's inventory. Being a decrease, the **Quantity** field for entries of the **Sale** type is a negative value. We want to reverse this sign because we want to see the quantities sold as positive values.

15. Save and compile the query. To do so, click on **File | Save** (or press *Ctrl + S*).

16. We will be asked for an ID and a name for the query. We will set the **ID** attribute to 50000 and the **Name** attribute to My First Query.

17. The **Query Designer** window will close and we will be taken back to the **Object Designer** window. We will now run the query and take a look at the results. To do so, select **Query 50000 My First Query** and click on the **Run** button.

18. The Windows client will open and the result of the query will be shown as follows:

So far, so good! We have defined a pretty simple query with a single data item, but we have already seen how we can filter the results and the different method types, and how the results are grouped.

Adding additional data to the query

We will go further into this example by *adding a couple of extra data items to the query*. Perform the following steps to do so:

1. In the **Object Designer** window, select **Query 50000 My First Query** and click on the **Design** button. The **Query Designer** window will open with the query we were creating.
2. On the first empty row, enter a **DataItem** value for the **Item** table.
3. Open the **Properties** window for the **Item** data item.
4. Click on the **Assist Edit** button for the **DataItemLink** property. Select **No.** as the field, the **Item_Ledger_Entry** data item as the reference **DataItem**, and **Item No.** as the reference field. Click on **OK**.
5. Back at the **Properties** window, the value for the **DataItemLink** property should be what is shown in the following screenshot:

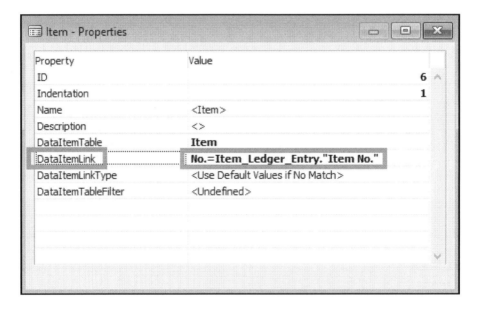

6. Close the **Properties** window.
7. For the **Item** data item, select the **Description** field as the **Column** type in the rows below the **DataItem** field.

8. On the first empty row, enter a new data item and select **Customer** as the **Data Source**.

9. Open the **Properties** window for the **Customer** data item.

10. Click on the **Assist Edit** button. For the **DataItemLink** property, select **No.** as the field, the **Item_Ledger_Entry** data item as the reference **DataItem**, and **Source No.** as the reference field. Click on **OK**.

11. Close the **Properties** window.

12. For the **Customer** data item, select the **Name** and **Customer Posting Group** fields as the **Column** type in the rows below the **DataItem** field.

13. Set the **DataItemLink** property to No.=Item_Ledger_Entry."Source No.". The final query should look like what's shown in the following screenshot:

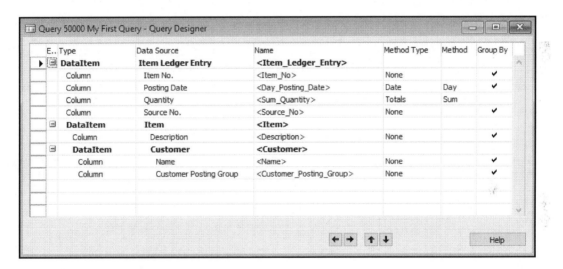

14. Save and compile the query.

15. Run the query to see the results, as shown in the following screenshot:

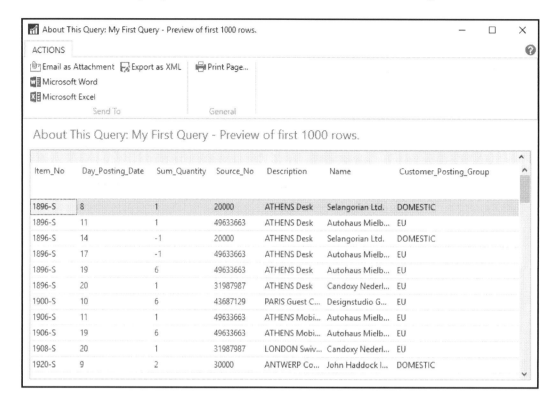

Queries object in Microsoft AL

It's also possible to create new queries from Visual Studio Code. The *tquery* shortcut will create the *basic layout* for a new Query object when using the Microsoft AL Language extension in Visual Studio Code.

Here is an example:

```
query Id MyNewQuery
{   QueryType = Normal;
    elements
    {
        dataitem(DataItemName; SourceTableName)
        {
            column(ColumnName; SourceFieldName)
            {
            }
```

```
            filter(FilterName; SourceFieldName)
            {
            }
        }
    var
        myInt: Integer;
    trigger OnBeforeOpen()
    begin
    end;
}
```

 For more information, you can visit `https://docs.microsoft.com/ en-us/dynamics365/business-central/dev-itpro/developer/ devenv-query-object`.

Business Charts

The Windows client and the Web client can display a set of predefined charts that use Microsoft Dynamics NAV and Microsoft Dynamics 365 Business Central data; *queries* can be used as data sources for those charts in both systems.

There are two types of charts:

- Standard Charts (available in Windows client only)
- Business Charts (available with JS add-ins)

 You can read more about business charts concepts and components at `https://docs.microsoft.com/en-us/dynamics-nav/displaying- charts-using-the-chart-control-add-in`.

Standard Charts in Windows Client

We will use the query defined earlier on in this chapter as the data source of a chart, and we will display it on the home page of the Microsoft Dynamics 365 Business Central On-premise Windows client.

To define a query as the data source of a chart, perform the following steps:

1. Open the Windows client for Microsoft Dynamics 365 Business Central on-premise.

2. Navigate to **Departments** | **Administration** | **Application Setup** | **RoleTailored Client**.

3. Select **Generic Charts**.

4. Click on **New** on the ribbon bar to add a new chart. The **New - Generic Chart Setup** page will open, as shown in the following screenshot:

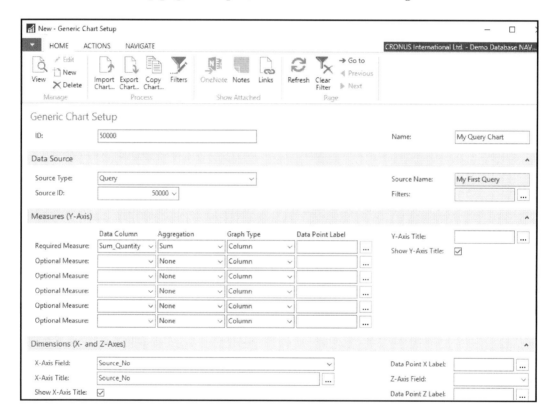

5. Give the new chart an **ID** value and a **Name** value. For example, set **ID** to 50000 and **Name** to My Query Chart.

6. On the **Data Source** tab, select **Query** as **Source Type** and **50000** as **Source ID**.

7. On the **Measures (Y-Axis)** tab, select **Sum_Quantity** as **Data Column** on the **Required Measure** row.

8. On the **Dimensions (X- and Z-Axes)** tab, select **Source_No** as **X-Axis Field**.
9. Click on **OK** to close the **New-Generic Chart** setup page.

To display the chart on the home page of the Windows client, perform the following steps:

1. Go back to the home page of the Windows client for Microsoft Dynamics 365 Business Central on-premise.
2. Click on the Microsoft Dynamics 365 Business Central on-premise icon, found on the upper-left corner of the page, select **Customize**, and then **Customize This Page**.
3. Select **Chart Part** from **Available parts**.
4. Click on **Add**.
5. A blank chart will appear on the **Role Center layout** section. Select the blank chart and click on **Customize Part**.
6. Select the **50000 My Query Chart** chart and click on **OK**.
7. Click on **OK** to close the **Customize the Role Center** page.
8. Back at the home page of the Windows client, the chart should be displayed as follows:

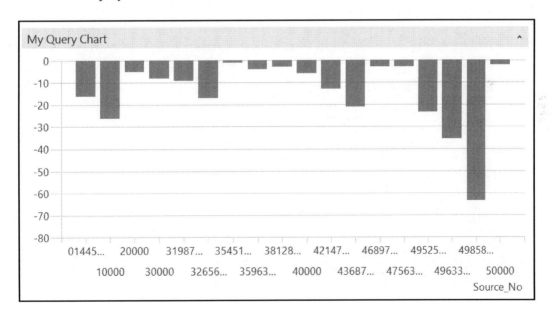

Web services

Starting from Microsoft Dynamics NAV 2009, it was possible to publish page and codeunit objects as web services to allow external applications to access Microsoft Dynamics NAV or Microsoft Dynamics 365 Business Central data and business logic. In the later releases of Microsoft Dynamics NAV and Microsoft Dynamics 365 Business Central, it is also possible to publish Query objects as web services.

Page and codeunit objects can be accessed through the **SOAP** (short for **Simple Object Access Protocol**) web services. Queries can only be accessed through the OData (Open Data) web services protocol.

 We will look at how to create and use Web service OData in Microsoft Dynamics 365 Business Central, since its the same for Microsoft Dynamics NAV.

First, you will need to enable the SOAP and OData services from the Microsoft Dynamics 365 Business Central Administrator; perform the following steps to do so:

1. Start the **Microsoft Dynamics 365 Business Central Administrator** from the Start menu.
2. Click on the service that's running Microsoft Dynamics 365 Business Central. If you did the full installation, the default service should be **BC130** (or **DynamicsNAV130**).
3. Select the **service** and click on **Edit**.
4. Place a checkbox on **Enable SOAP Services** and **Enable OData Services**.

5. Click on **Save** after you're done:

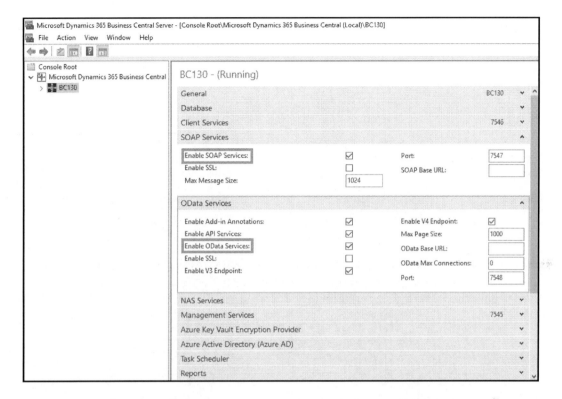

To publish a query as a Web service from Microsoft Dynamics 365 Business Central, perform the following steps:

1. Open the Windows Client for Microsoft Dynamics 365 Business Central.
2. Navigate to **Departments | Administration | IT Administration | General**.
3. Select **Web Services**.
4. Select **New** on the ribbon bar to publish a new web service. The **New - Web Services** page will open.
5. Select **Query** as **Object Type**.
6. Enter 50000 in the **Object ID** field.
7. Enter a name in the **Service Name** field. For example, let's use **MyQueryWS** as the **Service Name**.

8. Check the **Published** field, as shown in the following screenshot:

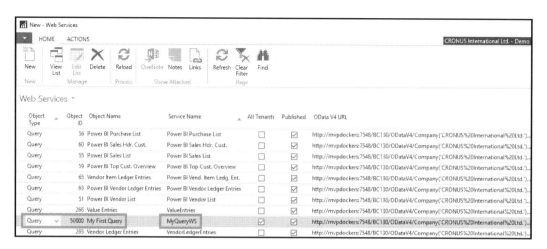

At this point, the query is already published as a Web service. You can check to see whether it is accessible using your browser by clicking on OData URL, and then clicking on the hyperlink symbol or copying and pasting the URL in the Edge browser:

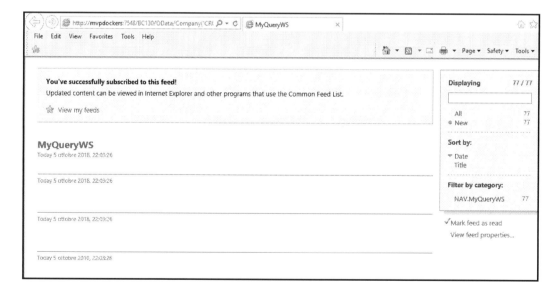

If you're using the Windows Edge browser from Windows 10, the Web service will not display. You will only be able to run it using Edge, Google Chrome, and other browsers.

Integrating external applications with OData web services

Because Microsoft Dynamics 365 Business Central queries can be published as web services, they can be accessed by absolutely any application that can consume OData web services. It can be an external application developed by you for the sole purpose of reading Microsoft Dynamics 365 Business Central data, or it can be a commonly used application that supports OData web services.

If you are integrating Microsoft Dynamics 365 Business Central with an external app via web services, it's always recommended not to directly expose the Business Central web services, but to use a custom Web service that talks with Business Central (via standard web services, exposed as described) and the external system.

In this section, we will look at how to use Microsoft Dynamics 365 Business Central queries in Microsoft Office Excel.

Microsoft Excel and PowerPivot add-in

Among all the applications that are out there, an extensively used one is probably Microsoft Office Excel. There is a free add-in for Excel called **PowerPivot** that can consume OData web services—we can do that as follows:

1. If you're using Microsoft Excel 2013 or later, you can enable **PowerPivot 2013** by going to the **Add-in** page from the **Options** menu. Alternatively, you can download PowerPivot by performing a quick search on the internet, which will lead you to the download page.

2. The installation of PowerPivot will create a new tab in the ribbon bar of Microsoft Office Excel:

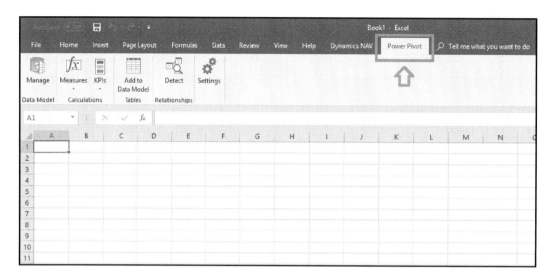

3. Open Microsoft Excel 2013.
4. On the **Power Pivot** tab, select **Manage**.
5. Select **Get External Data** | **From Data Service** | **From OData Data Feed**.
6. You will be asked to enter a friendly connection name and a data feed URL. (The standard path is composed by: `http://server:port/Service/OData/Company('Company Name')/Query`). Enter `NAVMyQueryWS` as the **Friendly connection name** and copy and paste the OData URL from the Microsoft Dynamics 365 Business Central web service screen. Alternatively, you can type in `http://mvpdockers:7548/BC130/OData/Company('CRONUS%20International%20Ltd.')/NAVMyQueryWS` as the value for **Data Feed URL**:

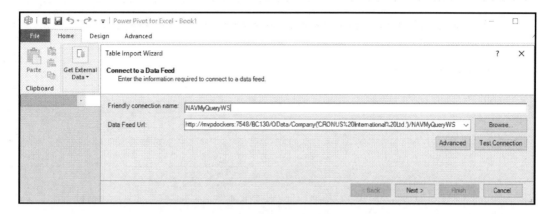

7. Click on **Test Connection** to check whether PowerPivot can access the published web service.

8. Click on **Next** and then click on **Finish**:

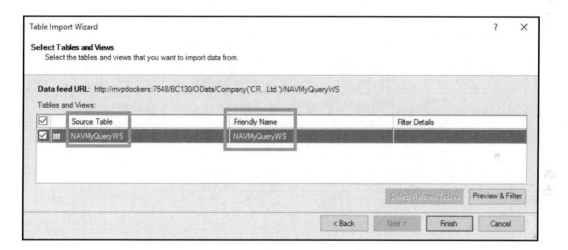

9. An import process will start. Once it has finished, click on **Close**.

10. The imported data will be displayed on the **PowerPivot for Excel** window:

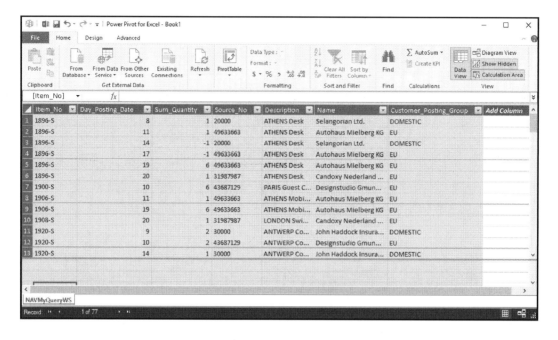

11. Select **PivotTable**, and a PivotTable that uses data from Microsoft
    Dynamics 365 Business Central will be created. Select the fields that you
    want to see on the PivotTable:

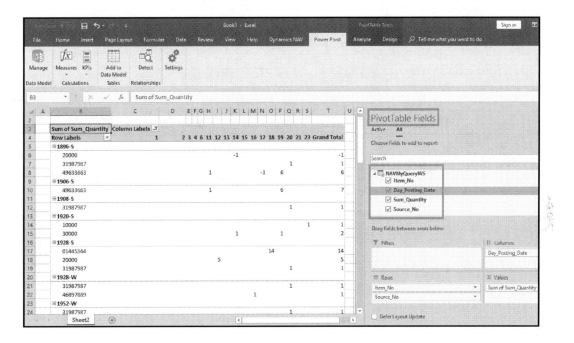

Microsoft Power BI

Microsoft Power BI is a tool that is part of the Microsoft Office 365 offering. It provides a *web-based analytical tool* for your data that can be set up to gather real-time data. The aim of Microsoft Power BI is to provide business intelligence to companies at a fraction of the cost of buying a regular business intelligence solution.

The following diagram shows the Microsoft Power BI layouts:

The Microsoft Power BI layouts in different devices

There are also content packs, which are specifically designed for Microsoft Dynamics NAV and Microsoft Dynamics 365 Business Central (Apps, in this case) within Microsoft Power BI in Office 365. Within the content packs and Apps, they provide some of the graphs and charts Microsoft believes most companies will want to see.

 You will need a Microsoft Office 365 account in order to use Microsoft Power BI. To access the content pack, proceed to `https://app.powerbi.com/getdata/services/microsoft-dynamics-nav`.

Once you sign in using your Office 365 account, you can find the Microsoft Dynamics NAV content pack and Microsoft Dynamics 365 Business Central Apps for Microsoft Power BI.

Screenshot showing the Apps (content pack) for Microsoft Dynamics NAV

You can also see the following screenshot:

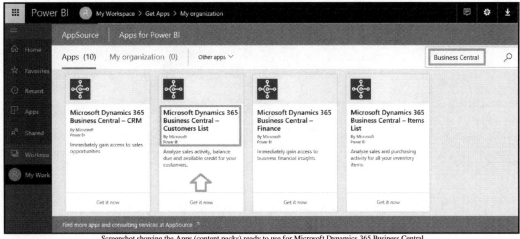

Screenshot showing the Apps (content packs) ready to use for Microsoft Dynamics 365 Business Central

Enabling your business data for Power BI

Microsoft has published the following content packs for Microsoft Dynamics 365 Business Central, and Microsoft is creating new ones in order to enhance the product offer (Apps that are ready for use), as is also the case for Microsoft Flow.

Currently, Apps are available for the following:

- Finance
- Sales
- Item List
- Jobs List
- Purchase List
- Customer List
- Vendor List
- Item List

 In the next example scenario, we will see a connector between Microsoft Power BI and Microsoft Dynamics 365 Business Central. For example, the Customer List app can show sales activities and a balance for customers.

How to get Power BI Apps

To get Apps, you need to go into **My Workspace** | **Get Apps** | **My organization** | **Apps for Power BI**:

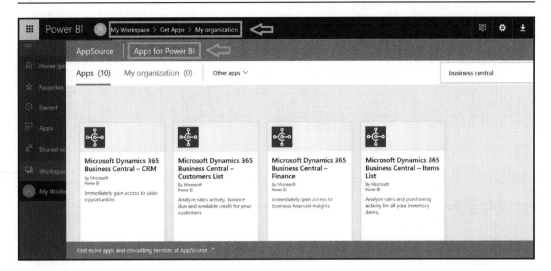

To install a Power BI App (in this case, for Business Central), perform the following steps:

1. Click on selected app—in this case, "*Business Central - Customer List*". Afterwards you will find your app installed in your workspace.
2. Once it's installed, configure **ExtensionDataSourceKind**, **ExtensionDataSourcePath**, and **Authentication method**.

The following screenshot shows the configuration of the: **Business Central – Customer List** app:

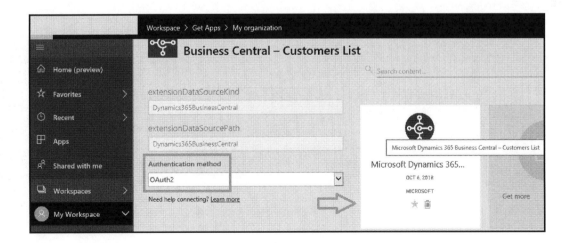

The following screenshot shows the **Business Central - Customer List** app configured:

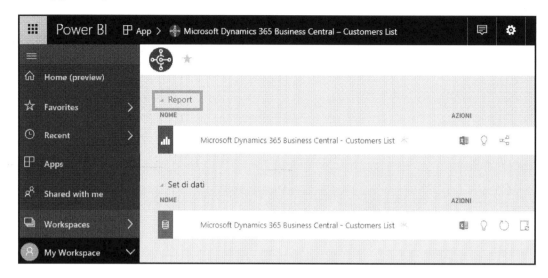

The following screenshot shows the **Business Central - Customer List** app in action—**Customer Sales Dashboard**:

Check out how to use and configure Apps for Power BI at `https://docs.microsoft.com/en-us/dynamics365/business-central/across-how-use-financials-data-source-powerbi` and `https://docs.microsoft.com/en-us/dynamics365/business-central/across-how-use-financials-data-source-powerbi`.

Connecting to Microsoft Dynamics NAV 2018

For Microsoft Dynamics NAV 2018 (and for previous releases), the connection mode is the same. The only difference is that you need to log in using a username/password, but for Microsoft Dynamics 365 Business Central SaaS, it is possible to use the same login for everything (Microsoft Office, Microsoft Dynamics 365 Business Central, and Microsoft Power BI). The following screenshot shows the Apps for Microsoft Dynamics NAV 2018:

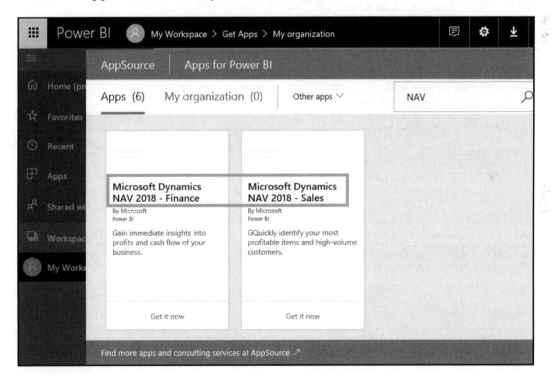

How to connect to Microsoft Dynamics NAV 2018

You'll be prompted to put in the OData web service. If you're using the default setting, it should look as follows:

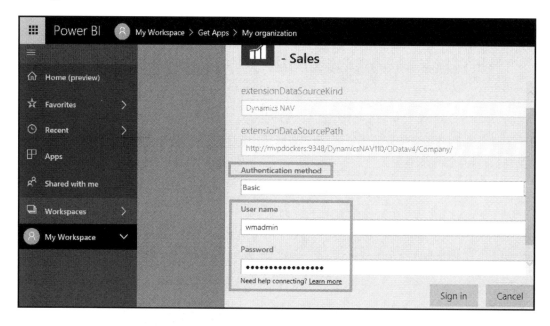

Use **Basic** as the **Authentication method** and type in the **User name** and **Password** that you've set up on your machine.

It will then prompt you that the system is importing the data from the web services. After the information has loaded, you will see the dashboard.

The following screenshot shows the Power BI Sales dashboard app for Microsoft Dynamics NAV 2018:

For more information on connecting with Microsoft Power BI, visit
`https://powerbi.microsoft.com/en-us/documentation/powerbi-c`
`ontent-pack-microsoft-dynamics-nav/`.

Jet Basics NAV (formerly Jet Express for Excel)

Jet Basics NAV for Microsoft Dynamics NAV is a business reporting tool that's meant to let users create high-impact reports in a familiar environment, such as Microsoft Excel. With Jet Basics NAV (formerly Jet Express for Excel), you can use all Excel capabilities, such as formatting, slicers, charting, and pivot tables.

The following is a product definition by the vendor: *"An extension included with Microsoft Dynamics NAV to give users a simple way to create basic reports and business queries inside of Excel"*.

Note that this is a free version of Jet Basics NAV. There's also a paid version of Jet Basics NAV (named Jet Reports) that you can purchase, so a lot of the functionalities have been stripped out of the free version; there is also a version that allows you to create reports in Microsoft Word (using an extension that's included with Microsoft Dynamics NAV to create custom documents with Microsoft Word).

Visit the JetGlobal website for updated information on this application. On the website, you will also find a few demo videos that show you how you can start using it.

Here are some links to get you started:

- `https://www.jetglobal.com/jet-basics/jet-basics-nav/`
- `https://www.jetglobal.com/jet-reports/`
- `https://www.jetglobal.com/jet-reports-financials/`
- `https://www.jetglobal.com/jet-express-for-word/`

Downloading Jet Basics NAV

The installation file of Jet Basics NAV can be downloaded from `https://www.jetglobal.com/jet-basics/jet-basics-nav/`.

You will need to provide your information to download the installation files. The installation file should be called `Jet Basics Setup.exe`.

Installing Jet Basics NAV

The step-by-step guides on how to install and enable Jet Basics NAV can be found at the preceding website.

Make sure that you use the guide that's appropriate for your version. Basically, there's a version prior to Microsoft Dynamics NAV 2013 and a version that's for Microsoft Dynamics NAV 2013 and above. The following screenshot shows the Jet Basics NAV installed as an Excel Add-in:

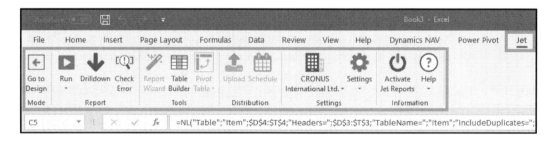

The following screenshot shows the Jet Reports in action:

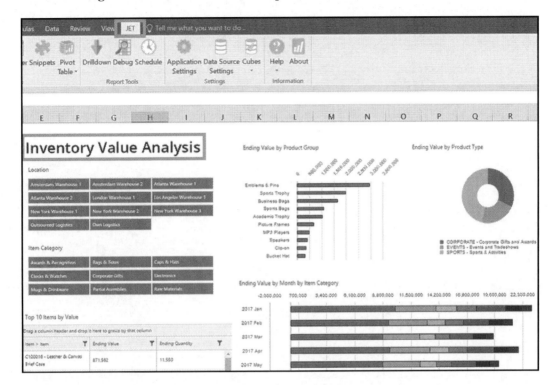

Screenshot showing the Jet Reports in action

Microsoft Flow

Microsoft Flow is a cloud-based workflow service for creating automated processes.

It can be used in many applications to automate processes; for example, it could be used to generate and send reports automatically, starting from a workflow; even if it is not a reporting tool, it could also be used for such purposes, perhaps integrated by the Microsoft Power BI.

Check out the Microsoft Flow page at `https://flow.microsoft.com`.

The motto of Microsoft Flow is, "work less, do more". With Microsoft Flow, you can create automated workflows between your favorite apps and services to get notifications, synchronize files, collect data, and more.

Microsoft Flow for Microsoft Dynamics 365 Business Central

There are numerous ready-to-use workflow templates, both for Microsoft Dynamics NAV and Microsoft Dynamics 365 Business Central. These templates are useful to understand how both of them work and also understand their potential. The following screenshot shows the ready-to-use templates for Microsoft Dynamics 365 Business Central:

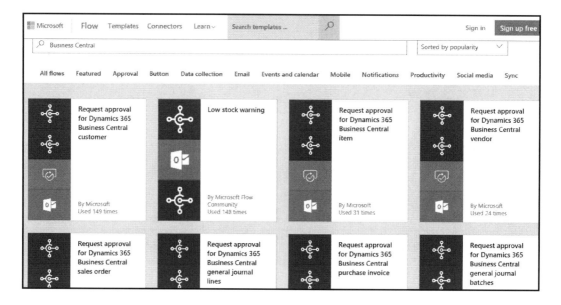

The following screenshot shows the example of a low stock warning report workflow:

The following screenshot shows the configuration of the **Low stock warning** workflow:

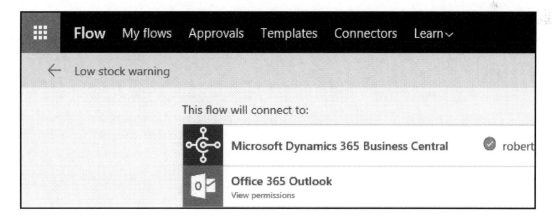

The following screenshot shows the structure of the **Low stock warning** workflow:

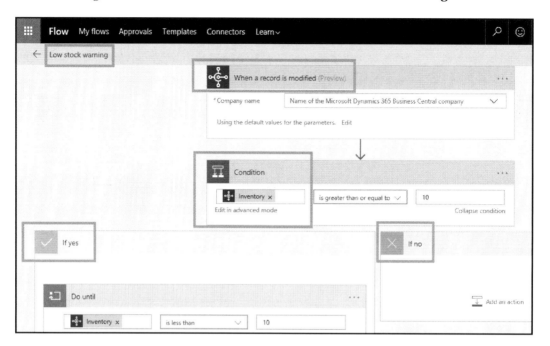

> If you are interested in Microsoft Flow, you can see how workflow works on my blog: `https://robertostefanettinavblog.com/2018/07/10/business-central-ready-to-use-microsoft-flow-templates/`.

Summary

In this chapter, you saw some of the reporting and analysis options that are included in Microsoft Dynamics NAV and in Microsoft Dynamics 365 Business Central that extend their functionalities and are very useful to users and companies. With web services, the options for analyzing your data are endless. We also explored some third-party tools that can be useful for creating reports in a simple and convenient way for users.

13
Microsoft Dynamics 365 Business Central

Microsoft Dynamic 365 Business Central is a cloud-based ERP (Enterprise Resource Planning) delivered with the **SaaS** (short for, **Software as a Service**) model through **Cloud Service Provider** (**CSP**) partners. Currently, however, it is available in different ways: cloud, hybrid, and on-premises.

Microsoft Dynamics 365 Business Central is born on the Microsoft Dynamics NAV platform and is integrated with several other Microsoft services. With Microsoft Dynamics 365 Business Central, Microsoft reinvents business productivity. Microsoft Dynamics 365 Business Central connects business processes with the productivity tools in Microsoft Office 365 to help SMBs grow sales, manage finances, and streamline operations. It is designed as a true multitenant public cloud service (SaaS) running on Microsoft Azure and sold through the Microsoft CSP program. Customers can access the service on the web, or using apps for Windows, iOS, or Android devices.

The following screenshot shows the Microsoft Dynamics 365 Business Central SaaS—Web client:

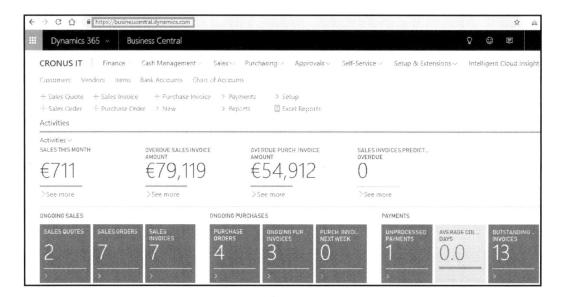

Check out more about the Microsoft Dynamics 365 Business Central service at `https://businesscentral.dynamics.com/`.

Microsoft Dynamics 365 Business Central specifics

Dynamics 365 Business Central brings the full power of Microsoft Dynamics NAV to the cloud. It is an all-in-one business management solution that helps you make smarter decisions and connect your business processes. Microsoft Dynamics 365 Business Central is easily adaptable and you can extend business applications to other Microsoft cloud services, such as Power BI, PowerApps, or Office 365. Thus, you can upgrade from all your other business application to this single, comprehensive solution to manage operations, finances, sales, and customer service.

Microsoft Dynamics 365 Business Central delivers functionalities in modules with a fixed price per month and with a per-user license model; the SaaS release is based on two license types: Essentials and Premium.

Microsoft Dynamics 365 Business Central is a modern digital business management solution that helps you streamline your processes and enable growth by offering the following:

- **Business without silos:** Automated tasks and workflows—integrated with familiar Office tools like Outlook, Word, and Excel—boost productivity and efficiency.
- **Business insights:** Get a complete view of your business with business analytics and intelligence, and Microsoft's leading intelligent technologies, so that you can take appropriate action for greater outcomes.
- **Solutions built to evolve:** Adapt in real time with this flexible business suite that allows you to scale to suit your business size, needs, and complexity.

Microsoft Dynamics 365 Business Central is usable anywhere on every device, as follows:

Usability of Microsoft Dynamics 365 Business Central across various devices

Microsoft Dynamics 365 Business Central's main pages can be found at `https://dynamics.microsoft.com/en-us/business-central/overview/` and `https://docs.microsoft.com/en-us/dynamics365/business-central/index.`

License types – Essentials versus Premium

Microsoft Dynamics 365 Business Central is sold with two license types with fixed prices:

- Essentials
- Premium

Premium licenses include all modules in the Essentials license, as shown in the following table:

Essentials	Premium
Financial management	Financial management
Customer relationship management	Customer relationship management
Project management	Project management
Supply chain management	Supply chain management
Human resource management	Human resource management
Warehouse management	Warehouse management
	Service management
	Manufacturing

The named user licensing model

Compared to previous versions of Microsoft Dynamics NAV (for example, perpetual licensing model), a new licensing model has been introduced in Microsoft Dynamics 365 Business Central: the **named user** license.

Named CALs are assigned on a named user basis, meaning each user requires a separate user license. Named user licenses cannot be shared, but an individual with a named user license may access the service through multiple devices.

There are three types of Microsoft Dynamics 365 Business Central licenses:

- Team Member (reads and approves, creates cards, quotes, and sales orders)
- Essentials (all except service management and manufacturing)
- Premium (all including service management and manufacturing)

Additionally there is:

- One external free license for an accountant
- One external free license for an administrator
- Annual or monthly billing, trials available, no storage limitations
- At least one Essentials or Premium user needs to be licensed

 CSP is the only method to license Dynamics 365 Business Central cloud license.

Fixed prices for Essentials, Premium, and Team Member license types

Currently, fixed prices are $70 per month for Essentials and $100 per month for Premium; here is a comparative pricing table:

There is a license called **Team Members** ($8 per month), limited to the use of a few features, which originated from the old Light User license that has existed since Microsoft Dynamics NAV 2013:

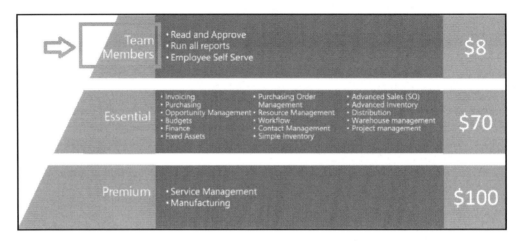

Dual use (SaaS and on-premise)

Dual use right is available only through the SaaS cloud licensing offering. Customers using the SaaS version can download a license key (in `.flf` format) from customer source by selecting the **My Products and Services** link from the drop-down menu and then clicking on the **Registration Keys** link beside the Microsoft Dynamics 365 Business Central product.

 You can download the Microsoft license PDF file from `https://go.microsoft.com/fwlink/?LinkId=871590clcid=0x409`.

Objects available in the licensed product

A series of objects is available under license, in the following numbers:

- **Objects in the 70,000,000 to 75,000,000** range are given by the vendor for free when registering an app in AppSource—inherited from Business Edition, and works only in cloud.

- **Objects in the 1,000,000 to 60,000,000** range are given by the vendor for free for ISV partner solutions (should match ISV requirements). This will be available for both on-premises and cloud versions of Business Central and will have possibility to be published in AppSource (not yet, but soon).
- **Objects in the 50,000 to 99,999** range are given by the vendor for free and could be used to deploy on-premises extensions per tenant, cannot be used in AppSource, but can be uploaded directly to a tenant.

By default, Microsoft Dynamics 365 Business Central on-premises sandbox is deployed with the Essentials type of user license. However, you can activate Premium functionality and enable manufacturing using this official guide: `https://blogs.msdn.microsoft.com/freddyk/2018/04/12/enabling-premium-experience-in-business-central-sandbox-containers/`.

Microsoft Dynamics 365 Business Central SaaS clients

For Microsoft Dynamics 365 Business Central SaaS, the Windows client is not available, only the Web client and the Universal App for the mobile world are available.

Innovative Web client

The Web client is the par excellence client of Microsoft Dynamics 365 Business Central, designed for the cloud but also usable in on-premises installations.

This innovative Web client has won prizes for better usability, innovation, intuitive utilization, and support for visual dysfunctions; Microsoft invests a lot in this product and improves it further. The following screenshot shows the Microsoft Dynamics 365 Business Central Web client:

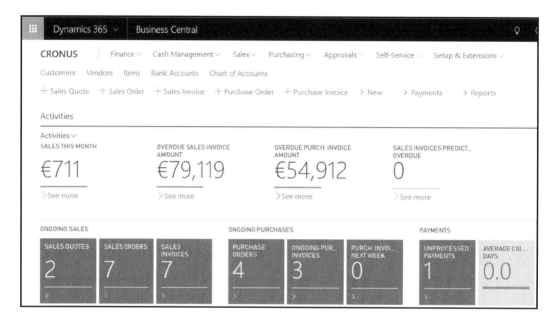

The Web client is supported by the following browsers:

- Microsoft Edge
- Microsoft Explorer 11 or higher
- Google Chrome 61 for Windows or higher
- Mozilla Firefox 55 for Windows or higher
- Safari 10 for Mac or higher

Universal App

The Microsoft Dynamics 365 Business Central Universal App is able to connect to cloud, on-premises, and hybrid deployments of Business Central. The app is available for the following:

- Windows 10 (desktop, tablet, and phone)
- Android (tablet and phone)
- iOS (tablet and phone)

The following diagram shows the availability of Microsoft Dynamics 365 Business Central:

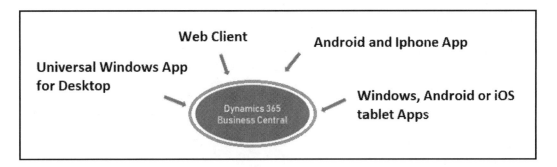

 Microsoft Dynamics 365 Business Central everywhere (`https://docs.microsoft.com/en-us/business-applications-release-notes/october18/dynamics365-business-central/business-central-everywhere`).

Dynamics 365 Business Central localizations

At October's release, Microsoft Dynamics 365 Business Central is localized and released for a lot of countries in many regions (Europe, North America, Asia Pacific). You can find a complete list of existing localizations with detailed specifics at `https://docs.microsoft.com/en-us/dynamics365/business-central/about-localization`.

Each partner can create a new localization, starting with the W1 (Standard Worldwide) release and distribute it as an app in AppSource.

 You can find more info about how to develop a localization at `https://docs.microsoft.com/en-us/dynamics365/business-central/dev-itpro/developer/readiness/readiness-develop-localization`.

Dynamics 365 Business Central SaaS architecture

Microsoft Dynamics 365 Business Central is based on multitenancy and Microsoft Azure-based features that make the infrastructure flexible and scalable.

The following key elements make this architecture flexible and scalable:

- Cloud technology
- Continuous update
- Monitoring and telemetry

All of these features allow you to always be updated and have a modern cloud-based system.

The architecture is essentially composed of two services:

- Database tier
- Service tier

Database tier: Each customer tenant (production or sandbox) is a single Microsoft Azure SQL database; a few application databases (for storing application objects and system tables) are used by the Microsoft Dynamic 365 Business Central service to share and serve different tenant databases with the same application code (useful for continuous upgrade). Azure SQL databases are managed and scaled using elastic pools.

Service tier: The application server, a set of Azure VM(s), where the Microsoft Dynamics 365 Business Central service and web server components are installed. Azure VM(s) use load-balancing to optimize process executions and are in the Azure Service Fabric Cluster to maintain redundancy and security.

Integrated telemetry: All these services are monitored to guarantee service health, availability, and performance. Telemetry permits Microsoft to collect and analyze data; you can use telemetry in CSP to monitor Microsoft Dynamics 365 Business Central Activities. A class A uptime SLA (Service Level Agreement) is guaranteed to all users:

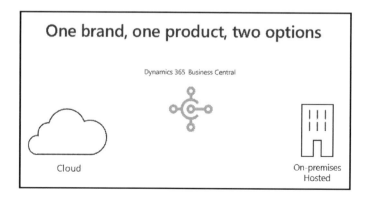

Dynamics 365 Business Central – on-premise versus SaaS

Microsoft Dynamics NAV and Microsoft Dynamics 365 Business Central have the same application base and the same functionalities; the big difference is in the type of deployment: on-premise or on SaaS.

On-premise versus SaaS Infrastructure—here are some differences related to the different aspects of on-premise and SaaS deployments:

- **On-premise:**
    - Initial costs exist
    - The on-premise product life cycle less than the one in SaaS; always updated
    - The hardware must be updated
    - You need IT support for maintenance

- **SaaS:**
    - No initial costs, only pay for what you use
    - The life cycle of the product is unlimited, always updated to the latest version
    - Maintenance in SaaS is done by Microsoft, no IT support is needed
    - There is no hardware to update
    - Performance and scalability

Scalability and performance in SaaS

Scalability and resource governor are in nature of SaaS-based solutions. Microsoft Dynamics 365 Business Central SaaS leans on Microsoft Azure cloud with a robust scalable infrastructure; in on-premise infrastructure, the scalability and minimal and a modern system needs scalability.

In on-premise systems, performance is related to installation, server configurations, and database servers. We need to monitor services to understand what's wrong. In SaaS, everything is controlled by Microsoft, with appropriate telemetry tools used throughout the infrastructure; if necessary, operations are scaled to optimize performance.

Upgrades and customizations in SaaS

In Microsoft Dynamics 365 Business Central SaaS, you can use only modern development tools to develop and install customizations as extensions. The extensions are checked before installing and there is no way to modify the standard code.

Software updates are managed by Microsoft; even the hardware is updated when needed, so the end user doesn't have to worry about anything.

Comparing Microsoft Dynamics 365 Business Central with Microsoft Dynamics NAV

The features and functions of both Microsoft Dynamics 365 Business Central and Microsoft Dynamics NAV are almost the same. The most significant difference is the platform. Microsoft Dynamics NAV is built for on-premise deployment, while Microsoft Dynamics 365 Business central is built for cloud deployment. However, you can host Dynamics in the cloud too, but it doesn't offer the same seamless experience as cloud-based software. Microsoft Dynamics 365 Business Central has all the capabilities of Microsoft Dynamics NAV, plus the cloud advantage. The functionalities of Microsoft Dynamics 365 Business Central are divided into two packages: Essentials and Premium:

Topics	Microsoft Dynamics 365 Business Central SaaS	Microsoft Dynamics NAV\Dynamics 365 Business Central on-premise
Accessing	Web client, Universal App for Mobile, Outlook client	Windows client, Web client, Universal App for mobile, Outlook client
Hosting	Cloud in SaaS	Microsoft Azure, local
Licensing	Monthly subscription, named users, including application, hosting, and maintenance	Perpetual, named users, subscription with included maintenance, but not hosting
Functionality	Dynamics 365 Business Central SaaS (Essentials and Premium)	Dynamics NAV Starter Pack and Extended Pack, Dynamics 365 Business Central on-premise (Essentials and Premium)
Extended Functionality	Extends through apps purchase on Microsoft app store or from partners, you can't modify standard features	Extends through extensions and from partners

Updates	Constantly updated on a monthly basis, with two major updates per year	Updates are the same as SaaS with the new policy (with cumulative updates every months and a major release on six months cadence)

Business Central Web client better than Dynamics NAV Web client

Microsoft Dynamics 365 Business Central Web client is quite different from Microsoft Dynamics NAV Web client; the new client has been introduced with very rich features in the October 2018 release. We looked at the Microsoft Dynamics NAV 2018 Web client in the previous chapters, so now, let's see some features of the Microsoft Dynamics 365 Business Central Web client:

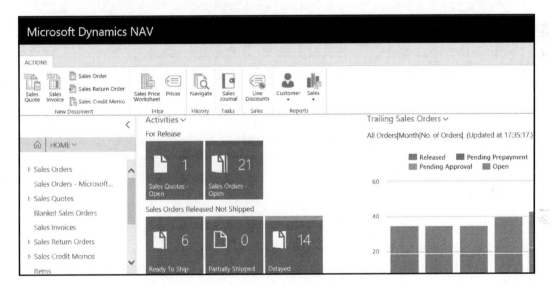

The following screenshot shows the Microsoft Dynamics 365 Business Central Web client:

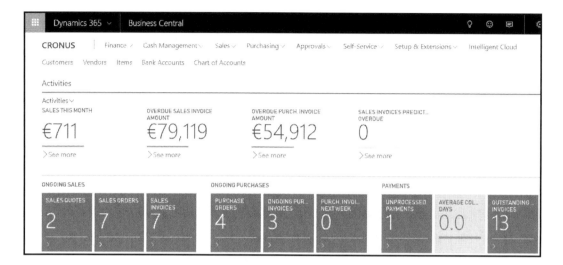

Business Central Web client – some improvements

The Web client is a new product, redesigned and implemented for the cloud, different in certain aspects compared to the Microsoft Dynamics NAV Web client, it has been modified to improve the user experience.

Best features and achievements by Business Central:

- For low vision or low mobility users
- Assistive screen reader support
- Full keyboard access
- UI element contrast
- VPAT review complete and passed—www.microsoft.com/accessibility

Some of the improvements in Business Central Web client are as follows:

- **Layout:** Generally different from Dynamics NAV (style, colors, navigability, and intuitive user experience).
- **Performance**: Light and faster, data paging improved, fast navigation, few icons, responsive.

- **Refreshed user experience:** Focus on improved layout of data, taking advantage of screen space, better data visibility and readability, and easier navigation through the entire application. Details pages (such as the customer card) also get a new look and feel, completing the visual refresh of all the application areas with further refinements across the application.
- **Home page:** Headlines with fast information on the latest events, the data is always under control.
- **Search:** Improved, has been optimized, the objects to look for are clearly visible and divided by category, shows links to documentation and suggestions.
- **Ribbon:** All icons have been removed, and the functions are grouped by section, so it is easier to find the commands to use.
- **Tiles:** Optimized, green is a catchy color and immediately brings the status of documents to the user's eye.
- **Activities in subpage:** The line functions were put in the subpages, before they were in the header, useful.
- **Filters on pages:** Very useful, you can use the advanced filters and filter the totals, but we are waiting for the saved views already seen on the Windows client.

 Take a look to my blog post, Mastering in Filters, at `https://robertostefanettinavblog.com/2018/09/07/mastering-filters-in-business-central/`.

Considerations on Dynamics 365 Business Central

In this section, we will look at some interesting general considerations related to Microsoft Dynamics 365 Business Central.

Why I will choose Microsoft Dynamics 365 Business Central

Both Microsoft Dynamics 365 Business Central and Microsoft Dynamics NAV are aimed at small and medium-sized businesses. While Microsoft Dynamics 365 Business Central is targeted more at small, growing companies that can do with fewer customizations, Microsoft Dynamics NAV is suitable for organizations that have more complex needs, require more customizations, and want an on-premise solution.

Here are some considerations on why companies should switch to Microsoft Dynamics 365 Business Central SaaS:

- **Latest technologies:** Microsoft Dynamics 365 Business Central has access to the latest technology.
- **Fast starting:** Microsoft Dynamics 365 Business Central will be installed and configured by the user. The user has the advantage of provisioning the server, for instance, in the cloud, and in a couple of hours, the application can be ready to use.
- **Integration with the full Microsoft stack**: Microsoft Dynamics 365 Business Central combines many Microsoft applications, such as PowerApps, Flow, Power BI, and Cortana Intelligence.
- **Open system:** Microsoft Dynamics 365 Business Central offers multiple ready-to-use APIs and institutes point-to-point connections between Business Central and a third-party solution or service (through Connect Apps).
- **Localizations:** With Microsoft Dynamics 365 Business Central, you can meet 100% compliance with your local regulatory bodies by molding it according to the requirements of the local market.
- **Powerful interface:** With the unified user interface policies of Microsoft, the application feels like a warm bath. Knowing other Microsoft applications the navigation will seem familiar will ease the learning curve of the application.

You can read this article published a short time ago, titled *Why I will choose Microsoft Dynamics 365 Business Central*: `https://msdynamicsworld.com/story/reasons-buy-or-move-business-central-2018`.

Main topics Microsoft Dynamics 365 Business Central:

- A lot of new documentation and training courses
- Cloud-first and automatic upgrades
- The New Modern Development Environment
- Sandboxes and Dockers
- Microsoft cloud services
- Improved Web client
- Business Central today is in Microsoft Public Cloud
- Scalability
- Cost

Microsoft Dynamics 365 Business Central – activating a demo license

You can test Microsoft Dynamics 365 Business Central SaaS from Microsoft trials portal, link: `https://trials.dynamics.com/`. The following screenshot shows the trials portal:

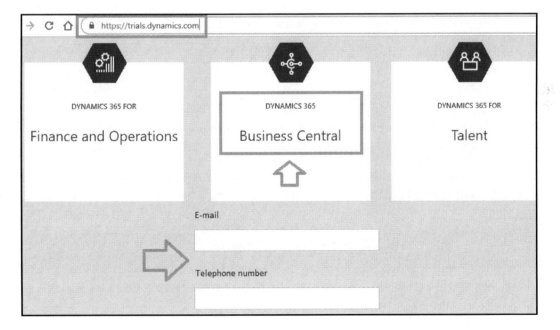

From this page, you can create a new tenant for Microsoft Dynamics 365 Business Central SaaS.

 Get a demo of Business Central (`https://community.dynamics.com/business/b/businesscentraldevitpro/archive/2018/11/08/get-a-demo-of-bc`).

Microsoft Dynamics 365 Business Central – October's major updates

The October release for Microsoft Dynamics 365 Business Central (on-premise and SaaS) included a series of new features and improvements that make the product even more user-friendly; the changes are of various types, I'll cover the ones I consider more important.

Many features included in this release originated as requests from users through Microsoft's social channels, which listen to requests to meet the real needs of partners and customers.

 Here's some information about Microsoft Dynamics 365 Business Central's October release: `https://docs.microsoft.com/en-us/business-applications-release-notes/october18/dynamics365-business-central/`.

The October release's best new features – technicals

Microsoft has published all the news related to the October release and the plan for the next releases on this page: `https://docs.microsoft.com/en-us/business-applications-release-notes/October18/dynamics365-business-central/planned-features`.

 Take a look at my blog for the best of the Microsoft Dynamics 365 Business Central October release: `https://robertostefanettinavblog.com/2018/10/01/business-central-october-release-whats-new-part-i/`.

Microsoft Dynamics 365 Business Central on-premise is available

The on-premise release of Microsoft Dynamics 365 Business Central was released (see the following paragraphs) with the same functionality of the SaaS release.

The Windows client, **RTC (RoleTailored Client)**, is still alive and has been renamed Microsoft Dynamics NAV client—connected to Dynamics 365 Business Central.

 To learn more about Microsoft Dynamics 365 Business Central Everywhere, visit `https://docs.microsoft.com/en-us/business-applications-release-notes/october18/dynamics365-business-central/business-central-everywhere`.

Keyboard shortcuts

Microsoft has updated the keyboard shortcuts and added new shortcuts, along with improved UI for better experience.

For example, with the *F8* key, users can rapidly fill in a new row by tabbing across cells and selecting *F8* on the cells where users want to copy the value from the preceding row. The following screenshot shows the new and updated keyboard shortcuts:

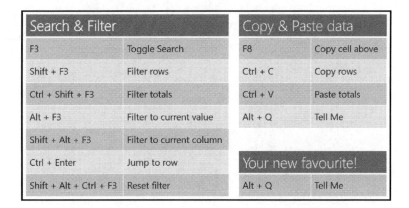

Search & Filter		Copy & Paste data	
F3	Toggle Search	F8	Copy cell above
Shift + F3	Filter rows	Ctrl + C	Copy rows
Ctrl + Shift + F3	Filter totals	Ctrl + V	Paste totals
Alt + F3	Filter to current value	Alt + Q	Tell Me
Shift + Alt + F3	Filter to current column		
Ctrl + Enter	Jump to row	**Your new favourite!**	
Shift + Alt + Ctrl + F3	Reset filter	Alt + Q	Tell Me

 Learn more about the new and updated keyboard shortcuts here: `https://docs.microsoft.com/en-us/dynamics365/business-central/keyboard-shortcuts`.

Refreshed and modern desktop experience

The refreshed desktop experience focuses on improved layout of data, taking advantage of screen space, better data visibility and readability, and easier navigation through the entire application. Details pages (such as the **Customer Card**) also get a new look and feel, completing the visual refresh of all the application areas with further refinements across the application.

The modern user experience navigation, with the back button displayed prominently on the left of the page, and with special dynamic system commands occupying the middle section move navigation closer to users.

Best layout improvements are as follows:

- The ribbon will be replaced with the action bar (including grouping)
- System actions will be promoted to the top of the page (as non-customizable)
- Previous/next will appear on the side of the card/document
- Sub-page-related actions will move to the sub-page
- List and fact boxes will be slightly restyled
- Data field controls look better

The following screenshot shows the back button on the left page—paper-like style:

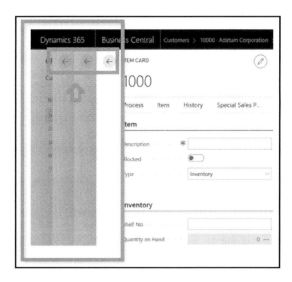

The back button view

The following screenshot shows the new look—buttons, shading, and date control:

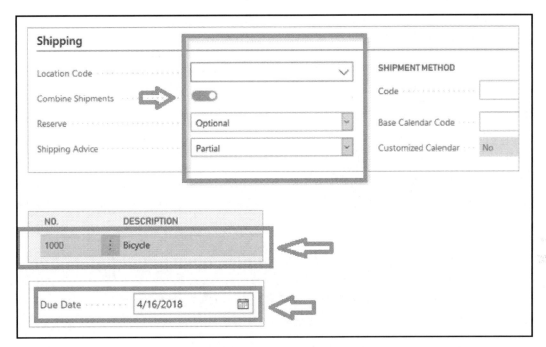

Improved search – TELL ME WHAT YOU WANT TO DO

The evolution of page search (*Alt + Q* to open from anywhere) shows the following:

- Actions
- Pages and reports
- Online help documents

The screenshot shows the **TELL ME WHAT YOU WANT TO DO** page—search for `remind` example:

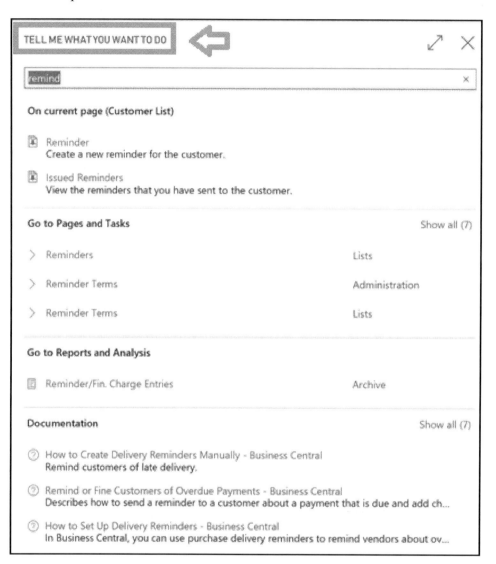

 You can find the FAQs about tell me at `https://docs.microsoft.com/en-us/dynamics365/business-central/ui-search-faq`.

Filtering list and advanced filters

The filter pane is available on all pages where a list represents the primary content, such as worksheets. Lists embedded as list parts continue to use simple filtering, and will adopt the filter pane at a later date. You can switch between predefined filtered views of your list, adjust a view by adding your own filters, or simply start from scratch.

Lists often display aggregated or computed values through FlowFields, such as currency amount totals. With this release, Business Central gives you a whole new level of control through which you can apply filters to one or more dimensions that influence computed values. Use this in combination with filters, sort, and search to explore and analyze your data.

The following screenshot shows the advanced filters:

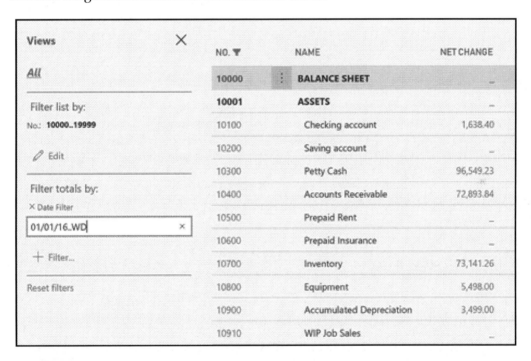

You can find more info here: https://docs.microsoft.com/en-us/dynamics365/business-central/ui-enter-criteria-filters.

Action bar replaces the ribbon

The action bar replaces the ribbon and has the following features:

- Modern presentation, follows Office
- Flexible, adaptive, clean
- Leaves more room for content

The following screenshot shows the action bar replacing the ribbon in sub-pages:

Permission sets are editable

End users can customize the permission sets and give them a structure that meets the specific needs of their business. From the list of permission sets, you can easily add new sets and copy an existing permission set. If you copy an existing permission set, you can choose to be notified if the original permission set changes.

Additionally, you can now import files with permission set definitions, such as files provided by a partner or copied from another company, or use RapidStart to add permission sets.

Copy and paste

The copy and paste feature enables you to do the following:

- Copy one or more rows in a list and paste them to the same (or similar) list.
- Copy one or more rows and paste them into Microsoft Excel, including the column captions. Not using Excel? Most applications, such as Microsoft Outlook, allow pasting tabular content where the column captions will be displayed.
- Copy one or more rows from Excel and paste them into Business Central.

This is one of the most important and useful features released, in my opinion.

The following screenshot shows the copying and pasting of Sales Orders lines on Excel:

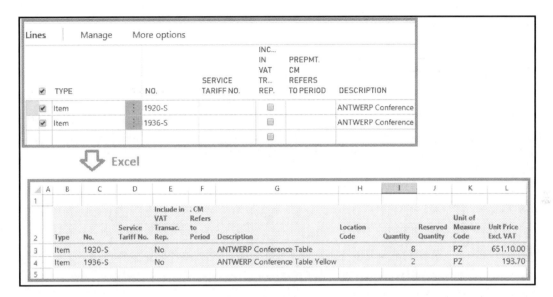

If you want to copy a single line, you can press *Ctrl + C* , to paste you can press *Ctrl + V*. If you want to copy more rows, you can press *Ctrl* + click on another row, or press *Shift* + click to select the row and all rows in between.

 For more information about the copy/paste feature, check out `https://docs.microsoft.com/en-us/dynamics365/business-central/ui-copy-paste`.

Improved grids

Microsoft has rewritten how lists are displayed and how they fetch data, allowing grids to scale to more rows and more columns. This improves the overall snappiness of navigating across grid cells, as pre-loading rows more frequently makes for a seamless scrolling experience.

Updated Universal App

The Microsoft Dynamics 365 Business Central Universal App is able to connect to the cloud, on-premises, and hybrid deployments of Business Central. It's available for Windows 10 (desktop, tablet, and phone), Android (tablet and phone), and iOS (tablet and phone).

Enhanced Microsoft Power BI embedded experience

Enhancements to the current Microsoft Power BI embeded experience include an automatic deployment of Power BI reports, default report selection, and the ability to manage their Power BI reports without ever needing to leave Microsoft Dynamics 365 Business Central. End users can customize the embedded Power BI reports as part of their Business Central home page.

Microsoft Power BI "Ready-to-use Apps" for Microsoft Dynamics 365 Business Central

Microsoft has published and updated the following Power BI content packs composed by "Ready-to-use Apps" for Microsoft Dynamics 365 Business Central and is creating new ones in order to enhance the product offer.

Currently, the following are the available "Ready-to-use Apps" reports for some topics:

- Finance
- Sales
- Item list
- Jobs list
- Purchase list
- Customer list
- Vendor list
- Item list

To search and get apps, you need to go in Power BI desktop: **My Workspace** | **Get Apps** | **My Organization** | **Apps for Power BI** and search business central:

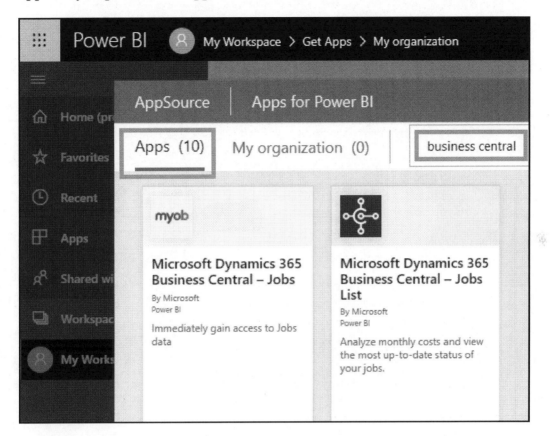

 Take a look at my blog post, *Power BI ready to use apps,* for Microsoft Dynamics 365 Business Central: https:// robertostefanettinavblog.com/2018/10/07/power-bi-ready-to- use-apps-for-microsoft-dynamics-365-business-central/.

Editing Microsoft Power BI reports in Microsoft Dynamics 365 Business Central SaaS

In the Microsoft Dynamics 365 Business Central SaaS fall 2018 release, Microsoft have already added Power BI reports on all pages where they were planned to be. It's nice to have, and it can be a time-saver, because you don't need to waste your time adding reports page by page. You don't need to leave your Business Central environment to manage reports. The following screenshot shows the **Manage Report** option in Dynamics 365 Business Central SaaS:

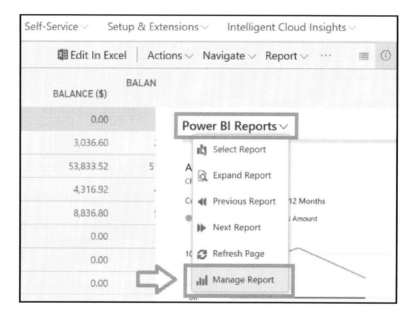

When you click on **Manage Report**, it will open Microsoft **Power BI Management** in Microsoft Dynamics 365 Business Central SaaS (the Microsoft Power BI designer) and you can design and save your reports. The following screenshot shows the **Power BI Management** report designer from Business Central:

Hybrid deployment

While Microsoft Dynamics 365 Business Central is a cloud-first service, customers who need to run their workloads on-premises or on the intelligent edge connected to the cloud.

With Microsoft Dynamics 365 Business Central, once customers sign up for the service in the cloud, they have the option to deploy it locally to their choice of hardware. While they are running Business Central on their own hardware, customers will have a tenant in the cloud, and the data from the customers' hardware will be replicated to the cloud for intelligent cloud scenarios. At all times, customers are informed of their cloud-ready status, so when they're ready to transition completely to the cloud, it's a simple step:

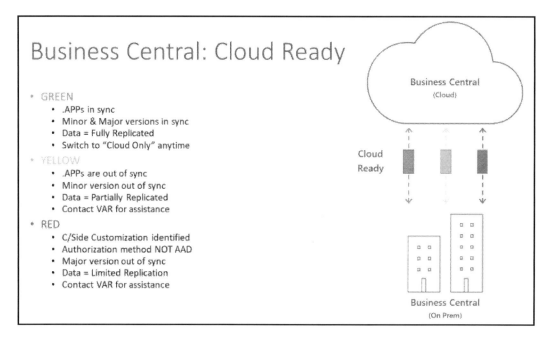

Take a look at my blog post on *Testing Intelligent Cloud Insights* at `https://robertostefanettinavblog.com/2018/10/14/testing-intelligent-cloud-insights/`.

Dynamics 365 Business Central Admin Center on the CSP portal and telemetry

Microsoft Dynamics 365 Business Central SaaS is now completely administrable from a dedicated section in the CSP portal.

From the CSP portal, you can activate the subscription, manage Azure reservations, create production and sandbox instance, manage users, nominal licensed and devices, manage and administer Business Central, configure mail for sending notifications, and use the telemetry service. The following screenshot shows the **Partner Center**—CSP portal:

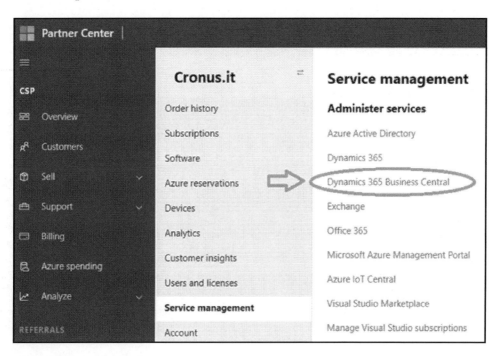

The following screenshot shows the Microsoft Dynamics 365 **Business Central Admin Center:**

The telemetry service allows you to monitor what happens in the customer's active tenants, so you can see the events released and what happens in the system.

The following screenshot shows the **Telemetry** service in **Business Central Admin Center**:

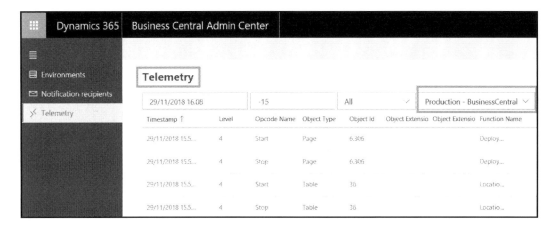

The notification service is very useful for sending automatic messages to users.

 Take a look to my blog post on sandbox and telemetry at `https://robertostefanettinavblog.com/2018/11/06/create-sandbox-based-on-the-production-environment-in-business-central-online/`.

Dynamics 365 Business Central Event Recorder

With the **Event Recorder** feature, you can register all the events *raised* when performing a certain action in Microsoft Dynamics 365 Business Central and then detect the best event for your needs.

To use this feature, you need to search for `Event Recorder` and then open the relevant page; here you have a **Event Recorder** menu with a start and stop button.

When you have finished the process, press the stop button in the **Event Recorder** page. All the raised events are logged in the exact order they were called, and you can see the event (name and type) and the object where the event is published. The following screenshot shows the **Event Recorder** page after **Stop Recording**:

CALL ORDER	EVENT TYPE	HIT COUNT	OBJECT TYPE	OBJECT NAME	EVENT NAME	ELEMENT
104	Custom Eve...	1	Codeunit	ClientTypeMana...	OnAfterGetCurrentClientType	
105	Custom Eve...	1	Codeunit	Office Host Man...	OnIsAvailable	
106	Trigger Event	1	Page	Sales Hist. Sell-t...	OnOpenPageEvent	
107	Custom Eve...	10	Codeunit	UI Helper Triggers	GetCueStyle	
108	Trigger Event	1	Page	Customer Statist...	OnOpenPageEvent	
109	Trigger Event	32	Page	Customer List	OnAfterGetRecordEvent	
110	Trigger Event	1	Page	Customer List	OnAfterGetCurrRecordEvent	
111	Custom Eve...	1	Codeunit	Data Migration ...	SkipShowingCustomerContact...	
112	Custom Eve...	1	Table	My Notifications	OnAfterIsNotificationEnabled	
113	Custom Eve...	1	Codeunit	Identity Manage...	OnBeforeGetApplicationIdentif...	

The best new features of October's release – functionals

Some functional changes have been added in the October release; I will discuss some of the most important ones here:

- **Catalog item (such as non-stock items)**: These pages have been renamed from non-stock item to catalog items.
- **Sales quotes (archive document)**: The functionality of archiving documents has been put in different places.
- **Send-to-email feature improved:** Preview is always embedded in the document, and has a nice layout.
- **Item sales blocked:** You have multiple options to block an item; in this case, you can block sales.
- **Items blocked** are not visible in sales or purchase orders. For example, in the Sales Orders Line, a blocked item is not shown in the item list.
- **Non-inventory items:** You can manage the non-inventory items directly from the Item Type option.

- **Copy account schedule:** Nice feature to copy Account Schedules.
- **More manual setups added**.
- **Finance charge interest rates changed**.

 Check out my blog for entries on what's new in October's release: `https://robertostefanettinavblog.com/2018/10/01/business-central-october-release-whats-new-part-i/` (part 1) and `https://robertostefanettinavblog.com/2018/10/04/microsoft-dynamics-365-business-central-on-premise-whats-new-part-ii/` (part 2).

Microsoft AppSource

AppSource is Microsoft's marketplace for your Microsoft Dynamics 365 Business Central offerings and there are several reasons why going to market with Microsoft AppSource is a great idea. For example, it allows you to promote your brand, expand your reach, accelerate the customer journey and upsell your solutions, and helps connect you with millions of Office 365 and Dynamics 365 business users. Whether you are adding a new solution to your existing cloud portfolio, or are taking your first steps in offering SaaS solutions, Microsoft recognizes that building a successful cloud practice around business-management solutions is a big investment and a strategic decision. It is not easy, but also that it is very achievable when the right commitment, investment, and guidance are combined.

AppSource for Dynamics 365 Business Central

AppSource is the launch pad for joint go-to-market activities with Microsoft and a flywheel for business growth. Using launch promotion, demand generation, and joint sales and marketing, your offer portfolio on AppSource can be the centerpiece of your cloud business engine. There are no fees for listing your offer in AppSource. Our goal is to connect Microsoft customers with solutions and services that our partner ecosystem offers.

By listing your offer on AppSource, you can enjoy the following benefits:

- Get started with confidence through a seamless on-boarding experience
- Use Microsoft's Go-To-Market services

- Customize your app listing page
- Connect directly with decision-makers and reach more customers
- Generate leads and sales opportunities
- Enhance business value and increase deal size with existing and new customers
- Get actionable insights on the performance of your listings via the cloud partner portal or the Office app publishing process

You can bring two types of offerings to Microsoft AppSource:

- **Individual apps:** Where you bring your industry expertise to market
- **Packaged consulting services:** Where you bring ready-made packaged engagements to market

The following screenshot shows the Microsoft AppSource marketplace:

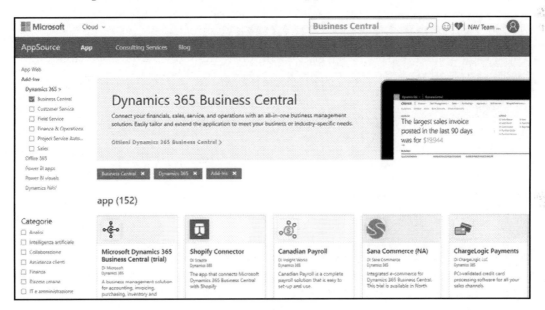

The Microsoft AppSource marketplace

 Check out the Microsoft AppSource specifics at `https://appsource.microsoft.com/it-it/marketplace/apps?page=2 product=dynamics-365%3Bdynamics-365-business-central`.

Get involved in communities and programs

Microsoft engagements programs and channels—Microsoft asks partners and end users to be active members using all channels available to improve the product, Microsoft listens to the requests arrived and if they are valid, implements them.

The following channels are currently available:

- The "Ready-to-Go" program
- Microsoft Ideas and Insider Ideas
- Microsoft Collaboration
- AL issues on GitHub

The "Ready-to-Go" program

The "Ready to go" program is designed to support you in the journey of bringing offerings to market. The program contains learning, coaching, and tooling.

You can find the *The "Ready to Go" Online Learning Catalog* here: `https://docs.microsoft.com/en-us/dynamics365/business-central/dev-itpro/developer/readiness/readiness-learning-catalog`.

 For more details about the "Ready to Go" Program, check out `https://docs.microsoft.com/en-us/dynamics365/business-central/dev-itpro/developer/readiness/readiness-ready-to-go?tabs=learning`.

Microsoft Collaborate

The Microsoft Collaborate (MS Collaborate) portal provides tools and services to streamline engineering collaboration within the Microsoft ecosystem.

Microsoft Collaborate enables the following:

- Sharing of engineering system work items (bugs, feature requests)
- Distribution of content (builds, documents, tools, specs)
- Ability to manage users of the system

The Microsoft Collaborate program is offered through the partner center and requires registration. If you already have an account in the partner center, it is best to use the same account to enroll in Collaborate. Here is the registration link: `https://docs.microsoft.com/en-us/collaborate/registration`. The following screenshot shows the Microsoft Collaborate page:

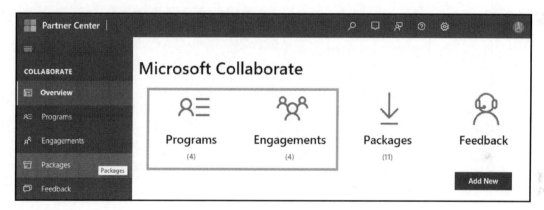

Microsoft Ideas and Insider Ideas

The Microsoft Ideas and Insider Ideas forums help Microsoft to improve Dynamics 365 and its family of products and solutions by discussing ideas, providing suggestions, and giving feedback. Many forums are available and some of them are listed here for the respective areas. The following screenshot shows the Microsoft Dynamics 365 Business Central—Ideas forum:

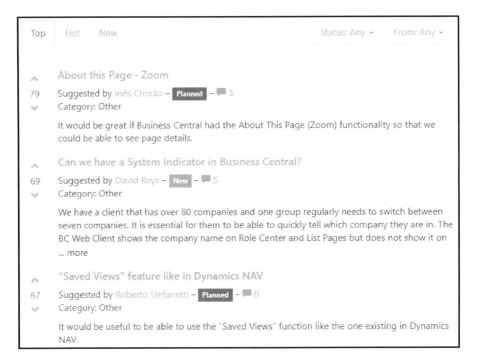

 Learn more about Microsoft Ideas at `https://experience.dynamics.com/ideas/`.

AL issues on GitHub

You can use the GitHub forum (http://github.com/microsoft/al/issues) to post questions about AL to the community and Microsoft experts:

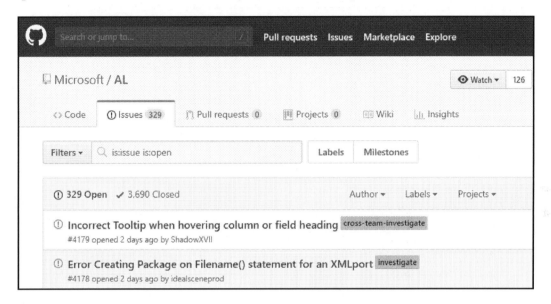

Microsoft Dynamics 365 Business Central on-premise

In this section, we'll look at how to install Microsoft Dynamics 365 Business Central on-premises. In this case, we'll be using the Business Central W1 Worldwide release.

Installing Microsoft Dynamics 365 Business Central on-premise

This installation is not very different from the installation of Microsoft Dynamics NAV 2018. It takes place through the image of the DVD downloadable from PartnerSource. The cumulative updates for product can also be downloaded from the NAV team blog with a direct link.

Perform the following steps to install Dynamics 365 Business Central on-premise:

1. Download from Microsoft PartnerSource and extract the files from package (`.zip`):

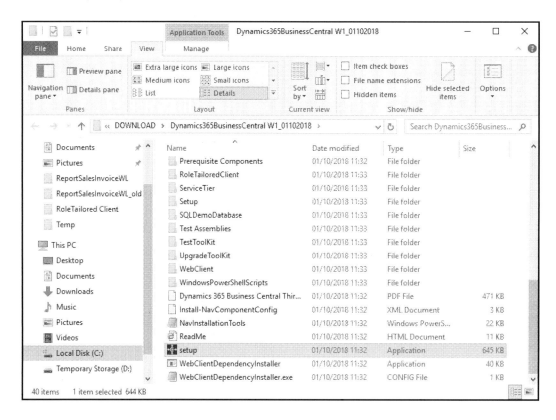

2. Launch the Microsoft Dynamics 365 Business Central `setup.exe` file, and the installation will start:

3. Choose an installation option (for example, **Developer**):

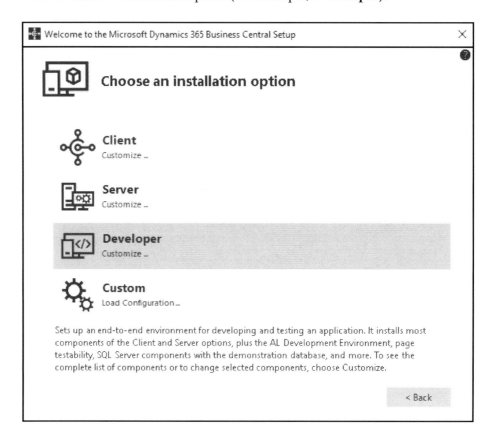

4. Select a customized installation (this example—for developer):

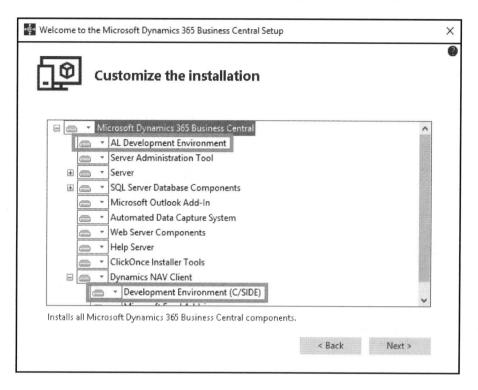

And select a customized installation (example—for client):

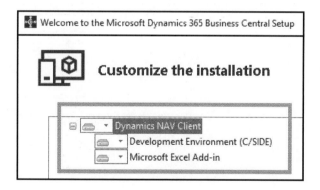

5. Select the installation folders:

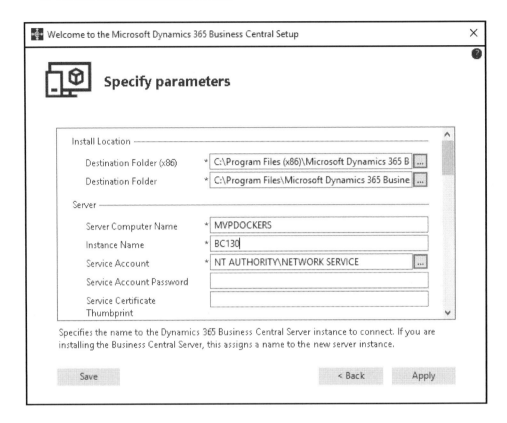

6. You will see some new icons available:

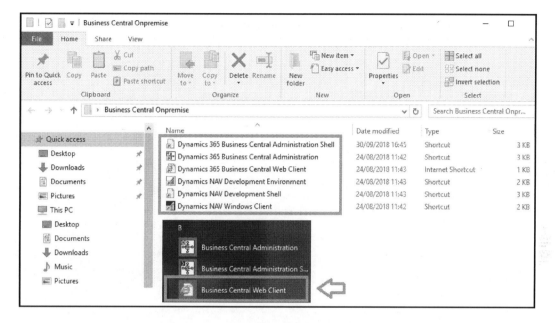

Microsoft Dynamics 365 Business Central on-premise is now installed.

7. Microsoft Dynamics 365 Business Central on-premise Web client:

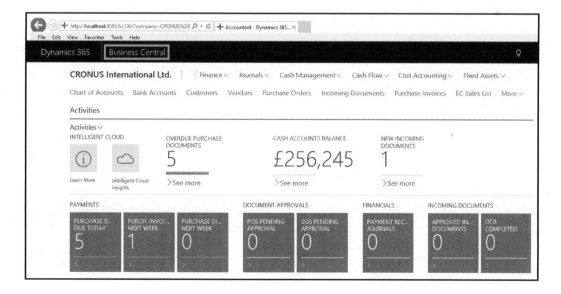

Enabling personalizations in Microsoft Dynamics 365 Business Central on-premise

Personalizations in Microsoft Dynamics 365 Business Central on-premise are disabled by default. To modify the `navsettings.json` file, you need to enable personalizations; after the change, restart your Business Central service tier and the IIS (short for, **Internet Information Server**) to see the **Personalize** option in the Web client.

You can find the `navsettings.json` file in this folder (for example `inetpub\wwwroot\<BC Folder>`):

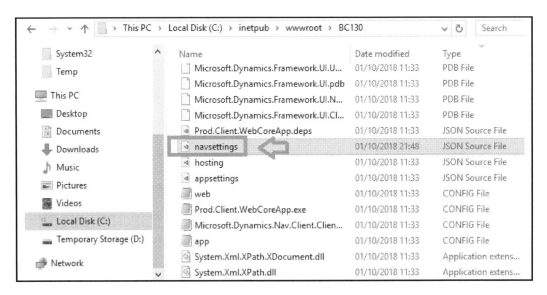

To enable personalization, you need to add the `"PersonalizationEnable"`: `"True"` setting in the `navsettings.json` file:

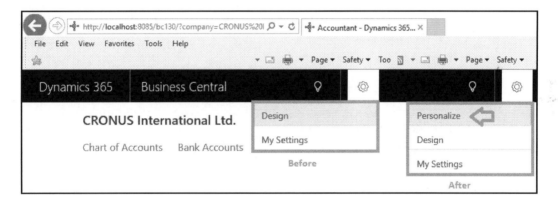

Then restart the service. Now the **Personalize** option is now available in the Web client:

> More info about personalization can be found here: `https://docs.microsoft.com/en-us/dynamics365/business-central/ui-personalization-manage`.

Features not implemented in Microsoft Dynamics 365 Business Central on-premise

Some features are available only in Microsoft Dynamics 365 Business Central SaaS and not in the on-premise release. Some features are available only under very specific circumstances, while other features are not intended for on-premise and there are no plans to implement these features in future.

 You can find the complete and updated list of features not present in Microsoft Dynamics 365 Business Central on-premise here: `https://docs.microsoft.com/en-us/dynamics365/business-central/dev-itpro/features-not-implemented-on-premises`.

Business Central data migration tools (RapidStart packages, intelligent cloud and APIs, and data migration extension)

For data migration, you can use RapidStart Services (configuration packages), export data from the original system in Excel files, and import them into Microsoft Dynamics 365 Business Central on-premise and SaaS.

The biggest problem is obviously rewriting code with the new extension model (which is mandatory if you want to go to the cloud, but not mandatory for Microsoft Dynamics 365 Business Central on-premise).

You can use these tools for data migration:

- RapidStart packages (configuration packages)
- Intelligent cloud (you can replicate data from on-premise to SaaS)
- APIs (you can use APIs to upload data)
- Data migration extension (not available to date, but is in development by Microsoft, and is already available for other products)

Dynamics 365 Business Central – integrations

We can integrate Microsoft Dynamics 365 Business Central using different technologies, such as:

- Microsoft PowerApps (you can make your Business Central data available on PowerApps)
- Microsoft Azure Functions (Azure Function is a way for handling integrations and you need to create your own functions)
- REST APIs (you can create Connect apps with third-party solutions using REST APIs)

Microsoft PowerApps

PowerApps is part of Office 365; it allows you to create apps (web and mobile) that connect to anything within the Microsoft ecosystem. We can considerate an application build platform for Microsoft Dynamics 365 Business Central; it is a cloud-based and no-code solution.

PowerApps is a suite of apps, services, connectors, and data platforms that provides a rapid application-development environment to build custom apps for your business needs. The following screenshot shows the PowerApps—customer app connected to Dynamics 365 Business Central:

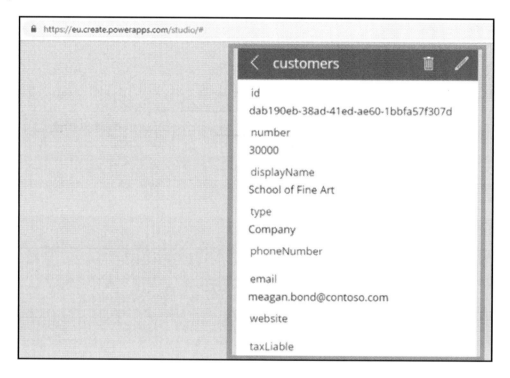

 Take a look to my blog post, *PowerApps integration with Microsoft Dynamics 365 Business Central Online*: `https:// robertostefanettinavblog.com/2018/11/22/powerapps- integration-with-microsoft-dynamics-365-business-central- online/`.

Microsoft Azure Functions

Azure Functions provide a serverless compute experience: a functional on-demand and event-driven code is invoked and executes a block of code or business logic. Azure Functions is actually the only way to run .NET code in the Dynamics 365 Business Central SaaS.

 Here is a great post on how to create an Azure Function: `https://demiliani.com/2018/03/27/serverless-processing-with-microsoft-dynamics-nav-and-azure-functions/`.

Rest APIs

With Microsoft Dynamics 365 Business Central, you can create Connect apps. Connect apps establish a point-to-point connection between Microsoft Dynamics 365 Business Central and a third-party solution or service, and this type of apps are typically created using a standard REST API to interchange data. Any coding language capable of calling REST APIs can be used to develop your connect app.

 Check out this link for more information on how to use REST APIs: `https://docs.microsoft.com/en-us/dynamics-nav/fin-graph/`.

Microsoft Power BI

We already discussed this topic in a previous chapter. With Microsoft Dynamics 365 Business Central, you can directly manage reports within the product with more integration.

 For more information, take a look at this post: `http://thinkaboutit.be/2018/10/how-do-i-add-and-link-a-power-bi-report-to-a-page-in-business-central/`.

Summary

Microsoft Dynamics 365 Business Central was born on the Microsoft Dynamics NAV platform and is integrated with several other Microsoft services. With Microsoft Dynamics 365 Business Central, Microsoft reinvents business productivity. Microsoft Dynamics 365 Business Central connects business processes with the productivity tools in Microsoft Office 365 to help SMBs grow sales, manage finances, and streamline operations. It's designed as a true multi-tenant public cloud service (SaaS) running on Microsoft Azure and sold through the Microsoft CSP program. Customers can access the service on the Web, or using apps for Windows, iOS, or Android devices.

It is possible to integrate the product with the whole Microsoft Office 365 world using different tools, such as PowerApps, Azure Services, Microsoft Flow, and REST APIs. In practice, it is possible to do anything in the Cloud with Microsoft Dynamics 365 Business Central.

14
Working and Developing with Docker and Sandboxes

In the previous chapter, we discussed, in detail, Microsoft Dynamics 365 Business Central, illustrating its features and the principles for which it was introduced, as well as how it works. In this chapter, we will talk about sandboxes environments, we can use to do the following:

- Develop and test
- Testing a demo company
- Testing copies of production data

These environments are useful for both Microsoft Dynamics 365 Business Central on-premise and SaaS.

Introducing Docker, sandboxes, and their benefits

In this section, we will start our discussion on containers, Docker and sandboxes.

Containers and Docker

Containers are tools that are widely used today because they are based on virtualization that can be used for different purposes. Container provides operating-system-level virtualization, they shares the host system's kernel with other containers. The only limitation to the number of containers that can be used on a machine are memory, the processor, and disk limits.

Docker is a set of tools for creating containerized apps, Docker for Windows is the best way to get started with Docker on Windows systems.

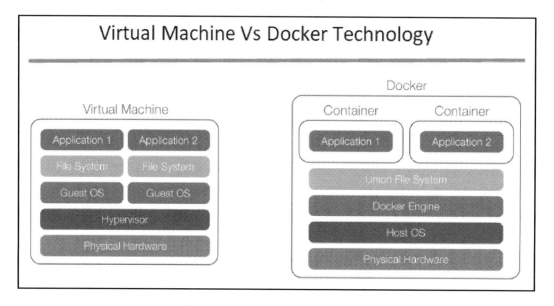

Comparison between virtual machine and Docker technology

 Got Docker for Windows? If you have not yet installed Docker for Windows, see `https://docs.docker.com/docker-for-windows/ install/` for an explanation of stable and edge channels, system requirements, and download and install information. You can visit the page for Docker for Windows at `https://docs.docker.com/ docker-for-windows/`.

Benefits of using Docker

The benefits of using Docker are as follows:

- Multiple systems and versions can be installed on the same machine
- It saves on the cost of new hardware
- It allows you to create, test and, develop applications
- It tests new releases and updates for products
- It offers the possibility to delete products when they are no longer needed

Starting from Microsoft Dynamics NAV 2016, Docker can be used for both Microsoft Dynamics NAV and Microsoft Dynamics 365 Business Central on-premise.

 A good book about Docker is *Mastering Docker,* published by Packt `https://www.packtpub.com/virtualization-and-cloud/ mastering-docker-second-edition` You can find a lot of information about Docker on their website, `https://www.docker.com`, and on the Docker Hub page at: `https://hub.docker.com/`.

Sandbox environments are environments that are totally isolated from a production environment where you can carry out many activities without disruption (that is, a sandbox is a safe environment).

From Microsoft, the sandbox environment feature is provided as a free preview solely for testing, development, and evaluation. You will not be able to use the sandbox in a live operating environment.

Benefits of using sandboxes

Sandboxes can be used to test data, develop and install apps, run demos, try new services, and test anything before bringing it into a production environment. You can also delete sandboxes when they are no longer needed, as with Docker containers.

 For more information on sandboxes, you can take a look to my blog post about how to use sandboxes for Microsoft Dynamics 365 Business Central at `https://robertostefanettinavblog.com/2018/ 06/25/how-to-business-central-sandbox-environments/`.

Using sandboxes for Microsoft Dynamics NAV and Microsoft Dynamics 365 Business Central

In this section, we will start by taking a look at sandboxes.

Sandbox types

There are two sandbox types that can be used for Microsoft Dynamics 365 Business Central—an online or on-premise sandbox that be managed locally or through Microsoft Azure. There are differences between the two types of sandbox and how they can be used, detailed in the following table.

The following table shows capability comparison:

SaaS sandbox	Local sandbox (container or Azure VM)
Managed by Microsoft	Managed by a partner
Uses VS Code only	Uses VS Code, C/AL, and SQL Server
The production and sandbox is in the same environment	Located in Docker container environments
Cost—subscription required	Costs—Charged on Azure; free on local
No database access (backups and load balancing is managed by Microsoft)	Full database access
Debugging	Debugging
Visual Studio Code and "In-client" Designer	Visual Studio Code, "In-client" Designer, C/SIDE, and SSMS

How to create online sandbox environments

An online sandbox is deployed as a Microsoft Dynamics 365 Business Central service in a separate tenant, so it's possible to create a new sandbox directly from the production environment or from the Microsoft **CSP** (short for, **Cloud Service Provider**) portal.

It's also possible to create a new sandbox by copying production data, which is a useful feature for testing your customer data and setting things up in a separate environment.

Creating a new sandbox from the production environment

To create a new sandbox environment, you need to follow some steps. First, search for Sandbox in the search menu, as shown in the following screenshot:

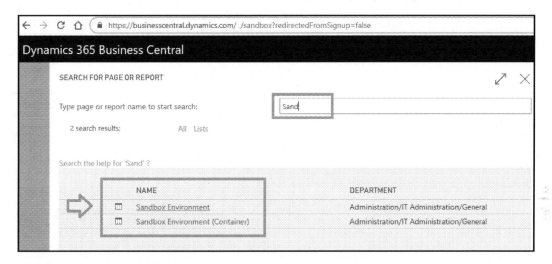

The search menu will show you the following two sandbox types:

- Online
- Container

Now that you've created one, it's time to move on and take a look at the actions available for your new sandbox.

Actions available for sandboxes

From the production environment (but not directly from a sandbox), it's possible to both create new sandboxes or operate on existing ones.

From the Microsoft Dynamics 365 Business Central production environment, you can do the following:

- Create a new sandbox
- Open an existing sandbox
- Reset an existing sandbox

Note that you can only activate online sandboxes only from a production environment. If you try to create a sandbox from a sandbox environment, you will receive the following message:

You can create a new online sandbox environment by clicking on the **Create** button on the wizard page, as shown in the following screenshot:

The description of each option is as follows:

- **Create**: When creating a new online sandbox, a new Microsoft Dynamics 365 Business Central sandbox tenant is deployed. The new sandbox will be created with a default demo company, which is Cronus.
- **Open**: This allows you to open an existing sandbox (for example, your development and data testing systems).
- **Reset**: Remember that it's always possible to reset a sandbox; in this case, it will be reset and recreated with the data of the demo company (Cronus), just like when a new sandbox is created.

You can switch between the production and sandbox environments when and however you want.

Once the sandbox has been created, a message will appear indicating that you are in a sandbox environment and not a production environment, as you can see in the following screenshot:

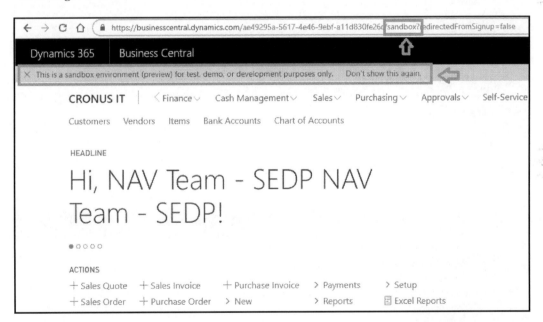

For more information, visit `https://robertostefanettinavblog.com/2018/06/25/how-to-business-central-sandbox-environments/`.

Creating a new sandbox from the CSP portal

From Microsoft Dynamics 365 Business Central October's release, it is now possible to create a new sandbox directly from the CSP portal.

The procedure in this case is fast and creates a direct copy (or snapshot) of your production environment. Whether you copy the production data or not is up to you; copying the production data is useful because it allows you to test setups, procedures, and apps.

To create a new sandbox from the CSP portal and Business Central admin center, take a look at the following screenshot:

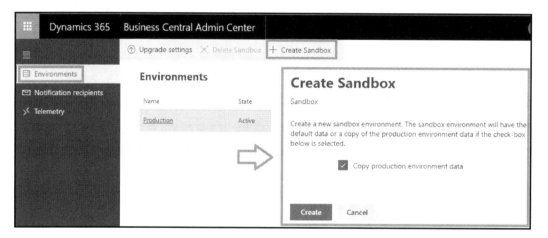

Once created, the new sandbox environment will be ready to use, as shown in the following screenshot:

If a sandbox is created with the production data option, a number of precautions should be taken for that sandbox. Note that the job queue is automatically stopped, any base application integration settings are cleared, and outbound HTTP calls from extensions are blocked by default and must be approved per extension. For more information, visit `https://robertostefanettinavblog.com/2018/11/06/create-sandbox-based-on-the-production-environment-in-business-central-online/`.

How to create Azure-hosted sandbox environments

You can create a new sandbox environment on a Microsoft Azure virtual machine. You can build it yourself or use an existing template. This sandbox can be created using Docker technology, and a container with the sandbox will be created on Azure Virtual Machine. Note that you will need an active Azure subscription in this scenario.

Creating a sandbox on Azure Virtual Machine (VM)

You can create the Azure VM sandbox by starting in the production environment, as is the case for online sandboxes. If you're already familiar with Azure and Docker, you can create a sandbox directly from the available templates in Azure.

To create a new sandbox on Azure VM, you need to follow these steps:

1. Search for `Sandbox` in the search menu and then select **Container Sandbox Environment (Preview)**, as shown in the following screenshot:

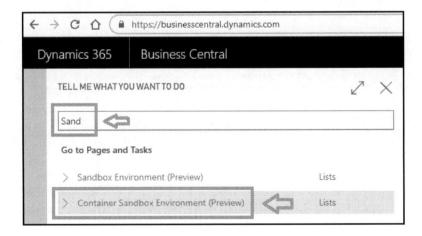

2. After selecting the **Create Sandbox Environment (Preview)** option, the page for creating the sandbox will open. There will be two options available: **Host in Azure** or **Host locally**. In this scenario, we will choose the **Host in Azure** option, as shown in the following screenshot:

To start the installation wizard, you need to follow these steps:

1. Click on **Host in Azure**. The system then runs the Azure portal and opens a new **Custom Deployment** page.

2. Configure your template if you have an active Azure subscription (select **Azure subscription** if you do). To configure the template and start the installation of the sandbox in the correct way, you need to set information such as the resource group, VM name, and the Docker image you want to use, as shown in the following screenshot:

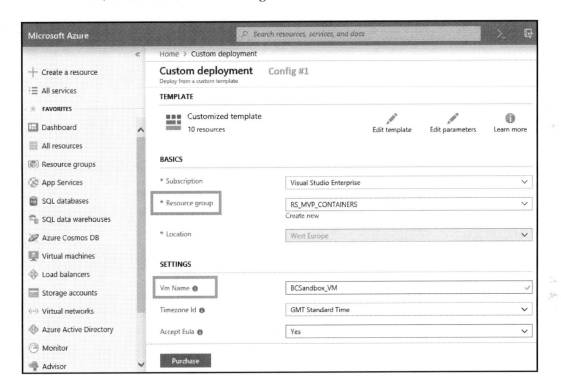

3. Select the required Docker image, which is **microsoft/bcsandbox:us** in this scenario, as shown in the following screenshot:

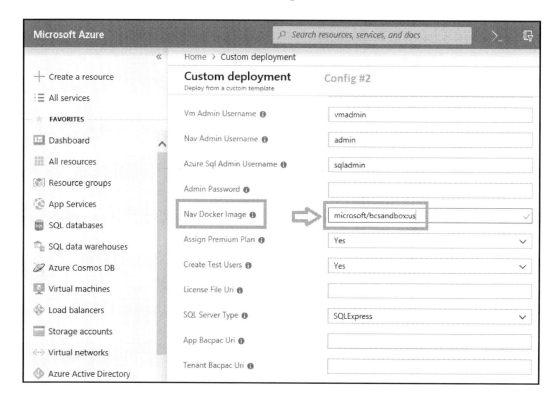

4. Now, start the installation and wait for completion. After the template is deployed, you can log in to Microsoft Dynamics 365 Business Central on-premises hosted on Azure.

How to create locally-hosted sandbox environments

A locally-hosted sandbox is the third option. In order to use a local sandbox, you need Windows 10 Premium, Windows Server 2016 or recently added Windows Server 2019, where Docker tools are already included as native tools. It is, however, possible to use Docker for Windows in previous versions.

You can download and install Docker for Windows from `http://www.docker.com`. After downloading it, it is necessary to execute "the switch to Windows Container" option in Windows 10 in order to use Docker. In Windows Server 2016, it's a server component.

To activate the local sandbox, click on the **Host locally** button, as shown in the following screenshot:

The system will then ask you to save a **PowerShell script (CreateBCSandbox.ps1)**. Open the PowerShell Command Prompt or PowerShell ISE to execute this script, as shown in the following screenshot:

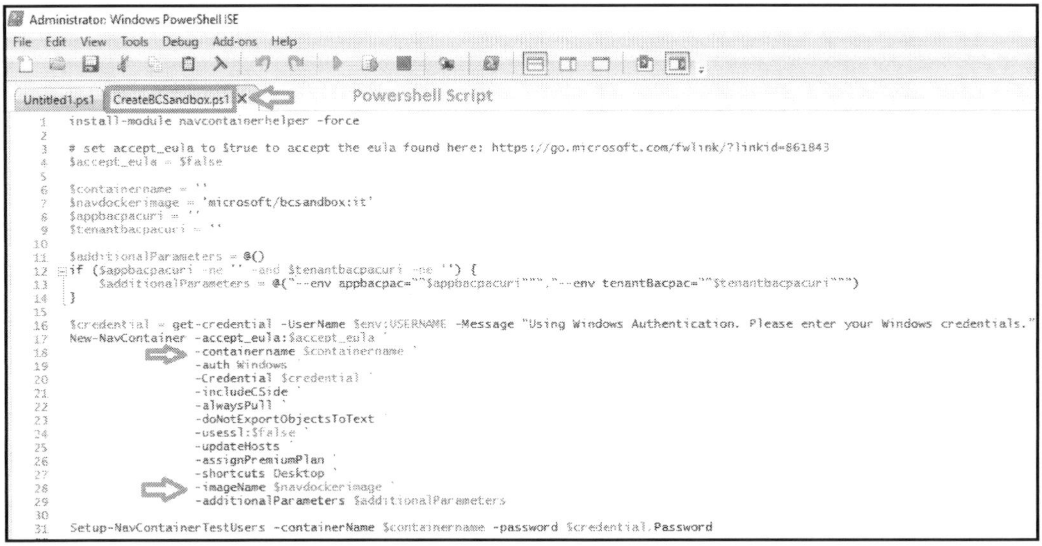

Here, you only need to define the following:

- The `$containername` variable, which is your `Container Name`, for example `MSDYN365BCSB`
- `$navdockerimage`, which is the image you want to download for the Docker container, for example `microsoft/bcsandbox:us`

The following screenshot is an example of the sandbox configuration:

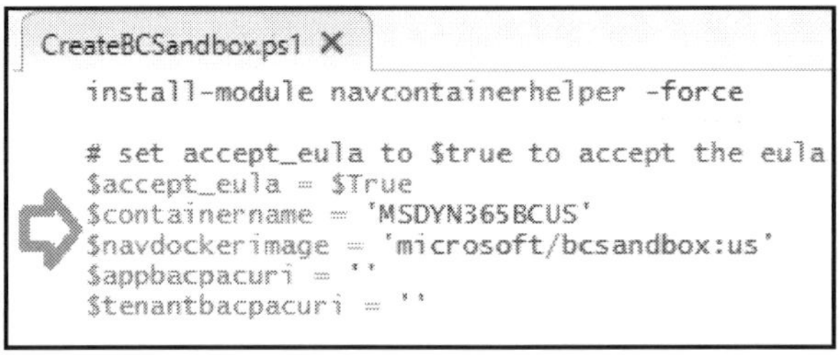

Now run the PowerShell script (press *F5*) and wait for it to complete. You should now have your local Microsoft Dynamics 365 Business Central on-premises, and locally-hosted, sandbox installed!

An example of a locally-hosted active installation in a ready to connect state is shown as follows:

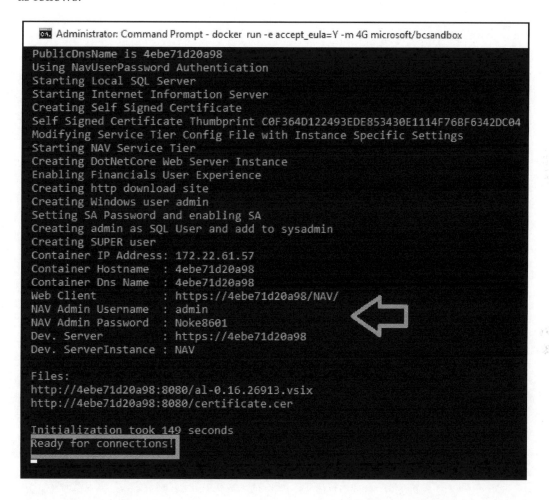

How to create sandbox environments from the CSP portal

From the October release of Microsoft Dynamics 365 Business Central SaaS (and it is currently being continuously updated), it's now possible to create sandboxes from the partners' CSP portal using the **ADMIN CENTER** page.

In practice, from this page, you can administer and manage some new features designed to manage the installation of Business Central SaaS for customers who bought it.

In the partner CSP portal page it's possible to do the following:

- **Create a sandbox** by copying data from the production environment (via an on-demand snapshot)
- **Provide and use telemetry** to monitor client servers and activities (activities on tenants, failure messages, GDPR activities, monitors on fired events, extension usage, and so on)
- **Set up an upgrade time window** that Microsoft will respect when pushing upgrades

Note that all of these feature will also be available through APIs.

The partner CSP portal page looks like the following screenshot:

To administer services for Microsoft Dynamics 365 Business Central, take a look at the following screenshot:

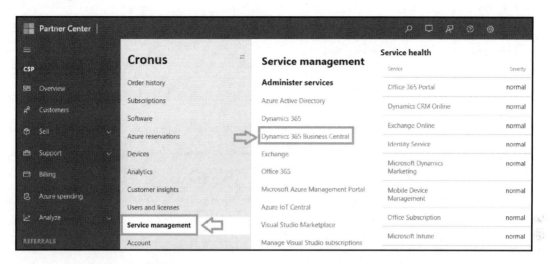

To create a sandbox from the Dynamics 365 Business Central admin center, take a look at the following screenshot:

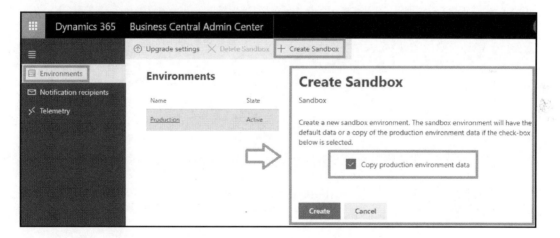

For more information, visit `https://robertostefanettinavblog.com/2018/11/06/create-sandbox-based-on-the-production-environment-in-business-central-online/`.

Using Docker for Microsoft Dynamics NAV and Microsoft Dynamics 365 Business Central

In this section, we will discuss how to use Docker for Microsoft Dynamics NAV and Microsoft Dynamics 365 Business Central.

Working with Docker for Microsoft Dynamics NAV 2018 and Microsoft Dynamics 365 Business Central on-premises

As we've already mentioned, it is possible to use Docker to install local sandbox environments; in these environments, it is possible to develop, debug, and test procedures and apps without touching the production environment at all. Deployments in Docker can be created, deleted, and recreated in a short amount of time, so they are a very useful tool for all developers and consultants who use either Microsoft Dynamics NAV or Microsoft Dynamics 365 Business Central.

Docker's best commands

The following list features some of the most useful commands in Docker:

- `docker images`: Shows the container list
- `docker pull`: Downloads an image
- `docker rmi`: Removes an image
- `docker run`: Runs an image
- `docker rm`: Renames an image
- `docker ps`: Runs containers
- `docker inspect`: Shows a container's content (ID)
- `docker logs`: Shows a log of a container's executions
- `docker start/stop/restart`: `<CONTAINERNAME>`
- `docker commit`: Saves a stopped container as a new image

You can run these commands from the Windows command prompt, as shown in the following screenshot:

Docker image distributions

As we've discussed, it is possible to run both Microsoft Dynamics NAV and Microsoft Dynamics 365 Business Central on Docker containers. When using the `docker run` statement, you just have to specify `microsoft/dynamics-nav:<country>` in the Microsoft Dynamics NAV Docker image field, and a Docker container will be provisioned in your local machine (Docker environment), making it usable a Microsoft Dynamics NAV sandbox environment with AAD authentication.

For Microsoft Dynamics 365 Business Central, you can also use the `docker run` statement to run `microsoft/bcsandbox:<country>`, which defaults to `bcsandbox` containers.

The end result for both systems is, however, the same, Docker only pulls for a docker image and it creates a container on your docker host with that image.

Docker images for Microsoft Dynamics NAV

Where can Docker images be found? Well, you can find Docker images on the Microsoft section in the public Docker hub (`https://hub.docker.com/r/microsoft/dynamics-nav/`). In the public Docker Hub, you will find all of the cumulative updates to Microsoft Dynamics NAV 2016, 2017, and 2018 and in all the different international versions. You can use the images simply by specifying the right tag.

The tagging used in `microsoft/dynamics-nav` is as follows:

```
microsoft/dynamics-nav:version-cu-country
```

Microsoft Dynamics NAV images are composed by listing the image name, release, and country, as follows:

```
microsoft/dynamics-nav
microsoft/dynamics-nav:2018-cu9-us
```

Docker Hub Microsoft Dynamics NAV's master page can be found at: `https://hub.docker.com/r/microsoft/dynamics-nav`.

Docker images for Microsoft Dynamics 365 Business Central on-premises

If you are developing extensions for the current version of Dynamics 365 Business Central, you will find Docker images on the public Docker Hub (`https://hub.docker.com/r/microsoft/bcsandbox/`).

You will find the current version of Dynamics 365 Business Central using the following command:

```
microsoft/bcsandbox:build-country
```

Microsoft Dynamics 365 Business Central images are composed by listing the name, release, and country, as follows:

```
microsoft/bcsandbox, microsoft/bcsandbox:us
microsoft/bcsandbox:12.0.21229.0-us
```

Docker Hub Dynamics 365 Business Central's master page can be found at `https://hub.docker.com/r/microsoft/bcsandbox/`.

Running Docker

As previously mentioned, you can run Docker by using the following two commands:

- `Docker Pull` (Windows will download a Docker image)
- `Docker Run` (Windows will run a Docker image)

Let's now consider how to run a `Microsoft/bcsandbox` w1 Docker image.

After executing the `docker run` statement, Windows searches (and downloads, if it hasn't already) the Docker image and runs it, as shown in the following screenshot:

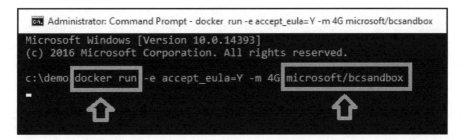

Microsoft Dynamics 365 Business Central W1's Docker image in action would look the following screenshot:

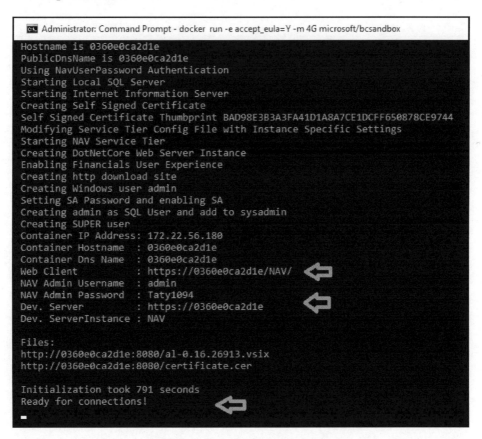

As shown in the previous screenshot, it is possible to connect to Docker on different service names and through different services names, which are generated at random when a Docker image is launched.

The following table shows an example of active services from the previous Docker image:

Service	Name, IP, Port
Container IP	`172.22.56.180`
Business Central server name	`NAV`
Web client	`https://0360e0ca2d1e/NAV/`
Development server (for Visual Studio and AL extension language)	`https://0360e0ca2d1e`
Credentials to connect	
NAV admin username	`admin`
NAV admin password	`Taty1094`

An example of connecting to Microsoft Dynamics 365 Business Central W1's Docker image (from the Web client) is as follows:

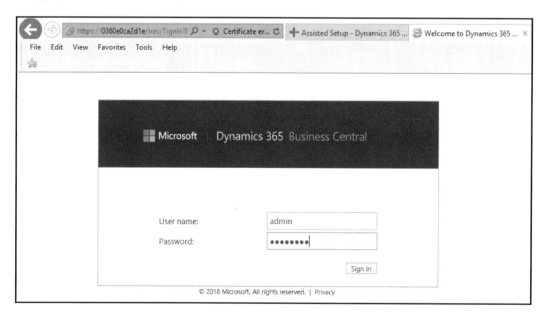

Microsoft Dynamics 365 Business Central W1's Web client in action can be seen in the following screenshot:

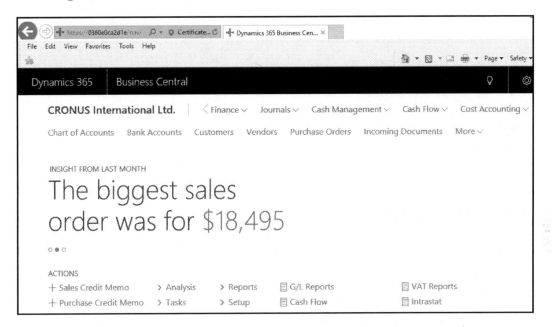

 You can also read a great post by Freddy, *What Docker Image is right for you?*, at: `https://blogs.msdn.microsoft.com/freddyk/2018/04/16/which-docker-image-is-the-right-for-you/`.

Working with Docker and sandboxes

In this section, we will talk about the differences in the development and deployment of apps between environments.

Differences in development and deployment

The likelihood of using Docker for development and application deployment depends on whether you are using Microsoft Dynamics NAV, Microsoft Dynamics 365 Business Central on-premises, or Business Central SaaS. With Microsoft Dynamics 365 Business Central SaaS, it is not possible to develop in the production environment—you can only do so in sandboxes.

The following table shows the differences between the development and installation of apps in these different environments:

Dynamics NAV 2018 and DYN365BC on-premises	DYN365BC SaaS
Local installations, Docker, and the production environment	Online sandboxes only
C/AL and A/L	A/L only
Internal objects and extensions	Extensions only
Apps can be installed anywhere (in production or sandbox environments)	Apps are installed in production (via manual upload) or in a sandbox environment by VS Code only

Developing with sandboxes on Microsoft Dynamics 365 Business Central

To develop extensions in Microsoft Dynamics 365 Business Central, you need to use sandbox environments, as previously discussed. So, to create a new development environment, perform the following steps:

1. Log in to Dynamics 365 Business Central SaaS.
2. Create a new sandbox environment (for development and the deployment and testing of applications).
3. Install Visual Studio Code and the Microsoft AL extension language from the **EXTENTIONS** button, as shown in the following screenshot:

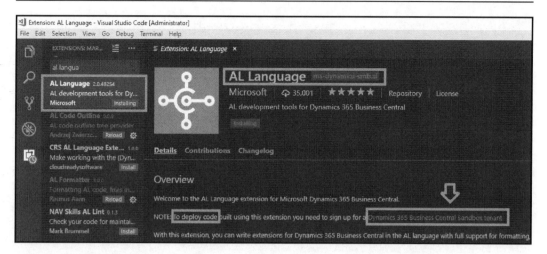

After installing the AL extension language, your New Modern Development Environment should now be ready to use.

To start operating Visual Studio Code and the Microsoft AL language extension, complete the following steps:

1. Run `al go` in the command palette to create a new Visual Studio Code workspace.
2. From the command palette, create a **New Project**, as shown in the following screenshot:

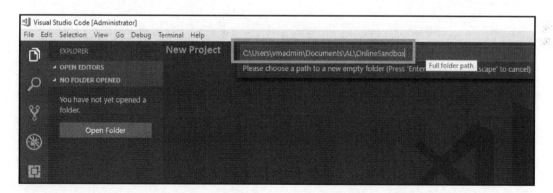

Then, choose **Online Sandbox** if you want to work with the Microsoft's hosted sandbox, otherwise choose local hosted and enter your login credentials.

Configure the `Launch.json` file to connect to **Microsoft Cloud Sandbox**, as shown in the following screenshot:

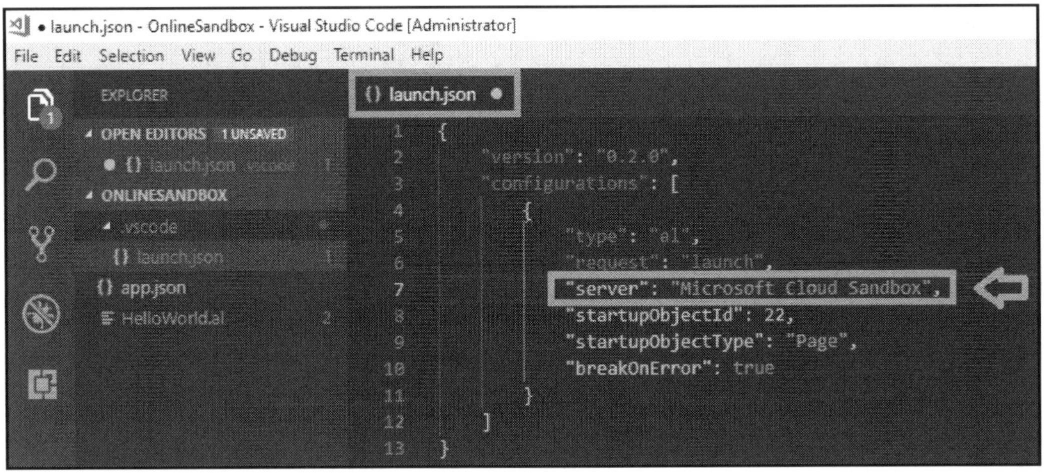

The new modern development environment should now be connected to **Microsoft Cloud Sandbox**, as shown in the following screenshot:

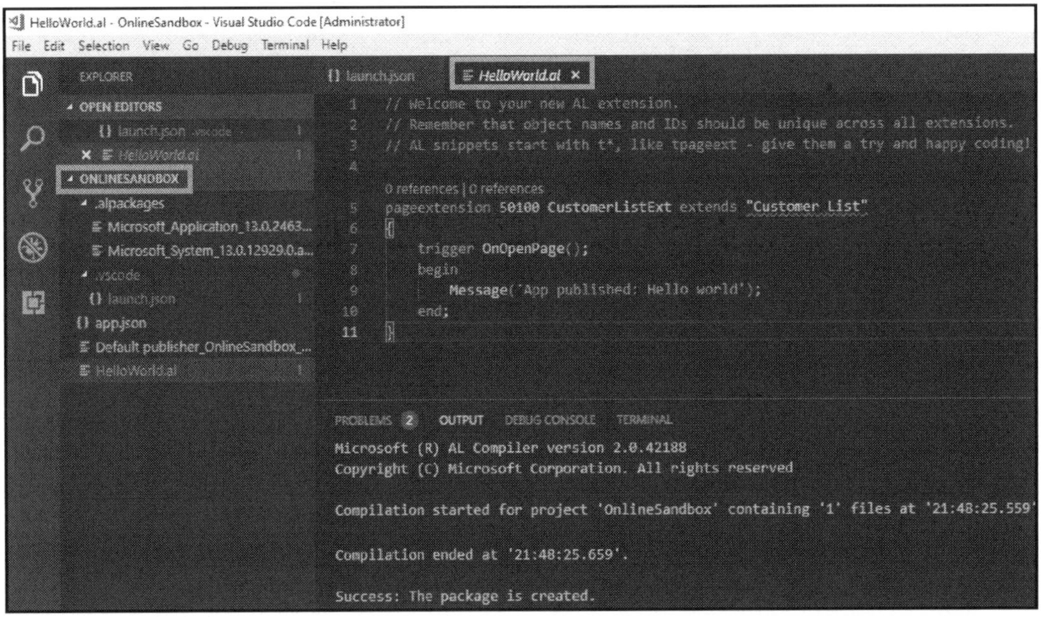

Note that after compilation, the package is deployed to the **Microsoft Cloud Sandbox**.

Summary

In this chapter, we offered step-by-step instructions on how to install, configure, and activate Docker and sandbox environments for test data, setup, and development in Microsoft Dynamics 365 Business Central and Microsoft Dynamics NAV. Sandbox environments are very useful for developing and testing data and applications before uploading them in a Microsoft Dynamics 365 Business Central SaaS production environment.

Sandbox environments, whether online or in Docker containers, are useful for everyone—customers, developers, and consultants—when studying and testing new product releases. They enable you to create, delete, and recreate products in a very simple way. In addition to Microsoft Dynamics 365 Business Central, Docker and sandboxes are also very useful for older versions of Microsoft Dynamics NAV when simulating upgrades, trying out new product releases, testing new cumulative updates, and so on.

Further considerations

Although this book is now finished, I would like to offer some considerations.

Remember that Microsoft constantly updates and changes its products, so some images and screenshots may not be as up-to-date as possible at the time of reading. The writing mode for this book is in line with my blog posts.

Thank you for reading and enjoy! 'Til we meet next time.

Other Books You May Enjoy

If you enjoyed this book, you may be interested in these other books by Packt:

Dynamics 365 Business Central Development Quick Start Guide

Stefano Demiliani, Duilio Tacconi
ISBN: 978-1-78934-746-3

- Develop solutions for Dynamics 365 Business Central
- Create a sandbox for extensions development (local or on cloud)
- Use Docker with Dynamics 365 Business Central
- Create extensions for Dynamics 365 Business Central
- Handle dependencies, translations and reporting

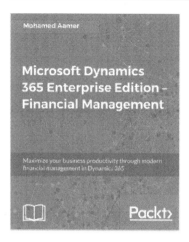

Microsoft Dynamics 365 Enterprise Edition - Financial Management – Third Edition

Mohamed Aamer
ISBN: 978-1-78883-929-7

- Become power user with the basic components and concepts of Docker
- Learn the best ways to build, store, and distribute containers
- Understand how Docker can fit into your development work
- Secure your containers and files with Docker's security features
- Solve architectural problems using the first and third clustering tool
- Leverage Linux containers and create highly scalable applications

Leave a review - let other readers know what you think

Please share your thoughts on this book with others by leaving a review on the site that you bought it from. If you purchased the book from Amazon, please leave us an honest review on this book's Amazon page. This is vital so that other potential readers can see and use your unbiased opinion to make purchasing decisions, we can understand what our customers think about our products, and our authors can see your feedback on the title that they have worked with Packt to create. It will only take a few minutes of your time, but is valuable to other potential customers, our authors, and Packt. Thank you!

Index

R

random data
  reference 250
Rapid Project Type 230
RapidStart Services Implementer
  profile, changing 282
RapidStart Services Wizard
  using 284
RapidStart Services
  Powershell cmdLets, using 308
  summarizing 309
  using, from PowerShell 308
Report Definition Language Client-side (RDLC)
  146, 380, 567
report definition language client-side (RDLC)
  19
report development
  about 566
  anatomy 567
  dataset, defining 569, 572
  RDLC reports 567
  visual layout, designing 572
  word layout reports 569
  Word layout reports, using 574
report transformation
  about 380
  classic reports, upgrading 381
  hybrid reports, upgrading 381
reports
  document reports 537
  executing 532, 533
  finding, in Web client 528, 531
  finding, in Windows client 528, 531
  list reports 536
  other reports 539
  posting preview reports 536
  posting reports 537
  scheduling 540
  test reports 536
  transaction reports 537
  types 535
  using 528
request limits 47
requirements
  obtaining 266

Requisition Worksheet
  changes, planning 500
  functional change 475
  implementation, for writing changes 489
  interacting, with other functionalities 478
  risks, analyzing 496
  time, selecting for change implementation 496
role tailored ERP 10
roles
  about 235
  analyst 239
  business consultant 236, 238
  developers 239
  end users 240
  implementer 240
  in customer team 236
  in partner team 235
  key users 238, 239
  project manager 236
  salesperson 236
  summarizing 240, 241
RoleTailored Client (RTC) 16, 77, 374, 661

S

SaaS infrastructure
  customizations 654
  performance 653
  scalability 653
  upgrades 654
  versus On-premise infrastructure 653
sales and marketing, Microsoft Dynamics NAV
  approval system 42
  customers 38
  marketing 44
  order processing 40
  pricing 43
sales tax, components
  tax area 35
  tax groups 35
  tax jurisdiction 35
salesperson 236
sample Windows PowerShell scripts
  for code upgradation 403
  for data upgradation 404